THE ENGLISH HEARTLAND

ROBERT & MONICA BECKINSALE

DUCKWORTH

First published in 1980 by
Gerald Duckworth & Co. Ltd
The Old Piano Factory
43 Gloucester Crescent, London NW1

ISBN 0 7156 1389 8

British Library Cataloguing in Publication Data

Beckinsale, Robert Percy
  The English heartland.
  1. Thames Valley – Description and travel
  2. Midlands – Description and travel
  I. Title   II. Beckinsale, Monica
  914.24   DA670.T2

  ISBN 0-7156-1389-8

Photoset by
Specialised Offset Services Limited, Liverpool
and printed in Great Britain by
Page Bros (Norwich) Ltd, Norwich

THE ENGLISH HEARTLAND

Contents

O pastoral heart of England, like a psalm
Of long days telling with a quiet beat
    (Sir Arthur Quiller-Couch, *On Eckington bridge*)

Preface

There is, as far as we know, no comprehensive book on the country between Warwick, Stratford upon Avon, Oxford, Northampton, Windsor and Reading, probably because it lies in many counties. Administratively it includes part of Warwickshire, Worcestershire, Gloucestershire, Wiltshire, Buckinghamshire and Northamptonshire, all of Oxfordshire and most of Berkshire. In recent years many of these boundaries have been changed and today, for example, much of the old Berkshire lies in southern Oxfordshire. The area does not fall naturally into counties and to describe it under such divisions may be convenient to authors but hides the unity of one of the most interesting and delightful regions in Britain. It lacks large cities and heavy industries and is essentially a rich farmland with small mediaeval market towns and rural residential villages. It drains mainly to the upper Thames and Warwick Avon and forms the transition zone between the industrialised Midlands and metropolitan England. It is, in fact, the southern Midlands and can rightfully be called the English heartland.

The authors of the present volume were born and bred in the region, one in the north Cotswolds, the other in the Vale of White Horse. They have lived for long periods at Chipping Campden, Burford, Reading, Castle Bromwich and Oxford. They wrote their first theses on the Cotswolds and upper Thames nearly fifty years ago and subsequently have continued to publish their researches on a variety of topics in specialist journals and several books.

In this wider survey, our aim, if we may revert to the personal, is to place before the reader the natural background and to trace upon it the historical developments which make up the present cultural landscape. The book is written for the general reader though some themes have been treated in depth to satisfy specialist tastes, and for those who want to pursue topics further we have added bibliographies of mainly post-1960 literature.

We have concentrated on the important aspects and have illustrated them from the finest local examples that can be visited today. There is enough here, we hope, to entertain and interest visitors and residents for a lifetime and to spur them on to wider comparisons. In addition to the charm of wolds and downs, the English heartland is especially rich in prehistoric monuments, in Anglo-Saxon survivals, Norman castles, fine country houses, landscaped gardens, and delightful mediaeval planned boroughs. Industrial archaeology, for long a special interest of ours, has been catered for by detailed chapters on windmills and watermills and a separate section on steam railways. We have inevitably also devoted special chapters to Stratford upon Avon and Shakespeare, and to the county capitals, Warwick and Oxford. Throughout we have tried to draw attention to attractive objects and to express their significance so as to entice a visit and to appreciate their wider value. Most of our observations are based on our own fieldwork done repeatedly at all seasons, during which we have on a modest estimate travelled nearly one million miles. For scenery, summer thronged with overseas visitors is not always the best time for residents to travel; spring and autumn bring delightful colours, and winter, to anyone clothed comfortably in modern plastics, gives wide views and unhurried viewing.

Our portrayal begins with general descriptions of the various distinctive regional landscapes that compose this heartland. We then go on in subsequent chapters to describe the successive cultural additions and alterations made to its landscape by its inhabitants from Neolithic times onward. Thereby we hope to provide a guide to the detailed understanding of the components and the complexity of the modern scene. Our survey will, we hope, also foster a wider and deeper appreciation of the existing environment and encourage visitors and residents alike to work for its preservation. Surely the residents should have the last word as they, with their own great efforts, beautify the components of the various landscapes and townscapes, but wise inhabitants will always be concerned with the whole region because they live:

> Not in Utopia — subterranean fields, —
> Or some secreted island, Heavens knows where!
> But in the very world, which is the world
> Of all of us, — the place where, in the end,
> We find our happiness, or not at all!

Oxford, 1980   R. & M.B.

Figures

Plates

CHAPTER ONE

The Countryside: Regional Landscapes

And view the ground's most gentle dimplement
. . . such an up and down
of verdure, — nothing too much up or down,
A ripple of land; such little hills, the sky
Can stoop to tenderly and the wheatfields climb;
(Elizabeth Barrett Browning)

Apart from the sandstone bluff at Warwick the English heartland consists of clay vales that alternate with limestone uplands. The clays tend to give flat or gently undulating scenery while the limestones are rolling uplands dissected by deep river valleys. The wolds and downs rise in steep scarps above the clay vale on their western flank and slope gently to the clay lowland on the east. The rocks become steadily younger toward the London basin, a tentative time scale being 220 million years before present (BP) for the beginning of the Keuper sandstone in the north, 160 million years BP for the Jurassic limestone, 130 million years BP for the chalk and 60 million years BP for the Eocene beds in the south. In contrast, large areas are today covered with glacial deposits less than 1 million years old. The westernmost clay lowland is drained by the Warwick Avon to the Severn while the other lowlands near Oxford drain mainly to the Thames.

The Lowland of the Warwick Avon

In the extreme northwest of the English heartland the Arden plateau is capped with Keuper marls that have weathered into a broken topography with many streams. Its small hills are due to local outcrops of sandstone and to patches of glacial deposits. It was the forest of Arden until cleared for farming and for fuel for Midland ironworks and today is mainly dairy pastures with arable and bush fruit on the more porous knolls. Neglected by the Romans, it developed fast in the twelfth century. About 1140 Thurston de Montfort built Beaudesert castle and soon after obtained a charter for a market. On the opposite bank of the river Alne facing this castle, Henley in Arden was laid out in 1185 as a planned borough along the Stratford-Birmingham highway. Probably at the same time the town of Alcester was created at the crossing of Ryknild Street and the Roman road from Stratford. The Keuper marl is interrupted by older rocks near Warwick and Kenilworth. The former stands on a riverside bluff of

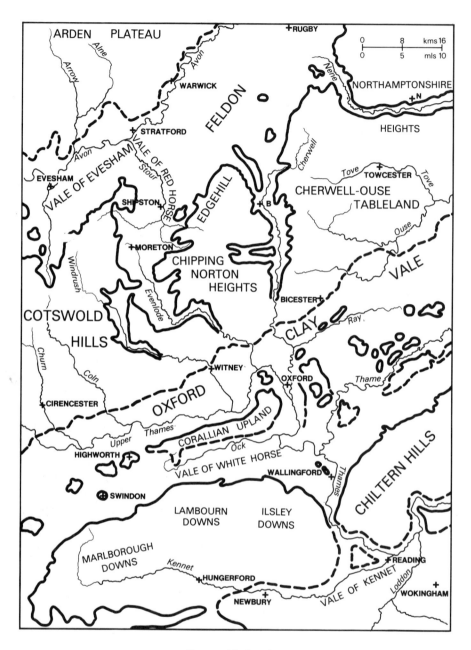

Geographical regions.

Keuper sandstone which gives an abundant water supply whereas Kenilworth is on unproductive coal measures that are impervious.

South of Stratford the Avon drains the Vale of Evesham, a wide expanse of Lower Lias clay with ribbings of Keuper marl. The landscape has been dissected into numerous hills, and the only flat land adjoins the Avon. The basal clay is stiff but is in many places covered with river gravels and nearer the Cotswolds by gravel that sludged down the scarp during glacial or periglacial conditions. These porous deposits and the relatively dry climate encouraged fruit and vegetable growing from monastic times onward. By the fifteenth century the vale was noted for perry and cider and by 1770 Evesham gardeners were hawking their produce as far as Bristol, Birmingham and Nottingham. After enclosure in the early nineteenth century, land drainage on the heavier clays was greatly improved, and in 1822 the Pershore yellow egg plum, which is self-rooting and flourishes on stiff clays, was propagated here. In 1852 when the Worcester-Evesham railway was opened, about 1000 acres (400ha) were under market gardening. In the 1870s a great agricultural depression due to cheap corn imports induced many large landowners to sell or lease fragments of their estates to small-holders who worked the plots intensively with the addition of much manure. Strawberries and tomatoes were successfully added to the asparagus, seeds and numerous other vegetables and fruit already grown. By 1900 about 5,000 acres

Market gardens in the Vale of Evesham.

(2,000ha) were under market gardening and within thirteen years, with the generous aid of Worcestershire and Warwickshire county councils, the intensively cultivated area had been doubled. The 'Evesham custom' proved a stimulus. By it the outgoing tenant gets generous compensation for all asparagus and tree plantings and for any other improvements, including the latent value of manures. He also has the right to nominate his successor or to be compensated fully for the privilege. In 1923 the custom received statutory recognition and on good market gardening land the tenant right is often more valuable than the freehold. Today there are a few large estates but about 80 per cent of the holdings are under 20 acres (8ha) and half are less than 5 acres (2ha). Some parishes have over 300 holdings or growers. Intercropping and the parcellation of holdings, each separate plot having its own small shed, are still not uncommon, and over some tracts the arable plots are neither hedged nor fenced so that the landscape assumes a mediaeval open field character. Many plots produce two and sometimes three harvests a year, and today at least forty different crops are grown and irrigation is common. The vale becomes a floral delight in spring when the plum, apple and cherry trees bloom and remains throughout the warmer months popular with motorists who enjoy its picturesque villages, wayside stalls and animated rural scenes. Of the towns, Evesham is unique in having over two hundred small-holdings within its administrative boundaries. It is also noted for sausages and pork pies.

From the Vale of Evesham the wide Lower Lias clay belt continues northeastward

Plum blossom in the Vale of Evesham.

to Southam and Rugby and southeastward as an embayment of the Cotswolds. This undulating country has acquired special names in different parts. The Vale of Moreton in Marsh, a flat plain covered mainly with glacial boulder clay, extends down the Evenlode valley almost to Charlbury and branches into the Windrush drainage basin in the Vale of Bourton where there are large patches of local river gravel.

The clay country immediately north of the vale of Moreton in Marsh focuses on Shipston on Stour and drains to the Avon near Stratford. It is known as the Vale of Red Horse after an equine figure cut, probably by the Belgae, out of the red marlstone rock on the side of Edgehill. The horse used to be scoured on Palm Sunday but was destroyed when the land was enclosed in 1798. The annual scouring fair was kept alive for a while by carving another horse near 'Sunrising Inn' but this 'miserable colt', as it was called in 1822, has vanished without trace. The Vale of Red Horse has a string of gravel patches and drift-capped hillocks that attracted early Anglo-Saxon settlers as the many -*ington* place name endings indicate. There are still clear signs alongside the main Shipston to Stratford road of the horse-drawn tramway that used to run from Moreton in Marsh to the tiny docks near the present theatre at Stratford.

Northeast of the Vale of Red Horse the wide clay outcrop forms an undulating tableland covered towards the Avon by extensive deposits of boulder clay. At the time of the *Domesday Survey* it was quite densely populated which probably explains why it is called the Feldon or open land as distinct from the Weldon or forest of Arden. Its large fields are under good mixed farming of grass and cereals. Michael Drayton, a Warwickshire man, in his *Poly-Olbion* (1612) included the Feldon in the Vale of Red Horse and praised its bounteous crops.

All the liassic clay lowland described above has a fascinating recent geological history.[1] Less than one million years ago the Stratford Avon rose near or far west of Tewkesbury and flowed northeastward to the Soar and Trent. Then icesheets advanced from the north and in various stages dammed up a large lake between the ice and the Jurassic escarpment and other high ground to the south. This magnificent sheet of water, called Lake Harrison after a Midland geologist, covered at its maximum extent about 750 square miles (2,000km^2). Normally it overflowed southward to the Tewkesbury area but at its fullest stage also spilled over down the Evenlode and Cherwell valleys and through other low gaps in the Jurassic scarp near Banbury. When the icesheets melted, the drainage of the former lake floor in the Vale of Evesham continued to flow southward toward Tewkesbury and so became a tributary of the Severn. The flat lake floor with its soft lacustrine deposits favoured the formation of large meanders and the meandering river soon cut a series of river terraces which later proved ideal sites for villages. In Anglo-Saxon times Evesham was founded on a spur projecting into a meander that acted as a defence on three sides. At the battle of Evesham (1265) Simon de Montfort's forces were trapped inside this river-bend by a ruse of the attackers who carried Montfortian banners (recently captured from the earl's men at Kenilworth) and so were allowed to march unmolested into the neck of the meander.

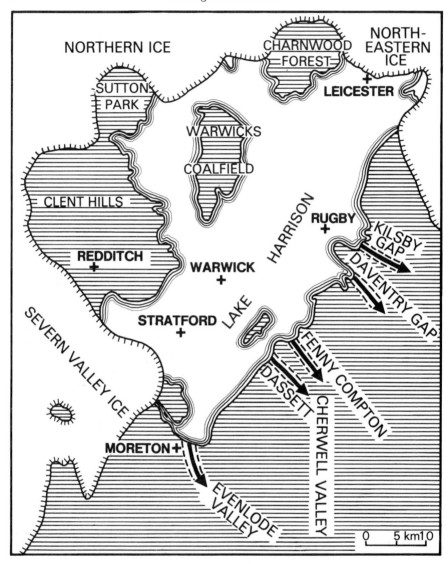

Glacial Lake Harrison at its maximum extent, showing main spillways (*after* F.W. Shotton and W.W. Bishop).

The Jurassic Limestone Hills

The greater part of the upper Thames basin is floored with Jurassic rocks which consist of a succession of limestones and clays with an occasional sandy bed that dips gently southeastward. The clays soon weather into hollows and into flattenings on the scarp and valley sides while the porous limestone and sands stand as plateaux, bluffs and steep slopes. The clays give rise to springs and surface streams which tend to dwindle or seep underground on the limestones. The main valleys are enormous because they are old and have been steadily widened by spring-sapping on their sides as well as by solifluction or soil-slipping and great floods during the Ice Age. Some of the chief valleys meander, a feature which probably originated upon the soft clays and then incised and imprinted itself on the harder underlying rocks. The present rivers are small and meander wildly upon a broad flood plain which hides the old valley floor buried quite deeply beneath the recent alluvium.

The topography depends largely on the thickness and porosity of the strata. When the sediments were being laid down, there was a north-south ridge or anticlinal axis through the present line of the Vale of Moreton and a deep basin to the south of it. Consequently the beds deposited were thick to the south, now the Cotswolds, and thin in the Moreton area, where erosion has been able to expose the Lias Clay beneath the former surface rocks. North of the Vale of Moreton the rocks are of moderate thickness only and contain a relatively high proportion of sands.

The southern upland, the Cotswolds, is the major Jurassic limestone plateau in Britain. Its western edge, where the strata outcrop above the Vale of Evesham, is stepped, first by a bastion of reddish marlstone and then, after a flattening on the Upper Lias clay, by the steep face of the oolitic limestone as may be seen to perfection from Dover's Hill near Chipping Campden. The scarp face is fretted by deep valleys especially of the Isbourne above Winchcombe where a tremendous combe begins near Charlton Abbots close to a narrow watershed whence the tiny headstream of the Coln rushes in the opposite direction down to Andoversford. Everywhere the marlstone is good for orchards while the precipitous limestone slopes are clothed with beech or coppice and scarred with quarries for building stone. The summit of the escarpment rises to just over 1048ft (319m) near Broadway tower and to 1083ft (330m) on Cleeve Common above Cheltenham. Eastward the Cotswold dip slope declines to the Oxford clay vale between Witney and Fairford. This slope flattens appreciably at 180-200m, where a wide bench may represent invasion by a sea in late Pliocene or early Pleistocene times, and again at 120m due, no doubt, in this instance to the relative softness of the cornbrash stratum.

The Cotswold upland provides good arable tillage with large fields divided by stone walls and with little treegrowth except in the deeper valleys and around estates. Most of the higher parts had been cleared of tall timber by about 1200 AD and not surprisingly sheep ranching flourished in later mediaeval times. The great wool merchants such as William Grevel of Chipping Campden (*ob*. 1401), the Forteys of Northleach and Tames of Fairford have left exquisite memorials while William Midwinter of Northleach was associated with the London dealers whose activities are portrayed so intimately in *The Cely Papers* (1475-88). After enclosure the open downs were criss-crossed with dry stone walls and an arable rotation with sheep-folding on roots became dominant. Railways avoided the higher uplands and the industrial revolution emphasised their non-industrial nature. The villages, with rare exceptions such as hilltop Stow on the Wold and Snowshill, cluster on the valley

The valley of the Leach in the north Cotswolds. The winding valley originated on a thin clay bed through which it was incised into the underlying limestone, and then widened and deepened by great spring floods in glacial times.

sides above flood level. The buildings are mainly of local stone and the domestic architecture, often with stone mullions and stone-slated roofs, has an appealing simplicity. The hamlets in the valleys of the Windrush, Coln, Churn and Leach have attracted favourable attention since at least 1726 when Alexander Pope found the prospect at Bibury pleasing. More recently the popularity of the region for retirement has added to its neatness and floral charm. Eventually the Cotswolds were recognised to be of great landscape value and finally in 1966 they were designated by statute an Area of Outstanding Natural Beauty.

Traditionally the Cotswolds are said to end northward at the Evenlode between Kingham and Hanborough but the upland immediately north of the Evenlode gorge is capped with Great Oolite limestones and its landscape, farming and cultural development are characteristically Cotswold. If there is a difference it lies in the lack of spaciousness as the dissected plateau near Chipping Norton and the Cherwell does not rise above 250m and the flat summits are never far from a deep river valley. Perhaps this region should be called the Chipping Norton heights.

North of Hook Norton the character of the Jurassic upland changes radically. Apart from the cappings of a few faulted hill blocks near Sibford Ferris, the Great

A large meander of the Evenlode valley near Combe, showing the present small stream meandering on a wide belt of alluvium that has buried the old valley floor. The railway crosses the meander (to left) in a cutting and then traverses the flood plain on an embankment.

Oolite limestones virtually disappear and the summits consist of Upper Lias clay and of Middle Lias marlstone. The buildings and arable soils change from grey to reddish brown and most of the steep-sided valleys are cut right down to the Lower Lias clay. The Swere valley is exceptional being a rift valley let down between two long east-west faults in which the oolitic limestones are preserved at depth. The marlstone rock bed locally is worked for its iron content which averages nearly 25 per cent, and the largest quarries, near Wroxton, have been worked opencast since 1920. From 1940 to 1965 about 30 million tons of ironstone were extracted, the peak production being 1,400,000 tons in 1955. Today the exploitable reserves in north Oxfordshire cover 5,000 acres (2,000ha) and contain about 250 million tons of ironstone. The British Steel Corporation, who own the present quarries, recommenced working in 1975 after a few years disuse but the rate of output then was only about 2,000 tons weekly, and the ironstone was sent for smelting to the north Midlands and Wales. After the

The escarpment at Edgehill. The steep marlstone outcrop is wooded while the Lower Lias clay on the Feldon (to left) is ridge-and-furrow pasture and cornland.

excavation the former top soil is replaced and the landscape soon reverts to its former pleasant character.

To the west the marlstone country ends abruptly at the straight, steep scarp of Edgehill which rises to 705ft (215m). Away from the wooded escarpment, the red soils of the dip slope yield excellent arable crops while the flat valley floors on the Lias clay provide lush pasture. This fragmented tableland, which nurtured a wealth of small farms and yeomen farmers with highly independent religious views, focused on puritanical Banbury and was noted for the making of plush. Its other products include Hornton stone, a rich brown or blue-grey marlstone, which is sent to many parts of the world for facings, fireplaces and paving and was used in the staircase of the Stratford Memorial Theatre. All the villages on this upland are built mainly of the same reddish ferruginous stone and their picturesque groupings on the upper lip of the valley sides are much admired. Commonly twin settlements face each other across the pastures on the floodable valley floors, as happens at Sibford Gower and Ferris, and Barford St John and St Michael.

The Cherwell valley from near Banbury southward to Kidlington almost severs the Jurassic cuesta. Although 3km wide near Banbury it narrows rapidly downstream and near Tackley cuts a winding gorge through Great Oolite limestone before entering the Oxford clay plain at Hampton Poyle. Its easy gradients are used by the railway and canal from Oxford to the north Midlands and today in the warmer months the waterway is busier than ever before.

The Jurassic upland northeast of Banbury lies mainly in the Northamptonshire heights, a rolling plateau floored largely with Upper Lias clays capped locally with Northampton sands. Here the marlstone outcrops mainly near the scarp and has been extensively quarried for ironstone at Byfield. Southeast of Banbury the Jurassic upland in Oxfordshire has much the same scenery but lacks a traditional name. It is hedged in large fields, with wooded hilltops and all the flatter land under cereals, except around Heyford and Brackley where the Great Oolite limestone forms a flat well-drained terrain used also for a large aerodrome and parks. East of Sulgrave and Brackley, especially in Buckinghamshire, the Great Oolite is capped with boulder clay from eastern icesheets, on which coppices and woods abound including the remnants of the former Whittlewood and Salcey forests near Stony Stratford. The Great Oolite grades into the Oxford clay vale across a wide belt of cornbrash, which is highly prized for corn and roots and forms a conveniently flat site for Bicester.

The Upper Thames Lowland

The Cotswolds and other Jurassic limestone plateaux described above are separated from the chalk downs by a lowland some 20 to 30km wide and floored mainly with clays which give smooth pastoral scenery and provide bricks for building. The general flatness and uniformity is interrupted by a thin line of Corallian limestone hills that runs lengthwise along the centre of the lowland (Fig. 1 on p. 2).

The flat vale, 10 to 13km wide nearest the Cotswolds and their continuation,

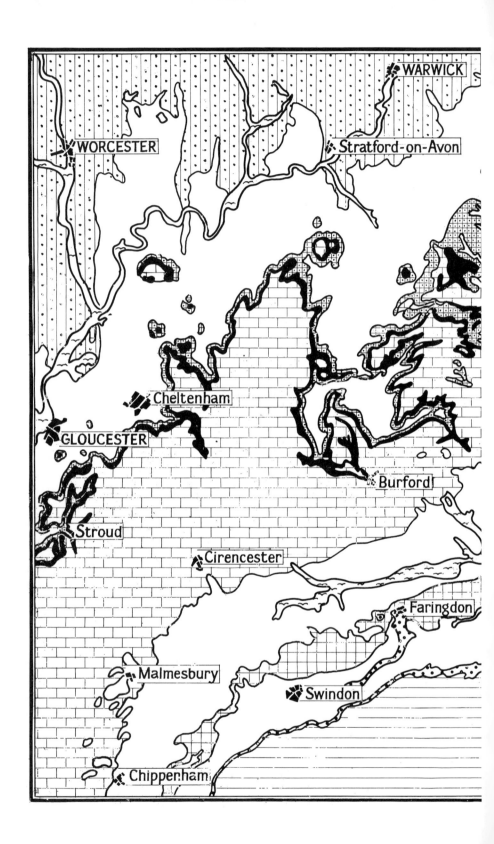

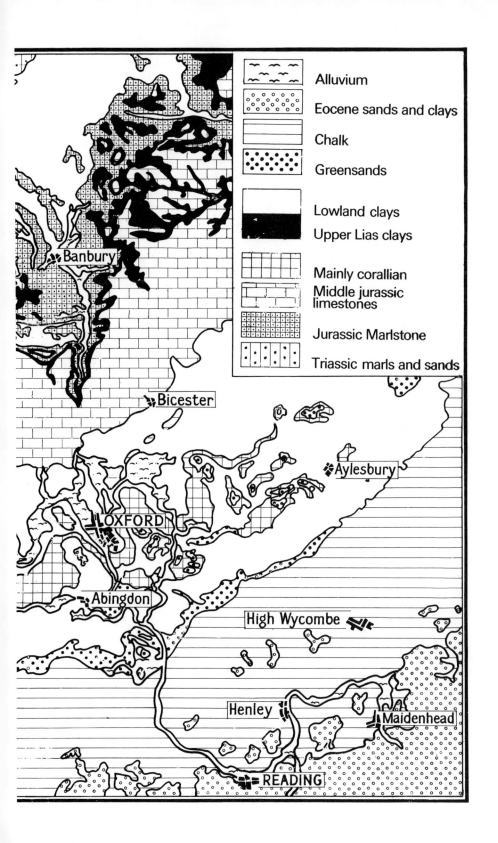

	Alluvium
	Eocene sands and clays
	Chalk
	Greensands
	Lowland clays
	Upper Lias clays
	Mainly corallian
	Middle jurassic limestones
	Jurassic Marlstone
	Triassic marls and sands

Banbury

Bicester

Aylesbury

OXFORD

Abingdon

High Wycombe

Henley

Maidenhead

READING

consists of stiff Oxford clay. West of Oxford, it drains to the upper Thames which downstream from Cricklade has a spacious alluvial floodplain flanked on each side by vast expanses of river gravels that are extensively quarried for construction purposes. The river is locked and navigable to Lechlade for boats drawing just over 1m but its prolongation in the Thames-Severn canal which tunnelled through the Cotswolds has fallen into decay. This upper Thames is often wrongly called Isis. Its name was always Tamesis or Thames, meaning a river but scholars knowing that the Thame entered near Dorchester thought the course above the junction must be the Isis. The ridiculous word Isis should be removed from all maps.

The Oxford clay vale northeast of Oxford is broken by a row of small cornbrash hills, or inliers, that partly enclose Otmoor, an alluvium-filled circular depression, 4km across, that was oak forest and marsh until enclosed and drained in the early nineteenth century. These peripheral hillocks carry a few pretty villages including Islip and recent plans or suggestions to submerge the basin beneath a water-supply reservoir have been strongly opposed by Oxonians. A short distance to the northeast near the Claydons patches of boulder clay appear as wooded mounds which form the watershed here between the drainage of the Cherwell and the Buckingham Ouse.

The Oxford clay vale ends southward at a sharp rise to a thin band of Corallian rocks, mainly ragstones, grits, sands and oolites which form small plateaux and high-level benches as at Stanton St John and Beckley above Otmoor and Headington above the Thames-Cherwell confluence at Oxford. West of Oxford the Corallian outcrop widens into a miniature cuesta followed by the main road from Cumnor to Faringdon. It is a delightful ribbon of woods, arable fields, and villages with many Cotswold characteristics in their house types. Variations occur near Faringdon where patches of Lower Greensand induce horticulture, and at Coleshill and Highworth where the Corallian deteriorates into isolated ridges and hillocks that have attracted many villages.

Everywhere south of the Corallian outcrop the basal rocks are Kimmeridge and Gault clay but there is a great difference between the scenery west and east of the Thames valley at Oxford. To the west the Kimmeridge clay has very few cappings of younger rock, the only notable eminences being a Greensand ridge at Fernham, and the small knoll at Bourton and Swindon where the old town sits on a hillock of Portland and Purbeck beds capped by Lower Greensand. The Kimmeridge grades almost imperceptibly into the Gault clay to form the Vale of White Horse which drains through the Ock to the Thames at Abingdon. The villages in the vale keep to gravel patches and some, as at Stanford, Goosey and Baulking, are built around greens. Mixed farming predominates except at Abingdon and at Didcot where light industries flourish near a huge thermal electricity-generating station.

Northeast of the Thames at Oxford the Kimmeridge clay vale is broken by numerous steep-sided tabular hills of Portland and Purbeck limestones capped locally with Wealden sands. The hills near Wheatley, Great Milton and Long Crendon are typical, while the ridge from Thame to Aylesbury is the largest continuous outcrop of Portland beds in Britain. The villages perch on spurs and hilltops and are built mainly of local limestone. The twin eminences of Muswell Hill and Brill are particularly clear cut, the former crowned with a Roman camp and the latter with a village standing nearly 100m above the adjacent clay vale. The Britons called it *bre*, a hill; the Anglo-Saxons also had no doubt it was a hill and knowing its name was *bre* called it bre-hyll. Most of the country dominated by these Portland and Purbeck hillocks is drained by the Thame to the Thames at Dorchester. The flatter land to the south nearest the Chilterns is a belt of Gault clay, 5km wide, much of which is covered with river gravels and large fans of flinty gravel washed down from the chalk scarp. Dorchester, although an Anglo-Saxon bishopric, never gained the strong control over the Thame valley that Abingdon did in The Vale of White Horse.

The Chalk Downs

The Gault clay vale steps up to the chalk escarpment through a bench of Upper Greensand or malmstone which is the site of a string of villages and towns, including Wallingford and Wantage. This fertile bench, in parts 2km wide, can be detected by its fruit orchards, especially near Harwell. Above it the chalk escarpment rises steeply in broad steps according to the hardness of the rock. Chalk consists largely of calcium carbonate, the microscopic fragments of broken shells (coccoliths) deposited in sea free of muddy sediments from rivers. The Lower Chalk is usually greyish-white and marly and in parts contains a harder bed of Totternhoe stone. The Middle Chalk has at its base a band of hard Melbourn rock and above it a great thickness of white nodular chalk. The Upper Chalk begins with a thin band of hard chalk rock and upward passes into a very white chalk rich in flints.

The various harder chalk bands provided an attractive building stone while the flints, set in mortar, were used in walls and buildings from Roman times to 1921 when Greyfriars, Oxford — of flint with red sandstone dressings — showed their enduring qualities to perfection.

The nature of the chalk scarp varies locally. South of Swindon the main road to Avebury leaves the Gault clay at Wroughton and ascends over the Upper Greensand and Lower Chalk to a bench 5 to 6km wide. To the east of this bench may be seen the precipitous scarp of the Middle and Upper Chalk rising in parts to over 250m in the Marlborough downs. If, as is generally thought, the bench is a marine platform cut by wave action in late Pliocene or early Pleistocene times, the inner scarp was once cliffs facing Atlantic rollers. The chalk escarpment is quite different at the White Horse above Uffington, where, except for a small bench on the Upper Greensand or malmstone, the main escarpment has a continuous steep slope. Here, south of the Port Way the grassy hillside ascends steeply up the Lower Chalk to about 200m OD at the top of the Manger, and continues smoothly up the Middle Chalk, in which the horse is cut, before flattening out at 250m upon the thin layer of Upper Chalk around Uffington Castle. Thus the White Horse is etched into a prominent spur of the chalk scarp and is visible from a great distance. The Lambourn downs to the south of it form open, rolling arable land with pasture on the steepest slopes only. In this tract

The Vale of White Horse from Uffington Castle.

nearly all the Upper Chalk has been denuded away and the scenery is more open than on the Marlborough downs and the Ilsley downs on either side of it.

East of the Thames between Wallingford and Reading, the chalk upland is called the Chiltern Hills. Here, as on the Ilsley downs, the Lower Chalk bench at 90-120m is wide and supports many settlements including Watlington and the incomparable Ewelme. But in the Chilterns the ascent over the Middle Chalk to the thick Upper Chalk at 200-230m leads to a landscape where cultivation is scattered among woodland. This lovely forested scenery was never fully understood by Wessex novelists such as Hardy. It depends on a surface deposit, clay-with-flints, formed by the dissolution of the chalk and of the sponge spicules in it by rainwater laden with carbonic acid from humus. Over tens of millions of years the chalk surface was lowered by solution of the lime and simultaneously the dissolved silica was re-

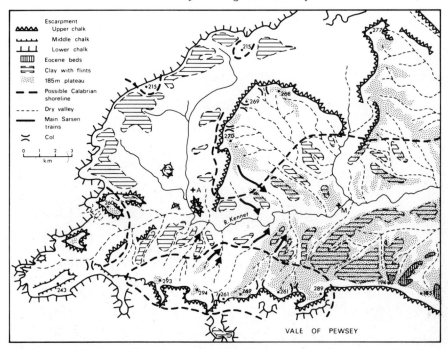

The Geomorphology of the Marlborough district (mainly after R.J. Small).

deposited as flint in the Upper Chalk. Later the clay-with-flints was covered by younger Eocene beds which in many areas have since been denuded away. The final result was a stiff, red-brown sandy layer that caps the higher parts of the Marlborough downs and Chilterns and covers vast areas in the basins of the Kennet and of the Berkshire Pang. The flinty matrix supports lush woods with ponds and bluebells, as near Nettlebed on the Chilterns and Savernake Forest and Westwood near Marlborough. Beech, which dislikes chalk, flourishes on clay-with-flints as do also oak and hazel. The rolling sea of short-turfed downs so beloved by Hardy is a minor variant stripped by erosion of its clayey cover. In parts, particularly near Avebury and the White Horse, the denudation was hastened no doubt by forest clearing by man in the last six millenia, but in areas below about 200m the erosion may have been largely the work of the Plio-Pleistocene sea as there are benches with gravels, resembling marine platforms, on the dip slopes at about that altitude.

The youngest rocks in the English heartland are the Eocene strata that once covered most of the chalk country. Today these Reading beds and Bagshot sands survive on the lower parts of the chalk dip slope in the valley of the Kennet and Thames all the way from Savernake Forest to Maidenhead but small isolated patches also occur on the upper dip slope at about 200m, as near Aldworth, Checkendon and Nettlebed. They are usually wooded and the extensive Bagshot sands in the Kennet and Loddon valleys are clad with pine, birch and heath.

The Chiltern escarpment viewed looking northeast from Aston wood. The steep slope on the Middle and Upper Chalk is clothed in beechwood and scrub, while at its base the Lower Chalk forms a wide platform with large hedgeless arable fields and substantial farmsteads, the scene of much enclosure in Victorian times (cf. Fig. 14). In the left distance are the Chinnor cement works and the track of the former Watlington-Chinnor railway.

Although eroded away over large areas of the chalk downs, the Eocene strata have left their mark. Their sandy beds were cemented by silica-enriched groundwater into a hard layer of sandstone, or a duricrust of silcrete, which on exposure broke up into the sarsens or grey wethers of today. During the cold periods of the last Ice Age when the soils froze and thawed frequently these blocks tended to slip downhill and to accumulate in the valleys. They abound in tens of thousands on Fyfield down and in adjacent valleys, particularly Clatford Bottom and Piggledene beside the main Marlborough-Avebury road. Throughout this area they supplied Neolithic tribes with their impressive megaliths and in later centuries were split into blocks for use in

Sarsens on Fyfield Down, with traces of Celtic fields.

walls and buildings. On the Chilterns most have soliflucted down the steep valley sides and are buried beneath the thick debris in valley floors. Samuel Pepys visited Fyfield down on 15 June 1668 when on his way by coach from Avebury to Marlborough, and wrote in his diary:

> It was prodigious to see how full the Downes are of great stones; and all along the vallies, stones of considerable bigness, . . . so thick as to cover the ground, which makes me think the less of the wonder of Stonehenge, for hence they might undoubtedly supply themselves with stones, as well as those at Abury.

CHAPTER TWO

Early Settlement: Prehistoric and Romano-British

And see you, after rain, the trace
Of mound and ditch and wall?
O that was a Legion's camping-place
When Caesar sailed from Gaul
      (Rudyard Kipling, *Puck of Pook's Hill*)

Neolithic Age

The clearing of forests by Palaeolithic and Mesolithic tribes was important but lack of detailed evidence forces us to begin our survey with the arrival of Neolithic colonists about 4000 BC when Britain was already separated from the continent by the Strait of Dover. The New Stone Age people entered southern England by two main routes: one up the Severn estuary on to the limestone Cotswolds whence they extended their domain along the Chipping Norton hills to the River Cherwell and beyond; the other from the chalk uplands of the south coast to Salisbury Plain and so to the Marlborough and Lambourn downs and Chilterns. The Cotswold settlers spread on to the river gravels of the upper Thames and lower Cherwell while the chalk down migrants spread similarly on to the scarp foot gravels, and the two groups probably merged near Dorchester on Thames.

The Neolithic peoples occupied and extended forest clearings on the hill tops that were within easy reach of springs. They practised shifting agriculture with a slash and burn technique, using picks and hoes and perhaps scratch ploughing. As the clearings expanded they began increasingly to herd sheep and cattle to ensure a more certain food supply. They also had pigs, goats and dogs and used stone querns for grinding. Their axeheads came from as far afield as Langdale Pikes in Westmoreland and Cornwall but the flints came from mines in the chalk. Their prime relics, apart from pottery and innumerable stone tools, are their camps and burial monuments.

The Neolithic causewayed camps at Windmill Hill and Abingdon were probably used for cattle pounds during periodic round-ups although less mundane tribal ceremonies are other possible uses.[1] Windmill Hill, 2km northwest of Avebury, is a dome-shaped chalk hill surrounded by three widely-spaced concentric ditches, the

Belas Knap long barrow.

outermost being 366m in diameter. The ditches are interrupted by numerous undug ramps or causeways probably to help in mustering the cattle but judging from the abundance of pottery and camp fires in them also used occasionally for social and barter purposes. Radio-carbon dating corrected by tree-ring evidence indicates occupation in 3350 BC and the earliest Neolithic culture yet recognised in England.

The Neolithic farmers are best known for their sepulchral monuments, particularly their chambered tombs or long barrows. The main groupings are on the limestones of the Cotswold-Chipping Norton hills, and on the chalk of the Lambourn and Marlborough downs. Each group contains at least one superb example carefully preserved and open to public inspection. Upon the Cotswolds, Belas Knap, an earthen mound nearly 52m long and over 18m wide, is reached by a circuitous field path on the top of the steep escarpment above Winchcombe. It has a fine false entrance at its northern end and four lateral burial chambers each entered only from the periphery of the mound. The curving containing wall of the highest part of the mound near the false entrance shows skilful use of Cotswold (Stonesfield) slates for drystone walling. The main portal, or false entrance, is blocked by a massive vertical slab in front of which were found the remains of 5 children and the skeleton of a young man as well as bones of pig and horse, a little flint and fragments of coarse pottery. The east chamber contained 14 skeletons of all ages; the west about 12 of middle aged persons probably resting on flat stones round the walls. The small chamber on the east side, with signs of corbel roofing, held 4 human skeletons while the long narrow passage at the south end contained only a skull and a few other bones. The tumulus was used over a long time and presumably the bodies had been exposed to decay in the open air before their skeletons were placed in the chambers.

Upon the Lambourn downs the most famous long barrow is Wayland's Smithy which reveals unique archaeological features. It consists of a burial chamber at one end of a long mound entirely covering an earlier mound that contained a wooden mortuary hut, constructed like a ridge tent over a sarsen floor on which fragments of fourteen bodies were found. The second or existing mound is today nearly 15m wide at the front and 6m at the rear. Four of the six large sarsens that formed the original facade of the wider end remain and flank the entrance to a stone-lined passage with a single chamber on each side. The gaps between the stones were filled with drystone walling. Excavations revealed parts of eight skeletons in the west lateral chamber, and showed that the material for the mound was dug from ditches on either side and held up by a kerb of sarsens. The finds also included what were thought to be two Iron Age currency bars until laboratory tests demoted them to eighteenth century barn-door hinges. Corrected radio-carbon measurements give datings of about 3500 BC for the burial mound.

Whereas Wayland's Smithy stands beside the well-trodden Ridgeway, the finest long barrow on the Marlborough downs, at West Kennet near Avebury, is reached by a long fieldpath with panoramic views. At West Kennet the grass-covered chalk mound is 101m long and 2.4m high and was originally held up at the back and sides by an edging of sarsens. The front, or eastern end, has a facade of gigantic sarsens, of which the massive central stone hides a semi-circular courtyard leading to a clover-leaf arrangement of five burial chambers. The gaps between the sarsen walls of these chambers are filled with drystone walling and the roofs have crude corbelling, or overlapping, capped in each chamber by a heavy stone slab. The barrow was badly damaged in 1685 when Dr Troope of Marlborough rifled it for human bones and carried off several bushels, of which he made a noble medicine that relieved many of his distressed neighbours. When completely excavated and restored by the Ministry of Works in 1955, the chambers contained skeletons and fragments of at least fortysix people irrespective of Dr Troope's bone snatching. The burials probably went on for a thousand years and eventually the tomb was sealed with earth and rubble.

In addition to these great chambered burial mounds, the equivalent of mediaeval cathedrals, neolithic peoples used simpler burial places that are marked by a single stone or by dolmen of a few megaliths only. The Hawk Stone at Spelsbury may have marked a single grave, while the Hoar Stone near Enstone and the Whispering Knights at Rollright probably mark portal dolmens or graves with a single polygonal chamber from which the covering earth has been entirely denuded.

During the Late Neolithic period (2500 to 2100 BC) the custom of building circular or oval enclosures with an internal ditch and outer rampart spread in southern England. Timber or stone circles were erected within the perimeter of many of these henge monuments, notably at Avebury and Stonehenge. The transition is associated with new invaders from the Rhinelands who buried their dead in single graves under round barrows, usually with pottery beakers and occasionally with trinkets of gold. These beaker folk were relatively round-headed and had a trade in and later a working knowledge of metals. The 7km strip of easily-tilled river terrace gravels beside the Thames between Cassington and Stanton Harcourt near Oxford has already yielded more than thirty beakers associated mainly with tribes from the middle Rhinelands who settled here after about 2200 BC. Under their influence, the late neolithic stone age merged gradually into the so-called Bronze Age.

Bronze Age

During this period the use of metallurgy was greatly extended and diversified especially in Wessex and the upper Thames. In addition to offensive weapons such as flint-tanged daggers, spearheads and axes, bronze was also used for agricultural implements and tools. Hoards of implements have been unearthed at Yattendon and Wallingford and many weapons and utensils dredged up from the Thames and its tributaries. Aerial photographs have revealed the outlines of many villages on river terrace gravels with hut circles and round barrows almost obliterated by the plough. Throughout the early (2100-1700 BC) and middle (1700-1200 BC) Bronze Age the changes in life and technology were due to native cultural progress and only in the closing stages (1200-700 BC) are there strong signs of invasion from overseas when newcomers, using globular rather than collared urns, spread as far north as the chalk escarpment and were buried in flat cemeteries or urnfields as at Standlake and Long Wittenham. About this time the casting of metal objects was improved by the introduction of a lead-bronze alloy.

The bronze-using peoples have left a rich legacy on the landscape and in museums. Objects discovered in the English heartland include trinkets of gold, amber and jet, splendid shields at Dorchester and Eynsham, a fine double-looped palstave at Garsington and a large cauldron at Shipton on Cherwell. The main landscape marks are the round barrows which began to be common in beaker or late Neolithic times and which, in spite of widespread obliteration by ploughing in the vales, survive in hundreds either as groups or singly especially on the downs and wolds. They have a variety of shapes and sizes, including large bell-shaped mounds for men and smaller disc-shaped mounds for women, and continued to be constructed for a long period but the majority are associated with Bronze Age cremation. They abound, for example, near the sanctuary east of Avebury and around Lambourn. Near the boundaries of Lambourn and Sparsholt parishes there are at least forty round barrows, including the Seven Barrows on the east side of the road from Lambourn to Blowing Stone Hill. Here two rows, each of five barrows, contain five bowl types, two saucer types, one disc type and two ditch-enclosed double mounds. About 230m north on the same side of the road is a large bowl barrow that had two cremations with

Avebury and Silbury Hill.

bronze tools at its core and over 100 secondary cremations in its surface, nearly half of which were in urns and the others under small sarsens.

It happens, however, that the largest round barrow, Silbury Hill near Avebury, is late Neolithic and dates from about 2500 BC. This, the highest man-made prehistoric mound in Europe remains a mystery.[2] It is a truncated cone, today nearly 40m high with a flat top over 30m in diameter. A short distance below the summit the sloping sides of the mound flatten into a distinct shelf or bench. The base covers over 2ha and is surrounded by a ditch once 3 to 5m deep and which today often fills with water leaving two narrow causeways to the main Bath road. Excavations and tunnels have not yielded any significant finds but were sufficient to suggest that the great mound was gradually built up as a series of stepped cones superimposed on each other. The final stage was the addition of chalk to smooth down the existing profile, except for the step near the top. The flat summit was probably used for ceremonial or astronomical purposes.

The most exciting landscape features popularly associated with the Bronze Age are the stone circles which, as noticed already, were in fact mainly the work of beaker or late Neolithic man. The greatest of them at Avebury and Stonehenge both originated about 2600 BC and continued in active use to about 1600 BC or the middle Bronze Age. Stonehenge was reconstructed in its present form by 1800 BC but here

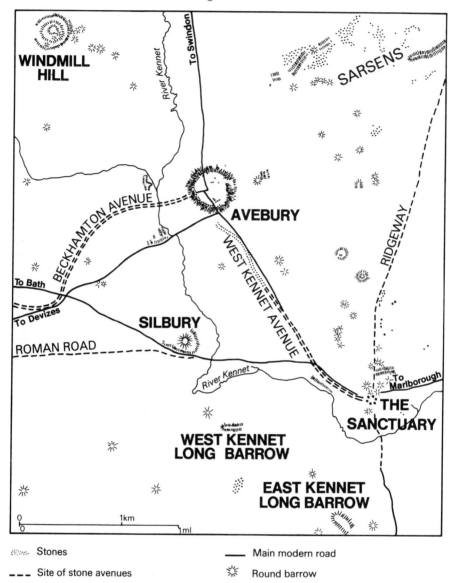

░░░ Stones	─── Main modern road
─ ─ ─ Site of stone avenues	☀ Round barrow

The archaeology of the Avebury district. Minor round barrows are omitted.

we are more concerned with Avebury which according to John Aubrey in 1663 exceeds it in greatness 'as a cathedral does a parish church'. The Avebury complex of prehistoric structures stands within easy distance of the upper Kennet and the henge monument with its stone circles does not command a wide view presumably because visibility was less important than water supply. The earthen part of the construction consists of an almost circular ditch and rampart over 1km long that encloses an inner area about 350m in diameter and covering nearly 10ha. The ditch, which just exceeds 21m in width at its lip, 4m at its base and 9m in depth, is steep sided but has silted up to half its original depth. The chalk excavated in digging the ditch was piled up about 4m from its outer lip into a bank with an average height today of about 5m and basal width of 23 to 30m. In parts at least the earth was retained on its inner side by a wall of chalk blocks. The banks are breached by four entrances, about 15m wide, that lead to causeways across the ditch and which today are followed by roads.

Within the enclosure at a few metres from the inner lip of the ditch a stone circle of about 100 huge sarsens was erected. They weigh up to 40 tons or more and were dragged, probably on wooden rollers, from the surrounding chalk downs. Within the great circle are the remains of two smaller circles. The northern inner circle was about 97m in diameter and contained originally about 28 stones of which only four survive. Within it was an inner ring of about twelve stones, at the centre of which, arranged as three sides of a rectangle, stood three huge sarsens, two of which survive.

The southern inner circle was nearly 104m in diameter and contained about 30 stones, five of which remain and the positions of four more are marked by concrete pillars. At the centre once stood a tall pillar stone and to the west of this stretched an alignment of small stones over 30m long which may have been associated with a single

Avebury, the great megalithic circle.

stone, called the ringstone, erected outside the inner circle but inside the main enclosure.

The southern entrance at Avebury, once marked by entrance stones, leads to an avenue about 15m wide of one hundred paired megaliths that stretches over 2km to the sanctuary on Overton Hill on the ridgeway overlooking the Kennet valley. This Neolithic sanctuary was either a circular wooden structure or an open air arrangement of concentric timber poles that was later replaced or extended by two stone circles.

Once an avenue of megaliths probably stretched from the western entrance at Avebury to the longstones near Beckhampton, but only the two longstones survive. The full story of the construction and reconstruction at Avebury has yet to be unravelled although many details have been revealed. In Anglo-Saxon times a village grew up within the large enclosure and thereafter destruction of the standing stones proceeded intermittently. As early as the fourteenth century a barber-surgeon was trapped and killed by the collapse of the stone he was trying to demolish. His instruments may be seen in the local museum. Most of the destruction occurred in the eighteenth century when the stones may have been connected with superstitious practices and an altogether too successful method of destroying them was devised; pits dug around them were filled with wood which was set alight thereby heating the stones which disintegrated when doused with cold water. The main scientific investigations at Avebury were carried out in the 1930s when the site was cleared of treegrowth, many fallen buried stones were re-erected and the known position of vanished stones marked with small concrete pillars.

Avebury is unique in its gigantic proportions and the only other famous stone circle in the Thames basin, at Rollright northwest of Chipping Norton has nothing in common with it except shape, proximity to an ancient ridgeway and a local supply of megaliths. The Rollright stones stand at about 220m OD on the scarp summit overlooking the Vale of Red Horse. The upland has near its surface a hard layer of oolitic limestone that breaks easily into large slabs, some of which have slipped down the steep hillslopes into adjacent valleys. The circle constructed of them is small, being 30 to 34m in diameter and consists of about 76 close-set stones mostly under 1m tall, with the larger on the northern arc. All the stones are deeply corroded presumably because they came from or near the surface where vegetation and humic acid had deeply etched the rock. A larger, isolated block, the King Stone, stands just to the east on the opposite side of the ancient Jurassic Way that in historic times became for much of its length the boundary between Warwickshire and Oxfordshire. Farther east overlooking the Salford valley are the Whispering Knights, a group of four standing megaliths and a fallen capstone that once formed the chamber of a burial mound. The Rollright circle, called the King's Men, has never been scientifically excavated and has acquired, with the outlying stones, an impressive folklore. Avebury is a metropolis set on flat land amid populated hilltops whereas Rollright is perched high on a narrow interfluve at the northern extremity of strong late Neolithic culture in the upper Thames basin. Here alone on the Jurassic limestones there was an abundant surface supply of local natural megaliths.

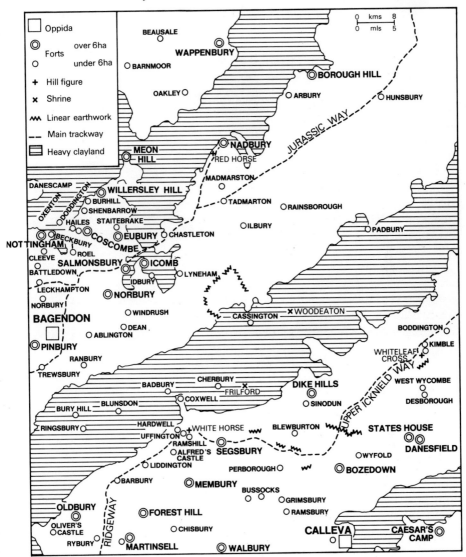

Main Iron Age camps and earthworks. For Willersley *read* Willersey.

Early Iron Age

The use of iron, rare in the late Bronze Age, increased steadily after about 700 BC but cultured life in the upper Thames basin changed little until the middle Iron Age (400-100 BC) when there was either a great increase of trading with the continent or invasions by groups of people from northern France who introduced the use of the wheel for transport. About 100 BC the invasions by Belgae from near the Rhine delta

Excavation in 1975 of Iron Age settlement site at Abingdon dating from 600-500 BC.

increased from traders and small raiding parties to groups of settlers who introduced a coinage of gold, silver and bronze. The English heartland was not seriously affected by these newcomers until the large-scale invasions in about 50 BC, after which the Belgae gradually gained control of most of southern and eastern England. It is impossible to disentangle cultural changes due to trade and the diffusion of ideas from those due to personal contact but the combined effects were highly significant.

Farming communities with distinct signs of the grouping of homesteads into embryonic village communities now become common on the river-terrace gravels, for example at Cassington, Stanton Harcourt, Radley and Long Wittenham. The inhabitants continued the late Bronze Age practice of scratch ploughing of small square fields outlined by low banks or lynchets except at their upper edge.[3] These so-called 'Celtic' fields survive best on the chalk uplands where large areas bear their mark, as near Streatley Warren on the Ilsley downs, near Ashdown Park on the Lambourn downs, and on Fyfield and Overton downs near Marlborough where in places the lynchets are up to 3m high.

The relative paucity of burial mounds denotes a simpler disposal of corpses and the Belgae, for example, usually practised cremation in urns in flat graves. Earth-moving activities were concerned mainly with the building of hill forts and later also of linear ramparts for outlining lowland settlement sites and territorial or grazing boundaries. The efforts of the natives to defend themselves against iron-using invaders and later of these invading groups to defend themselves against incessant attacks upon each other's cattle and tribal territory, led to the construction of earthworks on almost every strong natural eminence.[4] Many existing hill forts were strengthened and many new ones constructed. They range in size from 1ha to 50ha and in complexity from circular or square univallate types to multivallate with elaborate entrances. Most of them dominate a wide scene and form delightful viewpoints, particularly at Willersey Hill, Lowbury Hill, Uffington Castle and Sinodun Hill. The small univallate circular camps, as above the villages of Windrush and Chastleton, were probably used solely for cattle pounds but most others have storage pits and evidence of dwellings. In the last few centuries BC these earthwork forts were probably part of a tribal strategy, being barracks and cattle stockades for defence as much against neighbouring tribes as against foreign invaders.

On Edgehill and the Cotswold scarp hill forts abound but they are rare on the limestones east of the Cherwell. Yet it happens that one particularly interesting example, Rainsborough camp in Northamptonshire between Charlton and Croughton, stands on the lip of a small valley overlooking the Cherwell from the east. This camp of 2.5ha is bi-vallate and has a western entrance that consisted of a passage 18m long leading to massive double gates flanked on each side with a stone-built semi-circular guardroom probably once linked overhead with a wooden bridge or sentry walk. The skeletons excavated here indicate fighting, burning and rebuilding from 500 BC onward. Finally in 1772 the camp was landscaped by heightening its surviving ramparts and building a dry-stone wall along the top of the inner bank.

On the chalk cuesta, hill forts are rare east of the Thames on the clay-with-flint country in the Oxfordshire Chilterns, but west of the river they abound especially near the Ridgeway. Among the favourites are Barbury Castle, an oval bi-vallate earthwork, and Uffington Castle with a single rampart and ditch enclosing 3.2ha. At Uffington the bank, probably strengthened by timber and sarsens, curves outward along each side of the causeway leading to the western entrance. Nearby the White Horse has been cut out of the chalk turf. A disjointed beak-headed animal in full stride, it is the strangest prehistoric monument in England. Its loose limbed design, measuring 111.3m overall, resembles figures on some Belgic coins and metalwork and may have originated on coins of Philip II of Macedon. It dates from the first century BC and once had a counterpart, the Red Horse, on Edgehill. Michael Drayton in 1612 in *Poly-Olbion* laments the indifference shown to the Warwickshire Red Horse.

> Her roome among the rest, to White-horse is decreed:
> She wants no setting forth: her brave Pegasian Steed
> (The Wonder of the West) exalted to the skies:
> My Red-horse of you all contemned onely lies.
> The fault is not in me, but in the wretched time:

Today the Red Horse can be traced only on aerial photographs while the White Horse retains its startling clarity. A short distance to the east near the foot of Blowing Stone hill is a sarsen perforated by a natural hole — probably made by a tree root — that

Uffington Castle, an Iron Age hill fort beside the Ridgeway.

when blown the right way emits a trumpet-like sound. It was mistakenly incorporated by Thomas Hughes into his romantic accounts of King Alfred's exploits in this neighbourhood. Strange to say, that arch-romanticist Walter Scott often visited Hughes' grandfather at Uffington vicarage, where no doubt he was told the local legends about Wayland's Smithy and about Amy Robsart's death at Cumnor manor close to the wooded Cumnor hurst visible on a clear day from the White Horse.

Scott embellished the tales in his *Kenilworth* (1821). Thomas Hughes left his grandfather's house when he was eight years old but later wrote semi-historical books on Alfred and on the scouring of the White Horse and achieved lasting fame with *Tom Brown's School Days* (1857).

Folklore and imaginative legends seem peculiarly associated with hill-top structures while lowland sites of great significance suffer undeserved neglect and obliteration. The Iron Age lowland settlements include several notable camps that demonstrate the growing importance of the riverine plains. Cherbury camp on the low Corallian platform at the northern edge of the Vale of White Horse near Pusey was once surrounded on three sides by a small stream and marshes. It has triple banks and ditches and its entrance, on the north east, was lined with dry stone walling and closed with large double wooden gates. Of far greater size and importance were the camps between the confluence of two rivers at Dorchester and Salmonsbury. At Dorchester an area of 46ha between the junction of the Thame and Thames was enclosed on the land side by two massive banks and ditches. Here probably was a native tribal stronghold later transferred northward by the Romans. Salmonsbury Camp is a double-banked square enclosure of 23ha on the gravels between the junction of the Dikler and Windrush near Bourton on the Water, with earthworks probably dating from the first century BC.

The Belgae settlements called by the Romans *oppida* were on a similar grand scale and are also connected with tribal life in the lowlands. Calleva Atrebatum, later part of the site of Roman Silchester, was probably one of the earliest large settlements of the Atrebates, a Belgic tribe that came from the continent about 50 BC. Bagendon, the pre-Roman oppidum of the Dobunni, lies near the junction of the Cotswolds and vale of Upper Thames on the western side of the Churn valley. Several stretches of dyke or rampart partly outline an area of over 80ha. The finds of coin moulds show the existence of a mint here about 20-30 AD and the pottery and brooches reveal a considerable trade with the continent. Recently it has been suggested that the original oppidum was slightly farther north beyond the strong earthworks called Scrubditch and was moved south when the Cotswold Dobunni were overpowered by the Belgic-controlled Catuvellauni about 15 AD.

During this period the natives and invaders acquired tribal names and tribal territories. Belgic peoples dominated all southern England east of the Cherwell and south of the upper and middle Thames. The Atrebates controlled the territory south of the Upper Thames valley and the Belgicised Catuvellauni most of the land east of the Cherwell and of the Thames at the Goring gap. The non-Belgic Dobunni had control of the Cotswolds and their continuation as far as Edgehill. The upper Thames lowland lay between these three powers who apparently frequently invaded each other's domain. Probably attempts to stop these raids or to delimit grazing grounds are expressed by the long linear earthworks erected for the most part after 50 BC. Grim's Ditch west of the Thames on the Aldworth-Streatley downs is continued east of the river from Crowmarsh to the crest of the Chilterns and so for long distances northeastward. It seems to be some sort of barrier across the Ridgeway

The White Horse. View showing the combe-indented scarp mainly of Middle Chalk and (to right) the summit of the Lambourn downs.

and Icknield Way. In Oxfordshire the stretches of rampart called Grim's Ditch seem to demarcate a large area near the Evenlode and Glyme.[5] This earthwork, clearly visible in Blenheim Park where it is cut through by the Roman Akeman Street, may have marked the boundary between the territory of the Belgae and Atrebates.

Romano-British Interlude

After Caesar's brief invasion of southeastern England in 55 and 54 BC, there came a great invasion by the Belgae, of whom one tribe, the Atrebates, pushed northward probably almost to the chalk escarpment overlooking the Vale of White Horse. Inevitably the Romans returned to what they knew would be a rich source of corn and metals, and under Claudius in 43 AD about 40,000 troops landed. Within four years they had gained control by conquest and peaceful negotiations of most of lowland England. The Atrebates were among the tribes who came to friendly terms with the Romans. In 47AD the new governor, Ostorius, made the line of the Foss Way his civil boundary, disarmed the tribes to the east of it and built forts at intervals along it to repel raids by the Silures from west of the Severn. During the next four centuries the inhabitants of the English heartland progressed rapidly under a Romanised civilisation.

The general pattern of agriculture altered little, the 'Celtic' fields being in full use and extended but the emphasis changed toward cereals rather than cattle and the main farmlands were on the lower, milder slopes of the porous uplands and on the lighter soils of the terrace gravels of the plains. Many isolated farms and numerous nucleated villages have been located, particularly on the riverine gravels between Wallingford and Lechlade, and on the dissected marlstone plateau south of Banbury. Some of the isolated farms were crude wooden structures with ditched rectangular enclosures but the headquarters of larger prosperous estates developed into fine villae, built largely of stone. Most of these villae were carefully sited near to a good water supply, with a pleasant view and reasonable access to a metalled road for wheeled traffic. They demonstrate the great advances in domestic architecture introduced by the Romans. The drystone walling and circular stone huts of previous centuries were now gradually superseded by rectangular structures which in towns and on rich estates had walls of shaped stone bonded with mortar, often plastered and decorated, as well as mosaic floors, hypocaust heating, and a wealth of baths and damp-proof storage facilities. Most of the villae excavated have been covered in and some have been destroyed. That at Stonesfield on Akeman Street had fine mosaic pavements which the farmer broke up because they attracted visitors. That at Ditchley was covered in after careful excavation. Here, typically, between 80 and 300 AD the building developed from a timber, wattle and daub structure (? for workmen) into an elaborate villa with two wings and a colonnade or veranda in front, all beneath a roof of local Stonesfield slate. It stood at the northern end of a courtyard over 100m square that was enclosed first by a bank and ditch and later by a wall that also protected a well, threshing floor, workers' quarters and a granary capable of holding the produce of 400ha. New finds of Romano-British structures are constantly being made and include a bathing establishment at the Grove at Ebrington.[6]

Of the local villae that are still exposed, Chedworth and North Leigh are of outstanding quality. The former, best reached by a winding road from the Foss Way at Fossbridge in the Gloucestershire Cotswolds, is perched on a high bench overlooking the lovely Coln valley. It is noted for its fine mosaic of the seasons but is in all ways a superb example of Romano-British villa culture. The villa at North Leigh lies tucked away in the deep meandering valley of the Evenlode with a charming view of the floodplain. The courtyard plan, nearly 91m square, developed gradually from a small timber building into a grand structure with mosaic floors and painted plastered walls. It lies just over 1km from Akeman Street in a district abounding in

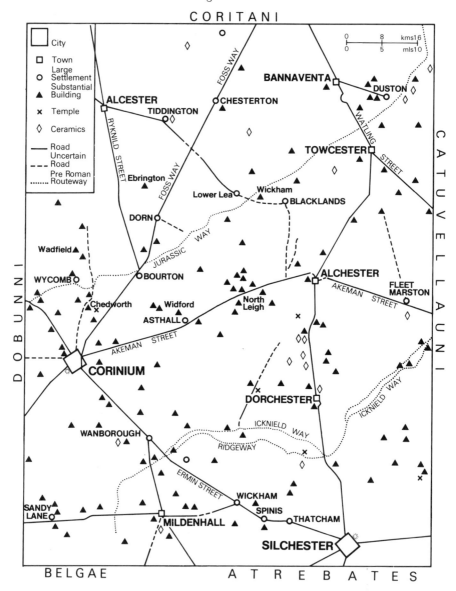

CORITANI

| City |
| Town |
| Large Settlement |
| Substantial Building |
| Temple |
| Ceramics |
| Road |
| Uncertain Road |
| Pre Roman Routeway |

BANNAVENTA
DUSTON
ALCESTER
CHESTERTON
TIDDINGTON
TOWCESTER
Ebrington
Wickham
Lower Lea
BLACKLANDS
DORN
Wadfield
WYCOMB
BOURTON
Chedworth
Widford
North Leigh
ASTHALL
ALCHESTER
FLEET MARSTON
CORINIUM
DORCHESTER
WANBOROUGH
ICKNIELD WAY
RIDGEWAY
ERMIN STREET
SANDY LANE
WICKHAM
SPINIS
THATCHAM
MILDENHALL
SILCHESTER

FOSS WAY
RYKNILD STREET
FOSS WAY
WATLING STREET
AKEMAN STREET
JURASSIC WAY
AKEMAN STREET
ICKNIELD WAY

DOBUNNI
CATUVELLAUNI

BELGAE   ATREBATES

Major constructional features of Romano-British times.

Romano-British remains. The nearby hamlet of Fawler derives its name from the Anglo-Saxon *faganfloran*, meaning variegated pavement or mosaic floor.

The Romans also introduced a more compact form of town plan and a more sophisticated town life. The main towns grew up on or close to pre-existing tribal centres, which they replaced in all ways. Thus Cirencester (Corinium Dobunnorum) was sited south of Bagendon at a spot where the deeply-incised valley of the Churn on the oolitic limestone broadens into a wide flat valley on the clayey Forest Marble that allowed a better lay-out and easier communications. The original Roman settlement here, a small fort called Chesterton where the Foss Way crossed the Churn, had by 100 AD been replaced by a well-planned town with a forum and large basilica. During the next century an area of about 97ha was enclosed by tall earthworks and masonry towers, and an amphitheatre was built to the west of the fortified city. Eventually the earthworks were fronted with massive stone walls. Corinium was the second largest Roman city in Britain and some of its glories are recalled in its excellent museum.

Silchester (Calleva Atrebatum) became a typical Romano-British cantonal capital. By the close of the first century AD the timber-structured capital of the Atrebates had been replaced by a new street plan, with a forum, town hall, baths, temples and many domestic houses, some of brick and stone set on flint foundations. The whole town of 93ha was enclosed by an earthwork still visible in Wall Lane near Rye House. Towards the end of the second century AD the city area was reduced to 43ha and the walls of the dwellings were being made entirely of masonry. This more compact town with its rectangular street plan of 39 *insulae* or blocks was surrounded first by a bank and ditch and a few decades later by a massive wall, over 2m thick at its base, from 6 to 8m high and topped by a rampart walk that was reached by internal stairs every 61m. The town had four main gateways, those on north and south (still visible) having single arches and those on east and west (now gone) double portals and guard rooms. There were in addition three small postern gates, the southeastern of which led to the extra-mural amphitheatre, an impressive oval earthwork now cluttered with shrubs and trees and once with its steep interior lined with tiers of wooden seating. Recently much treegrowth has been cleared from the town walls, long stretches of which survive, especially near Manor Farm, and are clearly visible from the adjacent lanes. A footpath leading from the parish church gives a full view of the whole town site, a vast gently sloping terrace of flinty gravels, naturally well-drained and ideally suited to Roman planning. In dry summers the outline of some of the Roman streets and larger buildings appears among the crops that cover the site which was excavated between 1869 and 1939 but returned to the plough. The modern churchyard of St Mary's overlies two of the three early temples here and has a sundial supported by part of a Roman column. A museum in the rectory garden at the north end of the drive contains models of buildings and many interesting finds including seeds recovered from pits and wells. The main collection of the wealth of objects found is nicely displayed in the civic museum at Reading, Berkshire. The parish with its mediaeval church and scattered farmhouses lies just within Hampshire. Silchester, although probably inhabited in a small way until the mid-sixth century, never proved attractive to Anglo-Saxon colonisers perhaps because it was too far from a copious stream. Today the open site yields good crops and encourages small excavations and schemes of preservation but modern society seems afraid of big decisions. Would it be too ambitious to consider the re-erection of a

Silchester, Calleva Atrebatum, aerial view showing Roman walls and traces of street plan revealed beneath the growing crops.

whole English Roman town? With Roman week-ends and gladiatorial contests in the arena, Silchester would prove a unique international attraction and, incidentally, would provide an exciting use for the millions of dead elm trees littering the countryside.

The other Romano-British towns in the English heartland were small and unimportant and essentially associated with the new road system. Roman Dorchester, an oblong enclosure of about 5.5ha sited just outside the older Belgic stronghold, was protected in the late second century by an earthwork that was faced by a stone wall about one hundred years later.[7] It controlled the crossing point of the Thames of the road from Silchester to Alchester and Watling Street near Towcester. Today the High Street of the village runs through the site of the north gate. Alchester was a new town, founded about 50AD near the junction of the Dorchester-Towcester road and Akeman Street. It was a square enclosure of about 10ha outlined at first by a bank and ditch and later also by a wall.[8] In Anglo-Saxon times it was superseded by Bicester and the only visible signs of its existence are a few low earthworks and a slight causeway. Towcester on Watling Street was a highway fort and posting station that in the second century was surrounded by a rampart and ditch, part of which forms the northwest angle of the present town. Alcester in Warwickshire was a small Roman town at the junction of Ryknild Street with a local road. Being at the junction of the Alne and Arrow its site proved attractive to Anglo-Saxon settlers.

The effect of these smaller Romano-British forts on the present landscape is less significant than that of the roads which they served. The English heartland was skirted on the north east by Watling Street and crossed on the west by the Foss Way. The latter ran from Bath (Aquae Sulis) to Cirencester and continues as a fine highway, in parts artificially raised and with flanking ditches, across the north Cotswolds to Bourton, Stow and Moreton in Marsh where it forms the wide main street. Thence it proceeded over low forested country via High Cross on Watling Street to its terminus at Lincoln. Near Bourton, at a large patch of gravels beside the Dikler at Chessels, a branch road, called Buckle Street or Ryknild Street, entered the Foss from Alcester by way of Bidford on Avon and Willersey Hill. At Cirencester a major road came in from Winchester and Silchester and crossed the Cotswolds to Gloucester, a *colonia* for veterans founded just before 100 AD.

The chief east-west highway in the upper Thames basin was Akeman Street which ran from London and St Albans to Alchester and Cirencester. Although a regional rather than national route it was carefully constructed and metalled and is still visible in the landscape, either excavated as at Asthall or as stretches of road, trackway, footpath and field boundary. The English heartland is ideal for the study of Roman roads. The place-names element *strat* or *streat* often reveals the existence of a metalled Roman road, as at Stratford, Stratton, Stratfield and Streatley. The roads are straight only in sections and have some difficulty in negotiating deep valleys. They were aligned on high points as was Akeman Street on Graven Hill near Alchester which in places they then had to swerve to avoid. Near Bicester by far the straightest road is the modern highway to Kidlington constructed in the 1930s. At Cirencester it looks as if originally the Foss Way was aligned toward the vicinity of Bagendon but before the road was completed it had to be diverted to the new capital several kilometres to the south.

The Collapse of Roman Colonisation

The withdrawal of Roman troops, internal dissensions and Anglo-Saxon invasions led to the decay of the more sophisticated objects and aspects of Romano-British culture. The raids of Saxon pirates had already become serious when in 410 AD Honorius told the tribes (civitates) in Britain to organise their own defence. No doubt civil and religious connections with Rome continued for a few decades and it was not until the 440s that the Roman emperor definitely refused military help and in the words of a Gallic chronicler, 'Britain, distressed by various defeats and other happenings, becomes subject to the Saxons'. Eventually Hengist and Horsa were invited to settle in Kent in order to help to repel the invaders, but the brothers quarrelled with and fought against the leading authority in southern England from 455 to 473. The disintegration of overall control opened the way for massive invasions by Angles, Saxons and Jutes.

Watling Street running north out of Towcester (Lactodorum).

As will be discussed in Chapter Three, the upper Thames now became the battle-ground between West Saxons to the south and Mercians to the north and during these troublous centuries the Romano-British towns and villae fell into ruin through either neglect or violent destruction. Eventually their exposed walls were pillaged for building stone and bricks of a very convenient size and the tilth of the ploughland surrounding them supplied downwash alluvium on slopes and encouraged tall tree growth that soon hid the lower structures, many of which were not discovered until modern times.

CHAPTER THREE

Anglo-Saxon and Danish Settlement

Early Anglo-Saxon Invasions

Although inland, the territory about the middle and upper Thames and middle Warwick Avon was affected quite early by new invasions. The two low oval mounds just east of Uffington Iron Age camp may be connected with early Saxon invaders as the one contained Saxon objects and the other 46 Romano-British skeletons, five with coins between their teeth to pay the ferryman for the passage across the Styx to the underworld. Although the many weapons found in the bed of the Thames at crossing places also seem to indicate numerous scuffles there appears to have been for some time a considerable overlap of the two cultures. At a villa at Shakenoak Farm near Wilcote, fragments of late Romano-British and early Saxon pottery were found together. Many burial grounds continued in use and place names combining bilingual synonyms are fairly common, among them *wīchām*, denoting a Romano-British *vicus* (village or street lined with houses) and a Saxon *-ham* (village).[1] Wilcote (originally Wyckham) had a large Romano-British village and Wycombe (also originally Wyckham) near Andoversford had a villa now partly buried beneath a modern bypass. Other *wichams* occur near Banbury while at Wickham, northeast of Newbury, the church with its Anglo-Saxon tower standing beside the junction of two Roman roads and the site of a Romano-British settlement strongly suggests continuity of occupation.

By the late fifth century burials of cremated pagan Saxons had occurred in several cemeteries often on riverine gravels on sites already used by Romano-British inhabitants as at Frilford, Reading and Long Wittenham. Within a few decades burials became common and signs of permanent settlement increase either in the form of isolated huts or of whole villages as at Sutton Courtenay. The invaders probably came mainly from the Wash along Icknield Street and in smaller numbers up the Thames valley and direct from the south coast. Whatever their route of entry, they settled largely on river-terrace gravels especially of the middle Thames and of the Avon near Bidford and Stratford. During these centuries the English heartland became increasingly the battleground between southern and northern influences, the former dominantly West Saxon or Wessex and the latter mainly Anglian and Danish or territorially Mercian and Northumbrian.

The Rise of Wessex: 550-830 AD

The expansion northward of the West Saxons was so spasmodic that the territorial changes could often be described as the southward expansion of the Mercians. The picture is vague but the turning point in either oscillation often stretched somewhere along the line of the upper Thames valley. The early advance of the West Saxons was halted when the Britons, or native inhabitants, defeated them at Mount Badon in about 500 AD. A possible site for this battle is Liddington Iron Age hillfort on the downs south of Swindon and recent excavations, although failing to find any evidence to substantiate the existence of King Arthur, did establish that the earthwork could have been occupied at the time. However, more examination of the pottery sequence is needed before any decision can be drawn as to whether Liddington was in fact refortified then.

Fifty years later in 552-6 the Marlborough downs and nearby territory were incorporated into Wessex after victories at Old Sarum and Beranburgh. The latter is Barbury Castle, a large oval Iron Age earthwork on the chalk downs above Wroughton near Swindon that probably was re-fortified by the West Saxons. In 571 a leader, probably Ceawlin, king of Wessex, defeated the Britons at Bedcan ford (unidentified) and gained control of most of present-day Oxfordshire and Buckinghamshire including the townships of Aylesbury, Bensington and Eynsham. In 577 Ceawlin and his confederate Cuthwine won a great victory at Deorham in the south Cotswolds and captured the cities of Bath, Gloucester and Cirencester. Ceawlin's successes continued and in 584 at Fethanleag near Stoke Lyne in north Oxfordshire he took many townships and countless spoil but his chief nobleman, Cutha, was slain and according to the *Anglo-Saxon Chronicle* the king returned 'in anger to his own'. This chieftain may have been buried under the *hoga de Cudeslowe*, a large earthen mound destroyed in 1261 by order of the Sheriff of Oxford because it was a favourite lair for robbers on the Banbury road just north of the town. In 592, after a great slaughter, Ceawlin was defeated at Wodnesbeorg, located at Adam's Grave where the Wansdyke crosses the ridgeway a few kilometres south of East Kennet. The Wansdyke or Wodnes Dic, a linear earthwork that once stretched from the Bristol Channel near Portishead to the neighbourhood of Hungerford or beyond, is still clearly visible in Wiltshire for long distances and consists of a strong rampart with a ditch on its northern side. It must be considered post-Roman and may well have been thrown up to protect the tribes to the south against advances of Anglo-Saxon invaders from the Midlands.

During the seventh century the frontier between Wessex and Mercia fluctuated widely. In 628 Cynegils, king of Wessex, had to make terms at Cirencester with Penda, the Mercian war lord, who then granted a large area of the north Cotswolds and adjacent tracts of the Avon drainage to Northumbrian princes. At this time there seems to have been here a vague territory of the Hwicce tribe, now recalled only by place names such as Wychwood and Whichford. Six years later in 634 the West Saxons established their bishopric under St Birinus at Dorchester on Thames but within a few decades had removed it to Winchester no doubt because of the pressure of Mercian advances from the north. In 666 Wulfhere, king of Mercia, drove the west Saxons south of the Thames and although Ine, king of Wessex, won a victory at Wanborough (near Liddington Iron Age camp) in 715, the Mercians swept on and within a few decades had overrun Wessex.

Yet the territorial control of the upper Thames continued to see-saw. In 752 Cuthred of Wessex revolted and recovered some territory by defeating the Mercians at Burford where a valleyside site is still called Battledge. In 779, Offa, king of Mercia crushed the West Saxons at Bensington and so regained present-day Oxfordshire and Buckinghamshire. Twenty years later Kenwulf, king of Mercia, founded an abbey at Winchcombe. However the tide turned again for the West Saxons between 825 and 830 when Egbert, their leader, defeated both the Mercians and Northumbrians and for the first time brought all English Britain under a single ruler. The triumph of Wessex was cut short by the arrival of hordes of invaders from the Danish peninsula.

Alfred and the Danes

The Danes, who had first forced a landing in England in 787, began a series of large-scale invasions in 834 and by 870 had conquered most of the territory north of the Thames. At this stage Alfred became prominent. He was born at Wantage in 849, the fifth son of king Aethelwulf by his first wife Osburgh and as a child showed great promise and was taken twice to Rome. From 868 to April 871 he assisted his brother Aethelred, now king of Wessex, in trying to repel the Danish horde. On the last day of 870 they won a skirmish at Englefield in Berkshire and in the following year fought six more battles, of which four were lost, one drawn and the other brilliantly won at Aescesdun, or Ashdown, probably in and around the Iron Age camp, now known as Alfred's Castle, at Ashbury. On Aethelred's death in April 871, Alfred became king and within a month had been defeated by the Danes at Wilton and forced to make peace with them. In 876 the Danes broke the truce and seized Wareham and Exeter, where, after a siege, they were eventually defeated and withdrew to Mercia. Alfred spent Christmas 877 at Chippenham and a few days later was almost caught there by a Danish commando. With a small band of followers he fled to the fort at Athelney which he used as a base for reorganising his forces and raiding the Danes. The silly fable about burning the cakes detracts from the skill and rapidity of his reorganisation. In May 878, with the pre-arranged help of levies from Somerset, Wiltshire and Hampshire, he crushed the Danes at Edington, and Guthrum their king with 29 chiefs accepted Christian baptism. The surviving Danish forces, which had retreated to their camp at Chippenham, went in the autumn to Cirencester where they stayed twelve months before moving on to occupy East Anglia. Then, as promised under the peace of Wedmore, all Wessex and English Mercia were free of Danish marauders and the territory north and east of Watling Street (London to Chester) became the Danelaw. The peace was kept until 885 when in opposing an uprising of the East Anglian Danes, Alfred succeeded in capturing and refortifying

Statue of King Alfred, Wantage.

London, which with the land as far east as the Lea, became part of Wessex. From 892 to 897 with the aid of his eldest son, Edward, he dealt successfully with a Danish invasion by sea of 330 sail and eventually drove most of the survivors out of the country.

On his death on 26 October 899 or 900, Alfred had established a secure military system in Wessex by three astute measures. First, the fyrd or national militia had been reorganised into two halves, which relieved each other at fixed intervals so ensuring the constant availability of a field army and of a home-guard. Secondly, the obligation of thanehood was enforced on all owners of 5 hides or more of land, thereby ensuring the king of a corps of highly skilled warriors complete with their own food and pay. Thirdly, he built a system of strongly fortified *burhs* at strategic points, which could be quickly garrisoned by nearby people in time of danger. Among these are Wallingford and Cricklade (described in Chapter Sixteen), both being square earthworks such as would be built by a leader acquainted with Roman forts.

Alfred's other achievements defy summarisation. He probably introduced the shire administration into English Mercia. He also built up the navy that Aethelwulf his father had founded, and in his later, less martial years translated many scholarly Latin texts into Anglo-Saxon. The manuscript of his translation of Pope Gregory the Great's *Pastoralis (Pastoral Care)* in his own hand is in the Bodleian library, Oxford. It was presented to Werfrith, Bishop of Worcester, who had translated the *Dialogues of Gregory* for which the king had written a preface. Alfred appears to have encouraged other arts. In 1693 a remarkable gold jewel decorated with cloisonné enamel and bearing the Anglo-Saxon inscription 'Alfred had me made', was unearthed at Newton Park near Athelney Island. It is attached to an animal-headed socket in which once a thin stem or pin was fixed. Its original use is doubtful; suggestions range from a pointer for following the lines of a manuscript, the face depicted in the enamel being a representation of Sight, to a long, decorated pin for a cloak. It is in the Ashmolean Museum at Oxford together with a similar, smaller Anglo-Saxon jewel from Minster Lovell in Oxfordshire. At Wantage the site of the royal palace is unidentified and at the Norman Conquest the manor ceased to be crown property. The marble statue of Alfred with a battle-axe now adorning the market square, was carved by Count Gleichen and presented to the town by Lord Wantage in 1877.

On Alfred's death his children undertook the conquest of the Danelaw using the same policy of constructing fortified *burhs* at strategic points. His eldest daughter, Ethelfleda, 'Lady of the Mercians', between 913 and 918 attacked the land of the 'five boroughs' and fortified Warwick, Tamworth and Stafford. His eldest son, Edward who succeeded him as king, took over the administration of the upper Thames district and fortified Oxford in 910 or 911, Buckingham in 914 and Towcester in 917. On Ethelfleda's death in 918, Edward went on to recover Northampton and to capture Lincoln, Nottingham and Stamford and when he died at Faringdon in 925 he was overlord of most of Britain. Alfred's aims were completed by his grandsons Athelstan, Edmund and Eadred and by his great-grandson Edgar (959-975), who was recognised as ruler of all Britain. During these reigns there were mints at Wallingford, Warwick and Reading.

Rulers of the House of Wessex

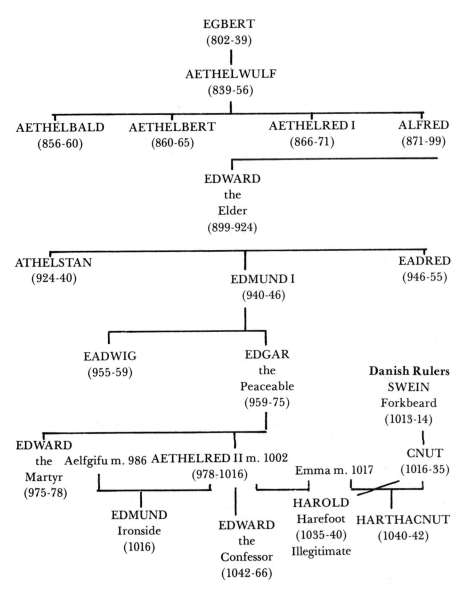

EGBERT
(802-39)

AETHELWULF
(839-56)

AETHELBALD   AETHELBERT   AETHELRED I   ALFRED
(856-60)   (860-65)   (866-71)   (871-99)

EDWARD
the
Elder
(899-924)

ATHELSTAN   EADRED
(924-40)   EDMUND I   (946-55)
                  (940-46)

EADWIG   EDGAR
(955-59)   the   **Danish Rulers**
                  Peaceable   SWEIN
                  (959-75)   Forkbeard
                                        (1013-14)

EDWARD   CNUT
the   Aelfgifu m. 986 AETHELRED II m. 1002   (1016-35)
Martyr   (978-1016)   Emma m. 1017
(975-78)

                                  HAROLD
EDMUND   EDWARD   Harefoot   HARTHACNUT
Ironside   the   (1035-40)   (1040-42)
(1016)   Confessor   Illegitimate
                  (1042-66)

Note: Aethelred II married as his second wife, Emma, the daughter of Richard I of Normandy, and their son was Edward the Confessor. This Emma later married Cnut.

The Overthrow of the Wessex Dynasty

The collapse of the political dominance of the house of Wessex, or lineage of Cerdic and Alfred, was more dramatic than its rise. Edward the Martyr, who held a witenagemot at Kirtlington, was assassinated in 978 and under Aethelred II ('Ethelred the Unready') England was invaded by a succession of large forces from Scandinavia. The unfortunate king tried to strengthen his cause by marrying Emma, daughter of Richard, Duke of Normandy, but ruined his chances of success when he secretly ordered the Danes living in England to be massacred on St Brice's day, 2 December 1001. The victims included Gunnhild (sister of Swein Forkbeard, king of Denmark and Norway) who was a Christian and one of the hostages for a peace arranged a few years earlier. Swein swore revenge and from 1003-14 he and his jarls harried southern England except when bought off by large ransoms. In 1006 Reading and Wallingford were burnt to the ground. From 1016-35 England was part of the Danish empire under Cnut but eventually hatred of his sons Harold and Harthacnut helped the recall of Edward the Confessor, then living at the court in Normandy. Edward had been born at Islip, Oxfordshire, in 1004. A small chapel, probably rebuilt in stone in the twelfth century, stood north of the church there until about 1780. Its font, traditionally said to have been used for the Confessor's baptism, was desecrated during the Commonwealth and after many changes of ownership finished up in Middleton Stoney church. Edward reigned from 1042 to 1066 and on

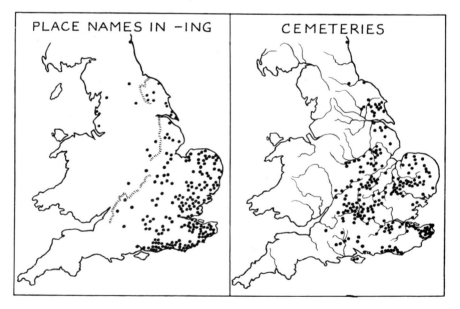

Anglo-Saxon cemeteries and place-names ending in -*ing*. In the English heartland the paucity of early place names ending in -*ing* contrasts with the numerous cemeteries.

his death the political pulse of England moved southeastward to London and Windsor.

The Anglo-Saxon Achievement

The new invaders, from across the English Channel and North Sea came to settle and occupy land on which to feed themselves by agriculture. They were patriarchal groups in search of sites with a water supply, meadow, pasture and ploughland and spaced themselves in small communities upon the richer, flatter land. Because many of the more desirable sites near springs and rivers had already been cleared and occupied by earlier settlers the same localities often show signs of occupation from at

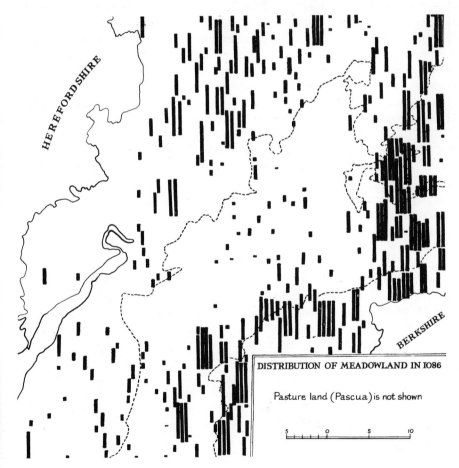

The distribution of meadow *(pratum)* in 1086 in the Cotswolds and adjoining vales. Meadow, often as water meadow on the valley floor, was highly prized. In the columns 1 cm is equivalent to about 50 acres.

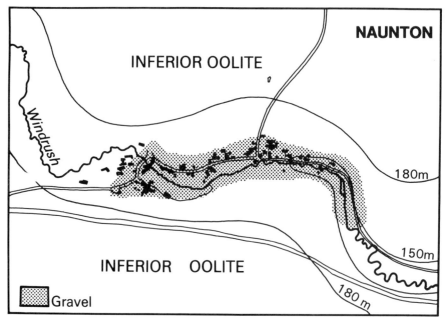

Naunton: a typical Anglo-Saxon riverside settlement. The original settlement kept entirely to the gravel terrace.

least the Bronze Age onward. Upon copious spring lines as at the escarpment foot of the Lambourn downs and in gravel-lined river valleys as on the Cotswold Coln and Warwickshire Stour, villages grew up every three or four kilometres, within easy reach of each other.

Early Anglo-Saxon settlement throughout the English heartland was especially attracted to gravel terraces on the valley floors which were light to plough and provided drinking water from shallow wells. These early villages may usually be distinguished by their place name endings of *-ing, -ington, -ingham, -ton* and *-ham*, the first three signifying a village, or home belonging to a certain person, and the latter two simply a village or township. The earlier settlers tended to avoid heavy clay soils and densely-forested tracts such as Arden and Wychwood. Almost everywhere in the English heartland each little group of settlers managed its farming originally or eventually in much the same way. Any form of grazing was grazed in common and the arable land was arranged in large 'fields', commonly two, one of which each year was ploughed and the other left fallow so that each 'field' came successively under crops and under fallow, when it could be grazed and manured. The ploughed field was subdivided into numerous blocks or strips held by individual farmers and all strips were open or unenclosed except for a temporary fence put up around the whole field to keep out stock until the crops had been harvested. So prevalent was this pattern of farming in the English heartland that it became known as the Midland open field system. How it originated remains a mystery. It may have begun in

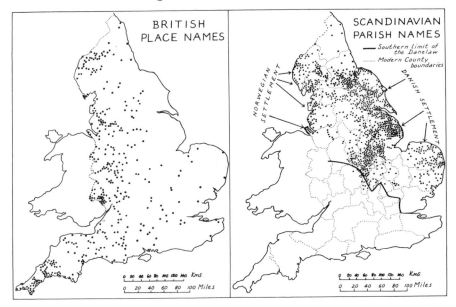

Surviving British place-names and Scandinavian parish names: showing marked paucity in the English heartland where Anglo-Saxon place-names ending in *-ton, -ington* and later forms predominate (after A.H. Smith). Details in Wales are excluded.

Romano-British times and developed gradually over the centuries from one field (infield) as the most practical management when a heavy plough drawn by several oxen forced individual farmers to combine their stock to make up a ploughteam. As the population of the village increased more common pasture or forest would have to be converted to arable and the ploughed 'fields' would increase either in size or in number and would become more subdivided. Eventually on the more populous areas the number of 'open fields' would increase to two or three or more. On the other hand the newcomers to the lowlands of the English heartland may already have been familiar with the use of two 'open fields' before they arrived.

Irrespective of the origin of the open field farming pattern, the villages grouped their houses together amid their own territory; the grouping may have been loose but it was definite and deliberate. Nearly all dwellings were constructed of wattle and daub or timber and thatch until masonry became more common in Tudor times.

The Danes in the late ninth century, once they had decided to settle rather than pillage, made similar settlements, usually distinguished by their place-names endings *-by*, signifying a village, and *-thorp*, implying a settlement near a village. However, the Danes created very few villages in the English heartland most of which lay south of the Danelaw and Watling Street. Danish place names are relatively rare and unimportant in the drainage basins of the Thames and Severn. The hamlet of Thrupp in Oxfordshire obviously occupied a space midway between the two older settlements of Shipton on Cherwell and Kidlington. It never grew into a village and

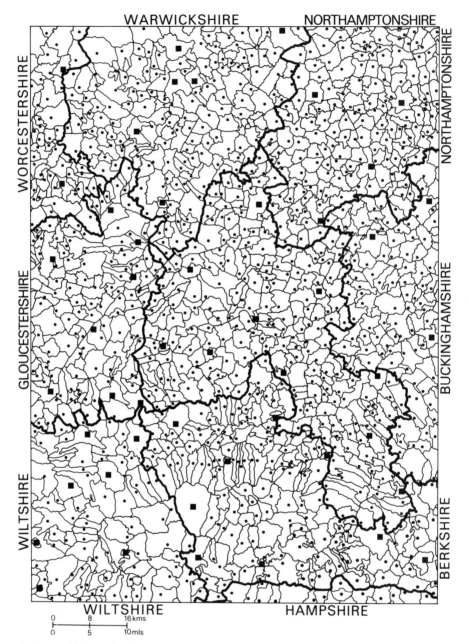

WARWICKSHIRE   NORTHAMPTONSHIRE

WORCESTERSHIRE

GLOUCESTERSHIRE

WILTSHIRE

NORTHAMPTONSHIRE

BUCKINGHAMSHIRE

BERKSHIRE

WILTSHIRE   HAMPSHIRE

0   8   16 kms
0   5   10 mls

The parochial mosaic; the unitary basis of local life; More than 1100 parishes are shown. Squares denote places that acquired administrative rights superior to those of a simple parish council. The county boundaries relate to the pre-1974 reorganisation when north Berkshire was transferred to Oxfordshire.

never had its own church and burial ground.

Between the sixth and eleventh centuries the population of many villages increased sufficiently for new communities to be set up in nearby uncolonised spaces, especially in wasteland and woods. This outward expansion of the family groups seems to be revealed by the descriptive classification of villages, such as Upper, Middle, and Lower Tysoe, and Great, Little and Wyck (dairy farm) Rissington. The clearing of woodland is often denoted by place names ending in *-leah* or *-ley*, *-holt*, *-hurst*, *-feld* and *-stoc* (stockade). King Alfred in the following passage describes one aspect of this expansion which for serfs provided the prime hope of obtaining land that might be recognised as freehold by the lord of the manor.

> We wonder not that men should work in timber-felling and in carrying and building, for a man hopes that if he has built a cottage on the *laenland* [land under the feudal tenure] of his lord, with his lord's help, he may be allowed to lie there awhile, and hunt and fish and fowl, and occupy the *laenland* as he likes, until through his lord's grace he may perhaps obtain some day boc-land and permanent inheritance.[2]

The overall effect of this new colonisation was that by the time of the Norman Conquest the spatial distribution of the settlements had become almost the same as it is today.

An important change in the social life of the villages began with the spread of Christianity, especially in Wessex after the arrival of Birinus at Dorchester on Thames in 634. At some time from the eighth century onward an increasing number of settlements came under the care of a priest and most of these *parochia* or parishes survive today, maybe slightly altered and in some cases subdivided. In time the parish acquired a church and a Christian cemetery and so there began the greatest single architectural feature of a village and its only truly communal building.

The earliest existing church masonry in the English heartland dates mainly from the tenth and eleventh centuries except at Brixworth (north of Northampton) where the church has been described as 'the most imposing architectural memorial of the seventh century surviving north of the Alps'. It was probably founded about the year 675 in the time of Saxulf, Bishop of the Mercians, as a monastery attached to Peterborough Abbey and was built on the plan of an early Christian basilica with a wide nave with aisles and a clerestory leading at the east end to a polygonal apse and presbytery. Between the nave and the presbytery was a tall triple arched arcade of which the north springer only remains. The western ends of the Saxon aisles also survive. These were the rooms forming the porticus to left and right of the two storeyed entrance porch which was raised in later Saxon times to make a tower. The pillars of the arcade leading into the former aisle from the nave are over 2 metres broad and their arches consist of Roman bricks as also do the arches over the clerestory windows and the doorway of the porticus that once led from the north wall of the presbytery.

Surrounding the apse is a half-sunken semi-circular ambulatory. Such crypts or ambulatories are characteristic of the early ninth to eleventh centuries on the

Brixworth, a largely seventh-century church, with most arches constructed of Roman bricks.

continent and are common in French and German churches but none exists there of
so early a date as this. Brixworth ceased to function as a monastery after Danish
devastation in 870. In Norman times as a parish church it was given a south doorway;
about 1300 a two-bayed south chapel was added and the Saxon tower heightened and
embellished with pinnacles and a spire.

Elsewhere in the English heartland early masonry survivals are more fragmentary
but are quite sufficient to show the quality of late Anglo-Danish stonework. In
Warwickshire at Wootton Wawen the church tower was built around an early
eleventh century structure and at Tredington high above the present arcades of the
nave are the remains of double-splayed Anglo-Danish windows and doorways. In
Oxfordshire the chief survival is at Langford where the tower, except for the parapet,
and the sculpture in the south porch are Anglo-Saxon. In Berkshire the early
stonework includes the projecting west tower of mortared flint with long and short
quoins at Wickham and a coffin lid at Stratfield Mortimer inscribed to Aegelward
who died in 1017 and is mentioned in the *Anglo-Saxon Chronicle*. In Wiltshire the
church at Avebury has interesting Saxon masonry, some of it reset, while in the
Gloucestershire Cotswolds, Coln Rogers, Daglingworth, Somerford Keynes,
Bibury, and several other village churches retain some long-and-short work and
early sculptures. When to this stonework are added the abundant local Anglo-
Danish treasures in the main museums, particularly at Oxford and Reading, the
artistic achievements of this early colonisation become quite impressive.

CHAPTER FOUR

The Norman Conquest and its Aftermath

Towers and battlements it sees
Bosomed high in tufted trees.
(Milton, *L'Allegro*)

The Norman Invasion

William of Normandy after his victory at Hastings on 14 October 1066 met with further opposition at London Bridge and decided to isolate London by devastating a wide belt of country around it on both sides of the Thames. With that aim he led his forces circuitously to Wallingford where they crossed the river by bridge and ford and encamped on the Oxfordshire side. Archbishop Stigand came here to swear allegiance to William who on the following day advanced with his forces along the Icknield Way and so entered London via Berkhamsted from the north.

The Conqueror willingly retained the services of other influential English collaborators, among them Aethelwig, Abbot of Evesham (1058-77) who was given general oversight of seven west Mercian shires, including Worcestershire, Warwickshire, Gloucestershire and Oxfordshire.[1] Aethelwig served the king well and at the same time ensured that very little of these territories was laid waste. It seems more than coincidental that one of the two native Englishmen who retained vast baronial estates was Turchil of Arden.

The reign of Edward the Confessor and the Norman conquest brought England into closer contact with west European ideas, the effect of which is seen in the resurgence of monasticism and the foundation of new planned towns. But the Norman invasion was a military conquest and led to the construction of many castles that later encouraged baronial warfare.

Norman Castles

The expansion of Wessex into the Midlands depended largely on defensive *burhs* or towns surrounded by ramparts as at Wallingford, Cricklade, Oxford and Warwick. In much the same way, the Norman conquest was based on castles, often sited at the same strategic points chosen for defence by the Anglo-Saxons. The unusual feature of the Norman system was the motte, a large circular mound of earth encircled by, and largely derived from, a wide ditch. The summit of the steep-sided motte was flattened to allow the erection of a timber fort or keep, and its perimeter was heightened by a wooden palisade. The motte was introduced into Herefordshire from Normandy by knights invited over by Edward the Confessor before the conquest. At the conquest the motte type of castle proved a quick and relatively easy way of garrisoning and controlling a district. Within a short time there were other variants, as for example castles standing on natural steep-sided eminences which could manage without mottes and those built of masonry in the form of a tall square tower, as at the Tower of London and Rochester and further defended by an encircling rampart, first of earth and later of stone.

But the changes in the motte castle are especially important as that type abounded. The climb to the top was laborious and soon it became common to add a courtyard, or bailey, on one or both sides of the base of the mound. Eventually, this defended courtyard was enlarged to surround the motte entirely, and, in time, proved so convenient that it was itself surrounded by a defended base court, the outer bailey. So the concentric rings increased from motte, to inner bailey and outer bailey. When masonry became common the wooden keep became a shell keep and, under the influence of the crusades, the walls of the baileys included towers with numerous intricate architectural features for defensive uses.

As far as possible castle sites were selected with some natural defences; Windsor is on a knoll of chalk overlooking the Thames and Warwick on a sandstone bluff above the Avon. Where steep-sided eminences were lacking, the castle would be partly or wholly surrounded by water, as at Kenilworth, Wallingford and Oxford. The bigger castles belonged to the crown and most others have occasionally passed to the sovereign through default of heirs and misdemeanours of their owners. Powerful lords, with large retinues, needed several castles since hunting in the nearby forests, for deer and other game, was an indispensable meat supply. Marlborough castle had the advantage of Savernake forest while Kenilworth and Beaudesert got supplies from the Forest of Arden. These hunting grounds needed to recover from the culling of the herds and also periodically the family and their retainers liked to move elsewhere temporarily to allow their living quarters to be cleansed and refreshed.

The story of castle building and castellar life is splendidly illustrated in the English heartland. During and after the Conquest the crown kept a tight grip on the counties or shires by building castles in the chief towns. The castles were often constructed ruthlessly upon the Saxon townships and within or astride the old fortifications of the *burhs*. *Domesday Survey* records demolition or 'waste' (unoccupied houses) at Warwick, Wallingford and Oxford. At Oxford, where the motte still dominates the west end of the city, the erection of the castle in 1070 must have contributed to the fact that nearly half of the 1,000 properties yielded no tax. At Wallingford the castle was constructed inside the town ramparts upon pre-existing Saxon houses and in 1975 when the site was threatened by some redevelopment for residential purposes

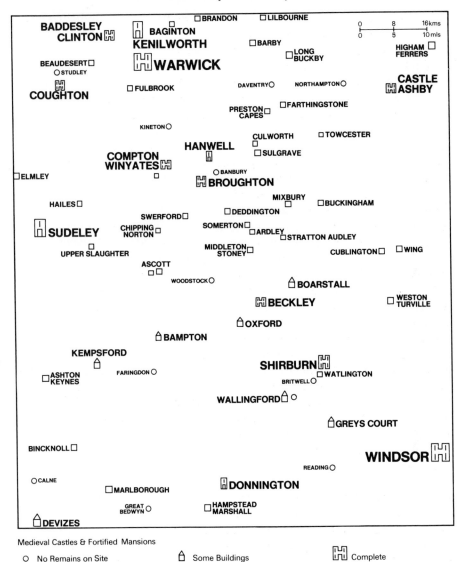

Medieval Castles & Fortified Mansions

O No Remains on Site
☐ Earthworks Only
⌂ Some Buildings
🏠 Extensive Remains
🏰 Complete

Distribution of mediaeval castles and fortified mansions.

involving deep foundations, archaeologists condemned the scheme as this was a key site for the investigation of the nature of a late Saxon town.

The kings also controlled the chief forests partly because they loved hunting.[2] Outside the main towns and royal woodlands the rural countryside was divided into manorial estates and on the larger of these, feudal overlords tended to erect their own castles. Soon the policy of the crown was to increase and strengthen royal strongholds and to keep in check baronial fortresses. The revolts of the barons and the struggle between Stephen and Matilda in the 'nineteen long winters' of 1135-54 led to the building of numerous unauthorised, or adulterine castles. In 1153 by the Treaty of Wallingford, when Stephen was recognised as king and Henry (the Second) his heir, unauthorised castles were to be razed, the crown lands restored and foreign mercenaries banished from England. But castles continued to be key points in rebellions against the king and in private wars between noble families and in 1217 instructions were again issued to raze unlicensed fortresses. Thus, it is not surprising that the remains of motte-and-bailey type castles are fairly common in rural districts. In Oxfordshire, they have been located and some excavated at, for example, Deddington, Beckley, Chipping Norton, Middleton Stoney, Stratton Audley, Ascott under Wychwood and Bampton. Similarly, in southern Warwickshire the earthworks and mounds of a motte and bailey are clearly visible on Castle Hill near Upper Brailes, also near Kineton, and on a hill at Beaudesert in the forest of Arden. The last named belonged to the de Montforts and has near it a small Norman church. At Upper Slaughter in the Gloucestershire Cotswolds the village partly surrounds a castle motte with a small bailey. The steep-sided motte is about 4m high and 25m (80ft) in diameter at its top which is nearly flat and originally centred upon a stone-lined well. A small bailey also about 25m across surrounds the motte and drops steeply to the floodplain of the Eye Brook on the north and east, and toward the manor house on the south. Excavation revealed that the upper 2m of the mound were artificial and that its base was probably supported by stone masonry.[3] There are signs of other earthworks outside the bailey but the most striking external feature today is the way the roads of the village encircle the base of the castle mound. The manor at Upper Slaughter was granted by William the Conqueror to Walter de Lacy, one of his foremost knights. It passed eventually to Walter's grandson Gilbert who fought in the wars in Stephen's reign and whose lands were restored to him by Henry II. Thus it is probable that the earthworks at Upper Slaughter were constructed in the twelfth century and slighted, including the removal of the timber keep at the top of the motte, soon after the Treaty of Wallingford in 1153.

In later centuries many landowners with royal favour and sufficient funds obtained licences from the crown to crenellate their manor houses. Such licences were given to Robert de Grey of Rotherfield near Henley on Thames in 1347, to Sir Richard Adderbury of Donnington in 1385 and to Thomas Wykeham of Broughton near Banbury in 1406. But many of these buildings have a peaceful aspect; they are domesticated castles rather than stark fortresses. The great strongholds belonged to the crown and a few powerful barons.

The Monastic Revival

The great Benedictine monasteries at Evesham, Winchcombe and Abingdon that managed to survive the Viking raids grew rich after the conquest. William

St. George's tower, Oxford castle.

celebrated Easter in 1084 at Abingdon. The monks at Eynsham abbey, which was founded about 1005, dispersed at the Norman invasion and were re-formed about 1095 by the Bishop of Lincoln. The new foundations included Reading Abbey created in 1121 for the Cluniacs by Henry I who endowed it with the hand of St James of Compostela. The king never saw its completion and was buried here in 1136 some thirty years before its final consecration by Archbishop Becket in the presence of Henry II. Its architects devised elaborate carvings and made much use of beakhead ornamentation in the arches which may explain why these fantastic northern motifs occur in nearby churches.

In the twelfth century most new monasteries were for Augustinians as at Northampton (1105), Cirencester (1117), an enlarged reorganisation of a ninth-century college of secular canons, Kenilworth priory (1122), and Osney priory (1129) which soon rose to abbey status and became the wealthiest monastic house in Oxfordshire.

In this century the Cistercians began to establish themselves on the relatively few open spaces still available for colonisation and sheep farming. In 1138 they moved a small house founded at Otley near Oddington a few years earlier, to a spacious site on the outskirts of Thame where it flourished. Within the next three decades, they successfully established abbeys on heathland near the upper Evenlode (since called Bruern from the French *bruyère*), at Stoneleigh near Kenilworth, and at Notley near Long Crendon. Their greatest local achievement came in 1246 when Richard, Earl of Cornwall, younger brother of Henry III, founded and richly endowed an abbey at Hailes at the foot of the Cotswold scarp near Winchcombe. The fine church was consecrated by fourteen bishops in the presence of Henry III and Queen Eleanor, many nobles and 300 knights. In 1270 Richard's son Edmund gave it one-third of a relic of Holy Blood which he had obtained on the continent and had been guaranteed by Pope Urban IV. Pilgrims then flocked to what Chaucer called 'the blode of Christ that is in Hayles'.

The twelfth-century monastic foundations included several nunneries and a few houses of the Knights Hospitallers of St John of Jerusalem and of the Knights Templar whose possessions were later incorporated into the Hospitaller estates. The early thirteenth century brought numerous groups of Mendicant Friars who settled especially in Oxford and Northampton. Add to these minor houses, various smaller establishments such as hospitals, hospices, granges and alien cells and add to the vast holdings of all local monastic houses the estates held here by distant abbeys such as Gloucester and Westminster, and the cultural and economic influence of the monasteries assumes gigantic proportions. They were great educators and until the introduction of printing into England by William Caxton before 1477 were the chief scribes and producers of manuscript books.

The Feudal Village, 1066-1216

Before the Norman conquest the countryside was, as we have seen, divided into vills or townships based on the needs of small groups of self-sufficient farmers. The limits of these holdings as shown by Anglo-Saxon charters were based wherever possible on definite landscape features such as streams, isolated trees, tumuli, earthworks and tracks. Upon this agrarian unit the church imposed the parish which was the vill or vills served by and paying tithe (one-tenth) to a certain priest. The Normans superimposed on this village system a tighter legal relation between the overlord or lord and other inhabitants on his estate. The new landlords, mainly barons, bishops and abbots, were given numerous estates — now called manors — in return for supplying trained knights for the King's service. The manors granted to a lord were usually scattered in various counties and an individual manor did not always coincide with a vill or parish. In Oxfordshire the parish and manor coincided in about two parishes out of every three whereas in Warwickshire and Buckinghamshire the proportion decreased to one in two. Where the manor and village or vill did not coincide, parts of the same village might belong to different manors or, on the other hand, a single manor might contain several adjacent vills. The agricultural affairs of each manor were settled at the manorial court which was held, usually in the hall of the manor house, every six weeks or so.

Place names now acquire a manorial tinge; villages of the same name instead of being distinguished by adjectives of their relative position could often be distinguished by different ownership, as in Oxfordshire where,

Cherwell winds with devious coil
Round Hampton Gay and Hampton Poyle.

Similarly the addition of Abbots, Prior, and Temple (Templars) denotes a monastic connection.

The Norman invasion hastened the building of parish churches and the typical village soon consisted of one or more manor houses, a stone church, a manorial water mill and a loose grouping of crude dwellings with their own garden plots. Outlying houses were rare and in most villages the dwellings were spaced in an almost haphazard manner around an open green. It is, in fact, hard to imagine how any sizeable farming community working a communal open field system could have managed without such a village green on which cattle could be temporarily kept or assembled within convenient reach of all fields and within sight of all dwellings. Many of these village greens survive today, some with a pond or watering place.

The church was usually erected at the expense of the lord of the manor who then owned the advowson or right of presentation to the living, which normally carried with it the tithe or one-tenth of the annual yield of all crops and stock. The cottages, mostly one-roomed and rarely long houses, were frail and although a few may have had stone footings, all have gone. Of the manor houses scarcely any have survived, except at Appleton and Sutton Courtenay. The former retains a fine deeply moulded, round-arched doorway leading to a hall from which two large doorways give access to service rooms, while Norman Hall at Sutton Courtenay has a grand south doorway also dating from about 1190-1200.

This paucity of domestic architectural survivals contrasts with the abundance of fragments of Norman stonework in parish churches, several hundred of which have incorporated into their later extensions round pillars and round arches, often decorated with zig-zag chiselling and beakheads. Among the numerous examples of rural churches with rich Norman masonry are Cholsey, which was given to Reading Abbey by Henry I, Salford Priors with an elaborate, doorway, Bucklebury with rosettes, faces, flowers and pellets as well as zigzag, Cuddesdon which belonged to Abingdon Abbey, and Cassington which was built by Geoffrey de Clinton before 1123 and appropriated soon afterwards by Eynsham Abbey. The wide choice of carved tympana includes the representations probably of David grasping two gryphons at Charney Bassett, of a very artistic angel holding a fluttering scroll at Halford and of the Harrowing of Hell and the Coronation of the Virgin in the richly decorated doorways at Quenington.

After the lapse of eight centuries village churches that remain largely Norman are rare and are virtually confined to small isolated parishes that never increased much in population. Presumably Beaudesert church retained so much late Norman work because the castle became uninhabited and most of the parishioners migrated to the new town of Henley in Arden. The fine Norman church at Elkstone on the highwolds north of Cirencester seems always to have been big enough for the few parishioners. At Crowmarsh near Wallingford the vill was divided at the conquest between Walter Gifford, Duke of Buckingham and King William's new foundation at Battle Abbey. About 1120 the burgesses of Wallingford founded a hospital for lepers and other unfortunates at Crowmarsh Gifford and built a small free chapel for their use. The generosity of the burgesses stopped there, for in 1214 they petitioned King John to close the thriving market that the parishioners had set up and the population of the tiny hamlet never outstripped the capacity of their church. The same may be said of the small, entirely Norman, church at Padworth near Aldermaston and of the still smaller one on the Cotswolds at Condicote which retains some good Norman work.

Two Norman survivals of exceptional quality confirm this conclusion. At Avington, a quiet secluded hamlet on the meadows beside a branch of the Kennet about 5km east of Hungerford, the small church is a harmony of round-arched windows and doorway and a chancel arch redight with zigzag, beakheads, gaping beasts and scallops. The simple rectangular plan measures about 75ft (23m) by 15ft (4.6m) and is divided into five bays, two in the chancel that once was rib-vaulted and three in the nave, each about 15ft square. At Iffley, now a suburb of Oxford, the Norman church is perched on the upper lip of the deep valley of the Thames. It was built between about 1170-80 as a gift from the St Remy family and was decorated inside and out in the Romanesque style then existing at Reading Abbey and characterised by traditional imaginative carvings of unnatural objects mingled with signs of a new naturalism. The west facade, with its rose window carefully restored to the original plan, is especially striking while the west doorway with exuberant carvings of rosettes, quatrefoils, fantastic beasts and fighting knights excites endless

The Norman font at Avington.

controversy of interpretation. The Norman plan of chancel, low central tower and nave remains unaltered except perhaps for a lengthening or rebuilding of the eastern bay in the Early English style before 1250.

The marked contrast between the abundance of surviving church architecture and the scarcity of surviving domestic dwellings cannot be entirely explained by the better building techniques of the clerics. In rural areas during the 'nineteen long winters' of Stephen's reign (1135-54) the barons expended much of their wealth and manpower in erecting unauthorised castles. After the Treaty of Wallingford (1153) most of these motte-and-bailey structures were razed, leaving only hummocky sites. The havoc wrought in the countryside by rampaging baronial troops during the struggle between Matilda and Stephen is shown, no doubt with some exaggeration, by the taxation accounts for 1156 in which nearly two-thirds of Warwickshire, two-fifths of Oxfordshire and over one-third of Berkshire were declared to be 'waste'. There can be no such doubts about the reality of the rapid recovery of prosperity during the late twelfth century.

The Great Expansion of Farmland, 1216-1335

The economic recovery mentioned above lasted throughout the thirteenth and early fourteenth centuries in the English heartland which, apart from the campaigns of Edward (later Edward I) and Simon de Montfort in 1264-5 in the Kenilworth-Evesham neighbourhood, enjoyed freedom from devastating armies. The peace and the increase of population brought about a remarkable expansion of farmland by clearance of forest and cultivation of the waste. This expansion was aided by a large decrease in the area recognised officially as royal forest and so subject to forest law. Soon in the English heartland there were only six or seven large tracts under forest law and none existed in Warwickshire, the Chilterns and the Gloucestershire Cotswolds. Assarting or forest clearing went on rapidly around the open fields, especially in wooded districts and on the fringes of royal forests. For example, the forest of Arden, which had never been royal forest, now experienced a large increase of population[4] while in both the manor of Witney on the fringe of Wychwood forest and the manor of Wargrave on the edge of Windsor forest about 1660 acres were cleared during the thirteenth century and scarcely any of their land remained unreclaimed. The assarting was organised in a variety of ways: the lord of the manor might employ his permanent workers or he might allow the villeins and freemen to lease the cleared land either for a lifetime or more, or on condition that part of the assart belonged to his desmesne and all of it was available for common grazing after the harvest.

The parish churches reflect the general prosperity of the period as well as the new architectural styles coming from England's large territories in France. In the first half of the thirteenth century the bishops made a great effort to improve the care, patronage and serving of secular churches. The chancel was the responsibility of the patron or of his representative the vicar, while the fabric and upkeep of the nave fell on the whole community. Under the new regulations, lay persons, except perhaps the patron, were forbidden to enter the chancel and eventually the custom grew up of separating it from the nave by a screen. During this period most parish churches were altered usually by extending the east end (chancel) and by adding side aisles and sometimes a tower at the west end or less commonly above a central crossing. The round arches of the Norman and Romanesque style gradually gave way to pointed

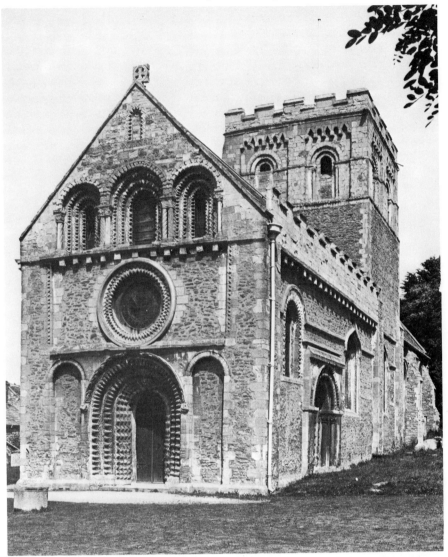

The Norman church at Iffley.

arches and, after a brief Transitional period, slim Early English lancet windows became common throughout Midland churches. Decoration was no longer important and the beauty lay in the elegant proportions of the smooth masonry and the brightness of the splayed lighting. The lancets, at first set singly, soon became grouped in pairs and triples beneath a single pointed hood mould as at Uffington. When the lancets were arranged in multiples of two or more, the blank spaces

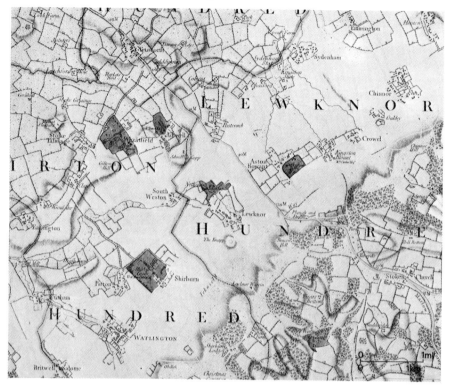

Enclosed and unenclosed parishes in southeast Oxfordshire in 1794. The enclosures lie mainly
on the clay-with-flints on the Chiltern summit to the east and Gault clay to the west. The open
field parishes are mainly on a flat wide bench of Lower Chalk cleared of woodland during prehistoric times (from R. Davis of Lewknor).

between their heads and the hood mould were filled, after about 1240, by one or more
tiny windows which within a few decades acquired geometrical shapes such as
curvilinear triangles, circles, trefoils and quatrefoils. Eventually there evolved more
decorative designs in which the mullions flowed freely into the upper tracery to form
a unified design. Ultimately the tracery took over and became decorative rather than
structural.

The variations and progressions of these designs may be seen in several hundred
parish churches and it is invidious to select examples, especially as several parts of the
sequence occur in most of them. Among the few that remain predominantly of one
style, those at North Moreton near Wallingford and Shottesbrook are outstanding.
At North Moreton the south chapel or chantry was built about 1295 by Miles de
Stapleton who with his two sons fell at Bannockburn (1314). It is lighted by five
graceful Geometrical windows of an unusual design and the large east window still
glows with its original stained glass. Various animals are carved in the cornice along
the external wall. At Shottesbrooke in Berkshire near Henley on Thames the flint

Uffington church, mainly of the mid-thirteenth century. A spire on top of the tower was 'beat down by a tempas, wind, thunder and liten' on 2 December 1743.

church, dating from about 1337 when Sir William Trussell founded a college here, is almost entirely Decorated in style with much elaborate tracery in its windows.

Several churches have fascinating exuberances and pleasantries. At Bloxham and Dorchester carved figures are combined with the tracery to give a three-dimensional effect. The magnificent choir at Dorchester Abbey was extended eastward in the early fourteenth century and the new windows included one with reticulated tracery bearing sculptured groups of Passion scenes at its intersections and another with tracery representing a foliaged tree springing from Jesse and bearing on its branches statues of his descendants. The carvings in some late Decorated churches reveal a touch of humour, as at Bloxham where a corbel table is carved in fantastic beasts, two men at fisticuffs and a pig with a litter, and at Harwell where the chancel arch rests on sculptures of comic figures being bitten by dragons and the side of the priest's doorway is adorned with a merry man with a bottle.

Parish churches now began to acquire memorials and tombs, the characteristic form in the beginning being a prone effigy of a cross-legged knight, a mailed crusader. Superb isolated examples of about 1280 exist at Dorchester and Stowe Nine Churches while at Aldworth near Goring the church was so famous for such tombs that Queen Elizabeth rode there pillion behind the Earl of Leicester to see them. These Aldworth 'giants', for they are more than life-size, suffered severe mutilation in the next century and the one in the outside of the church wall has vanished but nine effigies, all of the de la Beche family, remain. Five cross-legged knights and a lady lie under elaborate canopies in the north and south walls while two other knights, one with his wife, lie on table tombs between the arches of the arcade and as they do not have their legs crossed were presumably not crusaders. The last monument to be erected was to Sir Nicholas a constable of the Tower who died in 1346. The visitor will notice that one of the crusaders is not quite prone and another half reclines on one elbow, a rare departure from normal. Formerly, according to a local diarist, 'In ye E end of ye Syle did hang a table fairly written in parchments of all ye names of ye Family of de la Beche, but ye Earle of Leicester coming with ye Queen Elizabeth in progresse took it downe to show it her, and it was never broughte againe'.

The placing of tombs in churches was facilitated by the growing custom of adding side aisles and of dividing the chancel from the nave by a screen usually of oak as at Stanton Harcourt and rarely of stone as at Broughton and Baulking. This division was in fact highly desirable because the nave, which had no seats except stone benches round the walls, was used as a depository for communal utilities including the public coffin in which the corpses of paupers were carried to the burial ground, the military weapons of the able-bodied men, and the firehook for pulling thatch from burning cottages, a tool that in recent centuries was replaced by a man-handled fire engine.

The longevity of churches contrasts vividly with the rare and fragmental survival of domestic dwellings. Scarcely any parts of surviving half-timbered buildings can be safely attributed to before 1330 although the timbers of one cruck house (now faced with brick) at Steventon gave a radiocarbon date of about 1300. Stonework, with

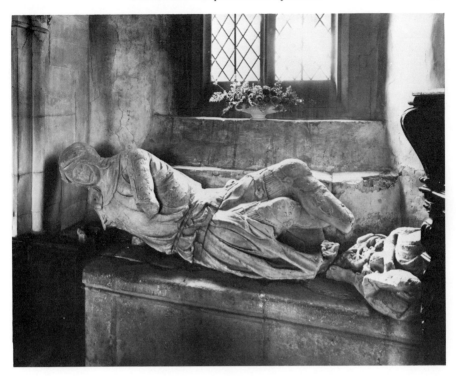

One of the Aldworth 'giants'.

pointed arches and tracery similar to that in the nearby parish church, has survived in several manor houses, a few rectories and an occasional monastic grange. Many of the surviving fragments are in former or present market towns as at Burford (Hill House and others), Deddington (Castle House and Leadenporch House) and Thame (Prebendal House) but rural districts are well represented. Broughton Castle is quite outstanding nationally and is described in Chapter 7. Stonor Park incorporates the four bay arcade of a two-aisled hall which originally had a south wing with service rooms on the ground floor and solar (upper living room) above. The manor house at Fyfield near Abingdon conceals behind its Elizabethan front a stone building of about 1320 complete with porch, hall and service wing, only the solar wing being missing. Among other manor houses with masonry of this period, sometimes as part of a private chapel, are those at Charney Bassett, Cogges, East Hendred, Ebrington, Sutton Courtenay and Swalcliffe.

The architectural survivals also include several large tithe barns, built of local limestone and roofed with local stone slates. That at Stanway manor was built in the fourteenth century for the Abbot of Tewkesbury and serves today as a meeting place and theatre. The following three fine tithe barns in the English heartland, each open daily until sunset, are cared for by the National Trust and still used for farming

The tithe barn at Great Coxwell.

purposes. That at Bredon in Worcestershire is exceptionally well constructed with a steeply pitched roof and on its east side two gabled porches one of which is surmounted by an upper room (tallat) with a fireplace, added in the fifteenth century. It makes a charming picture reflected in the nearby pond. The tithe barn at Middle Littleton near Evesham stands among market gardens close to the manor house and church. It is almost certainly thirteenth century and its ten bays extending over 140ft (43m) by 32ft (10m) originally stored crops for the abbots of Evesham.

The barn at Great Coxwell near Faringdon, was built in the late thirteenth century for the monks of Beaulieu who then owned the manor. A gigantic structure, over 152ft (46.5m) long and 51ft (15.5m) high to the apex of its roof, its roof timbers are supported by tall oak baulks standing on square stone pedestals about two metres in height. These supports divide the main body of the barn into nave and aisles, and the entrances for wagons were in the transepts until extra large doorways were inserted in the end walls in the eighteenth century. It is the finest surviving mediaeval barn in England and William Morris considered it 'as noble as a cathedral'.

An even larger tithe barn of slightly earlier age once stood near the church at Cholsey, a manor of Reading Abbey. It had the same maximum height and double the length of the Coxwell barn and its roof timbers were supported internally by tall stone pillars. Although the biggest tithe barn in the world it was replaced in 1815 by the present enormously long barn of stone and flint.

The High Tide of Mediaeval Prosperity

By the early fourteenth century the English heartland was, relative to the rest of England, at the peak of its prosperity. According to the lay subsidy of 1334, which taxed moveable goods at the rate of 1/5 in rural areas and 1/10 in boroughs and ancient desmesnes, large parts of mid-Oxfordshire and west Berkshire were assessed at over £30 per square mile. Oxfordshire was the second richest county after Middlesex and Berkshire the fifth, a reflection no doubt of their large production of grain and livestock.[5]

It is not known how long this exceptional prosperity lasted. In much of western Europe several poor harvests occurred between 1315 and 1321 due probably to wet autumns, but in the Midlands heavy rain is not necessarily disastrous on the porous soils of the downs and wolds. In several other regions of England agriculture and sheep farming were declining by 1330 but in the southern Midlands the wealth of new buildings, such as late Decorated churches, indicates continued prosperity. It is certain that at this time the population had increased greatly, probably three- or fourfold since *Domesday Survey* and that cultivation had spread on to the higher hills and deep into the waste and woodland.

The agrarian expansion was accompanied with improvements in farming and changes in the social system. The productivity of farms, often barely one-third of that of today, was gradually increased and in several parishes the old two-field system was turned into a three-field economy, so enlarging the proportion under arable. At the same time the tendency was to commute service duties for money rents, as most peasants produced in normal years enough grain for their own needs and to provide a surplus to market for cash. Occasionally the peasant might find himself short of food after bad harvests but he now had more opportunities of achieving freedom and advancement. For example the typical villein who owed a few mornings' work each week to his lord could become free or virtually free by commuting his labour for a cash rent, or by escaping to a borough for a year and a day, or by buying land from his lord, or by assarting in return for free land, or by becoming, with his lord's permission, a priest. Not surprisingly, by the mid-fourteenth century the unfree or serfs formed only half the labour force and they continued to decrease rapidly in number.

However, there is a less cheerful side to the apparent prosperity because the expansion of ploughland began to outrun the demand for grain and soon some of the newly-cleared tracts were not proving worthwile. By 1341 a considerable area of arable land had been abandoned because, it was said, of climatic hazards and poor soils. Probably an important contributory factor was the migration of villagers into the newly-created boroughs (*see* Chapter 16), the effect of which would first be felt in villages nearest the new towns and then ripple outward when people on marginal lands moved in to fill spaces and opportunities vacated in the lowland villages first affected. In Buckinghamshire many villages had some abandoned arable and poor soils were blamed in seven vills on the higher Chilterns. Upon the Cotswolds the small manor of Eyford and the hamlets of Harford and Aylworth near Naunton, which had 7, 4 and 5 ploughs respectively at Domesday Survey, went out of cultivation. Thus some of the less profitable ploughland had reverted to pasture before the Black Death brought disaster to towns and villages alike.

CHAPTER FIVE

General Decline and Recovery: 1335-1550

The Black Death and Abandonment of Villages

The bubonic plague came across the Channel into southwestern ports in August 1348 and spread via Bristol and Oxford to London. Its effects in the next two years were catastrophic. On manors belonging to the bishop of Winchester in the south of the English heartland the loss in population ranged from 30 per cent at Brightwell to 66 per cent at Witney. Elsewhere in Oxfordshire by 1350 at Steeple Barton 32 of the 36 customary tenants had died, the water mill was ruinous and more than 600 acres had fallen out of cultivation. Four years later the extent of uncultivated ploughland had doubled and the manor house was said to be worth nothing. At Tilgarsley in Eynsham, where 28 families were wealthy enough to pay tax in 1327, the whole population disappeared; at Hethe near Bicester 21 of the 27 villeins died and their lands remained untilled; at Tusmore the hamlet was virtually wiped out and with its church soon vanished. However, relatively few settlements were hit as hard as Tilgarsley and Tusmore and the majority struggled on as shrunken villages and stricken towns with half or two-thirds of their former population. The boroughs now had vacancies for more villagers and in villages and hamlets the more enterprising persons could acquire larger holdings and villeins could rise to freemen and freemen to yeoman farmers.

This great loss of population coincided with a rising demand for wool as well as for beef and hides, all of which began to fetch such good prices that livestock could prove more profitable than grain. In many manors pastoral farming solved the problem of shortage of labour which was made worse in some localities by further outbreaks of plague-like diseases in 1390-1 and 1407. Landlords began to enclose their land for livestock and to evict from hamlets and villages the serfs or peasants no longer needed to serve the economy. In Tudor times 8 or 9 per cent of the total area of the English heartland was thus enclosed, sometimes in square fields of about 10 acres which can still be recognised because their ridge-and-furrow reflects the pre-existing strips of the open fields. Enclosure and the abandonment of hamlets for the sake of sheep farming occurred most widely on the clay vales. In Warwickshire abandoned or 'lost' villages abound on the Feldon, a land of ancient settlements with an open field system, whereas they are rare in Arden where enclosed assarts were made direct from the forest. Similarly in Oxfordshire lost and shrunken villages are common in the

The English Heartland

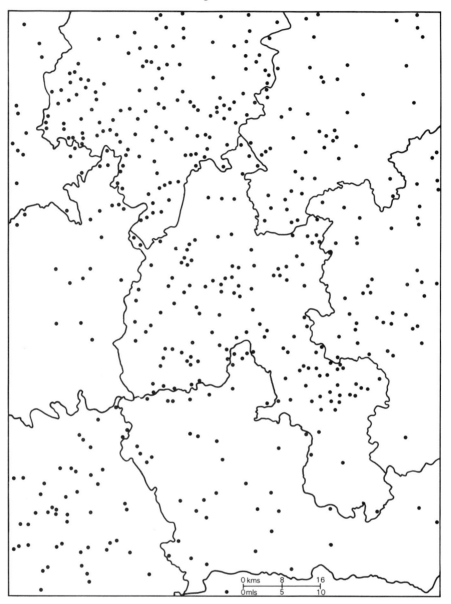

Distribution of unfortunate and unsuccessful settlements since about 1086. Some small hamlets, such as Signet, have been added to the official list of shrunken and deserted sites.

pastoral vales and uncommon on the Chilterns where enclosure from woodland had been active since Norman times. These abandonments and evictions went on from soon after the Black Death to late Tudor times when the increase of population raised the demand for grain and the national government began to heed the complaints against enclosures.

In southern Warwickshire over 113 deserted mediaeval villages have been identified and most of these were on the Feldon and abandoned between 1450 and 1485. Among the later or Tudor abandonments are Upper and Lower Radbourne, depopulated by the Catesby family about 1486, Compton (Wynyates) emparked by Sir William Compton in the reign of Henry VIII, and Wormleighton depopulated by William Cope about 1500. At the last named village the rather isolated church survived and when John Spencer, a large-scale grazier, bought the estate in 1506, he built his grand new manor house near the church and so some distance east of the mounds and hollows of the deserted village and original moated manor house. From his new headquarters he proceeded to acquire and depopulate the nearby hamlets of Little Dassett, Hodwell and Stoneton. Similar destruction of villages in Warwickshire continued for many decades and Shakespeare was well aware of it. In *Pericles* (Act II, sc. i), the first fisherman when asked how fishes live in the sea, replies:

'Why, as men do a-land; the great ones eat up the little ones. I can compare our rich misers to nothing so fitly as to a whale; a' plays and tumbles, driving the poor fry before him, and at last devours them all at a mouthful. Such whales have I heard on a th' land, who never leave gaping till the've swallowed the whole parish, church, steeple, bells and all'.

Evictions for sheep farming in the vales of Oxfordshire, Buckinghamshire and Northamptonshire are described in a pamphlet called *The Decaye of England only by the great multitude of Shepe* (c. 1550), which, in fact, underestimates the area put down to grass by over fifty per cent.[1] It complains that since the coronation of Henry VII, in Oxfordshire alone 'there lacketh 40 ploughs; every plough was able to keep six persons . . . and where that twelve score persons were wont to have meat drink raiment and wages now there is nothing kept but only sheep'. This eviction of weeping tenants, driven out to a life of crime, is a common theme in other contemporary literature. So sheep farming caused the abandonment of many villages already weakened by plague and migration to towns. In Warwickshire most of the lost villages had less than 20 taxpayers when they were abandoned. In Oxfordshire the grim struggle for survival is well documented. At Asterley, on the oolite northwest of Woodstock, the post-Domesday clearing supported 20 'farms' in 1279. In the mid-fifteenth century the chief landowner decided to leave the village and to build himself a new house in Nether Kiddington. Then the Bishop of Lincoln, in 1466, deprived Asterley of parish status because, he said, it was too poor to support a chaplain by reason of the barrenness of its soil, defects of husbandry and an unusual prevalence of pestilence and epidemic sickness. Today a solitary farmhouse marks its site.

Deserted mediaeval village sites of Nether Chalford and Over Chalford in the upper Glyme valley near Enstone, Oxfordshire.

The lingering decay of Brookend in Chastleton parish makes familiar reading. An eleventh century clearance of heath or waste under the control of Eynsham abbey, it had 16 households, growing mainly grain and pulses in 1279. It survived the Black Death and remained reasonably viable until about 1440 when all but three of the families left by night, with their goods and chattels to a nearby village. In spite of the abbot's efforts to get new tenants the settlement was virtually abandoned by 1470 and today is recalled by the solitary Brookend House.[2]

There are very few examples of the successful transference of a settlement to a more favourable site. Combe near Woodstock originally stood, as its name implies, in the deep valley of the Evenlode. This floodable site was abandoned about 1350 in favour of a new settlement on the slopes above, where a large area had been assarted. The Norman church on the valley floor continued in use till 1395 when the abbot of Eynsham, who owned the manor, erected a new Perpendicular church near the spacious green of the village on the watershed.

The cumulative result of over two centuries of abandonment, enclosure, emparkment, re-siting and migration was that more than 400 settlements in the English heartland virtually disappeared from the landscape. Some of their sites are marked by a lonely farmhouse or church or a few cottages; many reveal themselves only by sunken tracks and hummocks and hollows in the turf; a few have vanished without visible trace. The distribution of settlements that survived in 1550 has remained almost intact ever since.

Economic Recovery and Perpendicular Gothic Churches

By the late fourteenth and early fifteenth centuries many individuals and corporate bodies had wealth enough to spend on elaborate buildings. Wool sales from sheep runs were highly profitable and the poverty of landless serfs and vagrants went hand in hand with the opulence of wool merchants and large landowners. Ecclesiastic architecture now gradually adopted the Perpendicular Gothic, an essentially English style that originated at Westminster and was perfected after 1331 at Gloucester Abbey, whence it spread throughout England. Whereas the Decorated style embraced variety of form and detail, the Perpendicular was based on the uniform repetition of a single dignified motif. Windows were now arranged in a series of small panels (panel tracery) and soon they and doorways were surmounted by square-headed mouldings. Ceilings or vaults were usually either panelled in wood or beautifully fan vaulted. In rural parishes many new churches were built in this style and, more commonly, west towers, aisles and windows were added to existing churches but the fact that most of this work post-dates 1400 shows how slow was the recovery from the effects of the Black Death. The towns led the way because their guilds became powerful builders as at Stratford, Abingdon and Warwick. At Abingdon the fraternity of the Holy Cross, founded about 1389 in the church of St Helen, set up a rood screen there, built a new bridge over the Thames, undertook road repairs and in 1446 founded for thirteen poor people the hospital that still faces on to the churchyard. The church with its double aisles is mainly Perpendicular and retains a rare or unique panelled painted ceiling of about 1390. At Cirencester the abbot added a great three-storeyed south porch in 1490 and a few decades later the citizens replaced the thirteenth century nave with the present magnificent

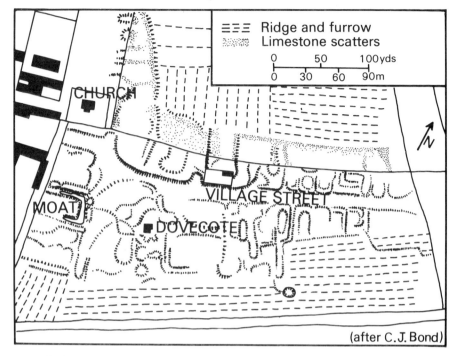

CHURCH

VILLAGE STREET

MOAT

DOVECOTE

≡≡≡ Ridge and furrow
░░░ Limestone scatters

0   50   100 yds
0   30   60   90 m

N

(after C. J. Bond)

* Billesley Trussell, a deserted mediaeval village near Stratford-upon-Avon.

clerestoried structure. In other boroughs on the wolds, as at Chipping Campden, Northleach, Burford, Fairford and Chipping Norton, glorious Perpendicular Gothic churches were raised mainly by wealthy woolstaplers. But such noble buildings were not restricted to the hills and the style is seen to advantage at St Nicholas', Newbury, raised in 1500-1532, by the munificence of Jack of Newbury the famous clothier, as well as at Henley in Arden and in the tower at Cricklade added by John Dudley, Earl of Warwick.

The prosperity of the boroughs filtered out to nearby villages. At Fairford, where the graceful church with its famous coloured glass was built by John Tame soon after 1492, the donor also rebuilt the parish church at Rendcomb. The urban influence on rural churches was especially widespread around Oxford where Perpendicular was introduced at New College chapel in 1379 to 1386. This college paid for the chancel at Adderbury, the work of Richard Winchcombe who later designed the Divinity School at Oxford. The same Richard was probably also responsible for the Melcombe chapel at Bloxham and the exquisite small fan-vaulted chantry chapel at North Leigh. Similarly William Orchard, the master mason of Magdalen College, may have contributed for Lord Harcourt, High Steward of the University, the excellent Perpendicular features at Stanton Harcourt and South Leigh.

Elsewhere in the English heartland remodelling of the parish church, as distinct

Cirencester parish church, the tall nave as rebuilt by the generosity of merchants and textile manufacturers between 1515 and 1530.

from minor alterations, depended on the presence of a rich resident landowner rather than of woolmen, merchants and clerics. The fine Perpendicular churches in Buckinghamshire at Hillesden and Maids Moreton reflect the wealth of a squire and of two maiden sisters respectively. The presence of important magnates was a chancy affair in an age when barons were likely to be soon out of favour at court and out of property but the results of such a concentration of wealth upon a certain parish may be seen to perfection at Ewelme, Minster Lovell and Stanton Harcourt in Oxfordshire. At Ewelme the manor was inherited by Alice Chaucer, grand-daughter of Geoffrey Chaucer the poet. She became the wife of Thomas, Earl of Salisbury and on his death at the siege of Orleans in 1428 married William de la Pole, his chief lieutenant who later became successively Earl and Duke of Suffolk. After fourteen years of continuous fighting in France, this Earl from 1431 onwards enjoyed dwelling in Ewelme 'for the love of his wife and the commodity of her lands'. About 1432 they rebuilt the body of the church and went on to found and endow a school, schoolmaster's house and almshouse, all of which are still used for their original purpose. The manor house of the Chaucers was less fortunate. After her marriage to the Earl of Suffolk, Alice enlarged it into a base court of timber and brick and an inner dwelling of brick and stone within a moat. In 1450, the Duke was beheaded and Henry VIII seized all the Suffolk estates and he and later Queen Elizabeth stayed at the house. It became ruinous in the next reign and eventually two of its brick buttresses and some roof timbers were incorporated into the present modest dwelling. Today Alice (*ob.* 1475) lies beneath a canopied tomb with a life-like effigy in a richly ornamented chapel and the charming village with its watercress beds culminates in the charitable legacies of the Suffolks.

The story of Minster Lovell is equally typical of the effect of the rise and demise of a powerful resident baron. The Lovells became lords of the manor here soon after the Norman conquest and in the early fifteenth century rebuilt the manor house and much of the church. Francis, ninth Lord Lovell, breaking from the family Lancastrian tradition, joined the Yorkists and managed to escape to Flanders after their defeat at Bosworth in 1485. His estates were confiscated by Henry VII who visited Minster Lovell house on three occasions. Francis returned secretly to England in 1487 to aid Lambert Simnel's rebellion but was again on the losing side and at the battle of Stoke was either slain or escaped by swimming on horseback across the Trent and living in hiding. Some confirmation of his survival comes from a letter of 1787 written by William Cowper, clerk to the Parliament, to Francis Peck, an antiquary:

> 'Apropos to this, on the 6th May, 1728, the present Duke of Rutland related in my hearing that, about twenty years then before (viz in 1708, upon occasion of laying a new chimney at Minster Lovell), there was discovered a large vault or room underground, in which the entire skeleton of a man, as having been sitting at a table, which was before him, with a book, paper, pen, etc etc; in another part of the room lay a cap; all much moulded and decayed. Which the family and others judged to be Lord Lovell, whose exit hitherto had been so uncertain.'

Northleach church, as rebuilt by the gifts of woolstaplers between about 1380 and 1500.

Somehow the incident became associated with the popular ballad of the Mistletoe Bough, in which the newly-wedded bride during the festal games hid herself in a chest that locked itself and she was never seen again. The legend is especially linked with Minster Lovell but Greys Court also stakes a claim because it has a large Flemish chest said to have come from Minster Lovell, that meets all requirements except perhaps age.

In 1602 Sir Edward Coke purchased the house and his family retained it until 1747 when much of it was dismantled by Thomas Coke, Earl of Leicester who was then completing his superb Palladian mansion at Holkham in Norfolk. The Lovell buildings were used partly for farm purposes until the government saved them in 1935 and made them safe for visitors. Today the ruins stand picturesquely beside the swift-flowing Windrush and make with the church, manor farmhouse, circular dovecot and large barns a delightful group rich in feudal romanticism.[3]

Stanton Harcourt also confirms our suggestion that for a village to acquire noble buildings it must have wealth from wide external sources concentrated upon it; or, inversely, that the normal rural parish cannot generate in itself exceptional qualities. Stanton, on a flat gravel terrace of the upper Thames near Eynsham was acquired in the twelfth century by the Harcourt family who lived there until they migrated to

Nuneham Courtenay in 1711. Their ancestral home was then allowed to decay and most of it had been pulled down by 1760. The parish church and three notable fragments of their great house bear witness to the opulence of the Harcourts. They maintained and beautified the Norman church which retains a rare thirteenth century screen and a lovely Perpendicular chapel added about 1470, probably by William Orchard, to take some of their tombs and monuments. Here lie the alabaster effigies of Sir Robert Harcourt and Margaret his wife (*ob.* 1471), both wearing the Order of the Garter, a distinction among female effigies in England shared only by Alice, Duchess of Suffolk, at Ewelme and one other. Nearby is the altar tomb of Sir Robert Harcourt (*ob.* 1490), the standard bearer of Henry VII at Bosworth Field. The church contains many other Harcourt tombs, earlier and later, as well as the richly-carved marble pedestal of a shrine brought by Sir Simon Harcourt, sheriff of Oxfordshire, from Bicester priory when it was dissolved.

Three important fragments of the mansion survive: the gatehouse, of about 1540, incorporated in the modern house, the north-eastern tower, now known as Pope's Tower, and the kitchen. The tower of about 1465, once part of the north range, has a vaulted chapel on the ground floor and three more storeys, the topmost being the room where Alexander Pope in 1717-1718 completed the fifth volume of his translation of the *Iliad*. The kitchen, a spectacular late fourteenth century structure re-roofed in 1485, stands detached as a square (31ft by 33ft), one-storeyed building with an embattled parapet and an octagonal pyramidal roof capped by a leaden griffin holding a weathercock. The cooking was done in three huge ovens and at two fire spaces, once with spits, along another wall. There is no chimney; the smoke went out through shutters (now windows) just below the roof that could be opened or shut from a passage round the roof on a level with the parapet. When in full roast the kitchen must have been a hell for the cooks in summer and as it stood on the west or prevailing wind side of the mansion the residents did not need a menu. Apparently the mansion was never moated and was protected by a battlemented wall round the whole site.

Church Memorials

The fine effigies of the lord of the manor at Ewelme, Minster Lovell and Stanton Harcourt are characteristic of the church memorials of the Perpendicular Gothic period. At first most of the effigies were of knights in armour and ladies in flowing dress and wimple carved in stone or rarely, as at Sparsholt, in oak. In the fifteenth century alabaster was the usual material and the less-costly tomb chest with decorated sides of Purbeck marble and lids inlaid with brasses, also became popular. The brass-rubber will find the English heartland a happy kneeling ground, there being nearly 90 figures dated before 1550 in Berkshire alone. Outstanding collections survive at Northleach, Chinnor, Cirencester, Chipping Norton and Thame. The chronologically minded will seek early examples, such as those to William de Leicester (*ob.* c. 1338) at Chinnor; to John Smith (c. 1370), with one of the

The tomb of Sir George Forster and his wife (*ob.* 1526) in Aldermaston Church. Realistic sculptures of their children occupy the front of the tomb. The painting on the church wall in the background is fifteenth-century.

earliest inscriptions in English, at Brightwell Baldwin; and to William Grevel (*ob.* 1401), probably the first to bear a merchant's mark, at Chipping Campden. The exceptionally artistic fifteenth century brasses include those of woolstaplers at Northleach, of Thomas de Cruwe and his wife at Wixford, Lady Clopton at Quinton, and the aristocratic Lady Philippa Bishopsden at Broughton.

Secular Building: The Typical Manor House

A few grand domestic buildings (described in Chapter 7) and numerous moderate-sized and small manor houses of this period survive little altered. Half-timbering was common everywhere and prevailed for a long time yet on the clay vales. The finest examples are in Warwickshire and outside this treasure land of half-timbered styles high quality specimens are rare, the main exception being Ockwells Manor near Bray in Berkshire which dates mainly from 1446 to 1466 and, with its cloistered courtyard and wealth of armorial glass, has been called by Pevsner 'the most refined and sophisticated timber-framed mansion in England'. Its timbering is constructed on a morticed post-and-truss arrangement which became popular in the early sixteenth century and superseded the older cruck construction.

On the wolds the use of stone for better-class dwellings became more common in the fifteenth century and the square-headed Perpendicular Gothic gradually developed in a simple form into the traditional or vernacular Cotswold architecture with stone mullioned windows beneath square mouldings or dripstones.

The typical manor house became associated with two or three interesting contemporary features, the tithe barn, moat and pigeon cote. The barns reflect the size of the manor and the available building material. The best preserved are of stone and include the magnificent structures built by New College about 1400 at Upper Heyford and Swalcliffe. Moats had sanitary and drainage advantages as well as defensive uses and did not require, as did crenellation, the permission of the Crown. They were especially common on the clay vales and sixty moated sites, exclusive of castles, have been traced in Oxfordshire alone,[4] as at Holton Park, Camoys Court at Chislehampton, and Gaunt House at Standlake which was fortified and besieged during the Civil War. At Yelford on the Thames plain near Standlake the moated manor house is a picturesque timber-framed structure, mainly of the fifteenth century, standing on a stone plinth. The timbering was infilled with lathe and plaster and the mullioned windows were wooden. At Beckley Park the present house, built by Lord Williams of Thame soon after 1540, stands impressively between the outer and middle moats of an earlier hunting lodge. It is constructed symmetrically of purplish-red bricks with black diapering and has stone mullioned windows under typical square head moulds. Moats also abound in the Vale of Aylesbury and in Warwickshire, where Baddesley Clinton hall with its embattled gateway and private chapel is incomparably beautiful.

Pigeon cotes far outnumber moats and in Stuart times probably 26,000 existed in England. They were usually the prerogative of the lord of the manor or chief landowner and were intended mainly to supply young birds (squabs) as fresh meat in the colder months. Cotes, circular or square, survive in most parishes and date mainly from the early fourteenth century onward. The large gabled pigeon cote at Naunton has 1000 nesting holes, that at Eastbury near Lambourn, a large octagonal structure of flint with brick quoins and pyramidal roof, has 990, but 500 was a more common number and a few score when the holes were inserted in one side of a farm building.

The Dissolution of the Monasteries

And thanne shall the Abbot of Abyngdoun
And al his issue for evere,
Have a knok of a kynge,
And incurable the wounde.
       (*Piers the Plowman* ? 1380)

The monasteries fell foul of Henry VIII who suppressed the smaller in 1536 and the larger in 1539. The destruction of their direct influence was virtually completed by the suppression of chantries in 1547 during the reign of Edward VI.

Although the number of monks had been drastically reduced by the Black Death, most surviving monastic communities profited later from the wool trade and undertook a considerable repair and reconstruction of their premises. Yet these fine buildings seem to have failed to attract enough novices and in Tudor times the number of brethren remained few. Reading Abbey, founded for 100 monks, had dwindled to 35 by the mid-fifteenth century. At the Dissolution, Bruern Abbey had 13 monks, Cirencester, a mitred abbey, had 17, Hailes, which started with 20 monks and 10 lay brothers, had 23, while Abingdon, with 78 monks in 1117, had dwindled to 25. Their income from property and estates ranged from £124 a year at Bruern to about £2000 at Reading and Abingdon. The communities who agreed without open dissent to hand over their properties to the king were dealt with generously. The last abbot at Hailes was granted a good pension, a prebend at York and a pleasant manor house on the Cotswold scarp at Coscombe. The abbot of Eynsham had £133 a year and was made Bishop of Llandaff. At Cirencester Abbey, valued at £1051. 7s. 1½d, the abbot had £250 a year whereas the abbot at Abingdon, also mitred, had £200 a year and the manor house at Cumnor. The abbess of Godstow received £50 a year, and lesser monks generally had smaller sums acording to their status. Dissent was brutally suppressed and at Reading, on a doubtful charge, the abbot and two priests were hanged, drawn and quartered before their own gateway.

All told about 240 monastic foundations were established in the English heartland and it is not difficult to find parts of fragments of more than half of these. This abundant survival is largely due to the many smaller buildings such as hospitals and granges that could be converted to secular uses. The large abbeys, except Reading, were ruthlessly destroyed as soon as possible. At Cirencester, for example, the buildings were sold on the express condition that they were pulled down and the

Evesham Abbey, the bell tower.

materials removed. So the only monastic remains here *in situ* not connected with the parish church are a twelfth-century hospital gateway and a fragment of wall. At Winchcombe Abbey, Thomas, Lord Seymour in 1539 made such a thorough demolition that only a park-like green and a doorway built into the parish church were left. Consequently, the English heartland lacks grand monastic ruins, such as those which grace the Yorkshire dales, although two of its abbeys ranked among the first five or six in England for wealth.

The most popular site, at Hailes, retains a few arches of the cloister garth and chapter house and basal masonry of the general structure. It is preserved by the Department of the Environment and with its museum and nearby church makes an attractive picture. Some monasteries fared better as at Evesham where the abbey tower still tops the meander core above the Avon and at Stoneleigh where the gatehouse and other parts were extended in Elizabethan times and incorporated into an imposing Italianate mansion in 1726. At Kenilworth, where the priory did not become an abbey until about 1450, the extensive fragmental ruins of the lower walls stretch over a considerable area but the guest house and gatehouse of the fourteenth century are well preserved. At Notley the main survival consists of the Abbot's Lodging, part fifteenth century and part built by the last abbot. Much the same happened at Thame Park where the present fine house was built on the site of the

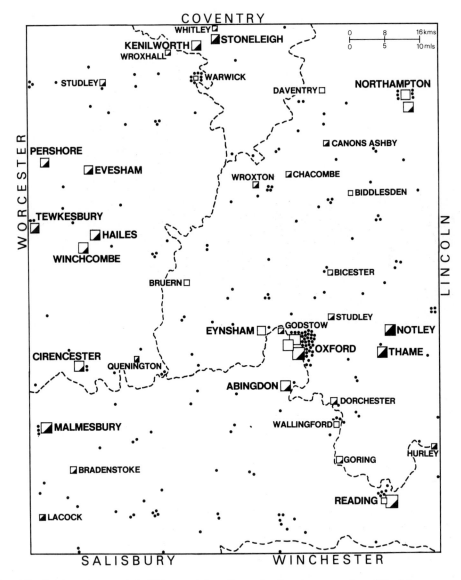

Distribution of monastic buildings and sites. For major sites the proportion of black in squares indicates approximate amount of structures surviving.

abbey. The north wing of the mansion incorporates some thirteenth century work. The south range, of the early sixteenth century, has a delightful facade with bay and oriel windows, and battlemented tower and stair turrets. Built for Robert King, the last abbot, its interior includes a large hall and on the first floor a small parlour of about 1535, sumptuously decorated with linenfold panelling surmounted by a

Hailes Abbey ruins near Winchcombe.

delicately carved frieze of Italian Renaissance style, a perfect gem unexcelled for its size and date in England.

Priories and smaller establishments were also occasionally incorporated into manor houses as at Wroxton Abbey near Banbury in the grand Jacobean house built in 1618 by Sir William Pope, the founder of Trinity College, Oxford; or at the gatehouse of the preceptory of the Knights Hospitallers at Quenington, and at the many timber-framed brick-and-plaster houses alongside the causeway between the church and village green at Steventon which were associated with an alien Benedictine cell. For later monastic tithe barns that at Enstone, erected originally in 1382 by the Abbot of Winchcombe, is outstanding. The search could also be extended to hospitals and to pilgrim taverns: 'The George' at Winchcombe, built before 1525 was an inn for pilgrims and 'The Shaven Crown' at Shipton under Wychwood, a delightful fifteenth century inn, could have been a guest house of Bruern Abbey.

The quality and destruction of monasteries can be illustrated from the Thames valley, a favourite location for monastic foundations, nearly all of which can be reached by boat and towpath as well as by road. At Eynsham the powerful Benedictine abbey, refounded at the Norman conquest, was sold off as building stone and allowed to crumble until only some doorways and a piece of arcade remain. A short distance downstream at Godstow a Benedictine nunnery, the burial place of

Stoneleigh Abbey, the west range built by Francis Smith of Warwick, 1714-1726.

Fair Rosamund, mistress of Henry II, survives as a walled enclosure with a small Tudor building, now used as a cattle yard. Within eyeshot, outside the city walls at Oxford and also beside the Thames, stood two large abbeys, Osney, of which a small building survives, and Rewley, of which a fragment of wall and one archway stand amid a coalyard. Oxford was fortunate in that monastic communities bequeathed to it its cathedral, formerly the church of the Augustinian Priory of St Frideswide, and a wealth of halls and colleges, particularly Worcester (Gloucester), Trinity (Durham quadrangle) and St John's, but the neglect or squalor of the sites of its Thames-side abbeys is unbelievable.

Farther downstream at reasonable intervals there were riverside Benedictine abbeys at Abingdon, Wallingford and Reading and an Augustinian establishment at Dorchester adjoining the magnificent monastic church now used by the parishioners. Abingdon Abbey was founded in 675 and, after destruction by the Danes, restored in 955. It soon acquired great wealth, having at *Domesday Survey* thirty manors in Berkshire alone. Some of its peripheral buildings remain, the chief being a long gallery, a chequer with a roof of about 1340, a square hall with a mediaeval chimney of about 1250, a hospital now the courtroom of the guildhall, a mill restored as a restaurant and an entrance gateway. The main site, adorned with an artificial construction of old masonry fragments, has been fashioned into a pleasant park beside the Thames.

Wroxton Abbey, a mainly early seventeenth-century house completed in Victorian times.

The abbey at Reading lacked the antiquity and scholarly reputation of that at Abingdon but soon equalled it in wealth and splendour, and because of proximity to Westminster played a regular part in national affairs. Most kings came here several times; here in 1359 John of Gaunt married Blanche, heiress of Lancaster, an event celebrated in Chaucer's *Dream*. In the abbey's peaceful and healthy buildings Parliament sat in 1440, 1452 and 1461-2 and the abbot had only to cross the cloisters to take his rightful seat in the council. After the Dissolution Henry VIII kept the abbey for his own use. In 1556 large quantities of stone were taken by barge to Windsor for building the Poor Knights' Lodgings there but succeeding monarchs used Reading occasionally until bombardment in the Civil War made it uninhabitable. In 1650 a survey of the premises ordered by parliament revealed, among many large gardens, orchards and closes, an 'abbey-house with the appurtenances . . . consisting of two sellars, two butteries, a hall, a parlour, a dining-room, ten chambers, a garret with a large gallery, and other small rooms, with two court yards, and a large gatehouse, with several rooms adjoining, and a small gardine with an old small house, . . . and a stable with sellars . . . , and a small tenement, and a dove house . . . in all by measurement two acres, value per annum fifteen pounds'.

On the east side of the abbey there was 'a great old hall, with a very large sellar under the said hall, arched, with some other decayed rooms, . . . with the ruins of an old large chapel, a kitchen and several other rooms, fit to be demolished, the materials valued at two hundred pounds. The ground on which the ruin stands is by estimation eight acres and a half, valued at eight pounds two shillings'.

There were in addition several small tenements, a malthouse, a large barn, formerly a stable, a granary and a porter's lodge at the west gate to Forbury. The property and rights included many fisheries and meadows, including the Great and Little Plummery, and the walled-in Forbury 'in which the town doth yearly keep four faires' and which although covering seven acres was worth only one pound annually because of the numerous public paths.

Within two centuries almost all the buildings had been pillaged for freestone and today only the inner gatehouse, restored in 1869 by Sir Gilbert Scott, and ruinous walls, largely of cemented flint infill, mark the outline of one of England's greatest abbeys. The exceptional quality of the stonework may be judged from the capitals and other carved fragments in Reading Museum and in the Victoria and Albert Museum. In the precincts much of the Hospital of St John survives and the original abbey site of thirty acres is outlined by the street pattern but most of the open spaces have been put to markedly non-ecclesiastic uses, the watermill being among the recent casualties. Only the outer court or Forbury has escaped and with its lawns and colourful flowers remains a peaceful oasis within a traffic-ridden perimeter. Near a monumental lion and a modest bandstand a path leads down to the scanty ruins of the abbey where over seven hundred years ago was written one of the first known English songs to be set to musical notation:

> Summer is a-coming in,
>   Loud sing cuckoo:
> Groweth seed and bloweth mead,
> And springeth the wood new.
>   Sing cuckoo, cuckoo.

CHAPTER SIX

The Golden Age of Domestic Building and Church Monuments: 1550-1645

Can storied urn or animated bust
Back to its mansion call the fleeting breath?
Can honour's voice provoke the silent dust,
Or flattery soothe the dull cold ear of death?
     (Gray, *Elegy Written in a Country Churchyard,* 1750)

The Steady Increase of Enclosures

The period between the death of Henry VIII and the Civil War, although generally prosperous, did not bring good fortune to all villages and towns in the English heartland. The most fortunate parishes were those where new lords of the manor brought in wealth acquired elsewhere, as did Hicks, a London financier, at Chipping Campden, Jones a woolstapler at Chastleton, and Shaw a clothier at Donnington. However, if the wealth were acquired locally its concentration in one fortunate parish might be at the expense of neighbouring parishes as happened when Spencer, a famous sheep grazier, built a great new mansion at Wormleighton and proceeded to depopulate surrounding villages.

Apart from changes from monastic to lay ownership and other land speculation, the farming system continued to develop on the same lines as since the Black Death. Serfdom was finally replaced by wage-earning labour, and enclosure, with the depopulation of hamlets, proceeded if at a slower pace. The steady introduction of root crops and of vetches allowed more stock to be kept throughout the winter and, although the open field system prevailed, the arable was in many manors now divided for rotation purposes into three or four fields (quarters) and in some into smaller units called furlongs.

The amount of land enclosed, compared with that in most other regions of England, was small, probably less than 10 per cent of the total area in the early seventeenth century. The proportion is greater if expressed in townships or vills because the smaller townships were most easily enclosed. In Oxfordshire the proportion ranged from about 13 per cent on the rich marlstone soils (Redland) near Banbury, to 15 per cent on the stonebrash of the wolds farther south, 21 per cent on the clay vales and 35 per cent on the wooded Chilterns. Of the 283 townships in the county only 51 (19%) had been entirely enclosed by 1630 and most of these were either small riverine manors with rich meadows, or forested estates with many assarts, or clayland parishes emparked for livestock, fallow deer, or purely residential reasons, such as spacious rural views and solitude. Whereas parliament did not object to enclosures for deer they did object in later Tudor times to enclosure for sheep. Every English county is said to have had a great plenty of parks, mainly for fallow deer which were kept in by wooden palings and later by stone walls. But of the 34 townships in Oxfordshire entirely enclosed at this time as residential estates, only 10 appear to have been deer parks. The same is true of adjacent counties and the English heartland must not be considered remarkable for the number of its deer parks.

Undoubtedly it was indeed remarkable for the relatively small amount of the total area enclosed and for the late date of the peasants' rebellion against enclosures. Whereas risings against enclosures began in Somerset in 1549 and quickly became important under Robert Ket in Norfolk, the Oxfordshire peasants did not revolt until 1596 when Bartholomew Steere of Hampton Poyle led an inglorious rebellion of villages from nearby parishes.[1] The plot failed miserably, the ringleaders being arrested and sent to London for trial and at least one was hanged and quartered. Yet it probably influenced parliamentary opinion because the last important Acts passed under the Tudors against depopulation, destruction of houses and conversion to pasture ordered that when houses of husbandry had been decayed for more than 7 years half the number must be rebuilt and 40 acres of land allotted. For this purpose the rearrangement by the lord of the manor and tenants of intermixed holdings in common fields and meadows was permitted. Land converted from tillage to pasture since the accession of Elizabeth should be reconverted and tilled land should remain arable on fine of 20s per acre per annum. The effectiveness of these Acts is uncertain but the clause about fines for conversion from tillage was not repealed, and appeared regularly in leases, until 1863.

The relatively small amount of early enclosure in the English heartland, except in the Chilterns and Arden and on the fringes of Whittlewood and Salcey forests in Northamptonshire, caused most villages to remain concentrated on their ancient sites near their manor house, church and village green. In most parishes outlying isolated farmhouses did not become common until parliamentary enclosure in the eighteenth and nineteenth centuries. These Georgian and Victorian dwellings are usually easily distinguishable from the isolated manor houses and shrunken hamlets associated with the enclosure and depopulation of small manors in Tudor times.

The Great Domestic Rebuilding

Except in depopulated parishes there was now a general improvement in the standard of living and houses, and the landscape was enriched by large numbers of domestic dwellings that have survived in part until today. The bigger houses of rich landowners, merchants, lawyers and manufacturers who invested their wealth in rural estates are described in Chapter 7. The Tudor peace turned baronial lords into courtiers and crown officials who did not need hordes of retainers and could spend more money on dwellings that could be designed solely as residences without

Woolstone, a typical scarp-foot village in the Vale of White Horse, showing the use of thatch, timber-framing, chalk blocks and brick.

castellation and moat. The sovereigns, formerly fond of the hospitality of monasteries, now visited more frequently their nobles who built big houses to impress their monarchs. The mansions built at this time include Yarnton manor, an enormous Jacobean house arranged round three sides of a courtyard by Sir Thomas Spencer about 1611 and since reduced in size. Another Spencer in 1613 added to his residence at Wormleighton a large detached gatehouse of stone with a five-storeyed tower that survives although most of the mansion has gone.

Homes of lesser landowners and yeoman farmers dating from 1550-1660 abound in the English heartland. In the lowlands timber-framed houses continued to be fashionable, often with brick infilling and with stone plinths or lower storey. These rural houses lack the intricate timber patterns of town houses, and dwellings of three storeys or more are almost restricted to the boroughs. Wherever easily available, stone was preferred to timber. In the Vale of Thame and Aylesbury where small limestone hills stand above the clays, the timber-framed houses were rebuilt of local stone. At Little Milton nearly all the older houses date from the early seventeenth century and are of stone, and traces of mediaeval half-timbering survive in two dwellings only.[2] On and near the downs west of the Thames, chalk blocks were commonly used in the construction of villages and churches as at Ashbury, Bishopstone and Sparsholt. In the Avebury-Marlborough district large fragments of sarsens formed an enduring building stone. East of the Thames where clay-with-flint caps much of the chalk downs, bricks were made from local clays, as at Pyrton at the

Arlington Row, Bibury, facing a mill leat of the River Coln. The cottages, built from local limestone and roofed with Cotswold slates, date mainly from the early seventeenth century.

foot of the Chilterns where in the early seventeenth century the mediaeval moated manor house was replaced by the present E-shaped house of brick with stone mullions. On the wolds a great rebuilding took place in local stone in the typical Cotswold style with mullioned windows, gabled dormers and stone-slated roofs. On the marlstone or redland area stretching from Edgehill into southern Northamptonshire the same style prevailed but gables were unusual, porches rare and roofs usually thatched.

Household inventories, mainly of lesser yeomen, husbandmen, and craftsmen, provide a vivid picture of smaller dwellings in Elizabethan times in Oxfordshire. Of the homes of these people who made wills, and so had property worth over £5, about 47 per cent had one room only, nearly 35 per cent had two to four rooms and 18 per cent had 5 or more rooms.[3] The hall, open to the rafters, was the principal living, dining and cooking room but was not slept in except in one-roomed dwellings. A common type of simple house had a hall with an entry or passage way and two chambers on the ground floor without rooms over them. In the better type houses with two storeys, which were unusual before 1570, staircases were beginning to replace ladders and in rare instances the windows were glazed. From late Elizabethan times bay mullioned windows were common in larger houses except in the redlands where mullions remained flush with the wall. From Jacobean times onward in the better houses the dripmould was often continued over windows and doorways.

Stanton, a scarp-foot village of the north Cotswolds, the buildings are of local oolite with Cotswold slate roofs, the older dating from 1570 to 1640.

Before discussing these admirable dwellings it seems fair to mention the humble cottages of the poor. The smaller landholders and labourers were indeed poor and although most probably had a few acres of land to work and a few stock to run on the common fields, they lived in one-roomed hovels. In Oxfordshire probably one quarter of the adults were too impoverished to need a will and over 16 per cent of the poorer landowners (presumably farmworkers and craftsmen) who made a will owned 5 acres or less. All told at least 60 per cent of the dwellings in the county had only one bay, measuring about 10 by 12ft. This cramped condition so disturbed Elizabethan politicians that in 1589 they passed an Act aimed at avoiding the 'great inconveniences which are found by experience to grow by the erecting and building of great numbers and multitude of cottages which are daily more and more increased in many parts of this realm'. In future no cottage was to be erected in the country without four acres of ground at least being assigned to it and no more than one family was to live in any cottage under a penalty of 10s. a month. Yet the cramped hovels of poor labourers persisted for a long time and in 1750 when Lord Harcourt displaced the village of Nuneham Courtenay it was in his words a collection of 'tumble-down clay-built structures'.

Against this poverty, the dwellings of the yeomen and larger tenant farmers seem truly palatial. Most tenants held 20 to 80 acres but many had over 80 acres and it was these and the yeomen with moderate-sized holdings and the lesser gentry with estates

Great Tew, an estate village in north Oxfordshire.

The Manor House, Wickhamford near Evesham. The sixteenth-century half-timbered building stands near the church and a circular dovecot.

of up to several hundred acres that built the small farmsteads and beautiful manor houses that grace so many villages today. A list of picturesque dwellings partly of this period would fill a volume. The earliest are irregular in horizontal plan and the later more geometrically shaped, in outline an E or L or H. They remain for the most part private residences with well-tended gardens and a few of the larger are open to the public a few times each year for charitable purposes.

Churches and Church Monuments

The outburst of domestic building contrasts with the rarity of new churches. At Shrivenham in 1638 Lord Craven erected around the existing central tower a large church in a Perpendicular style modified by Tuscan columns within. At Furtho near Towcester a new church of about 1620 eventually proved redundant and became derelict. Elsewhere the few changes were restricted mainly to the addition of an aisle or clerestory or the rebuilding of the tower. At Sunningwell, a fine seven-sided west porch, with unfluted Ionic columns at its angles, was added by Bishop Jewel about 1560 while at Winkfield near Windsor the remodelling of the interior was achieved by means of octagonal wooden columns. But apart from these and other rare exceptions, most existing churches were so adequate that little needed to be done to them.

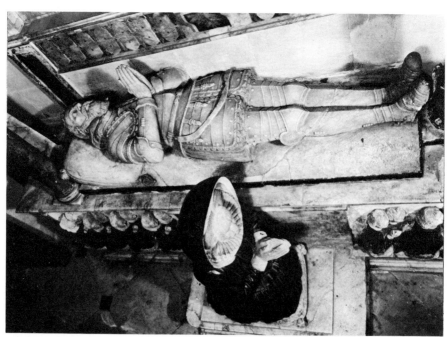

Alabaster tomb-chest of Sir Thomas Lucy (*ob.* 1605) in Charlecote church. His widow and their children are sculptured on the front of the monument.

Instead, rich patrons now found a popular outlet for their wealth in the construction of personal monuments to adorn church interiors. These tombs and memorials in the parish church form a fascinating commentary on the life and manners of Elizabethan and Stuart England. After 1560 when a royal proclamation forbade the defacement and destruction of such monuments, the idea of a permanent memorial became virtually a compulsion and tombs began to be looked upon as family portraitures suitably inscribed with the high qualities of the deceased. The memorial to Edmund Harman (*ob.* 1569) at Burford is not his tomb, and in several churches a monumental tomb was erected long before the death of one or more of the persons sculptured on it. Where the parish church was too small for adequate sepulchral sculptures the manorial lord, like Spencer at Yarnton and Knollys at Rotherfield Greys, added an aisle to the chancel. Recumbent effigies on a tomb chest, free-standing or less preferably set against a wall, were the most popular but their great size soon encouraged the use of kneeling figures at a prayer desk, single, double or even triple, as at Preston on Stour. In Stuart times the unoccupied wall spaces were used for frontal demi-figures showing the person's professions and achievements, especially of scholars and divines who lived mainly in the boroughs. The richer landed gentry preferred huge highly-coloured monuments with a lengthy history of the deceased, until the 1630s when more restrained work in white and black marble began to be popular under the influence of Nicholas Stone. The most beautiful of Stone's early tombs, and one of his best works ever, is that of Elizabeth Carey, erected about 1617 at Stowe Nine Churches in her lifetime. Realistically chiselled in white marble she lies sleeping, her head slightly turned resting on an embroidered pillow. Later sculptures by Stone may be seen at Compton Verney, Charlecote, Great Brington, Chesterton, Radley and Chipping Campden.

So many sepulchral monuments of this period survive that it is difficult to select outstanding examples. Oxfordshire is especially rich in sumptuous memorials worked in alabaster and marble by the Southwark school of sculptors. Among them are those of Lord Williams and his wife (*ob.* 1559) in the centre of the chancel at Thame and often attributed to Gerard Johnson the elder; of the Dormer family at Great Milton, with a relief of Sir Michael Dormer's exploits in the Spanish wars on the front of the tomb chest; of Lord Chief Justice Tanfield (*c.* 1628) in a small chapel in Burford church and notable for its magnificence and excellent sculptures of Virtues on its canopy; of the Knollys family at Rotherfield Greys; and of William Pope, Earl of Downe, and his wife at Wroxton. To these must be added Sir William Spencer's monument at Yarnton attributed to Jasper Hollemans, a Dutch sculptor, who settled at Burton on Trent and the Fettiplace monuments at Swinbrook.

Numerous parish churches in other counties of the English heartland have interesting collections of tombs but for artistry or for continuity of sequence those at Bisham, Fawsley, Great Brington and Lydiard Tregoze are outstanding. At Bisham, where the magnificent monuments to the earls of Salisbury and Warwick in the abbey church were destroyed at its dissolution, the estate and abbey ruins were acquired in 1553 by Sir Philip Hoby. Shortly afterwards he added to the parish church

Monumental tomb of Sir Baptist Hicks (*ob.* 1629), Viscount Campden and Lady Elizabeth, his wife, in Chipping Campden church. The effigies depict them in full state robes.

a chapel that within fifty years his family filled with exquisite tombs. The particularly beautiful and unusual monument to Margaret Hoby has a defiant swan guarding each corner of a high plinth that supports a slender obelisk crowned by a heart.

Longer tomb sequences inevitably cannot sustain such inspired artistry. At Fawsley the church stands isolated in a large park and protected by a deep ha-ha except on the lake side where a sunken track marks the road leading to the main porch from the former village. In this church the Knightley family immortalised themselves by a series of memorials starting with early Tudor brasses and proceeding through a superb free-standing alabaster tomb of 1534 to a huge Jacobean mural monument and so to architectural tablets and fine shallow reliefs of recent times.

Nearby at Great Brington, also in Northamptonshire, the parish church overlooks a green countryside dotted with grazing flocks as it was in the early sixteenth century when Sir John Spencer added a clerestory and rebuilt the chancel with the addition of a side chapel for his family tombs. Herein the Spencers from 1522 onwards erected a series of monuments probably unsurpassed for their grandeur in a rural church. They include five pairs of life-sized recumbent effigies on richly-canopied altar tombs as well as numerous mural monuments and sepulchral furnishings such as brass plates, gauntlets, coronets, swords, helms and hatchments. The monument, nearest the altar, to Sir John Spencer (*ob.* 1622) and his wife has in

Monument to Margaret Hoby (*ob.* 1605), Bisham church.

the apex of its canopy an angel similar to those on Henry VII's tomb in Westminster Abbey, which is why the design of Brington chapel has been attributed to Thomas Heritage, a rector here who later became surveyor of the king's work. Three of the largest richly-coloured tombs, each with a knight in armour and his wife in a deep ruff and wide projecting hood, are the work of Jasper Hollemans. The noble black and white marble monument of William Lord Spencer (*ob.* 1636) and his wife was erected in 1638 to the design of Nicholas Stone who was paid £500 for the work, including the materials, no doubt. The tomb sequence continues to modern times through expressive smaller reliefs by great artists such as Nollekens and Flaxman. Hidden in the chancel and nave are early seventeenth century floor slabs and small brasses to the Washington family who were friends of the Spencers.

Another remarkable collection of funeral monuments exists at Lydiard Tregoze near Swindon. This estate passed to the St John family in the reign of Henry VII but the earliest surviving local monument is to Nicholas St John and his wife (*ob.* 1592) who are depicted kneeling side by side under a Corinthian canopy. The next monument chronologically is a huge mural cabinet with two opening panels (triptych) painted on the outside with an heraldic genealogical tree showing thirty two ancestors of the St Johns, and inside with a group of full-length portraits. Erected in 1615, its genealogical tree has been extended to about 1700 when the splendid Italian ironwork rails and gates were placed across the front of the chancel. The tomb sequence continues with the mural monument to Sir Giles and Lady Katherine Mompesson (1633) who are shown in profile under arched niches, seated facing each other, he holding a book and she a skull. About this time the south chapel was remodelled and its stone arcade was replaced by round or classical columns of timber positioned and painted to fit in with the installation of the huge tomb of Sir John St John. This superb alabaster monument carries beneath its fine canopy the life-sized recumbent effigies of Sir John and his two wives, who occupy a slightly lower plane. Their dresses and features are delicately carved and the general design has great artistry. Margaret, the first wife was the mother of the five sons, three daughters and five infants who died in childhood and are so realistically sculptured here. She lies nursing in her arms one of the tiny infants neatly dressed in swaddling clothes and bonnet — presumably she died in childbirth — while the second wife lies serenely one hand lightly fingering a book. Facing across the chancel is the monument to Edward St John, the 'Golden Cavalier', who was killed in the Civil War in 1645. He stands in gilt armour life-size under a curtained canopy (baldacchino), a fine design that rather outstripped the execution of the details. Among the later tombs is one by Rysbrack to Viscount St John (*ob.* 1748) who largely rebuilt the adjacent mansion, Lydiard Park, which in 1942 was acquired by Swindon corporation. The extensive public grounds form a pleasant setting for the church and house.

The sumptuousness and size of church monuments declined during and after the Civil War and never again was so much money and effort to be spent on huge sepulchral sculptures and verses in parish churches. Many churches were already short of floor and wall space for big additions but in some rural parishes with strong traditions and rich patrons the custom persisted for several years after 1700.

The Mompesson monument, Lydiard Tregoze church.

CHAPTER SEVEN

Great Mediaeval Houses

The stately homes of England
How beautiful they stand!
Amidst their tall ancestral trees
O'er all the pleasant land.
       (Felicia D. Hemans, 1812)

Domesticated Castles

Until the mid-fifteenth century many manor houses were moated and castellated but thereafter the use of gunpowder and cannon undermined the security of such defences. By early Tudor times there was evolving a more domestic type of dwelling arranged as a courtyard with battlements and turrets for display rather than for defence. Outstanding among the examples in the southern Midlands are the courts at Coughton and Rotherfield Greys, the castle at Broughton, and the hall at Baddesley Clinton.

Coughton Court, 3km north of Alcester, has a fine central battlemented gatehouse built in 1509, with tall corner turrets and a large oriel window. Subsequently the moat was filled in and two battlemented wings were added. The base of the gatehouse forms the great hall which retains its fan-traceried ceiling. The interior of the house has several priests' hiding holes, which with its interesting contents reveal the associations of the Catholic Throckmorton family, particularly with Mary, Queen of Scots, the Gunpowder Plot, and the Jacobites. Here also is the famous coat made for Sir John Throckmorton on 25 June 1811 when two Southdown sheep were shorn and, under the direction of John Coxeter, manufacturer of Greenham Mills, Newbury, all processes of spinning, weaving, dyeing and tailoring were finished by that evening so winning a wager of one thousand guineas.

Rotherfield Greys, now known as Greys Court, stands on the chalk, west of Henley on Thames, amid lush pastures and densely wooded hilltops. It belonged to the de Greys in Norman times and in 1347 John de Grey was given a baronetcy for his services at Crecy, made one of the original garter knights and licensed to crenellate his home. Later descendants, through the female line, included Francis Lovell who fought for Richard III at Bosworth.

In 1518 Greys Court was granted to Robert Knollys whose son Francis was a friend, counsellor and for a time Lord Treasurer of the Household of Queen Elizabeth. There is a magnificent canopied monument to Francis (*ob.* 1596) and his wife in the

Coughton Court, Warwickshire, the west front.

parish church. Their son William became custodian of the Earl and Countess of Somerset after they had been convicted of the murder of Sir Thomas Overbury. This notorious crime happened because Robert Carr, Earl of Somerset, who was a patron of Sir Thomas and a favourite of James I, fell in love with Frances Howard, wife of the Earl of Essex, who tried to get her marriage annulled on the grounds of impotence. Overbury worked zealously to prevent the annulment so the lovers schemed to have him imprisoned in the Tower and in 1613 bribed a gaoler to poison him. Two years later, now married after a divorce, they were accused of the murder and thrown into the Tower whereupon Frances confessed to her part in the crime while Robert insisted on his innocence. Eventually they were reprieved and released on condition that, until further order, they were confined at or within three miles of Greys Court where Frances' sister was married to William Knollys. No doubt the verdict was awkward for William who was MP for the notoriously puritanical borough of Banbury, and strongly opposed to music, dancing or any other form of amusement. Shakespeare found in him the pompous original for Malvolio in *Twelfth Night* and in recent years Robert Gittings was inspired by the lovers' story to write the poem 'This tower my prison'.

Of the fourteenth century castle the chief surviving fragments are the great tower and three smaller towers, one of which is in the dower house or Bachelor's Hall. The outline of the courtyard and of two gatehouses can be traced in dry summers by lines of parched turf. The present house, erected within the curtilage, is a charming amalgam of different times and building materials. The kitchen with its massive oak beams and brick fireplace is mediaeval while the gabled east wing was added in the sixteenth century, the porch surmounted by an oriel window in the seventeenth century, and the elegant plaster ceilings, staircase and marble fireplace in Georgian times. The outbuildings include stables in which Cromwellian soldiers were billeted during the Civil War. At the other side of the former courtyard is a well 60m deep covered by an early Tudor wheelhouse that shelters a gigantic wheel, nearly 6m in diameter, once operated by a donkey walking inside its perimeter.

The gardens have some majestic trees and embrace walls and buildings that in places seclude and in other support a wealth of flowering plants. The walls of the old tithe barn enclose a garden of Japanese cherries; an archway, probably of Roman tiles, leads to a walled rose garden that in its turn gives access to an exquisite arbour of gnarled wistaria. In the Tower garden white flowers and shrubs are reflected in a lily pond and a scented growth of lavender, rosemary and cistus forms ground cover beneath venerable Scots pines. The whole is surrounded by rolling parkland of trees and meadows, clamorous with birds, and the visitor finds here what Robert Gittings has called 'an ancient content'.

Our third example of a domesticated castle stands at Broughton in north Oxfordshire in the deep valley of the Sor brook about two miles from Banbury. This, a castle only in name, is one of the finest and most complete mediaeval manor houses in the Midlands. The first building, much of which survives, was erected about 1306 and protected by a wide moat by John de Broughton, one of Edward the First's knights, whose resplendent tomb adorns the parish church. The house was sold in 1377 to William of Wykeham, the great architect, and from him passed to Thomas Wykeham who also lies, with his wife, beneath a fine monument in the adjacent church. In 1406 this Thomas, having obtained a license to crenellate, slightly altered and strengthened the gatehouse and perhaps added the stable wing with Perpendicular windows in the upper storey and arrow slits in the lower. In 1451 the property passed by marriage to William Fiennes, second Lord Saye and Sele, who, twenty years later, fell fighting for the Yorkists at Barnet, and whose family have held the estate ever since. Between 1550 and 1600 they transformed the mediaeval hall into an Elizabethan mansion mainly by skilful extensions to the existing structure and judicious alterations to its interior. Subsequently apart from repairs it has remained virtually unaltered, except that the moat is crossed by a stone bridge instead of a draw-bridge, although the raising wheels of the latter remain *in situ*. The gatehouse has two pairs of doors and its lower walls are pierced with slits for archers. It gives access to a turfed courtyard, with an incomplete partly battlemented curtilage, and to the dwelling house on its southern edge. The mansion centres on the baronial hall which had a typical plan with solar and oratory at one end, and at the other, kitchen, buttery and pantry behind a panelled screen with a musicians' gallery above. Originally this great room was open to the rafters.

The doors into the castellan's apartment still lead into the early mediaeval part of the house. The north door opens on to a vaulted passage from which a winding stair climbs to the great chamber or solar, and, farther along, to an undercroft now used for dining. The south door leads by a straight staircase to the garderobe tower and to the oldest domestic chapel in England. John de Broughton obtained a licence to build a private oratory in 1331 and it has been very little changed since, as the original stone altar with five consecration crosses and supporting brackets testify.

The great hall was given a flat ceiling and three floors were constructed above it in Elizabethan times. The first floor was designed as a gallery for walking and other exercise. It and the council chamber above were reached by two new staircases then constructed in two gabled projections added to the south front. Throughout Broughton the interiors are magnificent with fine plaster ceilings, panelled walls and handsome fireplaces most of which can be attributed securely to Elizabethan craftsmen. The wealth of historic contents includes Court Rolls for the manor since 1339 and the manuscript, edited and published in 1947, of Celia Fiennes' travels through England in the late seventeenth century.

The political influence of the Fiennes family reached its zenith in the reign of Charles I when from 1629 to 1640 the opponents of the divine right of kings met regularly here in the small upstairs council chamber. In these discussions William, Viscount Saye and Sele, became the oracle and pilot of the Puritans but proceeded with such caution that he was nicknamed 'Old Subtlety'. Leading Parliamentarians like Pym, Hampden, Brooke and Eliot, attended the meetings which were held partly under the pretext of forming a company to colonise New England. Eventually a group of emigrants set sail and founded in 1635 the town of (Old) Saybrook at the mouth of the Connecticut river, the name being derived from Viscount Saye and Lord Brooke, the chief shareholders in the company holding the land grant.

At Broughton the militant Parliamentarians actively prepared for the Civil War and soldiers were housed and drilled secretly in the rooms still known as 'the Barracks' at the top of a stairway called Mount Rascal. Although the viscount fought against the Royalists at Edgehill and had to surrender Broughton to them, he stoutly refused to countenance the execution of the king by the Cromwellians and at the Restoration was made Lord Privy Seal by Charles II.

Our last example of a domesticated castle, the Hall at Baddesley Clinton, is largely a fifteenth-century moated fortress as the frequent arrow-slits testify. In Elizabethan and Jacobean times it was embellished with better heating facilities, larger windows and rich artistic decorations, which, with few later changes, have made it a perfect mediaeval house. If present negotiations succeed, it will become a splendid addition to National Trust properties open to the public.

Tudor Mansions: The Landed Gentry

Where owners acquired considerable wealth and the same families occupied their traditional home for a long time, the older buildings were usually cased in later additions to form a large mansion. Some open their doors regularly or at regular intervals to the public and are preserved because of their high quality either by the National Trust or by their family heirs. Outstanding among these great houses are Packwood, Charlecote and Compton Wynyates in Warwickshire, Mapledurham in Oxfordshire and Althorp in Northamptonshire.

Packwood House, in Forest of Arden country a few kilometres northwest of Warwick, is a timber-framed structure of about 1550 that was encased in stone and brick extensions about a century later. The interior retains its great hall with mullioned windows and has a dining room rich in seventeenth-century Flemish glass, an inner hall with fine tapestries and a drawing room with excellent furniture of the time of Charles II and Queen Anne. The extensive grounds include many colourful garden courts, a Carolean formal garden and an assemblage of giant yew trees, planted in 1650.

Charlecote Park near Stratford represents the more formal Elizabethan mansion. It was built in 1558 for the Lucy family and the original gatehouse of mellow brick with stone cornerings and window frames survives. Much of the house, except the porch, was remodelled in the nineteenth century but so many of the old features were retained that the interior is a pleasant mixture of old and new. In the great hall Sir Thomas Lucy is supposed to have arraigned Shakespeare for deer stealing (*see* Chapter 17). Here and in other rooms may be seen the items bought by George Lucy when William Beckford's furniture was sold up at Fonthill Abbey in 1822. They include the superb mosaic table (*pietra commesse*), with an oval centre of the largest oriental onyx in the world surrounded by jaspers and breccia marble, that had come originally from the Borghese Palace in Rome. The elaborate base in oak, an incongruous wood for a classical piece, was designed by Beckford as also were four little oak tables nearby. The ebony state bed, of the seventeenth century, with its crimson damask hangings also came from Fonthill. Warwickshire furniture makers are represented by a wondrous gigantic carved sideboard by George Willcox of Warwick. The lovely park was laid out in a formal geometrical pattern, with canals, in the late seventeenth century and was redesigned in a naturalistic style by Capability Brown. Fittingly it keeps a herd of deer and also a flock of Spanish sheep. The brew house and coach house are Elizabethan and contain the tools of the brewing trade and a collection of coaches while the great kitchen of early Victorian times is amazingly complete. The Lucys, who have lived here for eight centuries, have also left some fine alabaster Jacobean tombs in the parish church. The house was saved from damage during the Civil War because Richard Lucy, MP for Warwick, was a Parliamentarian.

Packwood has charm and Charlecote grace whereas our third Tudor mansion, Compton Wynyates, represents the ultimate in the picturesque. This house lies off the Stratford-Banbury road in a deep wooded fold of the hills, set in a park formed by the enclosure of 100 acres (40ha) of ploughland and the destruction of three yeomen dwellings under a grant to Sir William Compton in 1513. Long before this emparkment the Comptons had a house on the site as they had been lords of the

Charlecote Park, showing Elizabethan gatehouse and east facade.

manor since 1204. The earliest part of the present mansion was erected by Edmund Compton in the late fifteenth century on the typical courtyard plan of four wings round a quadrangle. The substantial structure with walls four feet thick and stone-slated roof was almost certainly moated. Edmund's successor, William, was appointed boy page (aged 11) to the infant Prince Henry, aged two, afterwards Henry VIII. Later the king held him in great esteem and showered upon him honours, appointments, and privileges, among them the licence to empark mentioned above and the custody in 1509 of Fulbroke Castle near Warwick. This 'praty castle made of stone and bricks that was an eyesore to the earls that lay at Warwick castle', had been built in 1433 by Henry VI and later was granted by Edward IV to Warwick the Kingmaker who allowed it to decay. Fulbroke was the source of much of the stone and some of the roof timbers and bricks at Compton Wynyates although probably most of the bricks were made locally.

Work on the rebuilding began about 1520 and the house today is mainly Tudor with some ceilings and panelling of early Jacobean age. It was built on the same square courtyard plan closely surrounded by a water moat that was filled in after the Civil War. Around this stretched a flat forecourt with various outbuildings, also surrounded by a moat or ha-ha crossed by a drawbridge. The newer building is entered through a lovely porch with stone seats on either side and over its arched doorway the finely carved coats of arms of Katherine of Aragon and Henry VIII. This front of the house and the equally narrow north wing have turrets for garderobes and spiral staircases, the largest leading to the Council Chamber. Across the courtyard, in the east wing, directly opposite the porch is the entrance to the great hall, a splendid room floored with stone slabs set diagonally and topped by a raftered roof of four bays with timbering brought from Fulbroke. At one end of the hall a beautiful carved screen divides off the kitchen and pantry; at the opposite end a doorway gives access to a spacious parlour, now used as a dining room. The chapel occupies much of the south front, with the sanctuary projecting to the east and a tower on the southwest corner. Here the stonework of the windows and some fascinating carvings, maybe of scenes from mediaeval mystery plays, seem earlier than the date of the chapel. Another tower occupies the northeast corner and a range of buildings added in 1732 by James, Duke of Nottingham projects from it.

The whole mansion is low for its size and its roof line is markedly irregular. Above it rise like pinnacles forty chimney stacks widely divergent in age and detail, some octagonal, others ornamental or twisted but all beautifully simple. Add to this the lack of uniformity in the windows and window levels, and the effect becomes instantaneous: here is the unplanned perfection of the picturesque.

The house has survived threats of destruction by a hair's breadth. It suffered grievously during the Civil War when in 1644 it was occupied by Parliamentarian troops who killed the deer, mutilated the monuments in the church, and took '120 prisoners, £5,000 in money, 60 horses, 400 sheep, near 160 head of cattle, and 18 loads of other plunder, besides 5 or 6 earthen pots of money which they discovered in the moat'. In the following year the Comptons with a force of about 300 men made an unsuccessful moonlight attempt to recover the house. They cut down the drawbridge over the outer moat and stormed the outer court but, having lost the advantage of surprise, could not get across the inner moat.

After the Civil War, Lord Northampton (the Compton family) eventually regained his estates on payment of a fine of over £20,000. Although the main abode of the Northamptons was at Castle Ashby, the church in the park at Compton Wynyates was rebuilt in 1666 and refurnished with the battered monuments recovered from the moat. In the early eighteenth century James, afterwards 5th Earl of Northampton, lived here for a time and added an east wing but in 1768 the family were temporarily ruined by a spendthrift election for two parliamentary seats for the borough of Northampton. Lord Northampton supported one Tory, Lord Halifax another, and Lord Spencer a Whig who later withdrew in face of incredible opposition. The election and a long petition in parliament probably cost Lord Spencer £100,000 and the other two lords about £150,000 each. Lord Halifax was ruined and had to sell his house and estate at Horton, while Lord Northampton had to cut down £50,000 worth of timber on his great park at Castle Ashby and to sell much of the furniture there and all the contents of Compton Wynyates. He closed Castle Ashby and retired to a modest villa in Switzerland after ordering the demolition of Compton Wynyates. Fortunately, his steward, John Berril, wisely ignoring these instructions, blocked up

Compton Wynyates, with, on skyline to left, the windmill.

the windows to avoid window tax and managed to keep the main fabric of the mansion in tolerable repair. Its condition had become serious when the descendants of Lord Northampton directed some repairs from their seat at Castle Ashby. Eventually the fifth Marquess came to reside at Compton Wynyates and in 1895 laid out the garden on the south side of the house partly on the site of the outer moat. The delightful topiary dates from this time and, with the steep wooded slopes of the valley opposite, adds to the charm of this picturesque gem.

The finest Elizabethan dwelling in Oxfordshire is Mapledurham House, which stands most felicitously with rich parkland and Thames-side water meadows as a setting for its red and blue brickwork and grey stone-mullioned bay windows. The Blount family bought the estate in 1502 and Sir Richard Blount began the present mansion in about 1585. At first glance it may appear that he incorporated an earlier building on the same site but in fact the Elizabethan house was altered in the eighteenth and early nineteenth century in a Tudor style. The original front had a long facade with two projecting wings, behind which was a typical great hall with screen and dais now converted into an entrance hall flanked by a dining room and library. Among the many delightful architectural features is the fine staircase in the northern wing where on the ground floor the newel posts are continuous in the shape of Doric columns and on the first floor are surmounted with carved baskets of flowers

Castle Ashby, Northamptonshire, mainly of 1574-1635. The view shows the south and east wings, with their lettered balustrades of texts in Latin from the Psalms.

to match the pediments of the doorways. Several rooms have superb plasterwork ceilings of about 1612, with symbols of chivalry, dragons, portrait medallions, Tudor roses and mermaids. An eighteenth century Gothic-style chapel forms part of the back of the house and nearby in the garden are fragments of a much earlier building and a late Georgian Gothic fernhouse of banded red brick and flint.

During the Civil War Sir Charles Blount garrisoned Mapledurham House for the king and it was forced and plundered by the Cromwellians. Sir Charles later suffered a greater misfortune when he was shot dead at the north gate of royalist Oxford through either failing to give the correct password or advancing too soon after the sentry had challenged him. Alexander Pope became much attached to Martha Blount, a 'scornful beauty' with the brightest eyes in Britain, and bequeathed to her some of his books and other possessions. When she left London society to live at Mapledurham he sighed that

> She went to plain-work and to purling brooks
> Old fashioned halls, dull aunts and cawing rooks

but apparently Martha continued to treat him in cavalier fashion and refused to visit him during his last illness. Galsworthy used Mapledurham House as one of the settings in *The Forsyte Saga* and it figures also as Toad Hall in *The Wind in the Willows* by Kenneth Grahame who knew well the riverside seclusion of this lovely

Althorp Park, the south front.

parish with its picturesque watermill and unspoiled village.

Northamptonshire has numerous great Tudor mansions as at Kirby Hall, Drayton Hall, Boughton House, Deene Park and Castle Ashby, but most of them lie outside our survey. At Castle Ashby in 1574 Lord Compton began to erect a mansion on the site of an almost vanished castle. James I stayed here frequently and eventually the family was granted the title of Earl of Northampton. We have already mentioned the local political rivalry between the Northamptons and Spencers who lived nearby at Althorp. In 1508 John Spencer of Wormleighton bought an estate at Althorp and four years later was granted the right to empark 300 acres. In Elizabethan times the old house was extended by adding two projecting wings to form a courtyard and during the next two centuries the Tudor building was encased in stately alterations. In 1666 a grand staircase was made in the courtyard and within a few decades John Evelyn described it as a palace fit for a great prince. Yet the embellishments continued and in the 1730s the Palladian additions included a magnificent entrance hall and a huge stable block for nearly 100 horses, built of ironstone in a style inspired by Inigo Jones' church of St Paul at Covent Garden. This work was begun in the occupancy of the fifth Earl of Sunderland who on his mother's side succeeded to the title of Duke of Marlborough and the Blenheim estates. The Spencer branch at Althorp became earls and built a fine town house in London. During the canvassing for the spendthrift election of 1768 at a meeting at Althorp footmen stood by the main door handing to voters refreshments with a guinea concealed in each sandwich. The Spencers came out of the affair sounder than their rivals and in the 1780s they employed Henry Holland to alter and redecorate parts of the interior at Althorp and to line the red brick exterior walls with a light grey brick partly as 'mathematical tiles'. The wide range of decorations and furnishings includes a wealth of fireplaces, ceilings and panellings, some of them from London and Wormleighton. Recently the mansion has been opened at regular intervals to the public and visitors are generously catered for with ample facilities in the huge stable block. The park has some fine timber, especially of oak, with date stones of trees planted from 1576 to 1976.

Tombstone, with stars and stripes, of Lawrence Washington (*ob.* 1616) in the church of St Mary the Virgin, Great Brington near Sulgrave.

Tudor and Jacobean Merchants' Houses

In mediaeval England a prime means of acquiring wealth was the wool trade which provided finances for building fine churches, founding grammar schools and joining the ranks of the landed gentry. At Chipping Campden, William Grevel, a wool stapler, built a fine house about 1390 and also contributed generously to the new parish church. At Sulgrave, Northamptonshire, Lawrence Washington, a wool merchant and mayor of Northampton, bought the manor for £324. 14s. 10d. at the dissolution of the minor monasteries in 1539. About twenty years and eleven children later he built the modest manor house that is now a shrine to his descendants. His grandson Colonel John Washington emigrated to Virginia in 1656 and his great grandson George (1732-1799) became the first president of the United States. The Washington coat-of-arms is carved in the spandrels over the porch; it consists of three stars arranged horizontally over two horizontal bars or stripes and seems to have more than a chance resemblance to the American flag that evolved during George Washington's presidency. However, there is no supporting documentary evidence for a direct connection between the two and probably the 'Stars and Stripes' developed from a combination of pre-existing flags with either stars or stripes. The ancestral home at Sulgrave has been carefully restored and skilfully furnished with relevant documents, portraits and period pieces. 'Old Glory' flies boldly over the modest house and its English gardens.

Sulgrave Manor, the home of Lawrence Washington and his descendants 1540-1659.

During Elizabethan and Jacobean times the export of wool was gradually replaced by the manufacture and export of cloth. The homes of these manufacturers and merchants were on a grander scale than those of the earlier woolstaplers. Most parishes already had a large church so the newly-rich could conscientiously spend freely on domestic buildings. The largest Elizabethan mansion in Berkshire, Shaw House near Newbury, was completed for Thomas Dolman, a local clothier, in 1581. It has a graceful symmetrical exterior with a main facade arranged about a middle porch and flanked with two projecting wings of dark red brick with stone mullions and cornerings.

The mansions of merchants tended to become still larger in the seventeenth century as those at Chipping Campden and Chastleton exemplify. At Campden in north Gloucestershire the manorial and numerous other properties, including Grevel's house, were purchased early in James I's reign by Sir Baptist Hicks, one of the wealthiest and most influential of London mercers who had made a huge fortune chiefly in supplying stuffs and rich cloths to the Court on credit. The mansion was built of local oolitic limestone in an Italian style with terraced gardens covering in all about 8 acres (3ha). The principal front to the south faced on to a grand terrace flanked at each end with a graceful pavilion. The north front centred upon a porch with columns of the five architectural orders and was extended laterally, as were all

Garden terraces with flanking pavilion of Old Campden House.

other corners of the mansion, by a spacious bow window. The parapet was crowned with peculiarly shaped pediments and the whole structure was capped by a bulbous dome in which a lantern acted as a beacon at night to travellers on the wolds. The building cost £29,000 and the furnishings were valued at a further £15,000. Sir Baptist, having completed the house about 1613, began to beautify the adjacent properties. He spent £1,000 on an almshouse, about £90 on a commodious market hall and considerable sums on repairing the church and walling in the churchyard.

Thirty years later the main part of the mansion was destroyed. The descendants of Sir Baptist Hicks were ardent loyalists and in the Civil War the premises were garrisoned for the king, as they sat astride the best all-weather route from Gloucester to Warwick. The last commander here was Sir Henry Bard who during several months harrassed the neighbourhood ruthlessly irrespective of its inhabitants' allegiance. For example Winchcombe was plundered so thoroughly that the people lost all their cattle and 'had not a Sunday shift of cloathes left them'. Early in May 1645 the Campden garrison was called away to join the king's main army, and before leaving Bard had the mansion burnt in case it was used later by the Parliamentarians. Today only a small part of its south front survives but the outlying buildings remain, including the elegant pavilions or banqueting houses, the columbarium, almonry, dower house (once probably the stables) and on each side of the main entrance, the

Part of the Long Gallery at Chastleton. Such rooms were indispensable for exercise on wet and dark days.

two delightful gazebos or lodges with chimneys that cunningly emerge above the gateway. The curtilage still contains two original archways and the whole assemblage makes a charming scene when viewed from the almshouse terrace or from the quiet meadows of the Coneygree.

In Oxfordshire the most outstanding Jacobean house is that at Chastleton built between 1603 and 1614 by Walter Jones, a wool merchant of Witney. No doubt his surplus wealth came from flourishing sales due to the rapidly increasing use of white broadcloth as blankets for bed covers. He bought the estate from Robert Catesby, one of the planners of the abortive Gunpowder Plot, who needed the money to pay off a heavy fine. The mansion was built of local limestone to a skilled design probably by Robert Smythson, the architect of Hardwick Hall, Derbyshire. It and its outbuildings and most of its furnishings have survived intact so that it forms a perfect Jacobean piece. A fine arched stone gateway gives a full view of the main front of three storeys arranged under five narrow gables flanked at each end by a recessed staircase tower. The second and fourth bays project so as to flank at ground level a flight of steps that gives access to an entrance porch in the side of the bay, not visible from the front approach.

The interior decoration is lavish and exuberant in design, much of it based on Flemish pattern books still in the house. The porch leads by a door through a carved screen into the hall, the lower walls of which are panelled. Beyond the dais is a small parlour similarly panelled. The great parlour lies at the back of the house which is constructed around a quadrangle or court. On the first floor the many interesting rooms include the great chamber with opulently decorated walls, ceiling and fireplaces, and a Cavalier room with a secret chamber that was used by Arthur Jones in 1651 when a fugitive after the defeat of King Charles at Worcester. The whole length of the top floor at the back of the house is occupied by the Long Gallery which is panelled and graced with a barrel-vaulted ceiling with rich plasterwork.

In the grounds the interesting survivals include a quaint arrangement of topiary beasts within a circular hedge, a *hortus conclusus* or in common terms, 'the best garden'. The old bowling green is now used for tennis and the original brewhouse, bakery and stables serve less bucolic purposes, but little has changed in appearance since Walter Jones invested his wealth in Chastleton house and manor.

CHAPTER EIGHT

The Civil War and the End of Castles

The glories of our blood and state
Are shadows, not substantial things;
There is no armour against fate;
Death lays his icy hand on kings,
Sceptre and crown
Must tumble down,
And in the dust be equal made
With the poor crooked scythe and spade.
             (James Shirley, 1659)

The Civil War, 1642-1646

The central location of the English heartland acquired a new importance under
Charles I when London, the capital, was against the king and the country
disintegrated into a mosaic of different allegiances. The Civil War began and
virtually ended in the Midlands. The first bloodshed of the struggle happened at
Kilsby near Rugby when Royalist troopers searching for hidden weapons in cottages
killed two villagers and wounded others on 9 August 1642. The first notable
engagement took place on 23 August at Bascote Heath near Southam when a
Parliamentary troop from Warwick Castle under Lord Brooke attacked the
Royalists, killing 50 of them and capturing some artillery, before the King continued
on his way to raise his standard at Nottingham two days later. The first battle was at
Edgehill on 23 October when after a chaotic struggle the Parliamentarians withdrew
to Warwick and the king to Oxford.

    The university town occupied a convenient position between the mainly
Parliamentarian southeast and the largely Royalist north and west and was itself
fairly easily re-fortified. From late October 1642 to April 1646, when he went north,
Charles used the town as his headquarters and the seat of his court and government.
He borrowed or was given all the gold and silver plate that the dons could not hide and
from it minted a varied coinage including £3 gold pieces, the largest gold coins ever
circulated in Britain. Citizens and dons alike had a stirring time but the inhabitants
of neighbouring towns suffered much more from bombardment and pillage. The
walled borough of Northampton declared for Parliament and its garrison repelled a
minor siege and later made sallies to relieve other towns. Cirencester withstood an

early Royalist assault but was eventually taken and pillaged by Prince Rupert's troops, many houses being burnt and over 1,000 prisoners, with their leader Colonel Fettiplace, marched off to Oxford where some joined the King's forces and others helped with the extensive earthworks round the city. Banbury was battered by both sides: the Royalists captured it and then suffered two severe sieges which destroyed a large part of the town. Reading, situated strategically between London and Oxford, was flourishing exceedingly when the Civil War broke out. The King held the borough first whereupon the Parliamentarians under Essex marched from London and on 17 April 1643 began to bombard it with cannon ranging in calibre up to two of the heaviest guns from the Tower. The citizens surrendered honourably nine days later after much damage had been done especially to the abbey and St Giles' church. The Parliamentary forces pillaged the houses and the townsfolk had to pay heavy exactions and endure much quartering. Later the town was abandoned to the Royalists and the householders had to provide, in money or labour, for the rebuilding of their own defences. In May 1644 the king abandoned Reading to the Roundheads who forced the corporation to pay, among other things, for the re-erection of Caversham bridge. By the end of the Civil War the town's cloth trade was ruined, the corporation's property mortgaged and the citizens taxed almost out of existence. It took them more than a century to recover their former prosperity.

During the Civil War major battles were fought in the English heartland at Edgehill, Roundway Down, Newbury, Donnington, Chalgrove and Cropredy Bridge. The final battle that crushed the Royalist forces took place only just outside the region at Naseby on 14 June 1645 and happened when Charles' army was marching south to relieve the siege of Oxford. But the last notable open engagement occurred on 21 March 1646 when a new levy, three thousand strong, of Royalist troops under Sir Jacob Astley was routed just north of Stow on the Wold and several hundred prisoners were shut up in the church there. Oxford surrendered almost unscathed on 24 June 1646 but Wallingford castle, skilfully defended by Colonel Blagge, held out until 27 July when, after honourable capitulation, they were allowed to march out with horses and arms, colours flying, 'trumpets sounding, drums beating, matches lighted at both ends, bullets in their mouths and with bag and baggage'.

Although fortified towns suffered most, many villages and isolated manor houses experienced spasmodic skirmishes, quartering of troops and commandeering of food, fodder and livestock, especially horses. In 1643 about 2,000 horses were taken out of Oxfordshire for military uses, a loss which incidentally shows how much the farmers had gone over to horses rather than oxen for ploughing. The oppression of manor houses near roads frequented by troops may be judged from the account of damage and expenses listed by John Chamberlayne, squire of Maugersbury near Stow on the Wold.[1] Irrespective of great sums paid to stave off quartering, he could recall 58 main items of expenditure totalling over £446. Among these were large contributions to Royalists and Parliamentarians, the quartering of troops of both sides up to 150 in number at a time, the spoiling of his growing corn several times, and the loss to soldiers of 17 plough horses and at least 100 sheep. Eventually as a confessed

Royalist he was liable to a fine on his properties here which eventually — no doubt mitigated by his sufferings — worked out at £316 or about one-sixth their value. Chamberlayne also had to pay £930, a much higher rate, on his estate at Churchdown near Gloucester.

Parliamentary troops besieged and plundered the mansions at Compton Wynyates and Mapledurham, destroyed, for example, the manor houses at Milcote on Stour and Hillesden and seriously damaged the palace at Woodstock. The Royalists were equally and often more needlessly destructive. In order to deny comfortable lodgings to the Cromwellians, they set fire to the village of Chinnor and burnt down Godstow nunnery house, Cuddesdon palace, the mansion at Chipping Campden, and Spencer's great house at Wormleighton where Prince Rupert had stayed the night before the battle of Edgehill. Indeed apart from castles, city walls and some church interiors, the popular refrain 'I'm one of the ruins Cromwell knocked about a bit' seems often inapplicable.

After the war most castles were slighted including Oxford, Reading, Sudeley, Donnington, Wallingford and Kenilworth, but Warwick and Broughton escaped destruction because their owners had favoured the winning side. The fate of Banbury castle probably reflects the feeling of many townsfolk toward these supposedly protective fortresses: the citizens petitioned Parliament for its removal

The gatehouse (dated 1613) and tower of Spencer's mansion at Wormleighton.

and gladly demolished it for use in buildings nearby.

The loss of life was considerable and included Lucius Carey, Viscount Falkland who was killed at Newbury, and John Hampden who was fatally wounded at Chalgrove and died at Thame. The whole chain of events is commemorated in many plain monuments but produced even from the Royalists scarcely any artistic tomb memorials, except those of Colonel Glanville at Broad Hinton, of Edward St John at Lydiard Tregoze (*see* Chapter 6) and of Sir Edmund Verney at Middle Claydon.[2] The latter, a tall standing wall monument of dark and·white marble, commemorates a fervent Protestant who was MP for Chepping Wycombe when the Civil War broke out. Although convinced of the justice of the Parliamentary cause, Sir Edmund would not forsake a king whom he had served faithfully for nearly thirty years and at Edgehill he was the royal standard bearer. After the battle the only trace of his body found was a severed hand still grasping firmly the royal standard. At Radway on Edgehill, Captain Henry Kingsmill of the Royal infantry is remembered by a semi-reclining stone effigy, while at Naunton a long inscription on a marble tablet recalls a fortunate survivor whose father, Dr William Oldys, was 'barbarously murthered by ye Rebells in ye yeare 1645'.

Today the events, persons and ideologies of the Civil War period attract an ever-growing audience. The inns where Charles I stayed include 'The Red Lion' at Henley, which has a royal coat of arms dated 1632, and 'The King's Head' at Abingdon. Studley Priory, now an hotel, was the home of Sir George Croke, a noted jurist who declared in favour of John Hampden's refusal to pay ship-money. Numerous Civil War objects are displayed in museums at Oxford, Newbury, Cirencester and Banbury as well as in many of the Tudor and Jacobean mansions that we have already described. Littlecote House near Hungerford, then the home of Colonel Alexander Popham, a Parliamentarian, contains a superb collection of Cromwellian armour and a guardroom arranged in the contemporary way. The chapel here, of about 1637, has in the middle of its east wall an elevated pulpit instead of an altar and marks the transition to the 'preaching house' of the Puritans.

Burford was the scene of an interesting aftermath of the Civil War ideology. In May 1649 the Levellers, a highly democratic puritanical sect who postulated *inter alia* the abolition of all privileges, mutinied against Cromwell at Salisbury and Banbury. The Salisbury mutineers decided to join forces with those at Banbury and marched by way of Marlborough and Wantage to Abingdon where they collected more supporters before fording the Thames near Newbridge and proceeding in the evening of 13 May via Bampton to Burford. Feeling quite secure, they billeted themselves for the night in the town and two neighbouring villages.[3] About midnight, barely three hours after their arrival, the mutineers in Burford were utterly surprised and cornered by Cromwellian troops. After a desultory resistance they surrendered and about 340 of them were imprisoned in the church. Their comrades — a further 560 or so — in the neighbourhood managed to escape although most of them left behind their weapons and horses. On Thursday 17 May three of the prisoners were shot in Burford churchyard in full sight of the others who were then led

Monument to Edward St John (killed 1645), Lydiard Tregoze church.

back into the church and addressed by Cromwell. The Leveller mutiny virtually ended that morning as shortly afterwards Cornet Thompson, the ringleader at Banbury, was killed in a wood beside the road to Wellingborough after shooting dead three of his pursuers.

The End of Castles

The increased use of gunpowder and artillery in the fifteenth and sixteenth centuries weakened the defensive security of castles, and in 1464 the Earl of Warwick reduced Bamborough Castle in a week. Within a short time the erection of new castles in England virtually ceased and magnates built instead huge Tudor mansions and palaces. Probably the last true castle built in the Midlands was at Thornbury in the vale of Berkeley, Gloucestershire. Here in 1510 Henry VIII gave the third Duke of Buckingham permission to empark 1000 acres and to build a castle. The main gatehouse and great embattled tower were finished by 1514 but seven years later when the Duke was executed some of the other buildings were incomplete. Their late Perpendicular style and smooth-faced freestone give the surviving parts of the castle a grace and loveliness which belie its defensive intention. However, thereafter curtilage defences and high crenellated towers give way to purely domestic dwellings.

During the Civil War castles reassumed some of their former strategic importance as they could stand up for at least a short time to bombardment by lighter artillery, and direct infantry assault on them was likely to be extravagant of lives. At Donnington, Colonel John Boys fortified the castle for the king and threw up earthworks to the south to hold the enemy cannon fire at a safe distance. He had then a garrison of about 200 men together with 25 horses and a few guns. The second battle of Newbury in October 1644 followed the relief of the castle by the king's forces, but when the royalist troops withdrew to Oxford the Roundheads renewed the siege. Colonel, now Sir John Boys, held out for eighteen months and when, in April 1646, he was given an honourable surrender, the castle had been seriously damaged and within a few years was ruinous. Today only the massive gatehouse with its two flanking circular towers stands boldly on a chalk spur overlooking the Lambourn valley.

Wallingford castle suffered even more drastically. During Mary's reign it had been stripped of its lead and much of its stone and other building materials for works at Windsor. When the Civil War broke out, Wallingford castle's defences were hurriedly restored and in 1646 it was defended for the king for sixteen weeks with only 5 men slain, before its garrison was granted an honourable surrender. In 1652 the Council of State ordered its demolition and today the spacious site of 26 acres (10ha) has little to show of it except a window, a few fragments of wall, gateways, and foundations, and many fine earthworks including the motte and a double line of moats.

Fortunately some castles escaped or largely survived the Cromwellian demolition and it is to these that we now turn. Windsor Castle, although in Berkshire, belongs to the lower Thames vale rather than to the Midlands and sits astride the gateway guarding the easiest approach from the Midland shires to London. It is the supreme example of a royal castle and in its nine hundred years has acquired a wealth of

Fourteenth-century gatehouse of Donnington Castle.

treasures and beauty unparalleled in Britain. Anyone who has not visited it several times has missed a vital element in the English scene.

The prime surviving castles in the English heartland proper are at Sudeley, Kenilworth and Warwick. Sudeley stands on the lower slope of the Cotswold scarp near Winchcombe guarding old all-weather roads along the hills from Warwick to Gloucester and across the wolds to Cirencester and Stow. The present buildings date from about 1440 when the castle belonged to Ralph Boteler. It was forfeited to the Crown in 1469 and remained in royal hands until 1547 when Edward VI gave it to Thomas Seymour, his Lord High Admiral. In the same year Thomas secretly married Katherine Parr who had been widowed for the third time a few weeks earlier on the death of Henry VIII. Katherine had been married when thirteen and again when 18 and was already Seymour's sweetheart when in 1543 at the age of 31 she married Henry VIII. Now as Seymour's wife the ex-queen travelled to Sudeley in state, accompanied by Lady Jane Grey and Princess Elizabeth. Her marital misfortunes continued for in September 1548 she died of puerperal fever after giving birth to a daughter.

In 1554 the castle was granted to Sir John Brydges, later Lord Chandos, whose son rebuilt the outer court, except the gatehouse, and entertained Elizabeth here several times. During the Civil War Sudeley was taken twice by Parliamentary troops, who

Sudeley Castle near Winchcombe.

destroyed the interior of the church, and recaptured twice by the Royalists. In 1649 it was slighted and remained in ruins until bought in 1837 by the Dent family who proceeded to make the northern quadrangle habitable, to restore the church and erect there a fine tomb to Katherine Parr. In the 1930s the Dent-Brocklehursts continued the restoration and today various rooms of the castle are opened regularly to the public. Large parts of the fifteenth century buildings survive as well as the church and the picturesque ruins of a great barn. The treasures on display include items concerning Katherine Parr and a contemporary portrait of the young Queen Elizabeth. The Dents laid out a delightful garden in front of the ruinous southern quadrangle and the mature trees and stone balustrades of the water-lily pond and terrace blend pleasingly with the fifteenth-century backcloth. Details such as tall clipped yews, a formal flower garden with low box hedges and a replica of a mediaeval pleasance with an original sundial add to the charm of a loving rehabilitation.

Kenilworth and Warwick, the prime castles of the English heartland, lie far to the north. By a strange chance they stand barely 5 miles (8km) apart and their owners were often at daggers drawn, particularly during the time of Simon de Montfort and in the Wars of the Roses. Each since its foundation in Norman times has had the advantage of the Forest of Arden for timber and game but Warwick castle has always graced the county capital whereas at Kenilworth, the town, although today just outstripping its rival in population, has never achieved much importance on its own account. For this reason we will describe in a later chapter the castle at Warwick and its borough.

Kenilworth

A distinct knoll of gravel rising a few metres above the flood-plain of the tiny Rinham brook at Kenilworth was selected about 1125 AD as the site of a castle by Geoffrey de Clinton, chamberlain to Henry I. It was presumably of a simple motte and bailey type. Geoffrey also founded nearby an Augustinian priory which grew into a large abbey worth about £600 a year at its dissolution. Of this spacious and beautiful structure only a few late fourteenth century buildings and walls survive together with a fine Norman doorway now re-set in the parish church of St Nicholas. The fortress had a much longer life and although ruinous remains one of the most aesthetically pleasing of English castles.

The castle built by Geoffrey was taken over by the king and about 1170 to 1180 under Henry II a rectangular keep, 25m high, was erected. It has four broad angle turrets, one of which surmounted a well. Between the turrets the stone masonry is 20ft (6m) thick at ground level and is stepped back to a height of about 3m until the walls are over 4m thick. The lowest part with the receding wall is filled with earth, no doubt because it was built around the old motte. Above this the keep consists of two floors, each of one large room only, and with the outside entrance on the upper storey. There was also a small bailey surrounded by a ditch and probably also by a palisade.

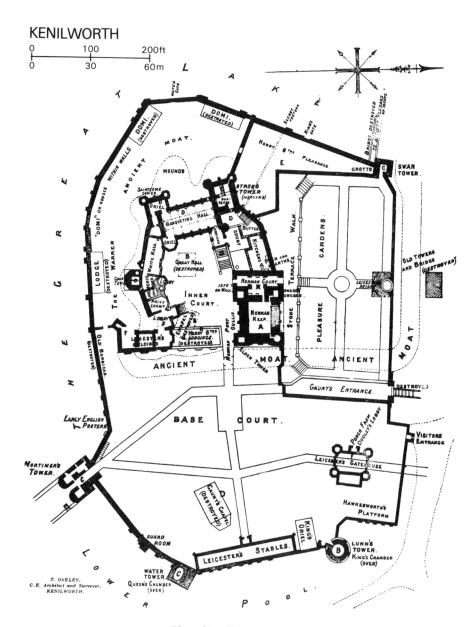

Plan of Kenilworth castle.

The castle was greatly enlarged and strengthened in the early thirteenth century by King John, who is said to have spent £2,000 on the work, and by his successor Henry III. Eventually the fortress consisted of a keep and inner bailey, with the living quarters, completely surrounded with a strong curtain wall and moat. Around this stretched a spacious outer bailey, itself defended by a stone curtilage with three towers and a strong gatehouse. Outside this castle complex of 9 acres (3.6ha) were wide water defences consisting of a great lake, covering 100 acres (40ha), connected on the west and south with narrower lakes and on the north and east with a wide pool. This water girdle was held up by a great dam, 120m long, across the Rinham Brook on the southeast of the castle. Here, until Elizabethan times, was the main entrance which consisted of an outer barbican in the form of a large half-moon shaped earthwork and a gatehouse, called Mortimer's Tower, with two round towers on the outside flanked by small guardrooms with cross-shaped slits for archers. It completely closed the outer end of the long embankment or causeway dam, which was topped by a wall on each long side and led to another strong gatehouse at its inner end in the wall of the main castle enclosure. In peaceful times this causeway made a splendid tilting ground.

Henry III leased Kenilworth castle to Simon de Montfort, Earl of Leicester, who had married princess Eleanor, the king's sister. On Montfort's rebellion and death at the battle of Evesham (1265) his followers under his younger son, Simon, withstood at Kenilworth a remarkable siege. Every form of attack then known was brought against the castle, including battering rams, siege towers, ballista and even naval warfare using barges brought overland from Chester and launched on the lake. For six months the garrison of 1,700 men held out until, decimated by disease and famine, they surrendered with 'honours of war' and as the besiegers entered, the stench of decaying corpses was said to have been overpowering. The king then annexed the castle to the inheritance of his younger son Edmund, Earl of Leicester and Lancaster. Edward II was imprisoned here for some months in 1326-7 before being secretly taken elsewhere, and here, according to Marlowe's play, the king was shaved in puddlewater to prevent him from being recognised by possible rescuers.

The castle now assumed great political importance because John of Gaunt made it his chief country seat and enlarged its living quarters in a most magnificent way. He was born in 1340 at Ghent (hence his name), the fourth son of Edward III and Queen Philippa. When he married his cousin Blanche, Duchess of Lancaster, in 1359, he became the greatest lord in England. From their children descended Henry IV, V and VI of England and the family that ruled Portugal until 1910. On Blanche's death in 1369 John of Gaunt married Constance, the elder daughter of Pedro the Cruel, king of Castile and Léon. From them descended Isabella, the queen of Ferdinand of Aragon, whose offspring ruled Spain until 1700 and who sponsored Columbus' voyage to the New World. When Constance died in 1394, Gaunt married Catherine Swinford who had long been his mistress. Their children, the Beauforts, were the ancestors of Edward IV, Richard III and all the other English and British sovereigns from Henry VII to the present day.

John of Gaunt, 'time-honoured Lancaster', spent most of his life campaigning with the Black Prince in northern France and at the head of his own large army in Aquitaine, Portugal and in Spain where he assumed, and vainly tried hard to win, the right to the kingship of Castile and Léon. But by the time of his death in 1399 he had quite transformed Kenilworth castle. Against the curtain wall of the inner bailey west of the keep he erected a large kitchen with three great fireplaces (the fourth was added in the fifteenth century). This led into a buttery or storeroom (now disappeared) and so to a strong tower used partly as a prison, and partly as service rooms. South of these the pre-existing hall was replaced by a magnificent banqueting hall excelled for the time only by that at Westminster. At Kenilworth, this fine structure 90ft (28m) long and 14m wide, forms the western flank of the inner bailey or courtyard. It has large windows, including a spacious bay window, both to the inner and the outer bailey, and its western side forms with the service tower a symmetrical facade that is virtually unknown in domestic buildings — as distinct from whole castles — up to this date. The great hall occupies the first floor and beneath it is a large vaulted undercroft, with a postern that led direct to a postern in the wall of the outer bailey. The hall was warmed by a large fireplace in the middle of each long wall but the southeast corner, near the polygonal bay window with stone seats, has a smaller fireplace presumably for the benefit of the potentates on the high table. At this end a passage leads into various living rooms.

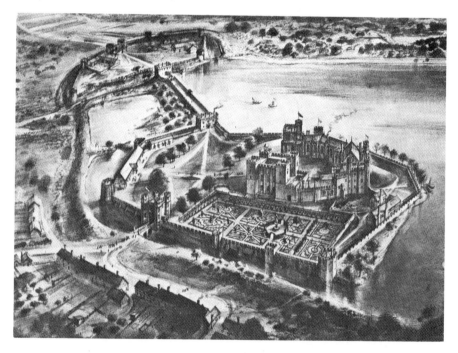

Kenilworth Castle, a pictorial reconstruction by Alan Sorrell of its probable appearance in 1575.

When John of Gaunt died in February 1399, Richard II confiscated the Lancaster estates whereupon Henry Bolingbroke, Gaunt's son, returned from exile and won the crown as Henry IV. Kenilworth now became royal and in the hall here, Bolingbroke's son, Henry V, threatened to 'mock French castles down' when he received the Dauphin's envoys and his gift of tennis balls. This Henry appears to have found the great banqueting hall too grandiose for about 1414 he ordered the construction of a rectangular earthwork surrounded by a moat at the northwestern edge of the lake. This pleasance has a timber-framed house that was used as state appartments until Henry VIII had it demolished.

In 1563 Elizabeth granted the castle to her favourite Robert Dudley, and shortly afterwards made him Earl of Leicester and Chancellor of Oxford University. Dudley spent lavishly in extending, repairing and beautifying the structure. He pierced the keep with wide mullion windows and built a small pillared courtyard on its original entrance. A large extension with a gracious facade of tall mullioned bay windows was added to the southeast corner of the inner bailey. A big new barn and stables were constructed against the outer bailey wall on the east, and nearby a magnificent new gatehouse was erected to allow a stately entrance from that quarter. The wide pool on this side was drained and converted into an orchard. Elizabeth visited Kenilworth several times but her fourth visit in June 1575 was especially notable. She stayed for seventeen days and Leicester spent £1,000 a day on entertaining her. He kept his own troupe of liveried players headed by James Burbage and it is widely believed that Shakespeare heard about or that he or his father actually saw a water pageant performed on Kenilworth lake. Arion appeared on the back of a dolphin carried in a boat with oars shaped like fins; musicians concealed within the dolphin played melodiously while Arion sang a delectable ditty. In *A Midsummer Night's Dream* Oberon says

> Since once I sat upon a promontory
> And heard a mermaid on a dolphin's back
> Uttering such dulcet and harmonious breath
> That the rude sea grew civil at her song
> And certain stars shot madly in their spheres
> To hear the sea maid's music.

The Queen no doubt was highly diverted by Leicester's theatricals but they did not induce her to marry him and as Shakespeare records

> the imperial vot'ress passed on
> In maiden meditation fancy free.

The Earl died in 1588 and lies buried beneath a magnificent memorial in the Beauchamp chapel at St Mary's, Warwick.

During the Civil War Kenilworth Castle changed hands twice in 1642 without much fighting and after the battle of Edgehill it was held by the Parliamentarians. In

1649 it was rendered defenceless with 'as little spoil to the dwelling-house as might be'. The outer walls were breached, one side of the keep blown up and the dam or causeway broken so that the lake was drained and the old tilting ground cut in two. The Elizabethan gatehouse became a dwelling and survives intact but the main part of the inner castle has remained uninhabited from the late seventeenth century.

The decay and desolation were far advanced when hope of salvation came from an unexpected quarter. About 1816 'a man of middle age, with lofty forehead and a keen grey eye, slightly lame but withal active, entered its gatehouse and passed many silent hours within its walls. That man was Walter Scott'. Sir Walter conceived a plot for an historical romance with small regard for historical facts. Amy Robsart crashes to her death at Kenilworth whereas she had in fact been found dead in 1560 at the foot of the stairs at Cumnor Place in Oxfordshire, three years before the castle was granted by the queen to Robert Dudley. The remarkable ceremonial details in Scott's *Kenilworth* were taken from two contemporary tracts that give in full the verses, masques and speeches. He touched up the verses and attributed characters to the speakers to suit his whim; for example, the gigantic porter which he made a rude, drunken hero was in fact 'Maister Badger of Oxenforde, Maister of Arte, and Bedle in the same Universitie'. However, Scott's novel was extremely popular. The Earl of Abingdon, then living at Wytham Abbey near Oxford, found it so thrilling that he arranged a party to drive over to Cumnor Place which he owned. Not till they reached the site did he recollect to his horror that he had had the place pulled down a few decades earlier. Scott's influence on Kenilworth castle was wholly beneficial. After the publication of his novel in 1821, to continue our quotation from T. Oakley (1886), 'The progress of desolation was to be arrested; the torch of genius again lighted up the spacious pile; visions of sorrow and suffering, of woman's weakness and man's treachery, all were to be for ever after associated with recollections of ancient splendour'. Inevitably Queen Victoria visited the ruins and finally on 17 November 1958, the four hundredth anniversary of the accession of Queen Elizabeth I, Lord Kenilworth gave the site and a generous gift toward its preservation to the people of Kenilworth. Now under the care of the Department of the Environment it is thronged with visitors who marvel at its mediaeval grandeur although so many of its structures stand

All tenantless save to the crannying wind
Or holding dark communion with the clouds.

CHAPTER NINE

Transformation of the Rural Scene and Life: 1660-1835

Oh let us love our occupations,
Bless the squire and his relations,
Live upon our daily rations,
And always know our proper stations.
                    (Dickens, *The Chimes*, 1845)

The Expansion of Squirearchy and Decline of Peasantry, 1660-1760

The hundred years following the accession of Charles II were of great importance in the life and landscape of the English heartland. During them the number of peasants, or owner-occupiers of small farms, declined still further and the power of squires or landed gentry rose rapidly. Prices for agricultural goods generally fell after 1660, except in years of poor harvests, and the land was heavily taxed but, on the other hand, the flourishing colonial overseas trade did not compete directly with home-produced foodstuffs and provided much capital for investment. Whereas in previous years, high profits had come mainly from sales of wool abroad or at home, after 1673 a bounty on corn exports, combined with a duty on imports, guaranteed farmers a reasonable return from arable fields. Between 1732 and 1766 Britain fed its own population and had a record surplus of cereals for export.

Agricultural methods continued to improve slowly with more turnips and leguminous fodders and more flexible rotations. Lord Townshend's four-course system of two cereals alternating with roots and clover became more popular and, with sheep folding, caused 'prodigious improvements' in the Cotswolds after 1730. The English heartland produced Jethro Tull (1674-1741) who was born at Basildon in Berkshire and perfected his mechanical seed-drill on his father's farm at Howberry near Wallingford. However, his ideas were not published until 1731, when *Horse-hoeing Husbandry* advocated sowing in regular drills wide enough to use a plough or hoe between them, proper pulverisation of the soil, and also the use of better seed. In fact, his theory spread slowly, becoming more important in the nineteenth century.[1]

Under a system of mixed farming and steady profits, the squirearchy or larger land-proprietors became supreme. They controlled administration and justice locally, and government nationally. Merchants, manufacturers, financiers and professional men showed a quickened desire to own estates and once established proceeded to enlarge their properties whenever the opportunity arose. The small freeholder was especially approachable, as he could stay on as a tenant or find alternative work in crafts and industries. Conditions at Adderbury in Oxfordshire are typical. Here the chief land purchasers were the Dukes of Argyll and Buccleugh who between them spent over £12,000 in buying up manors and numerous freeholds in the parish. Not far away the Duke of Marlborough was also purchasing manors to form the Blenheim estates. This kind of engrossment caused a marked decline in the number of small freeholders and owner-occupiers—akin to the European peasantry—and a rapid rise in the number of farms of over 100 acres (40ha). By the late eighteenth century in Oxfordshire small freeholders, paying 6s. to £20 tax a year, occupied only 10 per cent of the land. Tenancy dominated the farming economy and only the squire crowed in the rural roost. The attractiveness of the squirearchy may be judged from its effect on Sir Christopher Wren, who in 1713 when over eighty years old, bought the Elizabethan mansion, Wroxall Abbey, in order to provide a foothold for his family in the landed gentry of Warwickshire.

The richer landowners built for themselves fine houses with parks and landscaped gardens, such as are described in Chapter 11. The lesser squires and chief farmers continued to improve their homes and there was a great rebuilding or refacing of existing properties, many of which were still partly of timber and wattle and daub or some other earthy admixture. In most moderate-sized and smaller farmhouses the traditional local style persisted to well into the eighteenth century when touches of Classical details, and sash windows and hipped roofs reflecting a Dutch influence, became common.

The trade in oolitic limestone or freestone now reached its zenith for quarrymen, masons and local architects. The Cotswolds had long been famous for their building stone when a series of quite remarkable fires and a flurry of new mansions created a large market. Disastrous city fires in London (1666) and Warwick (1694), and the vast amount of rebuilding here, as well as at Oxford and at new country mansions, such as Blenheim palace (1705-1720) and Heythrop, stimulated local quarrying and local masons.[2] The Strong family of Barrington and Taynton, and Christopher Kempster of Burford were especially associated with the rebuilding of St Paul's and other London churches. They owned large quarries and sent vast quantities of stone to London and to Blenheim. In Gloucestershire, Edward and Thomas Woodward of Chipping Campden were noted mason-builders and designers. In Warwickshire, the chief builders and designers in stone were Francis and William Smith of Warwick, David and William Hiorn and Sanderson Miller. These master craftsmen dealt mainly with major projects but occasionally took an interest in minor buildings and employed groups of masons competent to supervise the construction of small traditional homes. The wealth of stone facades of this period forms the chief glory of the older nucleus of numerous villages on and near the limestone wolds. The persistence of the vernacular Cotswold style may be judged from the slow introduction of Classical details and sash windows. The late seventeenth century Medford House, Mickleton, combines the traditional and Classical styles while the manor house of the same date at Compton Scorpion near Ilmington has one symmetrical front with mullioned windows and another with sashed windows and a parapet.

On clay vales, far from cheap building stone and on chalk uplands capped with clay-with-flints, bricks formed the chief construction material although stone was often used for churches and for quoins, dressings and carved ornamentation. Here, too, destructive town fires, in Marlborough (1653), Northampton (1675), Hungerford (1680-5), Buckingham (1725) and Stony Stratford (1742) greatly stimulated the local brick and tile industries. These towns became a symphony of brick, red, blue and grey, sometimes vitrified and arranged chequerwise. The style spread to nearby villages, where brick facings were often given stone dressings as at Radley Hall (now College) of about 1726, or more rarely stone facings had brick dressings as at the manor farm at Stanford in the Vale. Along the foot of the chalk scarp and on the Marlborough downs, house walls were often made of chalk rock and of sarsen blocks. In some places fashion conflicted with the local provenance of building material as at Bicester (on the cornbrash limestone), where three disastrous fires between 1718 and 1730 led to much rebuilding and the refacing or facing of local coursed rubble with either stucco or variegated brick. The opportunity was also taken to insert sash windows and to add classical porticoes to the front entrances.

Very few new churches were built in this period except in connection with some large house. Most ecclesiastical construction kept to the traditional Perpendicular style and purely Classical churches are rare. That at Honington was erected adjoining the lovely hall of the same age in the 1680s except for the old tower. Similarly at Ayno the main body of the church was rebuilt in Hawksmoor style about 1725 when large parts of the Carolean mansion were refaced.

Church monuments tend to become more modest and less space-consuming, with standing mural effigies outnumbering tomb chests. The grand exceptions to this tendency include the heroic Baroque memorials at Blenheim and Steeple Aston. The stupendous monument of 1733 to John Churchill, Duke of Marlborough, in the chapel at Blenheim Palace was designed by William Kent and sculptured by Rysbrack. The very tall monument to Sir Francis and Lady Frances Page at Steeple Aston, although their white marble effigies are only life size, is equally impressive. It was commissioned from Henry Scheemakers in 1730 and erected in Sir Francis' lifetime after existing memorials had been removed to make space for it. The son of a Bloxham vicar, he made a fortune at the bar and bought an estate here in order to live the life of a country squire. His marble effigy portrays him in full legal dress, half-reclining alongside his graceful wife whose head and shoulders are propped by pillows. The superb craftsmanship instantaneously expressed the imperious mien of a judge, who according to Alexander Pope was noted for hard words and hanging. The strength of tradition among the squirearchy of rural districts may be judged from the monuments to the Fettiplaces in Swinbrook church. These include two large memorials, each with three tiers of reclining effigies of knights in armour. The first tier, erected by Sir Edmund Fettiplace (*ob.* 1613), is of local stone and

VI QVIBVS IN REBVS
IPSE OLIM SOCIVS INCLARVISSET
IN HSDEM MEMORIA EIVS POTISSIMVM CONSERVARETVR
HONORARIVM HOC MONVMENTVM
ANNA MARIA FILIA IONATHAN SHIPLEY EPISC ASAPH
CONIVGI SVO B M
P C

HE FORMED A DIGEST OF HINDU AND MOHAMMEDAN LAWS

Monument to Sir William Jones (*ob*. 1794) by John Flaxman in University College chapel, Oxford.

presumably by a local mason as the straight-legged effigies recline awkwardly on one elbow on a cushion; in the other, erected by Edmund Fettiplace (*ob*. 1686), the figures have a more realistic pose and were carved in alabaster by William Bird of Oxford. The eighteenth century monuments here to this family are small and artistic. The Fettiplaces owned or had owned estates in many parts of the south Midlands and had a large Tudor mansion at Swinbrook until their line died out in 1805. The house, which has been completely removed, stood beside the pleasant footpath that leads from Swinbrook south to the small church and deserted hamlet of Widford. By late Georgian times the formal effigies and contrived groupings on monuments had been superseded by evocative images and imaginative compositions, often informative and not infrequently sentimental.

The scarcity of new churches of this time contrasts markedly with the abundance of reconstructed, refaced and enlarged vicarages and rectories. The rector now began to live in a dwelling commensurate with his position as one of the chief freeholders in a parish, indeed often second only to the lord of the manor. At Burford, Stanton Harcourt, Inkpen, Hambleden, West Hanney, Fenny Compton and Whichford, to mention but a few, the vicarage was rebuilt on a grand scale, usually as a rectangular block with a hipped roof. In Buckinghamshire nearly all the rectories were rebuilt or refaced at this time, those in the north in stone and those elsewhere mainly by inserting brick infilling into a timber framework.[3] Many a vicar virtually became a squire with generous accommodation that was to prove far too palatial for his successors in the twentieth century.

The answers of parsons to their bishops' enquiries provide a percipient view of the nature of rural parishes. In Oxfordshire in 1738 on the Chilterns, as on the Arden in Warwickshire, most parishes lacked a considerable village. Rotherfield Peppard had about 40 houses, mostly scattered; Bix consisted of several small hamlets; Swyncomb had 'chiefly 3 villages or hamlets . . . consisting for the most part of poor inhabitants; the arrable lands . . . are mostly appendant to lone farm houses, as they are very much in all this hill or Chiltern part of this country. It comprehends about 40 houses and cottages. The chief family is Mr Greenhill now settled at Swyncomb; about 6 years ago he purchased what he has here . . .'[4]

Elsewhere in Oxfordshire parishes the dwellings were usually clustered together near the church and manor house. The vicars, although not asked to do so, differentiated between houses and cottages, presumably because the latter were too poor to be taxed and to contribute anything to church expenses. The answers also reveal the small number of owner-occupiers. Alkerton had 8 'town' (village) houses and 6 little farmers, four of which were rack-rented, that is to the outer limit of the worth of the farms. Ardley had 19 families of which 2 were small freeholders and the rest tenants of the Duke of Marlborough. Cuxham, with 24 houses in the village, had 1 parsonage, 4 farmhouses and the rest filled chiefly by day labourers in husbandry. At Idbury all the constant inhabitants except a few poor people were tenants of the lord of the manor. At Oddington the one village contained 25 houses, including the parsonage, 10 farmhouses and 14 cottages for labourers and poor people. At South Weston, of 20 families in the village, 2 were yeoman farmers and the rest labourers. At Mapledurham 23 of the 70 houses were cottages.

There seems no doubt that the housing conditions of the families of day labourers and of the poor were appalling. They had at worst one and probably at best two or three small rooms. The idyllic pictures of the cottager painted by poets such as Thomson ('Of happy labour, love and social glee') and Gray ('How jocund did they drive their team afield'), and the bucolic bliss of Goldsmith's *Deserted Village* are hard to reconcile with toil from sunrise to sunset and crowded hovels in a rainy climate. At Nuneham Courtenay the fine new semi-detached homes erected for the labouring tenants in 1760, had two small rooms below and 2 small bedrooms above, and were considered 'just what they ought to be, comfortable but unostentatious'. One old woman preferred, and was allowed to end her days in her 'clay-built cot' in the old village, but the others, in the words of William Whitehead, the poet laureate,

Had left their cots without a sigh,
Well pleased to house their little train
In happier mansions warm and dry.[5]

The Old Vicarage at Burford dated 1672.

However, this acclaimed solution to the problem of labourers' cottages was not adopted widely until beneficent landowners built model villages in Victorian times. By then, as will now be shown, almost the whole of the countryside had been enclosed as private property.

Parliamentary Enclosure of Common Land

Much of the present landscape of small fields enclosed with hedgerows and walls dates only from Georgian and Victorian times. Most enclosures of parks and farmland prior to the 1630s were enforced by powerful landlords against the wishes of poor parishioners or tenants and of parliament, but voluntary enclosure of common fields was always possible if all the commoners in a manor agreed to it. At Godington in 1603 the Fermors, lords of the manor, agreed with the rector and the one remaining yeoman that they had not yet bought out, to enclose the parish except the cow pasture of 100 acres.[1] By the early seventeenth century the Fermors had split the estate into eight farms, five let at over £40 a year and three at £20-£40 a year. Events were fairly similar at Bletchingdon where in 1623 Sir John Lenthall persuaded the rector and fifteen other freeholders with common rights to enclose and subdivide nearly all the remaining open land in the parish. Of the lay freeholders, one received 60 acres, another 56 acres and the other thirteen smaller amounts, five having less than 10 acres each. Within a century only five or six freeholders remained. Coleshill, Great Coxwell and Goosey were among other parishes enclosed wholly or largely by agreement before 1660.

After that date so many agricultural writers extolled the benefits of enclosure that parliament began to promote it. Where a majority of the commoners in a parish wished to enclose their common lands they could obtain a private Act of Parliament to do so. Later much enclosing was done under General Enclosure Acts, especially those of 1756, 1757, 1801, 1836 and 1845. The earliest enclosure Award for Oxfordshire was for Mixbury in 1730 and the last for Crowell in 1882. Steventon, then in Berkshire, was not actually enclosed until 1883.

In spite of Tudor enclosures scattered throughout the countryside, the English heartland was by far the largest area in England where the greater part of the common fields was unenclosed. It had remained the prime home of open field agriculture and benefited most from Parliament Enclosure Acts. The number of townships affected by such awards was remarkably high; in most districts two parishes in three underwent some enclosing and the proportion exceeded four in five on the redlands near Banbury. Appreciable areas of forest, 'waste' and heath were now also permanently fenced in as well as the remaining open fields. All told,

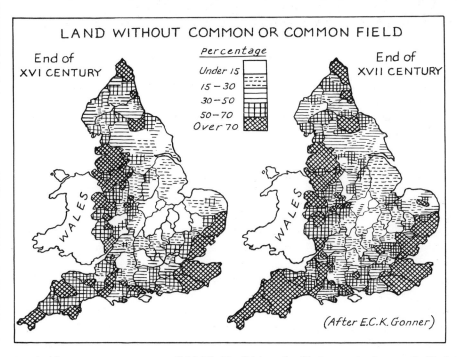

Land without common or common field. The English heartland is shown to be the stronghold of the open field system which is revealed by the relative abundance of land with common field.

counting common farmland and waste together, about 52 per cent of the total area of Northamptonshire, 46 per cent of Oxfordshire, 34 per cent of Buckinghamshire and about 25 per cent of Berkshire, Warwickshire and Wiltshire were enclosed under private or general Acts of Parliament after 1730.

The chief landscape effect of enclosures was the rapid erection of a chequerwork of fences. To keep out other people's stock and to define his boundaries, an owner now had to erect stout fences, a legal liability which had evolved since time immemorial and which was reflected in the custom of confining yew trees — poisonous to stock — to carefully enclosed churchyards. In rocky districts walls were built from stone quarried on the spot; elsewhere hedges of hawthorn and other quick-growing shrubs were planted. The land was now parcelled out into enclosed fields usually of 7 to 20 acres but occasionally of over 30 acres. The new field boundaries were usually straight and the fields rectangular except where they abutted on curving old enclosures and winding ancient boundaries such as stream courses and parish limits which frequently coincided.

With the spread of enclosures, vestiges of the old strips of the open arable land gradually disappeared beneath the mosaic of enclosed fields. Faint traces of the old system, recently much defaced, may be seen in a few low earthen balks beside the Burford-Stow road near the 'Merrimouth Inn' at Westcote in Gloucestershire. The allotment of strips in the common meadow survives at Yarnton as a living memorial to the ancient strip system and the high value of riverine meadows. Here on the flat floodplain of the Thames the lush pasture of Oxey and West Meadow and Pixey Mead is common to Yarnton and Begbroke parishes. Since mediaeval times at least 170 acres of this common tract have been divided into strips marked at each end by a post of stone or wood. For example Oxey consists of 3 batches or 'shots' of 13 strips each running from regular headlands and West Meadow of 5 batches. Each strip covers about one customary acre, or just under one statute acre, which is supposed to be as much as one man can mow in a day. Some of the strips are not rectangular especially near the winding river but they cover approximately the same acreage.[6]

The allocation of the strips was decided by lottery, so ensuring that each commoner had a chance of mowing the best strips. Since mediaeval times this lottery has been decided by drawing from a leather bag 13 balls corresponding with 13 'shots' or batches. Each of the small balls of hard polished wood has on it the name, abbreviated if necessary, of a 'shot', such as Water Molley or William of Bladon, and each represents the right to mow the grass of one lot and the subsequent right of common pasture from about late August to the end of November for 1 head of cattle per acre and 1 horse per 2 acres. The drawing which until recently took place on three separate days, is done at the head of each batch and the owner of the first ball out of the bag has the first strip of that batch of 13 strips, and so on. Most of the owners are local farmers or persons who have bought over the years rights or half-rights or even quarter-rights in a shot. The sale is held usually in early July when the grass is ready for mowing. In July 1974 the Nature Conservancy bought the rights of mowth and commons for that year, the grazing being sold as a single lot of 104 commons. The top

Ridge and furrow around the deserted mediaeval village of North Weston near Thame.

price for the mowth was £21 per acre for The Tidals. The origin of the system goes back to the days of strip farming but how the number 13 evolved is obscure. It may be connected with the fact that at Domesday Survey Yarnton and Begbroke together had 26 villeins but, irrespective of these uncertainties, it seems to represent an agreed simplification or rearrangement of an ancient meadow allocation.

Probably the most frequent relic of the ancient strip system lies in the ridge-and-furrow, particularly where arranged in curving lines reminiscent of the selions of the open fields. However, some ridge-and-furrow was made also for drainage on Tudor enclosures, and lacks the long curving lines of the old open plough-strips or selions. The latter, or curved type can often be detected by the way that the straight field boundaries of parliamentary enclosures cross them at right angles, showing that the new system was imposed on the existing landscape. Ridge-and-furrow is rare on well-drained soils and common on clays where ridges thrown up high by a fixed mouldboard provided drainage. It is soon obliterated by modern ploughing and survives mainly on pastures as at Water Eaton where the common fields on the stiff Oxford clay were abandoned about 1600 and have probably been under grass ever since.

The cost of enclosure was considerable although allocations were usually made so as to redistribute the land in compact holdings which were relatively cheap to enclose. In Warwickshire the costs per acre, other than those for fencing, averaged 11s. before 1760, 34s. in the 1790s, and nearly 62s. in 1801. In the English heartland generally, the ordinary costs (legal, surveying, clerical etc.) varied from 11s. to £5 per acre and averaged about £1. Many persons put the cost of fencing as high as £3 per acre but the small proprietor, who did his own labouring, probably paid no more than £3 per acre for all expenses.[7] The effort involved in a sizeable estate was enormous. At South Leigh (in Oxfordshire), which was largely enclosed under an Award of 1793, John Sibthorpe employed three horse teams and 54 men on enclosing and repairing. Within less than a year they felled and worked up between 2,000 and 3,000 trees to posts and rails for enclosures and for timber for the general repair of farmhouses and cottages. They planted over 12 miles of quickset cuttings and fenced half of it with posts and rails as well as providing the enclosed parcels with gates and gateposts.[8]

Enclosures such as these created the modern field landscape. On free-draining limestones the walls were easily repaired and proved virtually permanent except on tracts where poor quality stone weathered within a century or so into small rubble that became smothered by the bushgrowth it had sheltered. Elsewhere on clayey soils the hedgerows rapidly widened and became topped with trees, especially of elm, oak and ash, which regenerated themselves naturally and gave the clay vales a wooded appearance. In recent decades the increasing use of hedge-cutting machinery and the elm disease have seriously decreased the number of hedgerow trees, at the same time the use of larger farm machines and electric fences have favoured large fields which have been formed by uprooting hedges. Thus in parts, especially on the chalk, the farmland now resembles the open countryside of pre-enclosure days. The elm disease has been especially destructive in the clay vales which now appear startlingly flat and open without their chequerwork of hedgerow trees.

In the nineteenth century the main remaining areas of forest, waste and marsh were enclosed and improved for agriculture. The royal forests were not involved until Victorian times and their fate will be described in a following chapter whereas the drainage of marshes and floodplains was undertaken relatively early. In Oxfordshire the ill-drained bowl of Otmoor, a valuable waste of 4,000 acres, became famous for the local opposition to loss of common rights.[9] The villagers of seven townships on its periphery had acquired ancient rights of common and strove hard to retain them. Eventually the chief landowners obtained a bill in Parliament in 1815, but the ferocity of the opposition of cottage commoners who found themselves facing heavy expenses for draining and fencing their small allotments, delayed the final Award until 1829. Many cottagers sold their common rights for £5 to local farmers but, when in 1830 some of the latter became incensed with flood damage caused by the new drainage, the two parties joined hands in smashing embankments, bridges, hedges and fences. Not until police had been brought from London and the fences forcibly maintained intact long enough for ploughing and sowing in 1835 did the former commoners of Otmoor give up the struggle.

Another important effect of enclosure on the English landscape was the change in the distribution of dwellings in former open field parishes. Whereas previously it was every commoner's concern to see that the common fields were not encroached upon, after the awards the rearrangement and consolidation of strips into compact holdings allowed owners to erect dwellings on their own parcels. This had already happened in some seventeenth century enclosures as at Bletchingdon where several isolated farmhouses were built after 1623. In future the ancient idea of a central cluster of dwellings near the manor house and church persisted no longer and a scatter of isolated farmsteads appears, often with names reflecting British humour, such as Starveall, or national events such as Trafalgar and Waterloo. Sometimes the actual layout of the old Anglo-Saxon village was also directly affected. Many, if not most, had been loosely placed around some sort of green or gathering place for stock and in the award for some parishes this open space was subdivided largely among peripheral freeholders. In such villages at one stroke the prime original characteristic of the open field system of the Anglo-Saxon settlement was largely obliterated; Kidlington on the Green became Kidlington and in numerous other villages the manor farm was now fronted with a large private paddock and approached eventually by an avenue of horse chestnut or elm. In many parishes, parts of the old village green could now be built upon and although many extensive open greens still exist, as witness the cricket pitches at Greys Green near Rotherfield Greys, Steventon and Tetsworth, numerous others have been partly or wholly obliterated by houses.

Late Georgian Planned Estates and Model Villages

After the enclosure of a parish, progressive landowners found it easier to replan their estates and to increase their agricultural output. At Buscot in the late eighteenth century Edward Loveden built a mansion and completely reorganised the agriculture. His improvements embraced farm machinery, the quality of the livestock and the building on the Thames of a wharf with warehouses that he rented to London cheesemongers who soon were sending more than 2,000 tons of cheese annually downriver by barge.

About this time the most famous estate planner in the Midlands was John Claudius Loudon who, from 1809 to 1811, managed and replanned the estate at Great Tew. This parish which stood athwart the edge of the marlstone or redland country in north Oxfordshire was renowned for the oppression of the villagers by Sir Lawrence Tanfield, Lord Chief Baron, in the 1620s and for the cultural eminence of his grandson, Lucius Carey, Lord Falkland, who was killed in the Civil War. Of their house only the brick walls of three garden enclosures and perhaps the fine stone gateway, now the entrance to the churchyard, remain. In 1803 J.A. Repton was called in to plan a new house and to landscape the park, but for some unknown reason his designs were not used. Six years later J.C. Loudon was employed to transform the mainly pastoral estate into a Scotch-style farming system. His book, *Observations on laying out Farms in the Scotch style adapted to England* (1812), tells how he endeavoured to integrate aesthetically and economically, farmland, farmhouse, outbuildings and park. He uprooted the hedges of the existing enclosures and made larger fields each of 15 to 25 acres, each carefully drained but connected with a freshwater supply and with new haulage roads that were constructed along the contour to allow easy gradients between the fields and the home yards and barns. The northern boundary of the estate was already weather-fended by a long plantation so, wherever possible, he laid out the new field hedgerows, grown from hawthorn quicksets, in a north-south alignment to act as windbreaks against prevailing westerly winds. Today, the outlines of much of the scheme survive with some fine trees and rhododendron shrubberies skirting the park. More obvious are the improvements to the cottages most of which cluster around two greens in the wooded valley north of the park. Around the main green, with its stocks and Victorian Gothic school and teacher's house, the gabled stone cottages, for the most part thatched and of sixteenth or seventeenth century age, were embellished with Gothic porches and stone mullioned windows. The effect is idyllic as the old cottages are set within flower bedecked gardens fronted with neatly trimmed hedges. The other, smaller green at Great Tew was once a similar delight, but, alas, as farming became more mechanised and employment decreased, the dwellings became untenanted and most are now a sorry sight of utter dereliction, some of which bespeak the frailty of thatch.

At Great Tew the old village was incorporated fully into the remodelling of the estate but elsewhere, as at Nuneham Courtenay, landowners often preferred to resite the cottages outside the park, a preference greatly eased by the presence of new turnpike roads skirting the railed or walled emparkment. At Leverton near Hungerford the mansion at Chilton Park was rebuilt in 1800 and a delightful row of five pairs of thatched cottages with Gothic stone porches was placed alongside the nearby road. At Middleton Stoney until the early nineteenth century the nucleus of the village lay near the church and the site of a motte-and-bailey castle destroyed in 1216. The fifth Earl of Jersey, between 1814 and 1825 greatly enlarged the ancient park and demolished the old manor house and adjoining cottages near the church which was left in grand isolation. Lady Jersey personally directed the building, alongside roads fringing the park, of pleasant new cottages each with a rustic porch and small flower garden, as well as a new school and later a training institute and village reading room. A large new rectory was also built in a Tudor Gothic style alongside the Oxford-Brackley turnpike just outside the park. From examples such as these there developed the widespead custom in Victorian times of providing pretty cottages and model villages for servants and labourers on estates.

Population Growth and Poverty

The Civil War and the emigration abroad after it caused an appreciable loss of population in the English heartland, the main scene of its ravages. Consequently although the recovery in numbers was rapid its population growth during the seventeenth century was well below the average of 27 per cent for all England, being for example only 13 per cent in Northamptonshire, 15 per cent in Oxfordshire and 24 per cent in Berkshire. During the eighteenth century the rate of population increase in these counties almost doubled but again was far below the national average. Similarly between 1801 and 1841 although in most parts of the English heartland the number of inhabitants increased by about 7 or 8 per cent in most decades, this rate of growth was appreciably less than that for all England.[10] There could no longer be any doubt that this inland region devoid of coalfields was slipping back in the population race and that it, and the nation generally, was rapidly being dominated by the manufacturing, coalmining, commercial and metropolitan counties.

At this time the English heartland was grievously affected by underemployment and poverty. From 1800 to 1832 the average expenditure per capita on poor relief in most parishes ranged from 16s. to nearly £1 whereas the average for England and Wales was only just over 10s. In bad years such as 1802-3 about one person in every five was a pauper in need of poor relief and many of these were on permanent out-relief. This old poor law system had been based since Tudor times on rates levied on all householders in a parish and administered by overseers with the aid of the church-wardens. The funds went to build, if needed, cottages on the waste, to apprentice poor children and to set able-bodied paupers to work. In 1662 a law of Settlement and Removal tried to stop poor people from migrating from one parish to another where stocks of material for pauper work and perhaps waste land and woods were more plentiful. In future persons entering a parish could be sent back to their original home unless they rented a house worth at least £10 a year and could show that they would not need poor relief. After 1723 parishes were allowed to build and manage a workhouse but very few could afford this expensive solution to a problem that increased markedly with the enclosure of the common fields and waste. Many agricultural workers could only find part time or seasonal employment and in Berkshire in the 1790s the principle arose of giving supplementary poor relief according to the price of bread.[11] In 1795 the justices of the peace at Speen near Newbury issued a scale of supplementary allowances to earned wages up to a certain level and according to both the price of bread and the number of dependants. This bread scale principle, although never made statutory, spread throughout southern England under the name of the Speenhamland system. The scale of payments varied locally but everywhere proved expensive for householders, and the cost of Poor Law relief in England south of a line from the Wash to the Severn rose from under £2 million in 1785 to nearly £8 million in 1817 when it was equivalent to 13s. 3d. per head of population.

The differences between the economic conditions of the rapidly expanding manufacturing districts in coalfield England and the primarily agricultural counties in the English heartland now widened. The national contrast was symbolised in Warwickshire where by 1793 the hardy yeomanry of the country villages had been driven for employment northward into Birmingham, Coventry and other manufacturing towns. Everywhere in the rural areas of the south Midlands the natural increase of population had overtaken the employment available locally and the parish officers were more concerned with getting rid of people than admitting newcomers. All counties here had some migration to the coalfields and to London, the latter often being the offspring of middle class families. There was also some emigration overseas, as that to the United States sponsored by a Bicester committee in 1830, but the prevalent movements were of a short distance to nearby villages and towns. Many parishes under the control of one or a few powerful landowners refused entry to migrants and, under the settlement law, rigidly sent them back home. These 'closed' villages grew slowly and many of them remain small today. On the other hand some towns and villages with numerous landholders and empty or waste plots were more likely to accept some migrants and so to grow more quickly in population. One common way of housing more families was the division of larger houses into multiple tenancies, a practice which increased the risk of adding to the number of paupers, and which after enclosure was facilitated when some farmers moved to outlying farmsteads. Undoubtedly the chief recipients of this local movement of labourers were not the villages but the market towns and especially those at the junction of busy turnpike roads. The poor law now contributed to this growing urban dominance in a quite remarkable way.

The excessive burden of poor-relief rates, particularly in sparsely populated rural parishes, led to a new Poor Law Union Act in 1834. In future able bodied poor and their dependants were to receive public work and relief in a few large workhouses only. Each workhouse was managed by an elected Board of Guardians and was sited centrally amid a group of parishes called a Union thereby ensuring that no parishioner had more than a few hours walk to it. The building was spacious, carefully planned and well-constructed of the best local materials. Irrespective of the reputation for inhumanity which these workhouses later acquired, and which some of them deserved, materially they were fine additions to the townscapes: in some small towns the grandest public structural addition since the erection of the parish church. Not surprisingly when they were closed down in 1929 most of them were eventually used for other purposes. It is invidious to select superior examples. At Marlborough the building was completed in 1837 by the youthful (Sir) George Gilbert Scott; two-storied in stone, with a pedimented five-bayed facade and a rear of two symmetrical courtyards, it has been extended recently as a children's convalescent home. At Shipston on Stour the red brick structure in the latest Classical style is now Shipston House, and at Stow on the Wold the pedimented ashlar facade now fronts an old people's hospital. Oxfordshire was divided into eight unions and had the good fortune to employ as an architect George Wilkinson of Witney who liked a polygonal centre with four radiating wings of 9 bays each and, if possible, two pretty Italianate lodges beside the main entrance to the grounds. About twenty years later G.E. Street added a graceful chapel to most of these workhouses. Today these spacious structures form part of hospitals at Banbury and Chipping Norton, of Rycotewood College for agriculture at Thame and of Crawford Collets Ltd., mechanical engineers, at Witney.

The Poor Law Union Act of 1834 succeeded in greatly reducing the poor relief

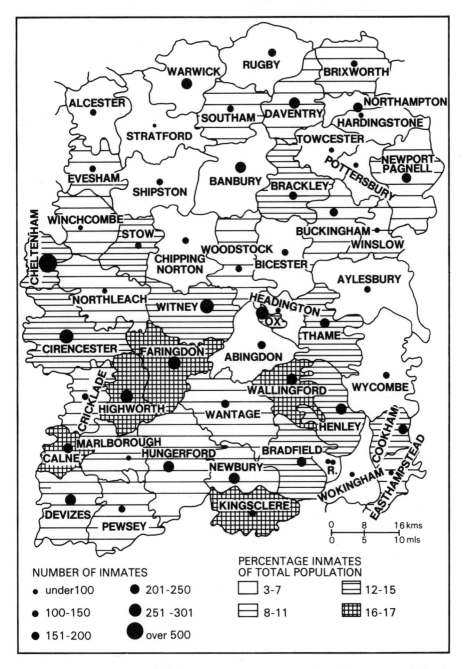

NUMBER OF INMATES

- under 100
- 100-150
- 151-200
- 201-250
- 251-301
- over 500

PERCENTAGE INMATES
OF TOTAL POPULATION

- 3-7
- 8-11
- 12-15
- 16-17

Poor Law Unions, with number of inmates and their proportion of the total population in 1851. The most populous Union districts were Cheltenham and Warwick (over 40,000 each) Northampton and Wycombe (34,000 each) and Banbury (30,000). All the other districts were under 24,000 population, and many were under 15,000.

rates in most parishes, but it did not solve the problem of widespread underemployment and low agricultural wages in rural districts. The poverty here would have been far greater but for the widespread development of domestic crafts, to which we now turn.

CHAPTER TEN

Turnpikes, Canals and Domestic Industries

You will hear more good things on the outside of a stagecoach from London to Oxford than if you were to pass a twelve-month with the undergraduates, or heads of colleges, of that famous university.
(Hazlitt, *On the Ignorance of the Learned,* 1820)

The Growth of Turnpikes and Hostelry

The period from 1660 to 1835 brought a remarkable revolution in transport in England, first in roads and then in canals. An Act of 1555 made each parish responsible for the upkeep of its roads but the parishioners seem to have made little improvement to road surfaces. In 1663 an Act was passed to allow justices of the peace of three counties on the Great North Road to levy tolls for the repair of stretches of the highway, but the tollgate or turnpike they erected soon ceased functioning. Towards the end of the century other Turnpike Acts were passed to subsidise the repair of a stated stretch of road under the control of a trust and the idea gradually became so popular that from 1735 to 1800 there was a flood of such Acts. The repaired surfaces proved especially beneficial for travel in winter and in areas where local stone and gravel were available for filling ruts and potholes. However, the perfection of a well-drained coherent road surface came in slowly under the improvements advocated by John Metcalfe (1717-1810), Thomas Telford (1757-1834) and John Loudon McAdam (1756-1836). The last named practised his notion of a compacted surface of small graded materials when surveyor for the large Bristol Turnpike Trust in 1815-1825 and probably the Bath to Bristol highway was the first to be 'macadamised'.

During these decades the enclosing of the open fields proceeded apace and the enclosure commissioners tried to define the main roads and the lesser tracks essential to life in the parish. Previously unenclosed land could be crossed at will by men and beasts; now fields and roads had to be enclosed. The normal width assigned to a main highway was 60ft, for a lesser highway 40ft; other carriage roads and bridleways were allotted a width of 20ft and public footpaths 4ft. These generous widths, intended to give space for manoeuvre round bad patches, created the wide grass verges bordering so many roads today. Where the enclosure award necessitated making new roads they were usually made dead straight to save expense. Frequently the award set aside gravel pits and stone quarries for material for mending the parish roads.

At the same time the flourishing state of the economy led to a great increase in

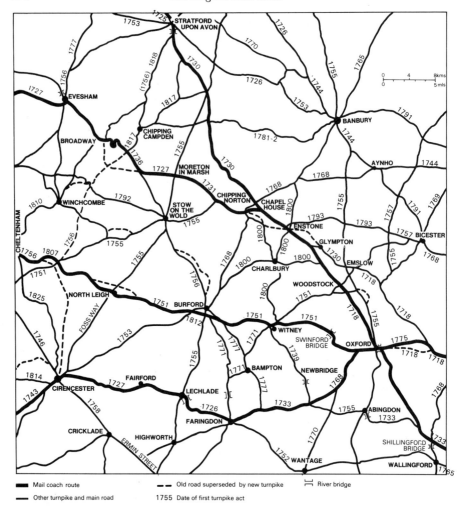

Turnpikes and mail coach routes. Some of the superseded roads were earlier turnpikes.

wheeled traffic which in its turn generated the need for better highways. Stage coaches did long journeys by stages, resting at night at an inn; thus in 1677 Anthony Wood left Oxford at dawn, spent the night at Beaconsfield and reached London on the following evening. A few years later by fly coach he made the journey in 13 hours. Such speeds and increasing freight traffic soon cut up the road surfaces and called forth the turnpike system. The first toll road directly affecting the Cotswolds was from Gloucester to the top of Birdlip and Crickley Hills under an Act of 1698 but its continuations over the dry limestones to Cirencester and Northleach were not turnpiked until 1746 and 1751 respectively. The important Bath Road was turnpiked in sections, from Reading to Theale in 1714 and from Speen westward in 1726. The first turnpike Acts for Oxfordshire date from 1718 and involved the London road between Oxford and Stokenchurch, the Oxford-Woodstock road and a section of the main highway from London to Worcester, Stratford and Warwick that ran north of Oxford from Wheatley to Islip. Road surfaces were now gradually improved. In 1769 Arthur Young thought the Witney-Northleach stretch 'the worst turnpike I ever travelled in' because it was mended with large blocks of stone that gave an excessively bumpy ride. By 1809 he found a 'noble change' in the condition of Oxfordshire roads, with the turnpikes 'very good and where gravel is to be had, excellent'.[1]

These and later improvements were associated with the building of many new bridges, causeways and new, straighter stretches of signposted road. On the deeply dissected uplands where the mediaeval roads wound in and out of deep valleys to serve the riverine villages and towns, the new turnpikes, being intended mainly for rapid through traffic between large cities, preferred to keep to the drier flatter watersheds. Thus, in 1730 the Oxford or London to Worcester and Stratford turnpike instead of winding in and out of the Glyme valley took a direct route from the Kiddington Turnpike at the 'Chequers Inn' to Chapel House above Chipping Norton. The new track was laid out by a team of eight oxen which ploughed the whole length in continuous furrows six miles long.[2] The straightening doomed Cleveley and several other small hamlets to remain 'deserted' while Enstone, through which the new turnpike passed, became the home of a noted firm of carriers and today, perhaps by more than coincidence, the headquarters of a private omnibus company. Another new straight stretch was constructed on the Moreton in Marsh-Evesham turnpike about the same time. From Bourton on the Hill it crossed the Cotswolds by the flat Five Mile Drive to the scarp above Broadway and so avoided the more hilly route via Snowshill. Today part of the A44, it is remarkable for the absence of dwellings and for the adjoining woodland strips clothing the roadside ditches that yielded the road metal. A similar avoidance of steep descents into deep valleys may be seen at Burford where in 1812 a new flat turnpike was built on the plateau above the town as a bypass for fast through traffic between London and Gloucester.

The citizens of some towns deliberately set out to attract traffic. At Wallingford new turnpikes were brought into the town, while at Northleach the burgesses appealed for a new turnpike to come through their market place rather than to continue to follow the much flatter hill-top bypass that had already been turnpiked through Hampnett and the 'Puesdown Inn'. However, in most places sharp gradients were avoided where possible. On the London-Oxford route the steep inclines on Shotover Hill were avoided after 1775 by a flatter turnpike from Wheatley Bridge to Headington which attracted into the university city much of the through traffic to Worcester, Stratford and Banbury that had formerly passed well to the north through Islip. In recent decades the tables have been turned and elaborate bypasses have been constructed to try to induce traffic to follow the mediaeval lines.

The tall escarpment of the north Cotswolds illustrates well the desirability of gradual gradients for coaches and heavy wheeled traffic. At Broadway in 1736 a 'well-formed serpentine road' provided a welcome alternative to the long straight climb of the old turnpike road to Snowshill and Moreton.[3] The village life readjusted itself to this new highway; the ancient church and nucleus on the older road lapsed into nonentity and eventually a new church was built in the lovely village at the scarp foot. Nearby at Stanway a similar serpentine road winds down the escarpment while the old cottages still align the straight stony ascent of the original trackway.

In many other towns and villages in Georgian times new building was attracted to the turnpike road and later their plan began to assume a markedly linear shape. After a parish was enclosed squatting became common on roadside verges, with dwellings squeezed in, sometimes side onto the routeway, as at Lower Heyford where, after 1802, an alignment of new cottages sprang up alongside the turnpike outside the old village core. But the well-to-do were equally sensible of the advantages of such a situation. At Kidlington where the Oxford-Banbury turnpike avoided the village green, several spacious dwellings and inns arose alongside the highway at some distance from the mediaeval core. A grander example may be seen in the fine Georgian buildings alongside the Bath Road at Speen, now part of Newbury, which included in 1769 'several inns to accommodate passengers on this road, particularly two erected of late years, one at each extremity of the street, which are exceedingly elegant and commodious'.[4]

Toll house on the Cheltenham to Evesham turnpike.

It is not surprising that improved road travel caused a tremendous expansion of hostelry and coaching inns. At the peak of turnpike traffic, in addition to numerous goods waggons, horsemen and local carriers, about 73 coaches called daily at Oxford, 54 at Banbury, nearly 50 at Charnham Street on the Bath Road at Hungerford, 42 at Marlborough, 39 at Burford and 22 at Enstone. All stage towns and market centres acquired numerous coaching inns, many of which survive and can be distinguished by their wide entrances and generous stabling. In small villages and open countryside inns arose or were perpetuated at road junctions and at wide intervals along lonely stretches of turnpike roads. The summits of long gradients called for a pause, as witness the 'Puesdown Inn' above Northleach.

The turnpike system created the toll house, a small three-faced low structure, occasionally two storeyed and invariably jutting prominently into the verge of the highway. A few have been removed in road widening but many survive as roadside dwellings. The takings at toll gates were usually auctioned annually, and in 1833 the leases of the Burford Roads Trust's gates fetched the following prices: Wykham £371; Chapel Heath £233; Burford £269; and Chipping Norton £162. Today the only active tollgate is at Eynsham bridge, a fine structure built over the Thames by the Earl of Abingdon in 1769. Many of the milestones and guideposts erected by turnpike trusts after 1773 have been lost or were defaced in 1940 but the numerous survivors include several dozen cast iron mile posts on the Great Bath Road.[5] The oldest

Cheltenham, the Promenade.

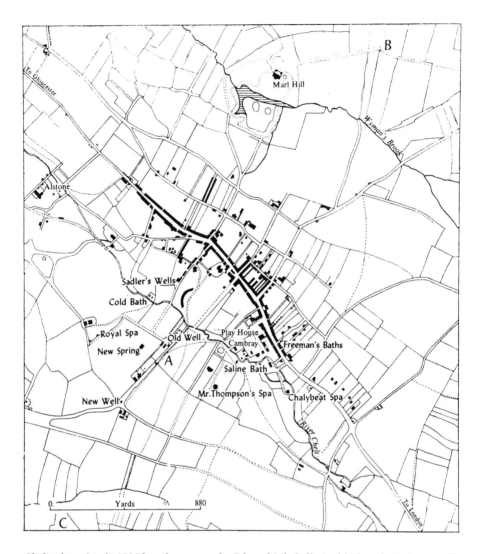

Cheltenham Spa in 1806 based on a map by Edward Mitchell. At this time the town was still largely confined to the line of the mediaeval High Street, but the widely dispersed nature of the medicinal springs and of the spas to which they gave rise is already evident.

At the Old Well, discovered in 1716, a Pump Room was built in 1738. Mr Thompson's Spa of 1801 became the Montpellier Spa but was later moved to New Well where the Rotunda was built. The Chalybeate Spa of 1803–4 moved in the 1830s to the Saline Bath where a Pump Room was built. The Sherborne Spa with a Pump Room of 1818 was built on the site of the present Queen's Hotel (A on map), while the Pittville Spa of 1825 (B) and the Park Spa of 1837 (C) were even more distant from the mediaeval nucleus.

surviving road sign is a private guidepost, provided by Nathaniel Izod in 1669 on a crossroads above Broadway Hill.

The extraordinary amount of through coaching traffic across the English heartland cannot be explained solely by the business connexions between London and the manufacturing cities of Birmingham and Coventry and the ports of Bristol and Gloucester. The fast coach traffic westward was greatly increased by the rise of watering places or spas. The popularity of Bath, especially after 1660, stimulated hostelry on the main highway to Bristol along the Kennet valley. On routes across the

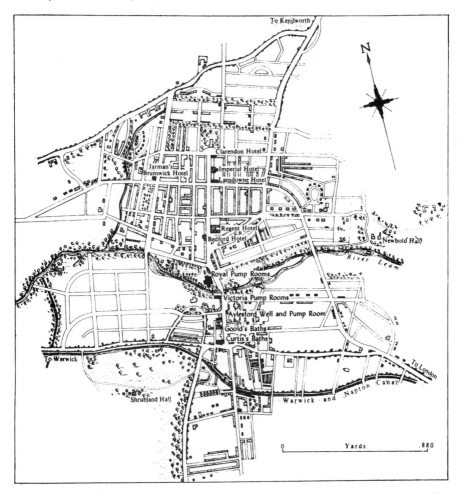

Royal Leamington Spa in 1843 (after S.E.K. Nicklin). The old town with its irregular layout lies south of the R. Leam and the new town with its regular spacious streets laid out in 1808 to the north. Pump rooms and baths are sited on several springs close to the river, but most of the larger hotels were built in the new town. Immediately north of the river are the Jephson Gardens, laid out originally in 1834 by the owner of Newbold Hall and acquired by the borough in 1896.

Chilterns and Cotswolds this spa traffic began in Georgian times with the growth of Cheltenham and Leamington. At Cheltenham mineral springs were discovered in 1716 and a pump house was erected about twenty years later. By 1788, over 1,300 visitors were coming annually when George III and his court stayed from 12 July to 16 August at Bays Hill Lodge and raised the spa to a new pinnacle of popularity. In the early nineteenth century over 2,000 visitors came each year to patronise the many chalybeate springs that had been found on the wide flat site. Eventually seven separate spas were made, each with its own appropriate buildings and surrounding houses, so creating 'the most open, spacious and varied of spa towns'.[6] Cheltenham grew fastest between 1750 and 1830 and retains in its wide tree-lined streets and gardens a wealth of elegant Georgian architecture, particularly of the Grecian revival phase of the Regency period.

Leamington is a later spa development although its mineral spring was known in Elizabethan times. Its tourist growth dates from about 1784 when a bath house and hotel were built near a mineralised spring. The old town, a collection of cramped streets on the south bank of the Leam, was greatly enlarged after 1808 by the addition of a new town laid out on the north bank to a formal rectangular plan of straight streets, wide tree-lined parades and dignified squares. In 1834 the Jephson Gardens were begun beside the Leam and today form a charming flowery enclave for a town that is still exceptionally rich in late Georgian architecture.

The Coming of Canals and Cheaper Coal

The carriage of goods by road was slow and expensive although by the early nineteenth century fly waggons with eight horses could reach London from Cheltenham (97 miles) in 2 days and regular, expeditious fly vans with 4 horses could do the journey in 20 hours. Heavy, non-perishable, cheaper goods were best sent by water and for this purpose the Thames had been made navigable to Lechlade, the Warwick Avon to Stratford, the Nene to Northampton and the Kennet to Newbury. The advantages of water transport became more obvious with the increasing use of coal as a domestic fuel in the seventeenth century and as a source of power for pumping after 1720 and general machinery after about 1781. The English heartland, utterly lacking in workable surface coalseams, now found itself midway between London, the prime port for northeastern seacoal, and the productive coalfields in Staffordshire to the north and Gloucestershire and Somerset to the west. Soon a network of canals was constructed to link up the navigable rivers and to bring in coal and take out local stone and agricultural products.

The first notable canal in the English heartland was the Thames and Severn, which after six years' effort was completed in November 1789. It started at Wallbridge near Stroud and ascended the Stroudwater or Golden Valley through 42 (later 44) locks to Daneway where it entered a tunnel 3,817 yds (3,490m) long through the Cotswold escarpment at Sapperton. After emerging on the Cotswold tableland at Coates, it proceeded to Siddington, where a branch went to Cirencester, and so to

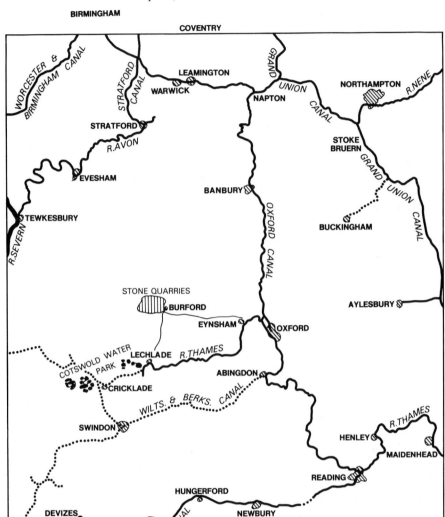

Canals and navigable waterways, showing land routes for transport of Cotswold stone to Thames-side water quays and London, and site of Cotswold Water Park. Dotted courses are abandoned except on the Kennet and Avon canal where reconstruction is in progress.

near Cricklade and along the Thames' floodplain to Inglesham, a total length of nearly 29 miles (47km). In its early days the canal carried much coal, mostly from the Forest of Dean, Staffordshire and South Wales, to towns and villages near the upper Thames but it was always plagued with excessive leakage in its broad locks and bed where it crossed the oolitic limestone and had continual difficulty in maintaining the water level at its summit. The company had to dig a deep well and install pumping gear at Thames Head, powered at first by a windmill and later by a Boulton and Watt steam engine. The dividends paid were small and ceased after 1864. Various subsequent attempts to revive the barge traffic, or to turn the bed into a railway, all proved either feeble or abortive. In 1911 the last commercial craft passed through the tunnel. In 1927 the canal was officially abandoned. Its course can be easily traced especially in the picturesque wooded valley on the Stroud side. The Sapperton tunnel is no longer considered safe and its two entrances, decorated with columns and niches in a simple classical way, have lost their parapets but the eastern end in Coates parish is being restored. The 'Tunnel House Inn' and 'Daneway Inn' at each end of the tunnel survive as well as five circular, tower-like dwellings of lengthsmen spaced at wide intervals between Chalford and Inglesham and thought to be copied from the tall stove houses used for drying wool in textile mills near Stroud. On the Cotswold side there are also three interesting buildings, of about 1789, which uniquely combine under one roof a wharfinger's dwelling and warehouse. The string of delightful villages in this stretch includes Kempsford which formerly had a castle belonging to the Duke of Lancaster whose heiress Blanche married John of Gaunt in 1359. The junction with the Thames near Lechlade borders a riverside park that provides a pleasant walk to Inglesham roundhouse and to the old church which was restored in 1889 'through the energy and with the help of William Morris who loved it'.

The Oxford Canal at the approach to Somerton Deep Lode from the south.

The coal traffic on the Thames and Severn waterway soon faced severe competition from the Coventry-Oxford canal. This direct route from the Midland coalfields was, in fact, encouraged by the unreliability of navigation on the upper Thames in dry summers, and its promoters promised in 1768 to cut the price of coal by about one-third. The canal reached Banbury six years later but was not completed to Oxford until 1790 when, on New Year's Day, the militia band, huge crowds and pealing bells welcomed the first Coventry barge to the wharves near the foot of the castle mound. James Brindley directed its construction and it was dug along the contour with several huge meanders as at Wormleighton where it almost encircles a large hill. The locks were built to a length of 72ft (22m) and a width of 7½ft (2.3m) which is suitable only for narrow barges. Below Cropredy near Banbury the course winds along the floodplain of the Cherwell and in parts makes use of the river channel. Just above Shipton on Cherwell the canal separates itself from the river by means of a wide hexagonal lock so shaped because the insignificant drop (2½ft) would not have allowed a standard narrow lock to pass enough water down to replenish the stretch below. The canal then runs along the valleyside well above the river, near Thrupp following the bed of an ancient valley that was occupied by water in the middle Ice Age and later abandoned. This abandoned channel provides an easy gradient to Oxford, where the canal now ends dirtily above an unsightly car park, and to the Thames above King's lock where formerly canal traffic proceeded to a wharf at Eynsham and a small industrial site near the 'Talbot Inn'.

The Oxford canal, as it came to be known, flourished and had no serious rivals until the Grand Junction canal (described below) was completed in 1805. Even then, it paid yearly dividends of at least 32 per cent from 1819 to 1839, partly because it exacted heavy compensatory tolls from the Grand Junction for traffic diverted from it. The Oxford-Coventry canal was improved in the early 1830s by cutting across meanders, so shortening its northern stretches by 13½ miles (22km) and by fitting the system with the present cast-iron bridges, with hexagonal patterned railings, supplied by the Horseley Iron Works. In 1868 the tunnel at Fenny Compton was replaced by a cutting. The canal has wharves, wharfinger's houses and lengthmen's cottages at wide intervals, and at important road crossings small hamlets with an inn, such as the 'Boat', 'Jolly Boatman', and 'Gibraltar' (then undergoing a famous siege). The waterway never became really moribund; its freight traffic in 1830 of about 475,000 tons, chiefly coal and building materials, had decreased in 1938 to 350,000 tons, mainly coal to the electricity generating station at Oxford. During the second world war a new wharf was constructed to serve the airfield at Kidlington. A few commercial narrow boats plied on it regularly in the 1950s, until the problem of sending their children to school began to defeat the barge families. When the coal traffic ceased in 1961, pleasure craft took over and today the canal is busier than ever before with gaily painted narrow barges and small boats. Its popularity has resuscitated nearby hamlets and its tow path, now horseless, attracts anglers and hikers who find here long stretches of truly pastoral scenery far from the noise of motor traffic.

The western end of the Kennet and Avon Canal near Bath.

A less happy fate has befallen the Wiltshire and Berkshire canal which was opened for narrow boats in 1810. It ran from the Bath Avon navigation near Semington to Wootton Basset and Swindon whence it continued at the foot of the downs along the Vale of White Horse to Abingdon on Thames. Its numerous branches included those to Longcot and to Wantage and after 1819 a longer extension, called the north

Wiltshire canal, from Swindon to the Thames-Severn canal at Latton near Cricklade. In 1837 this network carried about 66,000 tons of goods, of which two-thirds was coal from the Somerset-Bristol coalfield and the remainder largely grain and Bath stone. Traffic ceased in 1906 and the canal was abandoned in 1914. Its course can still be traced faintly in many parts but its main legacy is its feeding reservoir, Coate Water, which was taken over by Swindon corporation for recreation purposes.

The southernmost regions of the English heartland, between 1790 and 1810, depended on barge transport either upstream from London or downstream from Oxford for coal, the two supplies competing almost equally at Reading. The Kennet had been made navigable to Newbury by 1723 and more than half of its navigation channel of 18½ miles (30km) consisted of artificial cuts with, in all, 21 turf-sided locks capable of taking wide barges. Although the improvement benefited industries at Newbury, the waterway was not profitable. To bolster its finances it was extended by canal to the Bath Avon between 1794 and 1810, at a cost of nearly £1 million. The hope was to carry eastward not only coal from the Somerset and Bristol coalfield, but also anthracite from south Wales, Bath stone, lime and paving stones (? sarsens) from the Marlborough downs, in return for grain, other agricultural products and timber to go westward. John Rennie planned the canal with a width of 40ft (12m) and 79 locks capable of taking 60-ton barges. It runs from Newbury via Hungerford to Devizes, where a grand flight of 29 locks, with lateral side ponds, drops steeply to the flat Avon plain. The water supply to the summit level near Savernake was ensured by a reservoir and a large pumping station at Crofton which had two beam engines in regular use until 1959 when a diesel-driven pump was installed. Both original engines were made by Boulton and Watt but one was replaced soon after installation by a Cornish engine. Their beams are 30ft (9m) long and weigh 6 tons and 10 tons respectively. As they use 1¾ tons of coal daily, the British Waterways Board nowadays fire them only on special steam week-ends.

The Kennet-Avon canal proved successful for a while as a link between western coalfields and Reading and London. It handled 360,000 tons of freight in 1848 but four years later was bought by the Great Western Railway and eventually became derelict. However, it was never officially abandoned and recently an enthusiastic canal association has set out to repair it. Already the Kennet river section has been fully restored together with long stretches of the canal, as may be strikingly seen at Hungerford where a pleasant grouping of houses has been built at the old canal basin and the waterway is busy with pleasure craft. The repair of the great stairway of locks at Devizes is probably beyond modern resources.

The northern part of the English heartland, nearest the Midland coalfields, had its own canals direct to London, to the Severn and to the Warwick Avon. Its eastern half, draining mainly to the Wash, was served by the Grand Junction Canal which was constructed between 1793 and 1805 from London across the Chilterns at Tring and northwestward towards Northampton, and so to Braunston on the Oxford Canal near Rugby. Branches led off this artery to Wendover, Aylesbury,

Buckingham and to Northampton at the head of the Nene navigation. Later this waterway was extended northward to the Trent by the Grand Union Canal. The whole was amalgamated with various other canals near Warwick and Birmingham to form the Grand Union network. The Grand Junction in itself was a success and paid dividends of about 12 to 13 per cent until 1837. The combined Grand Union system carried 1½ million tons of goods in 1938 and today its main stretches have both commercial and pleasure traffic, although most of the rural side branches have atrophied, notably those to Wendover and Buckingham. On the old Grand Junction the Tring section, with its steep chalk slopes and large reservoirs, and the Towcester reach in the open, pastoral country are especially attractive. For walkers the towpath is wide and the sturdy bridges provide full cover in time of rain. The pleasure boats have stimulated catering and handicrafts in nearby villages, as in the artistic shop and the hotel restaurant at Grafton Regis. Canal technology has now created its own interest and at Stoke Bruerne near the southern entrance to the Blisworth tunnel, close to the A508 road, a mill building has been converted into a Waterways Museum.

Canal enthusiasts will not need to be reminded of the staircase of 21 locks constructed near Hatton just west of Warwick to allow the Grand Union to surmount the steep shoreline of glacial Lake Harrison (*see* Chapter 1), nor, to go farther afield, of the 30 lock flight on the Worcester and Birmingham canal at Tardebigge. The Birmingham-Stratford upon Avon canal, opened in 1816 deserves a separate pilgrimage. Stratford was a notable river port that could be reached up the Avon from Tewkesbury by 30-ton barges in 1662 and 40-tonners by 1770, when coal from its wharves was sold as far away as Chipping Norton and Oxford. This Avon navigation worked without horses, there being no horse-towing path, the pulling being done, when necessary, by gangs of men.

The early 1790s brought a canal mania, with a flood of proposals for new canals, some of which materialised, including the Grand Junction from the Oxford Canal near Braunston to the tidal Thames at Brentford and the Warwick-Birmingham canal, both authorised in 1793. In November of that year construction began on a waterway from the Worcester and Birmingham canal at King's Norton to Stratford. The cutting had reached Hockley Heath by 1796 when the company ran out of funds. Three years later under a new Act the work was extended to Kingswood where a short branch was made to the Grand Junction (Warwick and Birmingham) canal. Although Stratford corporation offered a loan, further progress southward from Kingswood ceased until William James, a rich canal fanatic living at Warwick, took over the concern. James already owned the Upper Avon navigation and was keen on a fantastic plan to make a canal from Stratford via Shipston on Stour, Bourton on the Water, Great Rissington and Bampton to Abingdon on the Thames whence various canals continued to Bath.[7] In 1812 he recommenced work on the Stratford canal and by June 1816 reached Stratford, where best Midland coal now sold at the Avon warehouse at 10d. per cwt.

The completed canal from the tunnel entrance bearing a carved head of

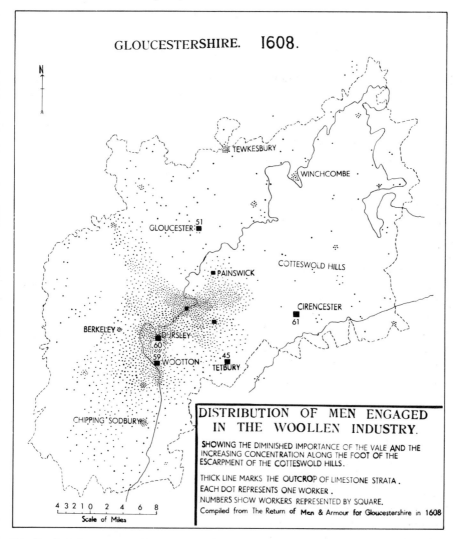

GLOUCESTERSHIRE.   1608.

N

TEWKESBURY

WINCHCOMBE

GLOUCESTER ■ 51

COTTESWOLD HILLS

■ PAINSWICK

CIRENCESTER
61 ■

BERKELEY

DURSLEY
60
59 WOOTTON 45
TETBURY

CHIPPING SODBURY

DISTRIBUTION OF MEN ENGAGED
IN THE WOOLLEN INDUSTRY.

SHOWING THE DIMINISHED IMPORTANCE OF THE VALE AND THE
INCREASING CONCENTRATION ALONG THE FOOT OF THE
ESCARPMENT OF THE COTTESWOLD HILLS.

THICK LINE MARKS THE OUTCROP OF LIMESTONE STRATA.
EACH DOT REPRESENTS ONE WORKER.
NUMBERS SHOW WORKERS REPRESENTED BY SQUARE.
Compiled from The Return of Men & Armour for Gloucestershire in 1608

4 3 2 1 0   2   4   6   8
Scale of Miles

Distribution of men engaged in the woollen industry in Gloucestershire in 1608 showing the un-importance of Cotswold towns except Cirencester.

Shakespeare at King's Norton to Kingswood is 12½ miles (20km) long and the section to Stratford a further 13 miles (21km). All told, excluding a broad lock at each terminus, there are 54 narrow locks, 25 of which occur in one flight at Lapworth. These constructions did not deter users; by 1840 the canal was carrying nearly 50,000 tons of coal annually and twice that amount of other goods. In 1856 the canal was bought by the Oxford, Worcester and Wolverhampton railway but in the 1860s in spite of railway competition it was carrying 110,000 tons of cargo a year. Within three

decades the water trade had dwindled to a few thousand tons; the canal slowly fell
into disuse. When railways were nationalised it passed to the British Transport
Commission and although pleasure craft used the northern section, the southern
section was unusable after 1945. In 1960 the National Trust took a lease of the canal
south of Kingswood Junction, and with the utmost support from local volunteers
restored it to full working order. Today it is deservedly popular for narrow boats,
anglers and towpath pedestrians. Technically it is interesting for its single storey
barrel-roofed lockhouses and its ingenious iron bridges that are split in the centre to
allow tow ropes to be passed through them. It has a narrow, grassy towpath amid
green countryside and ends in Stratford near the Shakespeare Memorial Gardens, a
perfect conclusion to any journey. The canal appears at its rural best at Preston Bagot
or at Lowsonford which, as Temple Thurston found on his boat journeys in *The
'Flower of Gloster'* (1911), 'lies alone in a cup of the hills like a polished pebble in the
deep pool of a twinkling brook. Right through the centre of the village runs the canal
under an old red-stone bridge, with the low tiled lock-house just beside it'.

The Heyday of Domestic Industries: 1660-1835

The improvements in transport described above had a stimulating effect on in-

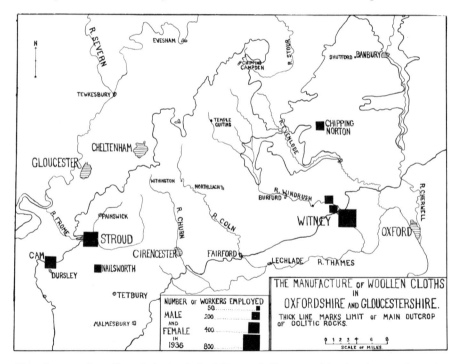

Manufacture of woollen cloths in Oxfordshire and Gloucestershire in 1936 as shown by
numbers of workers employed.

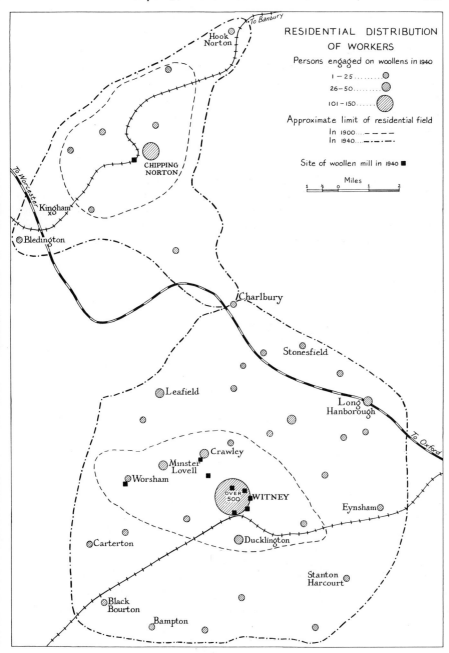

RESIDENTIAL DISTRIBUTION
OF WORKERS
Persons engaged on woollens in 1940

1 − 25 . . . . ◎
26 − 50 . . . . ◎
101 − 150 . . . . . . ◎

Approximate limit of residential field
In 1900 . . . . − − − −
In 1940 . . . . − · − · − ·

Site of woollen mill in 1940 ■

Miles

Residential distribution of textile workers at Witney and Chipping Norton in 1900 and 1940.

dustries in towns and villages near coaching roads and navigable rivers and canals. Whereas in coalfield counties manufactures tended to migrate to the coalfields, in the English heartland they continued to be concentrated on places with good communications, or, in other words, the old market towns. Coal was for them a fuel not a source of power, and most parishes had families working in watermills, many of which were equipped with new machinery in the eighteenth century and remained active into Victorian times. In addition many windmills were built or rebuilt and kept busy. (*see* Chapters 12 and 13.)

Each large parish also supported a considerable variety of skilled workers who supplied the craft needs of the primarily agricultural community. Usually rural parishioners either worked for wages or sold surplus farming products in the nearest market in order to pay their rents, if any, or to buy goods not produced locally. The increase of traffic and especially of road transport greatly increased the possibilities of local trade. Most sizeable villages had a smith and a harness repairer, as well as a wheelright and carpenter, and many, if not all, towns made saddlery and other horse equipment.

The faster transport opened up a new and wider market for local manufacturers, especially those nearer London. But it also meant that business-minded townsmen could more easily use the abundant cheap labour force in the nearby countryside for simple manufacturing processes, especially in textiles and leatherwork. The decrease in agricultural employment and large increase in population made any form of cottage industry attractive to the very poor; this became the great age of domestic workers who received raw materials from an urban distributor, returning them in a semi-finished or finished state. The nature of manufacturing depended largely on the local supply of raw materials and the influence of internal and external markets, but industrial progress in peripheral cities was also influential, as Coventry was on the north.

Textiles led the way, both in variety and longevity. The chief local developments in the manufacture of woollen fabrics took place on the edge of the south Cotswolds on the softwater streams near Stroud and Dursley, which became famous for fine dyed broadcloths. However these advances did not spread over the north Cotswolds except to a small degree at Cirencester, which soon ceased production, and at Witney which acquired an international reputation for blankets. Witney weavers had the advantage of the powerful Windrush for fulling and a position on the main London-Gloucester highway at a distance of 64 miles (103km) from Tyburn. When progressive clothiers in the Stroudwater and Bath areas went over to more elaborate, finer cloths the Witney workers continued to specialise in simple, undyed broadcloths that hitherto had supplied the traditional clothing.[8] The finer cloths and stuffs were sweeping the fashion market in Elizabethan times, while the simple broadcloth became increasingly popular as a covering at night. In 1677 about three score blanket manufacturers at Witney had amongst them at least 150 looms employing a total of nearly 3,000 people, from children eight years old to decrepit old age. In 1711 a guild or 'Company of Blanket Weavers of Witney and within twenty

The Bliss Tweed Mill, Chipping Norton.

miles thereof was granted a charter and its Blanket Hall, with clock, bell turret and arched carriage entrance still adorns the Windrush end of the High Street. By 1768 the number of looms was about 200, employing nearly 400 weavers and probably over 2,000 other workers from as far afield as Withington in Gloucestershire. Within a few decades, the introduction of the fly shuttle and the spinning jenny greatly decreased employment but not the output. In the nineteenth century the work was concentrated into water-powered factories strung out along the Windrush and under skilful management acquired its present world-wide trade and reputation. The Early family have been pre-eminent here since 1670.

A few miles to the north on the limestone wolds at Chipping Norton, the increasing waggon and coach traffic stimulated, as it did also at Witney and Banbury, the manufacture of webs, waggon tilts, and horse cloths as well as linsey-woolsey for women's petticoats.[9] This was at first a cottage industry and any fulling necessary was done 14 miles (22km) away at Swinbrook on the Windrush. In 1790 the owner, William Bliss, introduced a kersey check pattern for horse cloths that was used in the royal stables of George III; thereafter the business flourished. In 1804 an old malthouse in Chipping Norton was bought and equipped with carding and spinning machinery driven by horsepower, and six years later a water-driven flour mill was converted for fulling and spinning. In Victorian times the introduction of tweeds proved exceptionally popular and the present factory was built in 1872 to the design of a specialist mill-architect, George Woodhouse of Lancashire. It was intended to resemble a great house in a park. With its balustraded parapet, corner turrets and chimneystacks rising from a domed tower it still forms an imposing vista at the western approach to the town.

At Banbury the coach and waggon traffic created a web, girth and horse cloth factory in 1701, and the manufacture persisted until 1932. After 1750 the area became famous for plush, a shaggy stuff with a velvet nap on one side, that eventually dominated the textile industry in villages in four counties within twelve miles of the town. By 1831 the plush trade occupied at least 125 men in Banbury and over 400 men and considerable numbers of women and children in neighbouring villages. The specialities included superfine silk plush for liveries, embossed plush for upholstery and for lining omnibuses and cabs, and plush for covering top hats.[10] The hand-weaving flourished until plush and huge quantities of silk fabrics, a rival product, were made on steam-driven looms in Coventry in the mid-nineteenth century. The industry near Banbury eventually introduced power looms and together with handlooms continued to produce the gorgeous, richly-coloured cloths until the last factory, at Shutford, closed down in 1948.

The influence of Coventry spread southward also to the north Cotswolds where silk throwing or twisting was active from about 1718 onwards. As late as 1838 there were six silk twisting mills at Blockley and one each at Broadway, Chipping Campden and Winchcombe, all driven by small water wheels. The industry declined seriously soon afterwards but the mill buildings survive as interesting items in the village scene, especially at Blockley.

Throughout the clay vales where waterpower was scarce and in full demand for flour milling, the main textiles were flax, hemp, lace and straw. Lace was easily the chief and employed a phenomenal number of 'part time' workers, especially after its upsurge of popularity in the reign of William and Mary. Domestic handmade lace, or bone lace as it was known, gave work to many thousands of women and children aged six and upwards over a wide area stretching from northeast Oxfordshire, into Buckinghamshire, Northamptonshire and beyond. Probably at its peak 9,000 to 10,000 persons were engaged in it in Northamptonshire alone and in some parishes it provided the chief occupation, as, for example, at Hanslope north of Stony Stratford, in Buckinghamshire, where in 1801 no less than 500 of the 1,275 parishioners made lace. Cottage lace making did not begin to decline until mid-Victorian times and then in some areas its decrease was offset by the rise of straw plaiting.

The outstanding non-textile manufacture was leather working in a multitude of forms especially near forests where skins or pelts and oak bark for tanning abounded. Of the towns around Wychwood Forest, Burford was noted for saddlery and tanning, and Woodstock for gloves. In 1809 at the height of the glove trade in a wide area around Woodstock and Charlbury 1,500 women and a few score men produced by

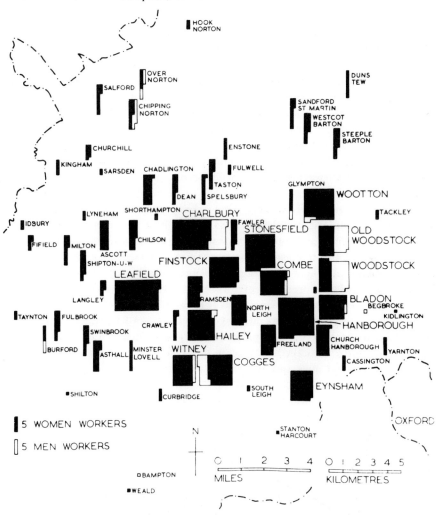

Distribution of adults engaged in gloving in Oxfordshire in 1851.

piece work in their cottages up to 400 dozen pairs of gloves weekly. Sales declined with the decrease of formal elegance and cold carriages and today only three factories with some home workers survive in Oxfordshire. One at Woodstock makes special quality items, and two others at Witney and Stonesfield specialise in golfing gloves for which there is a great demand.

The employment provided by gloving was always small compared with that in footwear and allied leather products in Northampton and neighbouring towns and villages. This district has been noted for boots since the fifteenth century, as the detailed exhibition in the central museum in Northampton makes clear, and soon leather working became its leading manufacture. By 1806 Northampton was the chief shoemaking centre in Britain and in 1961 leather manufacturing employed about 20 per cent of the labour force here and in some neighbouring towns.[11] Up to the mid-nineteenth century it remained a handicraft carried on in homes and small shops.

The long survival of domestic crafts and hand work, a few of which still survive on a small scale as at Woodstock, was characteristic of the economy of the English heartland which was slow to introduce the factory system, and slower still to use steam power. In 1800 it had only a handful of the 1,200 steam engines at work in England and its factories were almost entirely dependent on waterwheels until the coming of railways. Whereas steam power was in common use in the Stroudwater and other main textile regions, it was not installed at Chipping Norton until 1851 and at Witney till 1861.

Although most parishes had some ironworking crafts and several towns made agricultural machinery, metal industries made little headway in the English heartland. Oxford had an ironworks, that survives, in 1760 and several places near the Black Country had domestic industries in pins, needles and other small metal objects.[12] Thus in 1692 there was a forge at Clifford Chambers near Stratford; in the next century three small forges were at work on the river Arrow north of Alcester, and in the 1880s several of the mills here and near Redditch went over to needle making. But away from the Black Country influence, the chief metal manufacture normally involved farm machinery and for this Banbury was outstanding.[13] Here James Gardner patented a straw and hay cutter in 1815 and a very popular turnip cutter in 1834. The need for new industries and the depressed state of agricultural employment at the time may be judged from conditions in the nearby village of Tadmarton. The introduction of labour saving threshing machines and drainage ploughs caused a riot near Banbury in 1830 that was not quelled until regular troops were called in from Coventry. At Tadmarton some forty persons on poor relief and living in cottages rented for their use did not take part in the riots and were rewarded for their good behaviour by a gift from the overseers of twenty fat sheep and eleven tons of coal. With increasing mechanisation of agriculture and the eventual decline of domestic crafts in face of competition from mass production in steam-powered factories, such rural parishes were doomed to suffer severe distress and depopulation throughout the next one hundred years.

CHAPTER ELEVEN

Country Mansions and Landscape Gardening

Men come to build stately, sooner than to garden finely; as if gardening were the greater perfection
           (Bacon, *Of Gardens,* 1625)

For want of a better opening date we shall assume that English gardens began with the monasteries where within the cloister garth the monks grew medicinal and culinary herbs, had fishponds for fast days and, farther afield, planted vineyards for altar and table wines. Traces of these monastic gardens have virtually disappeared, but castle grounds contained similar garden elements, pools for fish, runnels of water, walks and herbage. Henry III commanded to be made at his royal palace at Woodstock 'a garden enclosed by walls, with a herbarium and a fishpond that the queen may be able to amuse herself'. It was a long time before gardens began to escape from behind defensive walls. At first English gardens were dominated by Italian ideas and were furnished with fountains, balustrading, stairways and statuary of which perhaps the modern dwarf figurines are lineal descendants. But the Italianate style was quickly subdued by Tudor conceits and devices, mazes, labyrinths, dovecotes, bowling greens and, above all, knot gardens, those small mosaics of 'pleasant delytes', of which a charming example exists at New Place, Stratford upon Avon. A much grander example of a Tudor garden may be seen at Kenilworth castle where its plan demonstrates the new popularity of formal designs. When, between 1564 and 1575, Robert Dudley, Earl of Leicester, began to modernise the castle and to make it elegant enough for the visits of Queen Elizabeth, he filled in the inner moat and laid out elaborate gardens between its original line and the curtilage wall nearest his new gatehouse (*see* p. 130). This garden has been recently restored to its original design.

Probably justice has never been done to the spread of gardening and fruit growing in Tudor times, nor to its associated popular interest in plants from Europe and later from the New World. The movement percolated down to small monasteries and inland districts. Thus at Burford the small Hospital of St John, today The Priory, had within its curtilage when it was dissolved in 1538, orchards and garden plots as well as meadows, pastures, stables and a dovecote. Five years later it was granted to Edmund Harman, one of the barber-surgeons of Henry VIII. In 1569 Harman caused to be erected in Burford parish church a mural monument (not a tomb) to commemorate the beneficence of God to him and his wife and their numerous children. The monument is decorated with carvings of athletic Red Indians and of tropical fruits including bananas and pawpaws.

Carolean and Jacobean Gardens: The Widening Vision

In the seventeenth century the close-knit symmetrical design characteristic of a Tudor pleasure garden became known as a parterre, or 'a level space in a garden occupied by flower beds ornamentally or geometrically arranged'. It was essentially a floral continuation of the house meant to be perambulated in and viewed direct from the living rooms. Such a seventeenth century parterre survives at Ashdown Park high on the downs above Ashbury. This interesting house was constructed of chalk blocks with brown stone dressings about 1660 for Elizabeth, Queen of Bohemia. It rises through three tall storeys to a hipped balustraded roof capped by a graceful cupola that is reached by a single staircase from the main hall and commands so breathtaking a view that the contemporary box parterre at the foot of the house tends to be overlooked altogether.

During this century there also arose signs of an extension of the pleasure garden into the orchards and meadows beyond the skirts of the mansion. At Chastleton (1603-1618) the small 'best garden' enclosed with tall yew hedges provided privacy and shelter from wind and adjoined the bowling green. At Packwood the various Tudor wall-enclosed gardens were continued outward in Carolean times, so as to terminate in an enclosure planted with a multitude of yews arranged about a central avenue that leads to an earthen mound up which a narrow path winds to the yew-topped summit. The assemblage of neatly clipped yews has been rumoured to represent various scenes from the New Testament, but the overall pattern seems to have descended directly from traditional rectangular designs. The mound, which gave rise to the rumour that this arrangement represents the Sermon on the Mount, is a fascinating addition to the garden scene. A similar mound existed at Wadham College, Oxford, which was built between 1610 and 1613 and four decades later had its gardens laid out with parterres, clipped yew hedges and an artificial mount, topped with a statue of Atlas, that survived until 1753. The large mound in New College gardens may well be, like that at Packwood, a survivor of a striking departure from, or actual revolt against, the flatness of the parterre. There is, of course, much else of interest to gardeners at Packwood. The tower at the corner of the brick-walled enclosure and terrace fronting the topiary garden is an eighteenth century furnace house for circulating hot air through holes in the wall to ward off frost from the fruit trees trellised against it. At the foot of the wall at one of the fine old gateways leading through the garden enclosure nearer the house are arched alcoves for sheltering beehives, or skeps, made of straw. The Carolean garden at Packwood seems an elaboration of the best garden enclosure at Chastleton. Both manifest not so much a quaint, mediaeval turn of mind as a truly English delight in trees and flowers which

Ashdown Park near Ashbury, now in Oxfordshire.

induced gardeners to venture out into the home orchards and meadows. Public interest in topiary and new plants increased rapidly during the seventeenth century and was closely associated with the founding of botanic gardens and the art of grafting.

Oxford Botanic Garden and New Species

The importance of herbs, or simples, in medicine eventually led to the making of physic and botanic gardens of which that at Oxford is the oldest survivor in Britain.[1] It was founded by Henry Danvers, Earl of Danby and a gentleman commoner of Christ Church, who 'being minded to become a benefactor in the University, determined to begin and finish a place whereby learning, especially the faculty of medicine, might be improved'. At a total cost of over £5,000, he acquired the lease of about three acres of meadow from Magdalen College and arranged for the building of 'a fair and sufficient wall' and of a grand gateway to a design by Inigo Jones. The opening ceremony took place on 25 July 1621 when the Vice Chancellor and other dignitaries paced from St Mary's Church to the low-lying site. In the following twelve years the ground was raised considerably to prevent flooding and the wall and main gateway were completed. The two statues, of Charles I and Charles II, were put up in the niches later, paid for it is said by Anthony Wood as a fine for libelling the Earl of Clarendon. At the outbreak of the Civil War the planting consisted only of 'divers simples for the advancement of the faculty of medicine' but Lord Danvers ensured the garden's survival by endowing it in his will with the rectory of Kirkdale in Yorkshire.

The first Professor of Botany, Dr Robert Morison, was appointed in 1669. He had been superintendent of the royal gardens at Blois for the Duke of Orleans, having studied anatomy, botany and zoology at the University of Paris, as a refugee, and taken a doctorate in physic at Angers. In 1660 he came to England at the invitation of Charles II and became a royal physician and superintendent of the royal parks, which posts he later held together with his chair at Oxford. Thrice weekly standing at a table in the middle of the Botanic Garden he used to discourse on the herbs and other plants growing there and in 1675 John Evelyn attended one of these lectures.

During Morison's professorship the head gardener was Jacob Bobart of Brunswick, who sported a long beard, tagged with silver on 'rejoicing days', and kept a goat as his usual walking companion. The prevailing fashion was all for clipped shrubs, geometric designs and prim symmetry, as Joseph Addison, an undergraduate and later a fellow of Magdalen, noticed with dismay. In 1712, a year after resigning his fellowship, he wrote in *The Spectator* No. 414, 'a Dial cut in Box was a rarity in New College: in Exeter Garden they fashioned their College arms in the same material. British gardeners instead of humouring nature, love to deviate from it as much as possible. Our trees rise in cones, globes and pyramids. We see the marks of the scissars upon every plant and bush'. These comments and Alexander Pope's lines

> The suffering eye inverted nature sees
> Trees cut to statues thick as trees

were particularly appropriate to the Botanic Garden where Bobart had excelled himself by cutting two large yews to represent giants guarding the entrance. To quote Thomas Baskerville (1683), 'Old Jacob some years past got two yew trees wich being formed by his skill are now grown up to be Gigantick bulkey fellows, one holding a Bill th' other a Club on his shoulder'. Inevitably these 'indefatigable sentries of the Physick Garden' became a constant butt for University wits. Yet it is worth noting that Jacob Bobart the younger, who succeeded Morison as professor, issued an important seed list and that, in spite of the short English flowering season, Celia Fiennes of Broughton in 1695 found here a variety of flowers and plants sufficient to entertain anyone for a week. This Jacob's brother, Tilleman, seems to have been keeper of the Botanic Garden for some time and also worked for the government laying out gardens at Hampton Court and planting the elms at Blenheim Palace in the same formation as the British contingent took up at the battle of Blenheim.

The Oxford garden was improved greatly by Dr William Sherard (1658-1728), who enlarged the conservatory, gave many curious plants, a famous herbarium, and a generous endowment to the Chair of Botany. In 1736 the Swedish botanist Linnaeus visited the garden and stayed a month with the new Sherardian Professor, James Dillenius, after whom he named a beautiful genus of a tropical plant. Thereafter eccentricity was not always confined to the unusual flora. Here in 1784 one of the first balloon ascents in England was made, and in 1847 at a party held by the British Association, Frank Buckland's bear dressed as a student of Christ Church in cap and gown was solemnly introduced to both Sir Charles Lyell and Prince Charles Louis Bonaparte. By then botany had become a respectable study and the garden was considered a source of information rather than of medicinal herbs, its health-giving properties being more associated with the spiritual benefits derived from experiencing 'Vegetative Philosophy'. So over the centuries it changed its emphasis from physic species in formal beds with clipped shrubs and yew lined walks to its present aim of being mainly a collection of geographical and economic plants illustrative of world floras. The conservatories or glass houses for ferns, water lilies, palms, orchids, cacti and so on tell part of the story just as the frequent addition of 'bred in the Garden' on name tags tells another. Although now extended to almost double its original size, it remains small compared with botanic gardens elsewhere, which may largely explain why it has such an undeniable charm and convenience.

The public concern with plants and trees evoked by botanic gardens was heightened by the advocacy of John Evelyn who, since his undergraduate days at Balliol in 1637 to 1640, had an enduring interest in horticulture. He often visited Oxford, where in 1654 he met John Wilkins and Christopher Wren, and eight years later was largely responsible for persuading Charles II to bestow his patronage on their scientific club, henceforth the Royal Society. In 1664 Evelyn, with the king's encouragement, published *Sylva, or a Discourse of Forest Trees . . .* in which he exhorted the English to plant trees to make good the deforestation caused by the timber requirements of the navy and by the Civil War. It was full of practical information and had appendices on the cultivation of fruit trees for cider and a gardener's almanac. The book became very popular and is thought to have led directly to the planting of nearly a million trees. Its influence was seen to perfection at Swallowfield Park in Berkshire where the mansion was rebuilt by the second Earl of Clarendon in 1689-91. Here, according to Evelyn, the gardens were 'as elegant as 'tis possible to make a flat by art and industrie and no mean expense'. He himself may have supervised the planting of the yew hedges, cedars and mulberries and already in 1685 he found the garden abounding in delicious and rarest fruit. 'There is one orchard of 1,000 golden and other cider pippins; walks and groves of elms, limes, oaks and other trees. The garden is so beset with all manner of sweete shrubs that it perfumes the air.'

The French Influence

Evelyn's patron, Charles II, was familiar with the landscaping carried out at

Versailles by André Le Nôtre who favoured a spacious design with radial tree-lined avenues and a magnificent Grand Canal. The king, on returning to England, introduced, as far as his limited purse allowed, some of these features at Hampton Court and St James's Park. Among the very few Midland landowners wealthy enough to landscape on this scale was Ralph Montague, Ambassador to the French Court, who owned an estate at Boughton just north of Northampton. Here 'with the aid of Vandertmeulen, a Dutch gardener, and money from dowries of two of the richest women in the kingdom, he laid out over a hundred acres in the pattern of Le Nôtre: branching radial avenues, water in straight geometric canals, endless parterres and a walled perimeter. Nothing now remains but a broken Pegasus in the fields, and traces of elm avenues stretching far into the country'.[2]

Chronologically our survey of gardens should now proceed to Dutch formal water gardens with straight canals, pavilions and yew hedges, but none survives in the English heartland, the nearest being the splendid example at Westbury on Severn, which happens to be the oldest survivor of its kind in Britain. The late seventeenth century gardens at Charlecote Park, shown below, seem an assemblage of Tudor

View of Charlecote Park in about 1696, painting probably by John Stevens. Showing a combination of parterre, long avenues of trees, and straight Dutch canals with tower.

PACKWOOD ⊠   ⊠ KENILWORTH   ▽   ▽   ▽   FINEDON ○

WARWICK ▽   ▽ALTHORP▽   ⊠ BOUGHTON   ▽
PRIORY△ □CASTLE   ▽   ○HARLESTONE   ▽

▽   ▽   ▽   ▽   ▽   CASTLE □
RAGLEY □   ⊠ CHARLECOTE   FAWSLEY ▽   COURTEENHALL ○   ASHBY
STRATFORD   ▽ □COMPTON   ▽
⊠   □VERNEY   ▽

▽   ▽   EASTON NESTON ▽   ▽
ETTINGTON▽   ◇RADWAY   GAYHURST□   △
◇   HANSLOPE ○   ⊡

HIDCOTE   COMPTON □   ◇WROXTON
BARTRIM +   WINYATES □

TODDINGTON▽ □SPRINGHILL   ▽   ADDERBURY□   ▽   ▽
▽ BATSFORD   ▽   □AYNHO
○SEZINCOTE   ▽   ▲   ▽

SUDELEY   ▽   ⊠CHASTLETON   ○GREAT TEW   △
▽ABBOTSWOOD+   ▽   HEYTHROP ▽   ▽CLAYDON   ASCOTT▽
▽   ○ADLESTROP   ○SARSDEN ▽   ROUSHAM ▽   ▽
DITCHLEY ▲   ▲   ▽MIDDLETON STONEY   ▽
CORNBURY △   □GLYMPTON   ▽
□KIRTLINGTON   WOTTON   ▽WADDESDON
▲GREAT   WILCOTE △   □BLENHEIM   UNDERWOOD □
BARRINGTON   ▽EYNSHAM   BOARSTALL □   □HARTWELL

▽RENDCOMB   ▽OXFORD   ▲SHOTOVER
△ ⊠ △   □RYCOTE
CIRENCESTER
PARK   ▽
△   ▽

BUSCOT   BUCKLAND   □RADLEY
⊠ Early gardens   +   NUNEHAM
Landscaping   FARINGDON △ ▽ △ ▽   COURTNAY □   ○WEST
△ Early   ▽   WYCOMBE
▲ Kent
□ Brown   ▽ ▽   ▽LOCKINGE   ▽   CLIVEDEN
○ Repton   FAWLEY □   □
◇ Miller   ▽ HARLEYFORD □
+ Modern   ⊠ASHDOWN   ▽
▽ Other parks   BASILDON△ ▽ ▽
PURLEY△▽
▽   □CAVERSHAM

▽   LITTLECOTE ▽ ▽   +▽ SULHAMSTEAD
□BOWOOD   △SAVERNAKE   BENHAM□
0   8kms   □TOTTENHAM   ▽SWALLOWFIELD
SANDLEFORD   STRATFIELD▽
0   5mls   ▽   SAYE

Distribution of parks and gardens landscaped by the most famous gardeners.

parterres and Dutch straight canals with a touch of spacious avenues of tall trees reminiscent of contemporary French designs. However, this was one of the gardens that Lancelot Brown found capable of improvement.

Eighteenth Century Mansions and Landscape Gardening

The eighteenth century was the great age of classical mansions set amid landscaped gardens and, fortunately, the English heartland has more than its share of them. There seem no reasons for this abundance apart from the general prosperity and the rapid spread of a fashion due to intense local rivalry between neighbouring landowners who liked to be better rather than different.

For example, the Corallian ridge near Faringdon has within a ten kilometre stretch three moderate sized classical mansions standing in landscaped gardens overlooking the upper valley of the Thames. Buckland House, built for the Throckmorton family in 1757 by John Wood junior of Bath, is surrounded by a fine landscaped park with lake, winding walks and surprise views of temples and grottoes. Faringdon House, built about 1780 for Henry James Pye, is also emparked and was no doubt partly beautified by its owner, who became Poet Laureate in 1790 and wrote, among other indifferent verse, a royal birthday ode so crammed with allusions to feathered songsters that it provoked the popular epigram:

> And when the pie was opened
> The birds began to sing;
> And wasn't that a dainty dish
> To set before a king.

Five kilometres to the east is Buscot House built in the Adam style about 1775, and noted *inter alia* for its salon adorned by large panels illustrating the story of the Sleeping Beauty, painted by Burne Jones when he was staying nearby at Kelmscott. This park too is a picturesque assemblage of woods, lawns, lakes and masses of flowering shrubs.

These and other graceful houses, such as Basildon Park and Kirtlington Park, reflect the apogee of an artistic movement that began elsewhere. Farther north several Midland mansions played a more influential part in the history of English landscape gardening and domestic architecture. Most of these are grandiose and none more so than the magnificent Ragley Hall two miles southwest of Alcester. Its main structure dates from 1680 but extensive remodelling and additions were made by James Gibbs after 1725 and James Wyatt after 1780. The fine decorations and stupendous proportions, especially of the classical portico and the great hall, match the spacious park that was landscaped about 1750 by Capability Brown, to whom we will return later.

Midland Landscape Gardeners

For Midlanders the history of eighteenth century landscape gardening must begin at Cirencester Park, where the mansion built by Henry Danvers, the founder of the Botanic Garden at Oxford, was purchased in 1695 by the Bathurst family. In 1704 Allen, first Earl Bathurst, succeeded to the estate of 3,000 acres and within forty years had rebuilt the mansion and landscaped or planted and enclosed most of the grounds. A man of wit and vivacity, he was a close friend of the leading literary figures of his day and retained his full faculties till his death at the age of ninety. Alexander Pope stayed here often and planned houses, avenues and glades, planted trees and contrived waterworks. The poet tells how the Earl enclosed with walls large expanses of open down and introduced the latest farming methods

> Whose ample lawns are not ashamed to feed
> The milky heifer and deserving steed;
> Whose rising Forests, not for pride or show,
> But future Buildings, future Navies, grow:
> (*Moral Essays,* Ep.IV. 1731)

Today this great estate is generously open to walkers who from the gates at Cecily Hill off Park Lane, Cirencester, may follow the Broad Ride, an avenue over 50m wide, for 2km to the focus of seven rides near Pope's Seat, a small stone rusticated

The Broad Ride, Cirencester Park with parish church tower in distance.

summer house designed by the poet. Westward the Park widens into the vast Oakley Wood where at one point ten rides converge on an eminence and at another several rides focus on Alfred's Hall, a sham ruin in which Pope also had a direct hand. Its irregular castellated walls, Gothic windows, half-collapsed doorways and shell of a tower acted both as an eye-catcher and, in the mood of ancient philosophers, a reminder of the rapidity of material decay:

> Alas, my Bathurst! What will they avail?
> Join Cotswold hills to Sapperton's fair dale,
> . . . .
> Link towns to towns with avenues of oak,
> Enclose whole downs in walls, — 'tis all a joke!
> Inexorable Death shall level all,
> And trees, and stone, and farms, and farmers fall.
> (*Imitations of Horace*, Bk II, Ep.II)

The modern visitor may be surprised at the longevity of the enterprise which would surely confound the poet's time scale. Avenues in the park still end in statues and masonry: here a statue of Queen Anne; there a pair of classical buildings on either side of the Broad Drive; elsewhere long avenues of graceful trees. But, as Pope said, 'No words or paintings, or poetry, can give the least image proportionable to it'. It is a vast landscape dominated by trees, a Fontainebleau type of forest with broad drives rather than a landscaped park and may well be 'the finest wood in England'.

The other notable eighteenth century squire-architect and landscaper in the Midlands was Sanderson Miller (1716-1780) who contributed much to the scenery of the area around Edgehill.[3] The son of a Banbury mercer, he succeeded to an estate at Radway Grange in about 1737 and soon began improvements. He remodelled the Grange with Gothic adornments including two bay windows and in 1744 built on Edgehill a picturesque thatched cottage with a marked irregularity of plan and pointed windows. Within five years the top of the scarp nearby was capped with a castle with a gateway and tower complete with tall battlements and machicolations. By now Miller was widely consulted as an architect and landscaper throughout the Midlands and East Anglia, and was a close friend of many writers including Henry Fielding. It seems certain that he influenced William Hiorn of Warwick who did much of the gothicising of Arbury Hall near Nuneaton, which many regard as the gem of all early Gothic revival houses. About 1750 Miller built, on Claverton down, Bath, a sham Gothic castle that survives, now looking remarkably new after being stripped of ivy. His surviving architectural masterpieces are undoubtedly the charming neo-Gothic transformation of Lacock Abbey in Wiltshire, and the Shire Hall at Warwick, while his chief estate improvements were at Hagley Hall, Worcestershire and Wroxton Abbey, Oxfordshire. At Hagley Park, from 1751-6, he built or laid out new plantations, large lawns, a ruined castle (of mossy stones from Halesowen Abbey), a small lake with cascades, a hermitage, a pretty well in a wood, as well as brakes of trees around the park and an abundance of shady walks. At

Wroxton Abbey he was called in by Lord North to remodel the chapel and to improve the park and the parish church. Here the existing house was partly completed by Sir William Pope, at a cost of about £6,000, between 1610 and 1618. Miller transformed the chapel by inserting an east window with a crocketed ogee hood, which proved ideal for taking Lord North's collection of Bernard Van Linge's stained glass of 1632. In the house itself the central pendant of clustered caryatids in the hall seems to be Miller's only mark. In the park, a formal design with long straight vistas and a pond had already been laid out by Tilleman Bobart of Oxford from 1729 to 1732 when major alterations began. Probably Miller did not play a significant role until after 1744 but the ultimate result was a large artificial lake with a dam over which a cascade spilled into a serpentine river winding through woods. A pillared Gothic rotunda (by Miller about 1750) stood on a mound near the cascade, and other eye-catchers included a Chinese summer house, bridge and shelter, and an obelisk to commemorate the visit of Frederick, Prince of Wales, to Banbury races in 1739. Belts of trees were planted especially along the perimeter of the estate and lines of trees along the approach roads, while in the far distance near Drayton a great Gothic archway, of two thin round turrets supporting a ruinated arch, provided a sense of perspective. The mansion was completed and enlarged in the mid-nineteenth century, and since 1965 has been a college for American students of Fairleigh Dickinson University, New Jersey. Inevitably several of the more fragile features of the Georgian layout have vanished but Miller's masonry seems to have endured well, as becomes a man who always used the best local stone even in ruins. He has other memorials in Oxfordshire apart from the plain tablet set in the floor beneath the tower of Radway church. In the Old Library at All Souls, Oxford, his wall panelling and door surround are truly delightful and at Upton House, only 2km south of Radway Grange, visitors who come to see the famous pictures and porcelain, will be aware of the fine terraced gardens and beyond them a pool with a temple fronted with thin Tuscan columns attributed to Sanderson Miller, 'that pioneer of the Rococo Gothic'.

The Master Landscape Gardeners

Eighteenth century landscape gardening was dominated by two great artists, William Kent (1685-1748) and Lancelot Brown (1715-1783). The former became renowned alike for his Palladian architecture at Holkham Hall, Norfolk and the Horse Guards building in Whitehall, for his superb interior decorations and furnishings at Chiswick House, Holkham Hall and Ditchley Park and his landscaped gardens which are seen to perfection in the Midlands. At Chiswick, now a public London park, Kent retained in the garden design several formal features already laid out by Charles Bridgeman under French influence. At Shotover Park near Oxford there are signs that this versatile artist was breaking away from the prevailing fashion. This house has today a formal garden of 1718-1730 with long avenues and cross walks, and a long canal on its eastern part giving a view of a large Gothic temple.

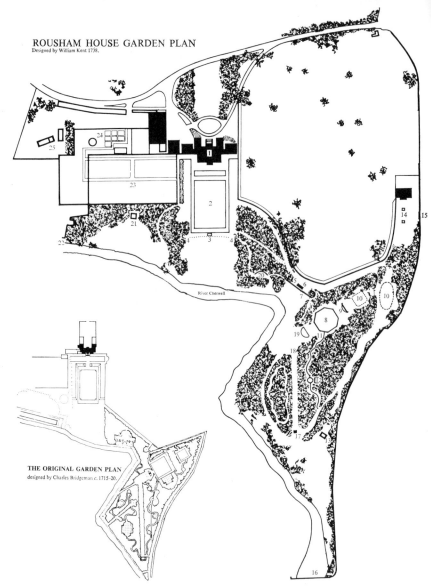

ROUSHAM HOUSE GARDEN PLAN
Designed by William Kent 1738.

River Cherwell

THE ORIGINAL GARDEN PLAN
designed by Charles Bridgeman c. 1715-20.

Key.

1. Rousham House 1636, 1740, 1877
2. Bowling Green c. 1720
3. Lion and Horse by P. Scheemaker, 1740
4. Four seats by William Kent
5. Praeneste Terrace
6. Dying Gladiator
7. Arcade by William Kent
8. Octagon pond
9. Upper cascade with Venus and Cupids
10. Site of upper ponds
11. Watery walk
12. Cold Bath

13. Temple of Echo by Kent and Townsend
14. Gothic seat by Kent
15. Palladian doorway
16. Heyford Bridge, 1255
17. Statue of Apollo
18. Long walk
19. Lower Cascade
20. Theatre by Bridgeman
21. Pyramid by Kent, 1720
22. Classic seat
23. Walled garden
24. Pigeon House garden

In the 1730s Kent took a hand in altering the garden facing the west side of the house and added here a domed octagonal temple and an obelisk separated by what appears to have been — for vegetation growth has blurred the detail — a wooded expanse with winding paths. But the great break from formality was yet to come and the traditional rigid axial designs still had powerful adherents in John Vanbrugh and Charles Bridgeman. Oxfordshire and Buckinghamshire were fortunate to be the scene of the change when geometrical rules gave way to naturalistic concepts wherein 'the three new graces, Poetry, Painting and Gardening should unite to dress and adorn Nature'.

The irretrievable step in this revolution was taken at Rousham, 20km north of Oxford, where about 1635 a modest house had been built for Sir Robert Dormer. Between 1738 and 1740 General James Dormer, a friend of Pope and Swift, called in William Kent to design two new wings, redecorate much of the interior and re-plan the gardens. Kent's interior work is seen to perfection in the painted parlour where in a grand manner he has left one of the most exquisite eighteenth century rooms in England on a miniature scale. Although adept at any form of decorative art he was at his best in garden design and here at Rousham his scheme survives unspoilt, the only one preserved intact.

Previous to Kent most English gardens were laid out on formal lines with groupings of geometrical patterns such as already existed at Rousham probably from the designs of Charles Bridgeman, the Royal gardener. Kent, however, had spent ten years studying art in Italy and was familiar with an Italian countryside dotted with classical ruins. He was imbued too with the dream-like landscape paintings of Claude, Poussin and Salvator Rosa then highly esteemed in literary circles. Addison had written in 1711 in *The Spectator* of the garden of Sir Roger de Coverley's lady friend, wherein rocks were shaped into artificial grottoes covered with woodbine and jessamine, woods were cut into shady walks and springs made to run over pebbles into a beautiful lake. On the basis of this marriage of Nature and Art, William Kent transformed the surroundings of Rousham into an idealised naturalistic landscape. To walk through the garden is to move through a series of landscape compositions with the scene changing at every turn of the path, utterly faithful to Pope's advice:

> Let not each beauty ev'ry where be spy'd,
> Where half the skill is decently to hide.
> He gains all points, who pleasingly confounds,
> Surprizes, varies, and conceals the Bounds.

The landscaping covers 25 acres (10ha) of the valley side dropping steeply to the curving Cherwell from the wide flat terrace around the house from which one gets no hint of the sylvan delights beyond. The temples and statues are set in intimate groves and leafy retreats like a succession of open air rooms. The Praeneste, an arcade of seven arches with alcoves and seats, overlooks a sweep of the river; on the walk above are statues of a dying gladiator and two herons; elsewhere a winding path leads through Venus Vale, a long wooded valley threaded by a tiny stream cascading through a chain of small lakes and ending in a grotto, the tomb of a favourite otter hound. On the skyline to the north across the river, a sham ruin acts as an eyecatcher. No wonder Horace Walpole thought Rousham 'the most engaging of Kent's works...the sweetest little groves, streams, glades, porticoes, cascades and river imaginable; all the scenes are perfectly classic'.

At Stowe, near Buckingham, William Kent produced for Viscount Cobham another masterpiece, this time on a gigantic scale.[4] There was already landscaping at Stowe, probably by Vanbrugh and Charles Bridgeman, when Kent was called in during the 1720s. By 1739 he had cleared away the formal gardens and parterres round the house, cut out broad vistas to temples, serpentined the lakes and added many new buildings, columns and statues. His numerous contributions to the forty classic 'enrichments' of the park include a Palladian Temple of Venus, a circular colonnaded Temple of Ancient Virtue, a sham ruin facing it known satirically as the Temple of Modern Virtue, and within eyeshot across a dam a temple with busts of sixteen British worthies. Eventually the gardens extended to more than 400 acres (160ha) and became one of the show pieces of Europe. In 1928 the mansion was taken over as a boys' school which continues to flourish, and which recently gave covenants over the main part of the landscape gardens and temples to the National Trust so ensuring the fulfilment of the prophecy of a visitor in 1769, 'my Lord Temple's gardens at Stowe, will continue the admiration of foreigners, and the boast of England, as long as liberality of mind and real taste adorn its natives'.

By chance Stowe's influence was to dominate the gardens of English mansions for centuries to come. During Kent's alterations a young man from Northumbria, by name Lancelot Brown, came to Stowe as a kitchen gardener. Capability Brown, as he was later known from his judgment that parks were capable of improvement, became the most famous English landscape designer and planned hundreds of estates. He left Stowe about 1750 and returned, when famous, about ten years later to widen and indent the central vista from the mansion to the lake and to complete the Grecian valley to the northeast. We will continue with Brown after interpolating a quite remarkable effect that 'the fair majestic paradise of Stowe' had on a neighbouring landowner.

About 13km to the southeast at Middle Claydon, Sir Ralph Verney, a merchant and former Lord Mayor of London, had bought the manor in 1463. His descendants came to live in the manor house in 1643 and their activities there are recorded in the well-known *Letters and Papers of the Verney Family*, edited in 1892 by Frances Parthenope who was Lady Verney and, incidentally, sister of Florence Nightingale. After the Restoration the Verneys grew rich from trading in the Levant and Far East; one of them, Ralph, second Earl of Fermanagh, was a passionate Whig who determined to outshine his political rivals, the Tory owners of Stowe. He spared no expense in enlarging and beautifying Claydon House and the costs, together with large political donations to Edmund Burke and others, exhausted the fortunes of himself and his rich wife. Bankrupted, he was sold up but managed to escape to France and when he eventually died in poverty in London was quite unrepentant of

Chinoiserie; detail of tea party at Claydon House.

the way he had spent his wealth. Never was a man more justified — Claydon is worth more than bankruptcy. The Earl's niece, Mary, who succeeded him in 1791 was sternly practical and proceeded to demolish two-thirds of the vast mansion but she spared the west wing overlooking the lake and park. This may have been built, and was certainly decorated, by Luke Lightfoot, an otherwise virtually unknown genius, variously described as carver, cabinet maker, master builder, surveyor, and victualler, who achieved at Claydon a masterpiece of rococo unsurpassed in Britain.

The present entry to the west wing opens directly into the Pink Parlour resplendent with Lightfoot's wood carvings on ceiling, cornice, mantelpiece and doorway. The room leads to a suite of three large chambers that occupy the existing west front. First comes the great eating room, designed as a large double cube with doorways and alcoves in a perfect symmetry and richly embellished with rococo wood carvings of the highest quality, a carved extravaganza emerging from a lemon yellow background with apple green in the frieze. This leads through mahogany doors with exquisite marquetry into the salon where the plaster decorations of the ceiling and coves are by Joseph Rose, who worked with Robert Adam at Harewood and Osterley. The library beyond is a double cube with an elegant plaster ceiling and cornice also probably by Rose. The great architectural treasure of Claydon lies in the exquisite staircase linking these fine rooms with the second storey. Its general design, probably by Sir Thomas Robinson and Lightfoot, dispenses with vertical supports, as the flights ascend gently twice round the side of the stair well, before reaching the upper landing. Their mahogany treads and soffits (undersides) are richly patterned with inlay or veneer of holly, ebony and ivory, as also are all communicating doors. The plaster walls, decorated with festoons, medallions, cameos and trophies in relief, were executed by Rose but the beautiful frieze upon the base of the glass dome is carved in wood and bespeaks of Lightfoot. The inlaid mahogany handrail rests on a balustrade of unbelievably beautiful ironwork wherein a continuous garland of wheat husks and ears, once gilded, climbs thin, curving scrolls and trembles delicately with each vibration of the stairs.

Today a supplementary staircase gives access to the upper suite of rooms decorated with rococo wood carvings by either Lightfoot or his master carpenter. In one of these ornate chambers, the combination of Gothic and Chinese motifs prepares the visitor for the Chinese room, a breathtaking mixture of rococo and chinoiserie. Here, among a wealth of wood carvings done to Chinese designs published about 1745, a Chinese pagoda-like alcove occupies almost all one wall. Carved with great delicacy and precision, tiny bells, once gilded, hang from its roof and in one place a finely moustached mandarin and companion sit at a table laid with teapot, cups and saucers, and what may be a sugar basin.

This west wing at Claydon faces on to a park designed and laid out between 1763 and 1776 by James Sanderson of Caversham at a cost of £3,399. At one stage the Verneys considered bringing down 'the Capability Brown, at least to give an opinion on intended piece of water'. Had they done so, Claydon would have joined Benham (Speen), Blenheim, Charlecote, Compton Verney, Ditchley, Kirtlington, Nuneham, Radley, Ragley, Sandleford, Stowe and Warwick as a major work of Britain's greatest professional landscaper.

During Brown's rise to fame the nostalgia for the classical ruins of Italy subsided and he was able to express the English love of nature and to bring out the subtle beauty of rain-washed wooded slopes and gentle stretches of greensward. He liked to enclose a whole park with a belt of trees of species suited to the locality and with an inner edge serpentine and irregular according to the contour. The middle distance was, if possible, enlivened with water to reflect the tree growth; the near distance up to the mansion had broad sweeps of turf accented by occasional groups of majestic trees. The patterns were clear cut and bright, with perspectives varied in detail and spaces vast without being awesome. Nowhere is this better exemplified than at Blenheim Palace, where from 1760 to 1770 Brown completed the most famous and grandest of his masterpieces.

The royal manor of Woodstock was given, with funds for a new palace, by Queen Anne to John Churchill, Duke of Marlborough, after his victory over Louis XIV's armies at Blenheim on the Danube in 1704. The manor covered 2,000 acres (810ha) and its limestone terrain was crossed by the deep gorgelike valley of the river Glyme. A

The skyline at Blenheim Palace.

royal hunting lodge, later enlarged to a splendid palace, had stood here since the early twelfth century but in 1554, when the young Princess Elizabeth was imprisoned in its gatehouse, the main structure had begun to decay.[5] This palace occupied a flat sunny valleyside terrace near the present bridge and faced southward to a causeway raised across the valley floor.

The new palace was designed by Vanbrugh who presumably also made the outline plan of the first formal gardens of 77 acres (31 ha). They were laid out (1705-1710) by Henry Wise of London, at that time the leading maker of gardens in Britain.[6] In 1758 the fourth Duke called in Capability Brown to complete the landscaping of the park that Vanbrugh had begun. Brown immediately removed the old causeway except for one stretch left to form a picturesque island, and built a masonry dam across the valley some distance downstream of Vanbrugh's magnificent Palladian bridge. The huge lake formed by the dam was naturally serpentine but, alas, submerged the piers of the bridge up to its main arches. Brown then proceeded to sweep away Wise's geometrical garden, or great parterre, from the south side of the palace, and bring greensward right up to the forecourts. Elsewhere the ground was left open or variegated with trees distributed with taste and discretion, although the wide avenue of elms stretching northward for three kilometres from the Column of Victory was retained. The High Lodge and Home Farm were refronted in a Gothic style. Subsequently landscapers have added a piece here and there to Brown's scheme, particularly near the palace and the cascade over the dam, but his aesthetic aims survive. There never will be agreement on the success of his landscaping here. Deep regret at the partial submergence of a magnificent valley and its splendid bridge must be weighed against some of the most beautiful humanised views in Britain. Seen across the park from the triumphal archway, the palace has an aura of misty romance and by some miracle of design Vanbrugh's baroque assumes a Renaissance charm. It is no wonder that Brown's influence spread abroad. Thomas Jefferson decided, after seeing Caversham, Blenheim and Stowe, to make the grounds of Monticello like an English park which he considered 'a beauty of the first order in landscape'. An anonymous poet summed up the general opinion when he wrote in 1767:

> At Blenheim, Croome and Caversham we trace
> Salvator's wilderness, Claude's enlivening grace,
> Cascades and lakes as fine as Risdale drew
> While Nature's vary'd in each charming view.
> To paint his works would Poussin's power require,
> Milton's sublimity and Dryden's fire.

The brightness of Brown's work at Blenheim and Warwick contrasts with its sad fate at Caversham (now largely built over), Nuneham Courtenay and dozens of other mansions. Nuneham Park occupied his last few years and embroiled him in an estate with a history characteristic in many ways of eighteenth century emparkments. The mansion was begun in 1756 on a bluff of Lower Greensand which gave desirable views of the Thames and the domes and spires of Oxford. Its dilettante owner, Simon, first Earl Harcourt, preferred the site to that of his family home at Stanton Harcourt on the flat vale of the upper Thames. For the foundations of his new Palladian house at Nuneham he took stones from his ancestral mansion and floated them by barge down the Thames. Stanton Harcourt village now lost both its mansion and its chief domestic employer whereas Nuneham Courtenay suffered a complete translation, as the earl destroyed the existing village and rehoused the villagers at a distance in new brick semidetached cottages spaced regularly in pairs along both sides of the Oxford-London turnpike. The old church was replaced by a classical temple suited to Italianate vistas designed in the park. The displacement is said to have influenced Goldsmith strongly when composing *The Deserted Village* although it seems hard to equate Nuneham on a sandy bluff with 'Sweet Auburn, loveliest village of the plain'. The next earl, George Simon Harcourt, was an artist and idealist who befriended Rousseau and generously patronised the cottagers in the model village. One of his poetic acquaintances, William Mason, laid out for him a large informal flower garden, probably the first of its kind, wherein floral beauty was linked to philosophy, aided by judicious inscriptions on urns and busts set discreetly in flowery recesses.[7] As there were still 1,000 acres (400ha) unimproved, the Earl called in Lancelot Brown to assess their capabilities and to blend the landscaped part with the untamed

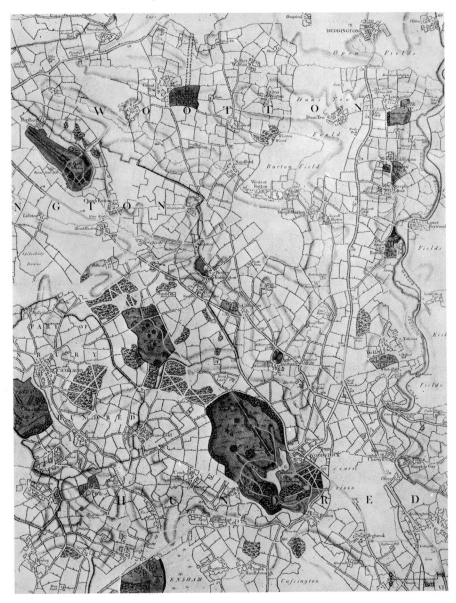

Parks near Woodstock showing landscape gardening at Blenheim, Heythrop, Great Tew and Blandford (Cornbury) Park in 1794.

woodland. Between 1779 and 1783 Brown and his son-in-law altered the mansion and devised a romantic walk winding parallel to the Thames and passing now through new groves and now through old, interspersed with clearings giving views of Abingdon church spire or Radley village or Oxford, and ending beyond a rustic bridge at an island where a picturesque thatched cottage provided earthly refreshments.

In the following century Nuneham Park suffered the fate of so many of the larger houses and landscaped gardens in England. The mansion was enlarged and in Victorian times almost surrounded by terraces, shrubberies and conservatories in which the nobility could walk protected from the naturalised landscape beyond. The flower garden, being superfluous, reverted to wilderness. Almost inevitably the estate passed to an educational institution, in this case the University of Oxford, who recently restored the mansion at a cost of £166,539 and leased it to a teachers' training college. To maintain the grounds to perfection was beyond the finances available and Brown's idyllic landscaping gradually faded in clarity and began to appear perfectly natural. Could a greater compliment be paid to any artist or a more subtle one to a gardener?

The Age of Extravagant Mansions

The landscaping tradition of Capability Brown was continued by Humphry Repton who differed little from him except in such details as a preference for mansions to be skirted by a formal terrace rather than by lawns which swept up to the facade. Repton made three thousand sketches for garden improvements and produced over 200 Red Books, now eagerly sought after because of the superimposed coloured flaps which showed cleverly by placing one on another the effect that the proposed alteration would have on the existing scene. However, he had relatively little influence on estates in the English heartland where so much landscaping had already been done. He worked at Adlestrop, Great Tew and Sezincote and is seen at his best at West Wycombe Park and Sarsden (Oxfordshire, *c.* 1795), each with a serpentine lake and one or more Doric temples.

During the nineteenth century, especially in the long reign of Victoria (1837-1901), purely classical building styles gave way to mixed Gothic eccentricities extravagant in style and size. The plutocracy showed a tendency to cling to the security of their vast mansions and to enjoy the seclusion and shelter of walled gardens, pergolas, fern houses and glass conservatories, where the vegetation expressed, the entwined, close-knit family group. The changing attitude is reflected in the poetry. Tennyson, who married Emily Sarah Sellwood at Shiplake church on 13 June 1850, rose to great poetic heights in *Maud*, where the garden is scented with musk roses and woodbine, the casement is draped with jessamine and the dawning light awakens lilies and rosebuds beneath a 'daffodil sky'. Deeper into Victoria's reign Thomas Edward Brown (1830-97), on a lower poetic plane, describes a more claustrophobic scene:

> A garden is a lovesome thing, God wot!
> Rose plot,
> Fringed pool,
> Ferned grot —
> The veriest school
> Of peace . . . . .

The variety of plants and seeds then readily available for gardeners had never been equalled and among the notable suppliers were Suttons of Reading, founded in 1806 by Martin Hope Sutton, an ardent botanist. Gardening now required skill in the detailed arrangements of colour and texture rather than a flair for spacious landscaping. But we are concerned with the combination of mansion and garden, and in Victorian and Edwardian times many new mansions were built in old gardens as well as new gardens around old houses, and new houses within new gardens.

Foremost among favourite estates in the Midlands where an ancient house has been surrounded by a new garden, is Compton Wynyates, Some of the early owners here were interested in botanical gardening and in 1632 when Henry Compton became Bishop of London he planted at Fulham Palace a remarkable collection of trees and plants, many of them from the eastern seaboard of North America. The present garden at Compton was laid out on the site of the former moats about 1895 as an arrangement of more or less regularly spaced evergreens clipped in a wide variety of shapes and placed in conjunction with a wealth of herbaceous plants and beds of roses and other flowers. With its lack of tall trees and quaint irregularity of yew-line it forms a perfect apron for the picturesque mansion.

At Cliveden, near Cookham, the garden is older than the mansion. Here the huge red brick terrace constructed in 1666 was topped in 1851 with its third house, a handsome Victorian mansion designed by Sir Charles Barry, and now let to Stanford University, California. The extensive gardens, with parterre and later terraces, were considerably altered by Capability Brown. The eye-catchers include a lovely fountain and several temples by Giacomo Leoni (*c.* 1735) who helped to introduce Palladianism into Britain. The estate is an arrangement of large formal layouts with long spacious drives, bounded on the river side by fine woods and shrubs, through which paths wind giving breathtaking views of the Thames at the foot of the steep valleyside. The notable scenes include magnolias, various conifers, a Chinese or Japanese garden with a pagoda from the Great Exhibition of 1851, and the massive Canning oak on the lip of the finest stretch of the Thames.

The Decline of Mansions and of Landscape Gardening

Since 1914 the maintenance of large houses has been so expensive that most owners have had little to spend on garden innovations. Many Victorian extensions to old mansions have been demolished and many great houses, old and new alike, have been saved from dereliction only by being taken over by institutions or corporations. Of the Victorian great houses the palatial Bear Wood is now a school; the flamboyant, castellar Gothic Wyfold Court is a hospital; and Waddesdon, built (1880-89) for Baron Ferdinand de Rothschild in French Renaissance style, was with its rich contents and fine park bequeathed with an endowment to the National Trust. Most large establishments managed reasonably well until the early twentieth century and a few new gardens were actually laid out then, usually of a terraced type. The favourites happen to be exceptional. At Buscot Park Harold Ainsworth Peto (1854-1933) developed a simple classical naturalness combined with high skill in the art of planting trees and shrubs. Here he designed an attractive water garden consisting of a long, wide tree-lined sward down the centre of which a narrow canal leads from the mansion to a large lake. The walk between clipped hedges varies in width and the canal itself varies in detail, with circular pools, fountains, bridge and vistas of lateral tree-lined avenues. The garden has been further adorned recently and, with its courtyard pool near the house, keeps its charm.

At Blenheim Palace, the original garden by Henry Wise, gardener to Queen Anne, consisted of a parterre near the house and a kitchen garden discreetly tucked away in the distance. The parterre was in a baroque design of swirling scroll-like patterns studded with small bushes clipped into geometrical shapes of a kind then popular on the continent. Capability Brown swept it away to bring greensward up to the palace, but in 1925 the ninth Duke of Marlborough employed a French gardener, Achille Duchêne, to restore the original plan and the great parterre, of a type unique in Britain, again skirts the sunny west facade.

As said, these formal designs were exceptional during and after Edwardian times when the over-formal style of Victorian gardens became unfashionable. The very popular books on gardens by William Robinson and Gertrude Jekyll led to admiration of informal designs with richly varied herbaceous borders. There was wide acclaim when Gertrude Jekyll wrote:

> I am strongly for treating garden and wooded ground in a pictorial way, mainly with large effects, and in the second place with lesser beautiful incidents, and for so arranging plants and trees and grassy spaces that they look happy and at home, and make no parade of conscious effort. I try for beauty and harmony everywhere, and especially for harmony of colour. A garden so treated gives the delightful feeling of repose, and refreshment, and pure enjoyment of beauty . . .
> (*Wood and Garden*, 1899, p.2)

With the ever widening facilities for obtaining an ever increasing variety of seeds, bulbs and flowering shrubs, the British became a nation of floral gardeners and much of rural England virtually became a garden. At the same time the creation of large new landscape designs on rural estates ceased when expense of upkeep and excessive taxation began to impoverish the owners of great mansions. Yet at least two memorable modern gardens arose. The first at Windsor Great Park is really outside the English heartland but is worth any amount of travelling to see. Laid out since 1932 by Sir John Savill, Deputy Warden, it has grown to 10ha on the side of the park near Virginia Water, and is famous for its colourful expanses of Japanese maple, rock

The Woodland Gardens, Windsor Great Park.

Gardens at Hidcote Bartrim.

plants, heathers, rhododendrons and azaleas.

The second modern country garden adorns the manor house at Hidcote Bartrim near Chipping Campden, and was made between 1905 and 1946 by Major Lawrence Johnston who from a basis of an old cedar, two clumps of beech and surrounding hilltop fields laid out piecemeal no less than 10 acres (4ha). The scheme consists of a series of about twenty interconnecting cottage garden enclosures, for the most part with wide borders profusely planted with flowers and shrubs, that extends outward into a stream garden and a woodland or wilderness that are resplendent with colour especially in spring and autumn. The whole shows a keen botanic knowledge of old, new and rare species, here grown to perfection, and an outstanding sense of colour and continuity of visual effect. The hedges, for example, have subtle variations of green, achieved by the use of yew, holly, box, beech and hornbeam; the topiary is just sufficient; the colour effects achieve the irridescence of a prism without the massed use of uniform planting. The garden was the first to be presented to a joint committee of the Royal Horticultural Society and the National Trust formed in 1949 for the preservation of gardens of outstanding merit. Although the creation of one man, Hidcote garden echoes the thoughts of millions with humbler aspirations, for, to trespass again on Gertrude Jekyll, 'The love of gardening is a seed that once sown never dies, but always grows and grows to an enduring and ever-increasing source of happiness'. Fortunately the same is equally true of the love of gardens planted by others.

CHAPTER TWELVE

Watermills

I loved the brimming wave that swam
Thro' quiet meadows round the mill
The sleepy pool above the dam,
The pool beneath it never still
The meal-sacks on the whiten'd floor
The dark round of the dripping wheel
The very air about the door
Made misty with the floating meal.
      (Tennyson, *The Miller's Daughter*)

Mediaeval Watermills

In mediaeval times the English heartland produced an abundance of grain for
flour and had plenty of rivers suitable for the erection of watermills. The river
gradients in the bigger valleys on the Jurassic wolds were steep enough to allow
mills to be placed at close intervals. On the clay vales the rivers were slower and
mills had to be spaced more widely although on the master watercourses a more
copious flow often compensated for relative slowness. Only on the chalk downs
were watermills seriously disadvantaged by lack of surface flow, especially in dry
seasons. Thus on the river Pang the first mill is at Frilsham, eight kilometres
downstream of the usual source. Even here in dry summers a duck could make
her nest under the mill wheel and hatch a brood before a drop of water passed.

The possibilities of erecting water wheels may be judged from *Domesday
Survey* where over 600 mills are recorded for the region. Most villages on streams
had one watermill and upon the stronger rivers many manors possessed three
mills or more. For example, four mills were credited to Kempsford on the upper
Thames, Sherborne on the Windrush system, Bidford on the Avon and
Honington on the Stour. Six mills were recorded at Sudeley manor south of
Winchcombe, at Shipton under Wychwood on the Evenlode and at Reading on
the Kennet near its junction with the Thames. Seven mills were mentioned at
both Letcombe and Hanney on small streams in the Vale of White Horse and no
less than twelve at Blockley manor upon swift tributaries of the Stour although
probably some of them were sited farther afield at Ditchford and Church Icomb.

The rent, or assessed annual value, of the mills seems to have varied according
to their output of flour. A single mill was valued at 6d at Saintbury, a tiny hamlet

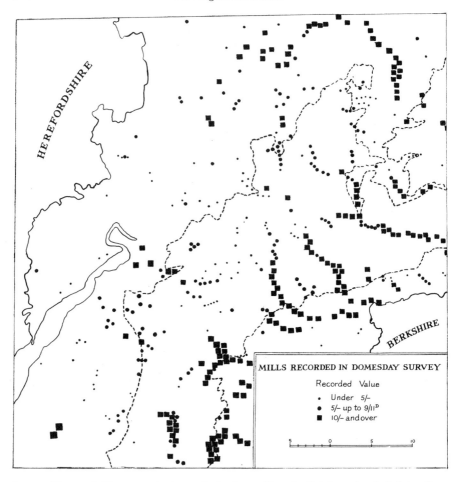

Watermills recorded in *Domesday Survey* in the Cotswolds and adjoining vales. Scale is in miles.

on the Cotswold scarp near Broadway and at 30s at Evesham amid the fertile lands of the Avon valley. Two mills were assessed at 6s 2d at Campden, 7s 8d at Stanford in the Vale, 10s 4d at Upton, 25s at Burford, and 32s 6d at Witney. The first two places are on small streams while the last three are situated successively downstream on the powerful Windrush where it leaves the eastern Cotswolds. Commonly on tributaries of the Severn system and less frequently elsewhere, mill rents were paid partly in eels, for which the Avon, Arrow and Alne were especially renowned. The mill at Stratford upon Avon was valued at 10s and 1,000 eels and that at Wixford at 10s and 20 stiches of eels, a stiche or stick containing 25 fish. On the Thames, Kennet and Loddon the kind of fish was often not specified although eels were highly prized here also.

The exact mechanism of these Norman watermills, and of their Anglo-Saxon

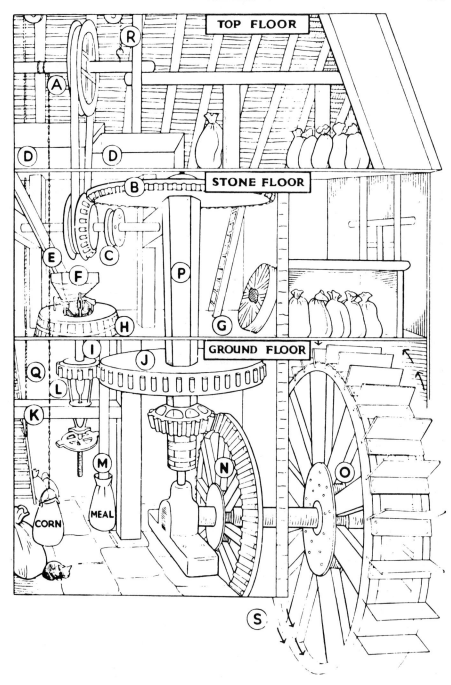

FOR KEY SEE P. 198.

Diagram of the fittings typical of many south Midland watermills.
A — sack hoist
B — crown wheel
C — cog wheel
D — grain bins
E — grain spout
F — grain hopper
G — spare millstone
H — grinding vat with bedstone and running stone
I — spindle
J — spur wheel
K — bridge
L — stone nut or pinion
M — meal spout and sacks
N — pit wheel
O — water wheel with spokes and paddles
P — central shaft
Q and R — gear cord
S — direction of water flow and wheel rotation.

predecessors, is not known. In a few the water wheel may have been horizontal in Roman or Norwegian fashion but probably most were undershot, that is pushed by the flow of water against the lowest ladles or paddles of a vertical rotating wheel.

Most of the *Domesday* mills were enlarged and, over the centuries, re-fitted with new and better machinery. In later mediaeval times, up to the Black Death, new mills were added to meet the needs of an expanding population and of monastic bodies, but for the most part increased output of grist was achieved by improvements in mill technique. No doubt these improvements included better quality millstones. On 23 July 1264 the sheriffs of London were ordered to buy without delay and without fail four millstones for the King's mills at Windsor Castle and to convey them thither by water.[1] The cost of such refitments was large and forms one reason why the lord of the manor insisted that his tenants had their corn ground at his mill. The manorial records for Cuxham in Oxfordshire demonstrate the large outlay of capital. The village stands on the fertile greensand belt at the foot of the Chiltern escarpment, about 2 kilometres northwest of the ancient market town of Watlington, which being on the chalk lacks surface water. The manor of Cuxham derives its streams from copious permanent springs thrown out at the base of the chalk. It had three mills at *Domesday Survey* but only two in the thirteenth century, one at the east end of the village and Cutt mill at the junction of two streams farther west. The former belonged to the priory at Wallingford while the latter from 1268 onwards was the property of Merton College, Oxford, who, as overlords of the manor, gradually improved it. Cutt Mill was at first a timber-framed building with walls of wattle and daub and a thatched roof. In 1299 it was rented out to Robert Newman at 40s annually, the landlord being entirely responsible for all repairs and all machinery. In 1330-31 the college purchased for installation at Cuxham and Holywell, Oxford, five foreign millstones at a cost of 63s 4d each. The stones, presumably made of pieces of chert or flint quartz from the Paris neighbourhood, were, after inspection, bought in London and there put on board a boat which carried them about 100km upstream to Henley, whence they were carted overland to Cuxham.[2] Apart from the penny (*argentium dei*) and 5 gallons of wine, costing 2s 1d, intended to seal the bargain and perhaps also to bring good luck, the further expenses were as follows:

At London:	loading in ship	5s
	wharfage and murage	1s 5½ d
London to Henley:	carriage on Thames	11s 2d
	murage at Mayden church	10d
Journey of bailiff, servant and horse, to and from London, taking 3 days		3s 0¾ d
Expenses on another occasion for 4 days in seeing to carriage of the stones		4s
At Henley: expenses of 3 men for 3 days boring the stones, and of 2 carters carrying 2 stones to Cuxham		3s 9d
Iron bought		2½ d
Steel for mill bills for boring the stones		9d
To smith for making bill and sharpening them again and again		2s
2 hoops bought for carrying 2 stones to Oxford		6d

Transport from London had increased the final cost of the stones by one-tenth and the expenses of the whole transaction were equivalent to the total rents for nearly eight years from a populous royal borough such as Woodstock. Yet this industrial installation proved highly profitable, as in 1349 the Cutt mill rent was increased to 50s a year and in 1358 the whole structure was rebuilt with a tiled roof. It seems remarkable that Merton College received from this one mill about the same income as the king had from his borough of over 100 dwellings at New Woodstock.

In the late twelfth century the use of waterwheels began to be extended from grinding corn to driving stocks or hammers for fulling cloth. By 1185 the Templars had built two fulling mills on the upper Windrush at Barton near Temple Guiting and within forty years at least another eleven fulling mills were at work in the English heartland. As will be described later, there now occurred a minor industrial revolution in the cloth manufacturing industry and by 1334 a further twenty three fulling mills were working, particularly on Cotswold rivers near Winchcombe and Cirencester and on the upper Kennet between Newbury and Marlborough. In this change the monastic influence was strong both on the Cotswolds and on the Thames as at Oxford, Abingdon and Reading.

Whereas some of the fulling mills were on new sites, most were adaptations and extensions of existing grist mills because the fulling hammers could be raised

The breast and undershot waterwheel at Lower Slaughter.

and dropped by means of a simple trip device on the rotating axle shaft.
Apparently some lords of the manor tried to impose on fulling the same
manorial custom (thirlage) as applied to grinding corn. At Sherborne, where

one of the four grist mills was given over quite early to fulling, the abbot of Gloucester in 1340 fined several of his tenants for taking their cloth to be fulled outside the manor.[3]

The sites of most of these mediaeval watermills, grist and fulling alike, can be readily identified today by their stream diversions and leats and in several places by masonry. Many grist mills and a few fulling mills continued in use until at least the late nineteenth century. A mediaeval fulling mill survives at Elcot near Marlborough.[4] A grist mill at *Domesday Survey,* it was adapted for fulling stocks and later refitted for flour milling. Its main gears are of wood and it retains an undershot wheel which, as will now be shown, became less common after Tudor times.

Modern Watermills

During the sixteenth and seventeenth centuries many books were published describing the great advances made on the simple undershot method of driving waterwheels. Probably the most influential of the publications in English was John Fitzherbert's small volume *Here Begynneth a ryght frutefull mater: and hath to name the boke of furveying and improvmentes* (printed by Richard Pynson of Fleet Street, London, 1523). The book was still being reprinted over two hundred years later.[5] After observing that mills can be made beside main streams and on small streams and artificial side waters by making a weir of timber and stone, it continues (if converted to modern spelling):

> Also there be other two manner of corn mills / that is to say: a breast mill and an overshot mill / and those two manner of mills be set and go most commonly upon small brooks / and upon great pools and meres. And they have alway a broad bow a foot broad and more and the ladles be alway shrouded with compost boards on both sides to hold in the water / and then they be called buckets. And they must be set much nearer together than the ladles be / and much more aslope downward / to hold much water that it fall not out / for it driveth the wheel as well with the weight of the water as with the strength. And the miller must draw his water according to his buckets / that they may be alway full and no more / for the longer that they hold the water the better they be.

Fitzherbert goes on to describe the best depth of sills and of water beneath the wheel (in the wheel trough), the latter being such as to give a free and ready flow and not to harbour still water. He recommends the number of cogs for the main gear wheel in the mill machinery. A corn mill on a large river should have 48 cogs and then the millstone will turn 8 times for every revolution of the waterwheel. For small streams 42 cogs is best, whereas with overshot wheels the main gear should have 36 cogs and in windmills the number should never be less than 48 cogs or 54. Mills properly built and driven will, concludes Fitzherbert, bring great profit to the lord of a manor and 'the most rent is raised upon the little ground'.

No doubt the profitability of watermills after this time was due partly to an increase in population, for England was recovering from the worst effects of the Black Death and the Wars of the Roses. However, the general interest in watermills can be sensed from their depiction in sixteenth century wooden panelling at University College, Oxford. All the methods advocated by Fitzherbert were already in use but wherever his suggestions were adopted or installed afresh they increased proficiency. The breast shot method allowed the water to fill the buckets at axle height whereas in the overshot they were filled at the top of the wheel. For these methods the normal procedure was to build a dam or mill pond and feed the water through a controlled sluice of correct width on to the wheel. In this way a stream could be carefully controlled and very little water was wasted. The weight of water forced the wheel round and the power generated depended largely on the width or capacity of the buckets and the diameter of the wheel. The general efficiency was about 60 per cent for the overshot wheel, 50 per cent for the breast shot and just over 20 per cent for the undershot. The first two methods were ideal for rapid streams in narrow valleys but proved more difficult to install in valleys with wide flat floors. In such situations the required head of water was usually achieved by enclosing a mill cut or leat in lateral embankments made largely from the earth excavated in digging the new channel. The results may be seen to perfection at Burford, where normally the water in the mill cuts stands well above the level of the adjacent meadows. Near the church, sedimentation over the centuries has steadily raised the bed of the mill stream and in efforts to prevent flooding the water frontage of the churchyard has been protected by heightening the artificial earthen levees.

When waterwheels and milling machinery became more efficient a manor with several mills could spare a mill, or part of one, for tasks other than grinding corn and fulling. The usual alternative was paper making which expanded rapidly from late Tudor times onward (*see* references on p. 409). By 1650 more than 40 paper mills existed in England and of these one was at Sutton Courtenay and no less than 12 near High or Chipping Wycombe in south Buckinghamshire, which lies for the most part just outside the English heartland. By the 1690s the total number of paper mills in England exceeded 100 and of these three (Wolvercote, Hampton Gay and Eynsham) were in Oxfordshire, four (Sutton Courtenay, East Hagbourne, Sheffield and Cookham) in Berkshire, one, Beoley, in Worcestershire, and 17 in Buckinghamshire. After 1712 English-made paper had to pay excise duties but this did not halt the expansion and mechanisation. For example in 1743 water-driven engines for beating rags were installed at Wolvercote and in the following year at Colthrop, Berkshire, where Joseph Lane, paper maker late of Horton in Buckinghamshire, took the lease of a paper factory that had been set up recently at or upon the site of two grist mills. About two decades later paper making was first recorded at Postlip, near Winchcombe. By 1800 the number of paper mills in England had risen to 415 and included just over 50 in the English heartland

Derelict overshot waterwheel. The water filled the buckets from a controlled sluice in the facing wall.

and as many again in the adjacent territory in south Buckinghamshire. There were then, for example, two mills (Upton and Widford) on the Windrush, four on the Cherwell system, six on the Kennet and eleven or twelve on the middle Thames. The number of mills declined rapidly after the bigger factories installed the Fourdrinier paper making machine in the early 1800s although these establishments, as at Wootton Wawen, Eynsham, Hampton Gay, Wolvercote, Sandford, Sutton Courtenay, Henley, Shiplake and Marlow, continued to flourish for several decades at least.[6] By 1911 there were 26 active paper mills in the English heartland and about the same number in south Buckinghamshire. Today only five mills in the English heartland manufacture paper, namely, Postlip near Winchcombe, Wolvercote and Sandford both at Oxford, Temple mills on the Thames near Henley, and Colthrop mills on the Kennet near Thatcham. In south Buckinghamshire the industry still flourishes in six factories in High Wycombe and at single factories at Taplow, near Maidenhead on the Thames and near Horton on the Colne. Needless to say, these mills are large modern manufactories that use great quantities of water and no water power, although one large waterwheel is preserved on the river Wye at High Wycombe.

The increasing mechanisation of paper making is also typical of the increasing improvement of waterwheels and grist milling machinery. Waterwheels for any purpose were, apart from metal strengthening hoops, constructed entirely of wood until the late eighteenth century when iron working parts were gradually introduced. In the following century new wheel installations were usually of metal and by 1861 iron overshot wheels 2ft wide and 20ft in diameter could be bought for £340. A local example survives at Bucklebury[7] where the foundry, now used for light engineering, derived power for the fan for its furnaces and forge bellows from an existing undershot waterwheel cast here in about 1875. Iron also became common for at least the main shafts and main gearing of the interior machinery of grist mills. A detailed account of interior mill mechanisms will be found in Katharine S. Woods' *Rural Crafts of England*[8] from which the accompanying diagram is taken.

The disuse of small grist watermills became common in late Victorian times when the introduction of grinding by iron rollers had proved especially suited to hard wheats imported from North America. Then large steam-driven grist mills were erected at the ports and within a few decades these giant concerns were producing nearly two-thirds of all the flour consumed in England. The result was that in the country as a whole only one mill was grinding wheat in 1906 for every nine in 1884. The English heartland being farthest from the chief ports suffered less than seaboard regions from this commercial competition and, although many of its watermills closed, a considerable number continued operative into the 1920s when bread delivery by motor van began to encroach upon the domain of local bakeries restricted to horse and van deliveries. The number of active watermills had dropped rapidly in 1939 when large-scale steam bakeries with special flours began to monopolise the bread market. Thereafter in the English heartland a score of ancient mills managed, often with the aid of

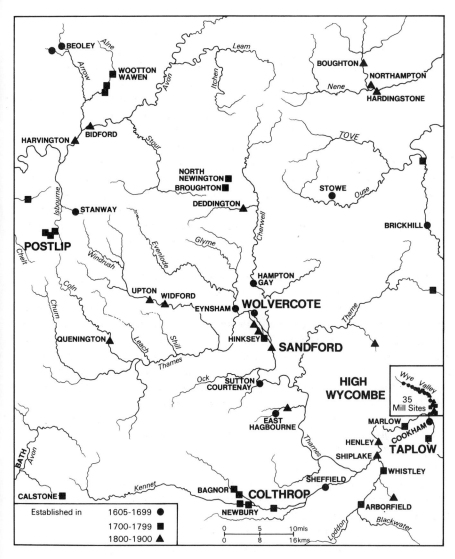

The distribution of paper mills. Existing mills are shown in large type.

auxiliary steam power, to retain some grist activities for a few years at least, and some found other uses. But the majority of the survivors were closed for ever. At Burford one mill was used to pump water to the hill-top reservoir and the other was converted to supply the town with electric lighting which at times waxed and waned from a moderate brightness to the faintest glimmer. When fire gutted the mill it was then used as a laundry. Similarly at Thame the ancient grist mill called Lashlake, which had been active with water and steam power up to 1923, fell into disuse and within a few years had become a laundry.[9]

The general fate of watermills may be judged from a survey made in 1963 by J. Kenneth Major in Berkshire where about 120 sites could be readily identified.[10] On 30 of these sites the buildings, as distinct from the leats, dams and millponds, had disappeared or fallen into an utterly ruinous state. A further 47 mills had been converted into private dwellings, a process which still continues. About 30 inactive mills had been given over to non-domestic uses such as agricultural stores, joinery, and other light industries or had been incorporated into modern factories as at Simonds Brewery, Reading. The remaining 15 watermills were either active or in a workable condition. They included several modern mills which incorporated extensive older buildings of the water-power age, as at Sindlesham, and Marsh Mills near Henley and Temple mills near Hurley. These last three, together with complete mills recently inactive, at East Hagbourne (long famous for paper making), Hamstead, Eversley New Mill, Woolhampton and River Barn at Bucklebury, were, it was suggested, worthy to be placed under preservation orders. The ultimate outcome of the survey was that five mills in Berkshire were listed as ancient monuments under Town and Country Planning Acts.

Throughout the English heartland recent changes in mill use have been to residential rather than industrial purposes; today several hundred former watermills have been converted into charming dwellings with stream-girt gardens, and with the mill leat actually beneath the building in the older structures. Often in the conversion the milling rooms have been stripped of their machinery and the waterwheel removed or allowed to decay. The names Mill Street and Mill End abound and the physical alterations of the river courses also remain visible.

Thus the watermill still forms an important feature of the landscape of the valley floors. It has also played a significant role in the life and literature of the region. The miller, although sometimes derided as a rogue in mediaeval tales, was usually a man of substance, who in many rural manors was the chief industrialist and one of the few freemen. The mill itself was inspiring to writers, artists and other viewers. On fine days its foaming tail race and overflow weir, its rotating wheel, calm mill pond and picturesque reflections provided the most exciting prospect in the cultural landscape.

Existing Mills on the Warwick Avon

The large abbey mill on an artificial leat of the Avon near its confluence with the Severn at Tewkesbury, although just outside the English heartland, is near enough to warrant a visit. A mill has stood on this site since before 1200 and was used continuously for grist until 1920. The present building is a fine specimen of early nineteenth century mill architecture and its milling machinery, driven by two large undershot waterwheels, is interesting even to the non-mechanically minded. It acquired literary fame and a new name on being made the industrial premises of Abel Fletcher in Mrs Craik's *John Halifax, Gentleman,* written in 1856 and since printed in nearly thirty foreign languages. She describes the lazy whirr of the mill 'which made a sleepy incessant monotone' and how it was built on piles in the centre of the narrow river, only a few steps of bridgework to either bank. The miller, Abel Fletcher, a stout-principled Quaker, apprenticed a little ragged boy, John Halifax, whose sterling character caused him to become owner of all and more than his master had.

The mill fell into disuse in the 1920s partly because another mill within eyeshot upstream captured the trade and even today, completely modernised, supplies flour to a wide region. Since 1965 the abbey mill, now called Abel Fletcher's, has been transformed. The building is carefully preserved as well as the two iron waterwheels but most of the interior milling machinery, apart from a main shaft or two and a fixed millstone, has been removed to make way for a spacious mediaeval banqueting room above and a restaurant below. The citizens with a touch of civic pride typical of Tewkesbury have gardened the bank below the mill race, and the river authorities have constructed a modern dam with an automatic tilting weir sill across the river opposite the mill. The whole forms a worthy conclusion to Shakespeare's Avon.

Far upstream at Guy's Cliffe near Warwick the Avon is controlled at a picturesque mill where the timber-framed and stone millhouse, rebuilt about 1750, is now joined to a younger building also of great charm. A waterwheel has been retained but the main machinery rooms have been cleared to form a restaurant. The various waterworks here show clearly, in an idyllic way, how a river in a wide vale could be harnessed for power.

Mechanically-minded readers will be glad to hear that the Avon drainage is not entirely devoid of workable watermills. At Haselor on the river Alne a short distance above its junction with the Arrow at Alcester, Hoo mill retains a remarkably complete set of milling machinery as well as its late Georgian miller's house.

Watermills on the Jurassic Wolds

Most of the numerous watermills in the north Cotswolds have been converted into delightful dwellings and few have preserved their waterwheels and interior machinery. At Donnington in Upper Swell parish near Stow, the watermill on the Dikler has been converted to a modern brewery, perhaps the smallest in England with only 17 'houses'. At Lower Slaughter, one of the prettiest villages in Britain, the mill stands beside a millpond on the Eye Brook, a tributary of the Dikler. Here flour was made until 1948; subsequently the baking has continued as a high-class confectionery with outside flour supplies. The charming millhouse is now partly the local post office. The waterwheel with its sluices, plainly visible from the village street, had two couplings, one for breast shot and the other for undershot when the pond level was low. When the water level

The Abbey or Abel Fletcher's Mill at Tewkesbury. One wheel is in the millrace to the right of the building; the other, in a derelict condition, is on the left.

dropped too low to fill the buckets a steam-engine was used to drive the machinery which still survives including two pairs of millstones. On the Coln at Bibury, Arlington mill has recently been restored in a most commendable way and is now a folk museum, re-installed with old mill machinery brought from North Cerney, containing rooms with exhibitions of farm implements, various tools and furniture from Ernest Gimson's workshop at Sapperton. It faces on one side across a lush island to the famous Arlington row and on the other to a thriving trout farm, which emphasises that one of the chief advantages of a mill was the excellent fishing in its waters.

The lower Windrush powered the densest concentration of mills in rural Oxfordshire. From just above the mediaeval bridge at Burford to the river's junction with the Thames at Newbridge, there were in the mid-nineteenth century 22 watermills, of which six were concerned solely with blanket manufacture. The bifurcation of the Windrush below Witney may well be

Blakedown watermill near Leamington.

artificial, dating largely from Saxon times. Of the grist mills, that named Gaunt was active until about 1946 and Church mill near Standlake retains in good condition one of its two separate wheels and sets of machinery. The wheel, completely enclosed within the building, is undershot with a cast iron frame fitted with wooden paddles, the overall diameter being 8ft 4 ins (2.5m).

In north Oxfordshire and the adjoining lands of Buckinghamshire and Northamptonshire, there are several surviving mills in working order.[11] That on the Evenlode at Combe is the sawmill and workshop for the Blenheim estates. An energetic local society has endeavoured to turn part of the mill into an industrial museum to celebrate Architectural Heritage Year, and hope to get the old 14ft waterwheel, last used in the 1950s, turning again. They have already fully restored a fine beam engine, installed here in the mid-nineteenth century, and have acquired the massive wooden main upright drive shaft from an old watermill at Wootton that was converted into a dwelling in 1954. Farther north in the Cherwell drainage mills at Little Barford, Adderbury, North Newington, Heyford and Kirtlington, are in full working order and can be used occasionally for private grist requirements. Flight's Mill, Kirtlington, claims to be the only watermill on the Cherwell now in regular operation for generating electricity.[12] A

The watermill at Lower Slaughter.

mill was mentioned here in *Domesday Survey* and the present name dates from about 1692 and the existing mill house from 1730. The sill or sluice provides 5ft (1.5m) head of water but the iron undershot wheel, 16ft in diameter, will rotate with only 3 inches of water against the paddles. In the 1930s the mill was harnessed with a Crompton-Parkinson generator for electricity, which provides the house with lighting, hot water and central heating. During the Second World War the old mill stones were used for grinding corn. More recently a steam engine has been installed to generate electricity when the stream is too high to drive the wheel. The construction of a new weir with three sluice gates gave the opportunity to incorporate an eel trap which in a single night during floods in July 1968 yielded one hundredweight (112lb; 55kg) of eels, then retailing at 11s. 6d. a lb.

To the east on the streams draining to the North Sea several mills survive intact. That near Buckingham at Tingewick on the upper Ouse, close to the crossing of Akeman Street and the site of a Roman villa, ceased to grind corn in 1966 and has now been renovated as a pleasant dwelling. The head of water, about 4½ft (1.4m), drove the existing steel breast shot wheel that was installed

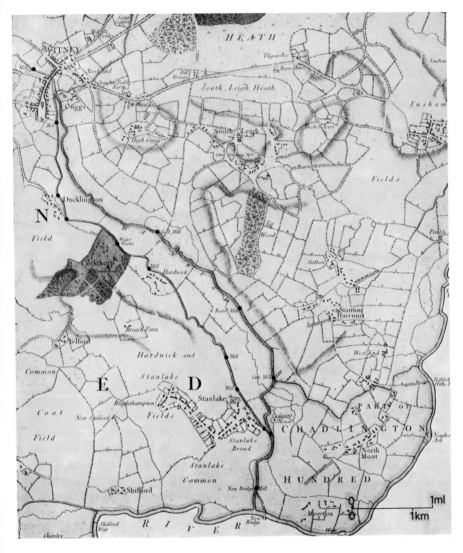

Mills on the lower Windrush in 1794.

in 1930 in place of an old wooden wheel. Electric power for the house is now generated by a water turbine set obtained from Deddington mill in Oxfordshire.

On the Ouse fine mills survive also at Maids Moreton and Thornborough near Buckingham, and in the same drainage basin, farther south, the molinologist will find near the foot of the Chilterns, at Ivinghoe, an interesting mill on display, powered by a tiny headstream of the Ouzel.

Another fascinating survival, the ultimate in watermill preservation, lies much farther north at Little Billing on the river Nene near Northampton.[13] Here connected with a large aquadrome, the mill house and mill, complete with its machinery, eel trap and relevant exhibits, have been preserved as a Museum of Milling, which in 1975 attracted 30,000 visitors.

Watermills and Navigation on the Thames

On the Thames the first waterwheel below the source was at the mill near Somerford Keynes and the last 158 miles (254km) downstream under old London Bridge where undershot wheels were used for pumping domestic water supplies from the late seventeenth century until 1817. This river, by far the longest in England, illustrates clearly the conflict between the needs of navigation and of milling. The millers constructed weirs across the channel to increase the head of water for their waterwheels and so hindered or blocked the navigation. If the mills were sited on backwaters they took, when working, much water from the main channel. For these reasons in 1065 Edward the Confessor issued a decree ordering the destruction of mills and fisheries on large rivers, and the repair of the watercourses. About this time Oxford merchants came to an agreement with the abbot of Abingdon, whereby in Lent each boat would pay a toll of 100 herrings for the right of using a new navigation channel dug through a meadow to the south of the abbey church. Although the abolition of weirs on the Thames was decreed in Magna Carta, powerful riparian owners continued to obstruct the channel and in places to charge heavy tolls. In the fourteenth century the normal upstream limit of navigation for bigger craft was at Henley; boats laden with victuals were unable to get to and from Oxford, 'as they have been accustomed to do', because the abbot of Abingdon and others had obstructed the river with weirs. By 1620 although the upper Thames was already navigable and passable for boats of 'good burdens' for many miles upstream of Oxford, barges from London could only ascend to Burcot 'within six or seven miles' of the university town. An Act of Parliament of 1623-4 appointed commissioners to tax the city and university to provide funds for making the intervening stretch navigable.[14] The citizens had great difficulty in meeting the costs, which is not surprising since the commissioners had to tackle more than 14 miles (22km) of channel, for although Burcot may be 7 miles (11km) from Oxford by road, the river actually meanders round the large greensand hill at Nuneham. A form of pound lock with 'folding doors, floodgates and turnpikes' was constructed at Culham, Sandford and Iffley, and soon the river between Oxford and Abingdon was 'full of barges and lighters'. In the late seventeenth century much stone was sent from quarries at Taynton and Upton, by road, to Radcot and thence by barge downstream to London for the rebuilding of St Paul's. But in dry seasons the navigability of some shallow reaches remained uncertain, and the favourite method of deepening them by flashing, or the sudden release of water by opening flash gates in weirs, never proved very satisfactory. In 1751 the Thames Commissioners were appointed and they and their successors, the Thames Conservancy of 1866, gradually built the succession of pound locks above Staines. The last surviving weir on the navigable channel, at Eaton near Kelmscott, was removed in 1937. Today the river is navigable for boats drawing 4ft (1.2m) to just beyond Lechlade bridge, and there are forty four locks on the freshwater course, including that at Teddington, the upper limit of tides.

The possibilities of erecting efficient waterwheels on this non-tidal stretch may be judged from its total descent of just over 231ft (70m) in a course of 125 miles (200km). On an undivided channel there could be at most about 60 mills with a 4ft (1.2m) head of water or 40 mills with a 6ft (1.8m) drop. The present locks provide a good guide to this waterpower potential: their average drop is 5ft (1.5m) but, as the river gradient varies, they range in fall from 2ft (0.6m) at Buscot to nearly 9ft (2.6m) at Sandford. Except on the upper Thames most of these locks had to be built alongside or on the sites of old mills and weirs. The upper Thames is rather exceptional as it winds slowly in a wide flat vale of Oxford clay. Here most of the villages avoided the extensive floodplain and sought gravel patches off its edge at some distance from the main channel. Many of these villages had mills on the Cotswold tributaries of the Thames as the succession of mills on the lower Windrush shows. These copious tributaries had a steeper gradient and were easier to harness than the main stream. At Eynsham the Abbey mill was on the lower Evenlode, which was cleverly controlled. Here the mill had gone over to paper making by 1686, later becoming closely associated with the Wolvercote paper mill and with technical innovations in paper production. The power available enabled James Swann to install a Fourdrinier machine about 1807; fifty years later the mill-owner, Thomas Routledge, did much to develop the use of esparto grass as a raw material in paper making. A prospectus for a share issue of 1888 describes the mill as in good working order and recently extended. Some part of its motive power came from two powerful turbine wheels driven by the Evenlode, the remainder from steam. The modern paper-making machine could turn out 25 tons of paper weekly and the average annual profits over the previous sixteen years had been £2,712 4s. 4d. The mill ceased operation in the early twentieth century and the weir now provides the water authority with a means of measuring the flow of the river.

With sites such as this available, the main river hereabouts was not harnessed in early times, and the locks were not connected with ancient mills. They are purely navigational structures that form isolated spots of gardened glory in a truly pastoral landscape. Their keepers are green fingered and, encouraged by a prize competition, turn them into multi-coloured floral islands.

The setting is quite different on the middle Thames from Godstow to Old Windsor. Here most of the locks were preceded by ancient mills and weirs and, as below Oxford the flood plain is narrower and the river more incised, hamlets could find non-floodable sites near the watercourse; often the mill stands in or close to its village and conveniently near to an inn. Upon the broad alluvial flats between Wytham and Cumnor hills and the gravel terraces on which old Oxford has expanded northward, the Thames breaks into distributaries, some no doubt largely or partly artificial. On the west the shallow, rapid Seacourt stream drove mills at Wytham (now a house), Botley and South Hinksey. The central main channel or branches from it had mills at Wolvercote, Osney, Oxford castle, Grandpont, the Weirs and Iffley.[15] The active mill at Wolvercote, once part of the endowment of Godstow nunnery, has, since the seventeenth century, been closely associated with paper making and the Oxford University Press. Its mill cut leads off the Thames just above King's Weir which was mentioned in 1189 as a trap for fish and actually remained some form of weir, with sluices that were opened to let boats pass, until replaced by the present lock in 1928. The mill had about 4ft 6ins head of water in winter and 3ft 3ins in summer. In 1885 for tax purposes its average water power was reckoned to be worth £50 a year. The waterwheels ceased to be used in 1943 and were removed seven years later. Today the large modern factory specialises in fine white papers for printing.

A short way downstream at Osney lock the wide lasher pool of the former abbey mill and its mill stream enclose a small suburb, providing a pleasant frontage to a new light industrial estate. The former mill sites at the Castle, Grandpont and the Weirs can be easily identified either by millhouses or by dams and sluices. The mill beside the castle or St George's tower was, with the fishery, held in mediaeval times half by the burgesses and half by the abbots of Osney. Eventually the citizens bought complete control for £566. At Iffley mill also the tenants had the right to catch eels and used to set down 'pudgets' below a sluice opened for that purpose which commonly yielded enough fish to pay the rent until the Thames Conservancy stopped the old custom about 1870. This picturesque mill was burnt down in 1908 and in 1924 a new lock was built at the spot, which remains a delightful terminus for the gravelled towpath from Folly Bridge, Oxford. Downstream almost within eyeshot, the Thames re-unites its distributaries into one master channel and eventually at Sandford is controlled by the deepest lock and one of the most powerful watermills on the Thames. The ancient mill, which went over to fulling as well as grist in 1219, turned to paper making with Fourdrinier machines about 1816. Some eighty years later this mill and another at Loudwater, Buckinghamshire, imported from the United States and installed the two earliest multi-cylinder board-making machines erected in England. Today, extended and modernised, Sandford mill manufactures mainly buff and coloured manilla for labels, cartridge paper and tickets without the aid of water power.

The next mill-weir-lock complex downstream is at Abingdon, 4½ miles (over 7km) away, the second largest stretch between two locks on the freshwater Thames. Here the feeder for the twelfth century Abbey mills leads off upstream of the lock and weir and goes on to enclose a flat island, once part of the abbey grounds and now a pleasant public park. The main surviving range of monastic buildings was concerned with worldly goods and manufacture and faces on to the wide mill stream. The buildings include the mediaeval granary, the long gallery, the chequer, mill house and reconstructed mill. The last named was a powerful installation with nearly 6ft (1.8m) head of water and two waterwheels, and when the great monastery was dissolved it was eagerly sought by Tucker, a clothmaker of Burford on the Wold, who in 1538 begged the king to lease to him the two fulling mills, now decayed, the floodgates, fishing, a farm and a house convenient for his occupation, whereupon he would bestow weekly during his life in wages to cloth makers in Abingdon 100 marks which should much enrich the town and keep the people from idleness.[16] To assist the royal decision Tucker offered to lead at any time twenty tall men in the King's service and to give his majesty £20 to buy a saddle. Later the mill reverted to grist only, and some animal food was ground occasionally until 1950. Today the building has been converted into the elegant Upper Reaches restaurant, part of which stands over the waterwheel housing and has glass panels providing a full view of the waterfall. Some of the old millstones and machinery have been placed against the facade and forecourt, and include a nice variety of well-worn millstones, among them one of millstone grit, another of carboniferous limestone (also from the Peak) and one composed of several pieces of silica-impregnated rock (chert; presumably from the Paris basin), bound together in the traditional manner by an iron hoop. Assuming they date from about 1860, their original cost would have been £70 for a pair of French 'burr' stones and £30 for a pair of Peak stones.

Downstream from Abingdon the mill at Sutton Courtenay still controls the whole of the natural channel and has recently been bypassed by a new cut with a lock for navigation. It demonstrates clearly the strong influence some millowners had on waterway traffic. This mill took up paper making as early as 1631, being probably the first on the Thames to do so. In the late seventeenth century its premises had four corn mills and a paper mill under the one roof, and from 1697 to 1724 it made the paper for the printing of Bank of England currency notes. In 1802 its paper mill with one house, stable and outbuildings was rented at 75s annually, and its corn mill, stable and store at 52s 8d, whereas the tolls paid by boats and barges in the previous three years had totalled £1,335, and expenses for repairs and toll collection had been only £50 annually. The proprietor was indeed a man of substance judging from his income and the magnificent pilastered mill house in the village.

Below Sutton or Culham lock the Thames winds wildly over flat claylands and the next surviving mill is no less than 10 miles (17km) downstream at Preston Crowmarsh, where two water wheels exist in one building. In this meandering stretch most of the mills are situated on tributaries, particularly on the Thame, which powers the important Overy mill near Dorchester, and on the two Mill Brooks. The Mill Brook that enters the Thames at Sutton Courtenay had eight mills on it, including the two in workable condition, at Drayton and at Upper Mill, Sutton Courtenay. The tiny Mill Brook that enters the Thames at

Wallingford drove five mills, of which that at East Hagbourne, always important, is still perfect, while that at Wallingford is a warehouse.

South of Wallingford the Thames quickens its flow where it threads its 'gorge' through the chalk hills, and mills now become frequent. Near Cleeve lock a beautiful backwater with weir, lasher and picturesque miller's house is associated with a mill that still generates electricity by its waterwheel. In close succession downstream come the sluices of the former Streatley mill facing on the Oxfordshire bank, the lock and mill at Goring, and the charming weir-mill-lock clusters at Pangbourne and Mapledurham, in a stretch made famous by Kenneth Grahame' delightful fantasies. Readers of *The Wind in the Willows* will recall how near the locks close to the bridge joining Streatley and Goring there is an old watermill with steep gables and high set dormers alongside a huddle of boat-builders' sheds. Here Rat and Mole, on leaving the main stream, 'passed into what seemed at first sight a little land-locked lake. Green turf sloped down to either edge, brown snaky tree-roots gleamed below the surface of the quiet water, while ahead of them the silvery shoulder and foamy tumble of a weir, arm-in-arm with a restless dripping mill-wheel, that held up in its turn a grey-gabled mill house, filled the air with a soothing murmur of sound, dull and smothery, yet with little clear voices speaking up cheerfully out of it at intervals'. The delightful fantasy was evoked by one of the most beautiful reaches of the Thames. At Mapledurham the mill, weir and lock adjoin a fine Tudor mansion, the fictional home of Toad of Toad Hall. Here the watermill has a Tudor timber framed core with later brick extensions, all weather-boarded beneath a half-hipped gable roof of red tiles. It has weathered into a most agreeable old age, and had Constable's father been miller here instead of at Flatford it would rightly be the most famous watermill in England. The mill had two water wheels driving four millstones, but one wheel was replaced by a turbine about 1913 to generate electricity and pump water for the estate; the other as late as 1947 was still supplying power to grind about twelve sacks of corn weekly for local use. The miller's house stands in the hamlet where its five-bay front of flints and red brick dressings demonstrates the high esteem in which the chief industrialist of a rural manor was held in early Georgian times.

Seven kilometres downstream from Mapledurham, the modern flour mill near Caversham lock faces across the river to the site of the former mill of Reading abbey. This monastic mill, which stood at the end of Abbey Street on the Holy Brook, an artificial side cut of the Kennet near its junction with the Thames, dated from about 1140 and in various modernisations, including rebuilding with iron rollers for finer flour in 1860, was in continuous use as a grist mill until 1959. It was demolished in 1965 to make way for urban development, and all that remains of the original mediaeval building is a length of masonry with three arches, one with chevron moulding.[17] During the demolition the two undershot waterwheels, 13ft 6ins (4m) in diameter, together with seven pairs of stones and the main gear were removed for preservation elsewhere.

From Reading to Windsor, mills, weirs, locks and millhouses occur at close intervals. Many of the mills are old foundations with early monastic connections; most eventually went over to paper making and continued active at least until the early twentieth century. At Sonning Eye in Oxfordshire the old mill installed iron rollers and turbines and continued producing flour until 1969. Recently its machinery has been removed, and its buildings are already derelict although well worth preserving as part of one of the most colourful and attractive mill-lock-weir-hotel clusters in England. At Shiplake and New Mills, Henley, paper making had ceased by 1910 whereas Marsh Mills near Henley produced flour until 1966 and Temple Mills near Bisham, like Marsh a modern factory with excellent older buildings, still remains active. In Hambleden parish, the Thames-side mill, recorded in *Domesday Survey* and granted about 1235 to Keynsham Priory, forms the most striking element of a noted beauty spot. At Marlow the mill ceased work in 1941 and its site is now occupied by dwellings which form the end or beginning of an exciting lock-weir footbridge that all river lovers will enjoy.

And so the story goes on to Cookham, Boulter's Lock, Bray and Clewer, each with its own history and charm, and with its surviving mill or millhouse, if any, incorporated into a bankside cluster of pleasant dwellings. These and all other mills on the Thames are best approached on foot along the towpath or in leisurely fashion by boat, but so many of them lie accessibly in lovely valley floor villages at the foot of steep wooded slopes in the chalk downs, that inevitably they also form havens of quiet for motorists. On fine days they are the jewels of the riverine landscape and at any time provide a restorative pause in an age of speed.

CHAPTER THIRTEEN

Windmills

Take care, your worship, those things over there are not giants but windmills.
(Cervantes, *Don Quixote*)

In the English heartland there are several wide areas where streams are too feeble or too variable to justify the erection of watermills or where if such mills were built they lacked adequate power to satisfy the needs of the parishioners. Chief among these regions are the summits of the chalk ridge high above the level where groundwater breaks out in strong springs, and the undulating minor watersheds in the wide clay vales, where, at some distance from the main rivers, the tributary streams rise in surface seepages that soon dwindle in time of drought. The largest lowland tracts afflicted with this lack of reliable waterpower lie in the wide hill-dotted vale northeast of Oxford and on the Feldon at the foot of Edgehill. Consequently, windmills are, or were, especially common on the windy tops of the escarpments and on isolated hillocks and high watersheds in the wider vales. For obvious reasons, they were seldom built within a short distance of a watermill, and the adjunction of the two at Edlesborough is unusual although the situation at Wardington on the Cherwell and at Doolittle mill, Totternhoe (just outside the English heartland), where the watermill carries on its roof a completely separate windmill, must be rarer still.

The earliest record of a windmill in Britain was long thought to be that in 1191 when Abbot Samson pulled down the *molendinum ad ventum* that one of his deacons, Herbert, had built.[1] But this East Anglian reference is probably preceded by one to Steeple Claydon in Buckinghamshire where, according to the *Cartulary of Oseney Abbey*, Henry D'Oilly, constable of Henry II, granted to the abbey free entrance and exit across his land at 'Claydone' to the abbot's windmill there.[2] The charter, which is not dated, presumably predates the king's death in 1189. In fact, the evidence now available suggests that there was a spate of windmill building in southern England between about 1180 and 1350 when it was halted by the Black Death.[3] For example, in Ploughley Hundred in north-eastern Oxfordshire by 1345 windmills are recorded at Bicester (two), Charlton on Otmoor, Cottisford, Launton and Oddington. At Bicester one of the mills belonged to the priory and was rebuilt or replaced entirely by a new mill in 1396-7 at a cost of £20 14s, and then farmed out for 26s 8d a year. These early windmills were constructed of timber fixed to a central post that was kept upright by means of side props or quarterbars sunk into the ground or partly buried beneath a low mound of earth.

During and after Tudor times when the population of many parishes began to recover from the ravages of civil war and plague, windmill building again became popular. Probably the oldest survivor in England is the 'beacon' or look out tower on the isolated hill-ridge at Burton Dassett north of Banbury. It consists of the two lower storeys of a stone tower· windmill (now with a conical cemented roof) and dates from the fifteenth century. About 1498 a windmill, that managed to survive until 1666, was recorded at Norham Gardens, Oxford. The first local representation of a windmill occurs in the east window of Corpus Christi chapel at Fairford church and may be assigned to about 1500.

By now the technique of windmill building had improved although not so fast as that at Burton Dassett would indicate, since this mill was quite exceptionally well built of local stone, hence its survival. Most later mediaeval windmills were wooden postmills raised upon a timber foundation of two crosstrees laid horizontally either upon the ground or resting at each end on a short pier of masonry. Near these four ends a stout timber baulk (quarterbar) was fixed so as to slope upwards and be jointed into a massive central post that was thereby kept upright and suspended just above the crossing of the crosstrees. To prevent vertical tilting of the main post its base or heel was cut into four prongs that fitted over the centre of the crosstrees. The top of the main post was fitted loosely into a massive horizontal beam (crown-tree), about which the framework of the whole mill was constructed so as to balance horizontally. Thus the complete mill rested upon the top and upper part of the great central upright and could be rotated upon it to face the wind. These rotatable timber structures were strong but were liable to damage from foundation rot and sudden changes of gale direction, as they could not be turned quickly into the wind. Not surprisingly, they were for the most part gradually replaced by tower windmills in which a stationary tower was surmounted by a cap that with its sails and windshaft could be rotated to face the wind. These towers could be much taller than post mills and provided superior storage and other facilities.

Tower mills are classified according to their building materials, which seems quite irrational as all have a rotating cap and much the same basic shape and internal mechanism. If constructed of wood with timber corner posts and weather boarding they are called smock mills because, when painted white, they often resembled a man in a smock; if of masonry, they are simply called tower mills. The timber framing of the many-sided, tapered smock mill required great skill in carpentry especially as the curb on which the cap rotated had to be level. To prevent the corner posts rotting these mills were often placed on a brick plinth but relatively few have survived, among them the fine structure at Lacey Green in Buckinghamshire.

Masonry tower mills were more durable and usually larger than smock mills. They represent the pinnacle of windmill design, and the finest examples were built in late Georgian times. Most of them survive in some form ranging from decapitated ruins to rare almost complete restorations.

By the time the tall stationary tower with a rotating cap had become the dominant type of windmill in Britain, a new improvement, the fantail, had also been introduced from Scotland. Throughout western Europe the wind changes repeatedly in direction, and millers always had difficulty in turning their sails square toward it. After 1745 many mills in Britain, Denmark and north Germany were equipped with a fantail, a small windmill fixed to the back of the cap, or more rarely to the post mill, at right angles to the main sails. This fantail was sheltered and had no effect when the main sails were head on to the wind but when the wind direction changed the fantail came under increased airflow and its small sails then rotated and turned a gear which moved the mill cap, together with the main sails, to face the wind. Although these fantails were geared low and took some time to turn the cap, or the post mill, they were quite sufficient in normal weather conditions. Henceforth the miller's main atmospheric dangers were turbulent gales and sudden wind-reversal during heavy thunderstorms, when if the cap or post mill could not be turned in time it might become tail-winded, and the cloth or shutters might be ripped from the sail frames or, more disastrously, the cap twisted off and post mills blown over forwards. In 1975 the sailframes at Brill mill, although unclothed, were damaged by hurricane-force winds. Stories of millers trying desperately to pivot their main sails at least at right angles to strong winds read like accounts of captains on schooners in typhoons.

In spite of these abnormal dangers, exposure to prevailing winds or height was essential to the success of all windmills and this frequently led to isolation which later hastened their neglect. In lowlands any small windy eminence might be utilised for them, as at Weston on the Green near Bicester, where the parishioners seized on an existing mound as a possible site for a windmill only to find that the main supports often collapsed and excavation of the mound is said to have revealed the graves of Cromwellian soldiers. Not uncommonly windmills elsewhere were raised upon artificial mounds, as may be seen at Blackthorn Hill and Bradwell. However, some of these mounds may have been old post mill mounds while others may be raised stages from which the miller could adjust the sailcloths.

The popularity of windmills reached its peak from the late sixteenth to the early nineteenth century, partly because they were cheap to erect and in parishes with old watermills did not interfere with existing water rights. In towns they provided freemen with milling exempt from manorial control. Thus at Bicester on a low, flat, cornbrash tract with feeble streams, the priory until its dissolution had its own windmill. There was also a manorial windmill. Two such mills, presumably successors of the above, existed in the parish in 1819 and one of them was advertised for sale as a working post windmill about twenty years later. In 1881 the manorial mill, the last survivor, was blown down.[4] About this time at

Thame the windmill that the citizens of the borough had erected at the end of Windmill Road was incorporated into the isolation hospital, now a farmhouse. The difference in survival is typical: the wooden structures have vanished without visible trace whereas the masonry building ensured material salvation. The result is that without detailed historical research into the records of all parishes it is impossible to tell how many windmills ever existed in any area.

The total number is surprisingly large. At the time of William Cobbett's *Rural Rides* (about 1830) some 10,000 windmills were said to be active in England. No doubt this was a gross exaggeration, typical of the deep impression lofty isolated structures have on the mind, but in Kent alone over 400 mills existed between 1596 and 1930, exclusive of replacements on the same sites. Windmills were never as abundant in the Midlands as in East Anglia and the south east, yet over 120 sites are known to have existed in Northamptonshire and about 300 in Warwickshire.[5] Although only the southern parts of these two counties lie within the English heartland well over 310 windmill sites have already been recorded in it, and continued research will raise the number considerably. By the late nineteenth century on about two-thirds of these heartland sites the mills had vanished without visible trace other than a few minor mounds and displaced millstones, and many are recalled only by names such as Windmill Hill, or merely Mill Hill, Windmill Hill Farm, Windmill Road and Windmill Inn.

Windmill Destruction in the Twentieth Century

Of the 100 windmills in the English heartland that survived until the close of the nineteenth century nearly half have been destroyed utterly either by decay, accident or deliberate demolition. Commonly their destruction was hastened by disuse and their isolation which before motorcar transport made them unattractive for conversion to dwellings. A few examples must suffice to illustrate the whole sad story.

At Nettlebed the old windmill, shown on eighteenth century maps, was replaced in 1822 by a mill brought from its original site at the escarpment foot near Watlington which had proved too low to catch sufficient wind. A smock mill, with octagonal weatherboarded sides, it stood prominently on Windmill Hill until burnt down on Good Friday night, 1912.

Misfortune also struck most of the surviving post mills. Those in Oxfordshire at Charlton on Otmoor, Wheatley and Great Milton had been destroyed by 1910. In south Warwickshire during the twentieth century post mills collapsed or were pulled down at Avon Dassett, Marton, Shrewley Common, Stockton, Upton and Warmington. The former Burton Dassett post mill shows the difficulty of maintaining exposed timber structures. Built probably in 1664 it worked until 1912 and was fully restored by the S.P.A.B. and public contributions in 1934. Twelve years later it was blown down in a gusty summer storm and today the massive main post and a crosstree lie in a hollow below the site. In

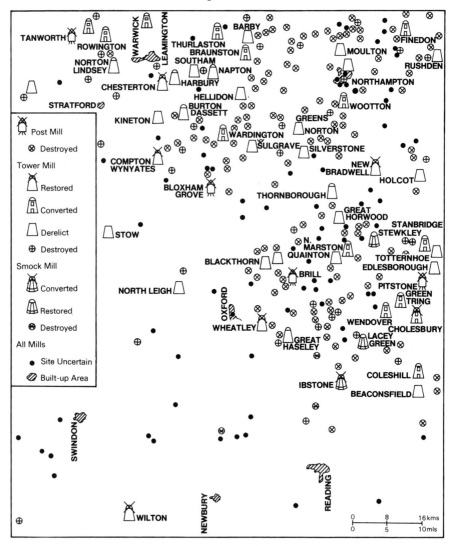

Distribution of windmills and windmill sites. The unnamed mills in the north west are Kenilworth and Packwood, both converted, and Holberrow Green partly derelict. Tanworth post mill is now in the Avoncroft Museum at Stoke Prior near Bromsgrove. The complete tower mill at Balsall Common (west Midlands) lies just north of the map.

Buckinghamshire at Cuddington the post mill, with a roundhouse protecting its post and quarter bars, was demolished in 1925. At Hillesden, the mill with six sails was destroyed in the 1930s. At Haddenham the wooden mill was demolished in 1919, while the disused tower mill survived for another decade. This order of longevity was reversed at Long Crendon where the tower mill vanished first, and the post mill, which escaped dismantling because it was on copyhold ground, did not collapse until 1930. These two localities illustrate a fascinating aspect of windmill distribution in the Midlands. Parishes on large hills commonly had over the centuries two or more windmills, the one, presumably the older, a post mill isolated on the most exposed southern slope, and the other, a tower mill erected more conveniently near the village. However, at Brill there were three post mills, and at Blackthorn eventually two tower mills.

The last great post mill in Oxfordshire was the 'giant' on top of the steep hill at Upper Arncott. It continued active into the early twentieth century but by 1925 was rotting away, with its weatherboarding so decayed as to expose the machinery and only two of its four sails, each over 2m wide and 9m long, remaining. Its post and quarter bars were protected by a roundhouse and it was turned into the wind by pressing on one end of a massive projecting beam which provided enough leverage to rotate the whole structure. Apparently its huge frame lacked sufficient tie rods or braces, for it collapsed in 1950.

The disappearance of this giant and of certain post mills with advanced building techniques must be especially regretted. The mills at Bledlow Ridge, Stokenchurch and Chinnor achieved greater vertical stability by having 3 crosstrees and 6 sloping timbers (called in other mills quarterbars) to keep the main central post upright. A strong timber curb was mounted on the top of these supports and may have helped to prevent any excessive tilt of the body of the mill. These improvements seem to have been beneficial for the Bledlow Ridge mill was not pulled down until 1933. The Stokenchurch mill, built entirely of wood in 1736, was in excellent working order in 1925, fully equipped with two pairs of millstones and four sails, two ordinary and two with longitudinal shutters. Rather surprisingly it was blown down in the following year. The Chinnor mill had been brought, mainly by barge, from Chatham in 1789 and continued in work till 1923. It had four patent sails and a fantail and its cap and massive frame survived until 1967 when it had to give way to houses. So the last post mill with three crosstrees in England was dismantled and there was talk of incorporating it and its machinery into a mill in Essex.

Tower mills also suffered many casualties during this period. For example, the red-tiled brick structure at Waddesdon, noted as the starting place in 1835 of a steeplechase won by Captain Becher, and later converted into a dwelling, was demolished in the 1930s, while the stone tower at Hornton and brick tower at Whitnash, Leamington Spa were destroyed in 1968 at a time when the British public was taking a keener interest in industrial archaeology. Perhaps it is surprising that 52 windmills still exist, in various states of preservation, in the English heartland.

Surviving Windmills

In south Warwickshire the surviving windmills included until 1969 the impressive framework of a post mill with sails at Danzey Green near Tanworth in

Arden. This has now been re-erected in the Avoncroft Museum of Buildings at Stoke Prior near Bromsgrove, Worcestershire, where fully restored it makes a splendid sight. Four of the surviving tower mills in southern Warwickshire—at Packwood, Rowington Green, Tainter's Hill near Kenilworth, and Thurlaston—have been converted into charming unconventional residences. The late-mediaeval building at Burton Dassett has been truncated to two storeys and capped with a conical cement dome and sealed up but the pleasant site is open to the public. The tower mills at Kineton and Southam are partly derelict, that at Harbury is a magnificent six-storey mill in fair condition but without sails, while those at Norton Lindsey and Napton on the Hill are well preserved although the last named has had two of its sails snapped off in a gale since its restoration in 1973. Three tower mills, at Balsall, Chesterton and Compton Wynyates (Tysoe parish) remain in perfect working order.

At Balsall Common (West Midlands) the red brick three-storeyed mill, with two common and two shuttered sails, stands on a mound in the garden of Mill House. Built in 1826, it worked by sail for over a century and is now open to the public on Sundays from Easter to the end of September.

The Chesterton mill stands isolated near the treeless summit of a minor watershed.[6] A fine stone edifice, it was built in 1632 probably both as an eye-catcher and as a working mill for Sir Edward Peyto who, with his wife, is commemorated in a delightful memorial in the parish church. It has an open ground storey with six tall columns surmounted by arches that support a floor with the milling machinery. Its cap, which is now covered with aluminium, is turned by means of a geared hand winch fixed to the framing inside it. The mill, complete with its four sails, has been restored to full working order by the Warwickshire county council and volunteers and occasionally has special working days. The nearby village has proved less enduring since its mainstay, the grand mansion built about 1650, was pulled down in the early nineteenth century. Windmill Hill Farm and only a few outlying tenements survive, among them the stone millhouse of about 1660 with a handsome three-bay front and a doorway pedimented on Tuscan columns. A diagram of the mill machinery will be found in Rex Wailes' authoritative volume *The English Windmill*.

Tysoe mill stands upon the escarpment of Edgehill about 1km north of the picturesque mansion of Compton Wynyates. A stone tower mill complete with sails, it is notable for the curb beneath its cap which instead of cogs has holes for the insertion of a pin. Two horizontal ungeared winches on either side of the tail of the cap were used to wind up a chain attached to the pin and so to turn the cap in either direction until the sails faced squarely into the wind. It is private and has recently been completely restored at the expense of the Marquess of Northampton.

The only other surviving windmill on the Edgehill wolds is a very small post mill on the hilltop above Bloxham Grove in Oxfordshire. Erected in 1869 by Herbert Warrender, a London engineer, perhaps on the site of a windmill

Chesterton windmill.

mentioned in 1618, it is complete with four sails and open trestles on red brick piers.

Farther south on the Cotswolds the abundance of waterpower in most parishes rendered windmills unnecessary. Apart from windpumps, the sole surviving windmills here are the derelict stone tower mills at Martin's Hill near Stow on the Wold and on the summit of the broad watershed between the Evenlode and Windrush at Northleigh. The latter was restored in 1932 by the S.P.A.B. but today its cap has gone and its sails are fragmentary.

Windmills become less scarce on the hills protruding above the wide clay vale east and northeast of Oxford. On Littleworth Common near Wheatley an octagonal tower mill, built of limestone with some red brick, was active with two sails only in the early nineteenth century when in addition to corn it also undertook the grinding of ochre quarried locally, the edge runners for stone grinding being outside the mill. Its cap and most of its sails had been destroyed and it was in a poor condition when restoration began in 1976. Nearby on an isolated hill at Great Haseley, another three-storeyed stone tower mill has been a well-known landmark since about 1764. It had lost its ogee cap and three of its sails and become partly ivy clad before being repaired and generally tidied up from 1975 onwards.

Great Haseley tower windmill, viewed from Great Milton, with the Chilterns in the background.

Farther north, where the steep sided hill blocks are larger, at least nine sites retain some remains of windmills that were working in the late nineteenth century. Those at Blackthorn, Great Horwood, North Marston, Stewkley (a smock mill) and Thornborough are only one-storeyed, being the bases of tall towers that were dismantled down to that height largely for safety reasons. All are built of red brick and when crudely roofed now form farm sheds, except one of stone at North Marston which has been lovingly converted with a red-tiled conical roof topped with a weather vane.

The larger survivals in this region comprise three tower mills and a post mill. On Blackthorn Hill, a four storeyed tower mill stands near the main road just east of its truncated neighbour. Strongly constructed with its lower part of white limestone and its upper part clad with red tiles, it has in recent decades lost its sails and the copper covering of its cap so exposing the interior and machinery to decay. It provides a fine viewpoint and seems a worthy candidate for complete restoration.

The same could be said of the very tall red brick tower dominating the village of Quainton from a spur of Quainton Hill. Built in 1830 as a six-storeyed red brick tower, it was nearly 21m high to the top of its metal dome cap. The mill was almost sail-less and its floors partly gone but the machinery and exterior were in a tolerable state when restoration started in 1975. Three years later the large steel-sheeted dome and sail machinery had been placed on the ground and the mill top covered in plastic. For once the great strength and weight of the massive ironwork could be fully appreciated.

Good fortune has blessed more quickly the windmill standing on the lip of the slope leading down to the Ouse and the Grand Union canal at Bradwell near Wolverton. A three-storied mill built of local stone in the late eighteenth century, it was erected on a mound and had sails nearly 8m long until they were repaired and shortened in 1950. It has two pairs of 'Peak' stones and was a trading mill that purchased grain to grind and sell as flour. Since 1974 it has been thoroughly repaired, complete with four sails and a new large boat-shaped cap, by Milton Keynes Corporation whose commendable foresight has preserved for posterity this important example of wooden machinery typical of the time before iron gearing came into common use.

For an equally complete timber windmill in this vale one has to go far southward to Brill where an impressive post mill stands on the west-facing brow of a steep high ridge. The sole survivor of three windmills on Brill Common, it lost its last companion in 1906 when Parson's mill, built in 1634, was demolished. This elevated ridge has had a windmill on it since the thirteenth century and the existing post mill probably occupies the site of a mill erected by John de Moleyns in 1345. The present structure was built in 1688, probably then to the latest designs, and remained in regular use until 1916 although latterly for coarse grains only. The need for it may be judged from the distance to the nearest watermill which is 9km away at Cuddington on the river Thame. The mill has been altered slightly during its long life but its essential features remain intact. In about 1865 a low circular brick roundhouse was added to protect the main post and its supports (two crosstrees and four quarterbars) from the weather. The whole structure was deteriorating rapidly when in 1947 Stanley Freese completely repaired it. In 1968 the main post was found to be tilted slightly out of the vertical and the Buckinghamshire County Council, now the owners, righted the fault and strengthened the mill's stability by adding a steel stanchion to each corner. The complicated nature of this seventeenth century post mill is fully discussed by Stanley Freese in his *Mills and Millwrighting* (1957) from which the following diagram is taken. The mill is open at weekends and visitors soon appreciate the skill with which the massive body was carefully balanced to be rotated horizontally on the top of the huge central post. The mill was pivoted into the wind by means of a great oaken tail pole or tiller beam attached to the massive base of the weather-boarded building and extending slantwise to the ground where its end was formerly fastened to a cartwheel. The interior machinery includes a powerful brake that could, when necessary, be applied to the windshaft to slow down or halt the movement of the four sails. The pair of millstones geared to the windshaft are intact and another millstone (of millstone grit from the Peak district) now forms a doorstep to the brick roundhouse. This post mill at Brill is not only one of the oldest in the Midlands but is unique in being close to a populous hill-top village. It overlooks a grazed common which

Brill post mill. The exposed site also attracts fliers of kites, even during clear days in summer when the hill generates its own strong breezes although the flat vale remains calm.

until recently was extensively quarried for clay. The adjacent brickworks have now been replaced by pleasant housing, and the tidy village flourishes with a wide range of services and shares with its large common at the end of Windmill Street, the enjoyment of lovely panoramic views across the oak-studded vale to the green bowl of Otmoor and beyond to the Cotswolds and Edgehill.

The chalk country in the south of the English heartland provides a mysterious blank for windmill addicts. On the rolling open downs near Lambourn and Marlborough windpumps are common and windmills rare, the only notable survivor being the tall tower mill that with its four sails and fantail and new domed cap makes a splendid picture on an isolated hill at Wilton, south of Great Bedwyn in Wiltshire. It is in full working order and is open every Sunday afternoon and Bank Holiday Mondays, from Easter to October. Yet in the wooded Chilterns adjoining the Vale of Aylesbury and Thames many windmills survive, some on the windy escarpment and most others on steep-sided narrow watersheds upon the plateau, here plastered with clay-with-flints.

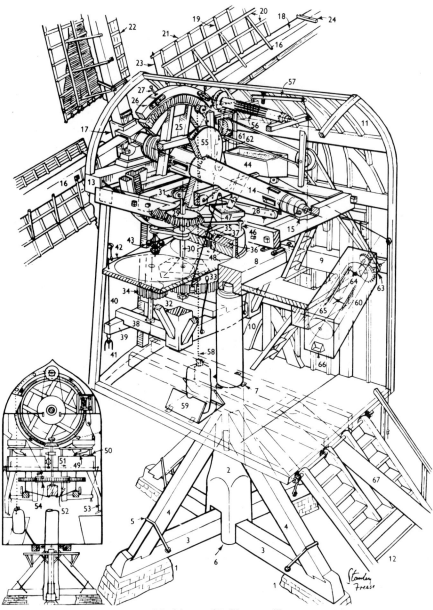

Machinery of Brill post mill.

1. Brick piers	6. Heel, or tongue, of main-post	11. Cap-ribs
2. Main-post	7. Centering wheels	12. Steps or ladder
3. Cross-trees	8. Crown-tree	13. Weather-beam
4. Quarter-bars	9. Side-girt	14. Wind-shaft
5. Retaining straps	10. Diagonal brace	15. Tail-beam and bearing

16. Sail-stock
17. Poll-head or canister
18. Sail-shaft or whip
19. Sail-bars
20. Uplongs
21. Hemlath
22. Wind-board
23. Curtain-rail
24. Sail cleat
25. Brake-wheel
26. Brake
27. Brake-chain
28. Brake-lever
29. Wallower
30. Upright shaft
31. Glut-box on spindle-beam
32. Bridge-beam
33. Great spur-wheel
34. Stone-nut
35. Cross-bar or bridge-piece
36. Upper or runner-stone
37. Rhynd or mace
38. Bridge-tree
39. Brayer
40. Tentering rod
41. Tentering screw
42. Steelyard
43. Governers
44. Grain bin
45. Great spout
46. 'Horse'
47. Hopper
48. Damsel
49. Feed shoe
50. Spring stick or 'rabbet'
51. Feed adjustment cord
52. Feed adjustment screw
53. Meal spout
54. Bell alarm
55. Sack-gear 'take off'
56. Sack bollard
57. Sack control lever
58. Sack chain
59. Sack trap
60. Dresser case
61. Auxiliary 'take-off'
62. Auxiliary gear-frame
63. Dresser gears
64. Dresser
65. Wire brushes
66. Dresser spout
67. Tail-pole

Today four windmills stand on or near the Chiltern scarp in Buckinghamshire. That at Loosely Row or Lacey Green above Princes Risborough is the oldest surviving smock mill in Britain, as it was built about 1650 at Chesham and moved to its present site in 1821. It has an octagonal three-storeyed body resting on a shallow brick base and retains most of its original gearing and equipment. It had become seriously derelict, with only one ruined sail of its former two common and two patent sweeps left, when the Chiltern Society began to restore it in 1973. The mill now makes a perfect complement to a superb viewpoint overlooking the beechwoods of the Chilterns and the farmland of the Vale of Thame.

A few kilometres northeastward at Wendover, a large six-storeyed octagonal windmill rises boldly above nearby dwellings. Stoutly built of red brick, it continued working with steam power until 1926 and five years later was converted into a house. Its imposing tower has a gallery round its upper rim and is surmounted by a large ogee cap recently re-roofed with aluminium sheets.

Still farther northeastward in Buckinghamshire, two windmills stand at the foot of the escarpment, one at Edlesborough and the other at Pitstone Green near Ivinghoe. The former is a derelict four-storeyed brick tower mill adjacent to a watermill; the latter, probably the second oldest standing post mill in England, is a mecca for molinologists. This Pitstone windmill, standing alone in a cornfield on the flat chalk platform at the foot of Ivinghoe Beacon, dates from about 1624 or 1627 and did not cease work until damaged by a gale in 1902. Some thirty years later it was presented to the National Trust and, after partial repairs, has since 1963, been completely restored by a local committee. Now it is perfect inside and out, with four common sails, a roundhouse, conventional ladder entrance and a wheel at the end of its tailpole. It is opened to the public on the afternoons of Sundays and Bank Holiday Mondays from May to the end of September and being close to the busy Icknield Way attracts many visitors who admire both the perfection of the mill and the devotion of its restorers.

It seems that in rural south Buckinghamshire the general attitude to windmills has long been friendly and practical. On the Chiltern plateau here, four tower mills that ceased work in the early twentieth century have been converted for domestic uses. At Cholesbury a tall slender brick tower, white plastered, with a green ogee cap and four white dummy sails and fantail forms a graceful part of a residence.[7] At Coleshill a red brick tower with a boat cap and the framework of a fantail is now a house. At Fulmer the lower two storeys of a brick tower, also emptied of machinery, have been battlemented and are undergoing renovation. The latest domestic conversion, at Cobstone mill near Ibstone, also demonstrates how modern transport, flexible services and panoramic views make windmills highly desirable dwellings. Here, the smock mill on the narrow crest of Turville Hill was bought in 1973 by the film director, Roy Boulting, who spent about £125,000 on restoring it and on extending and modernising the miller's house.[8] The tower, now a delightful home, is twelve sided, with a lower storey of brick, painted black, and two white upper storeys of timber, surmounted by a green copper ogee cap terminating in a torch finial. It retains the original windshaft and great spur wheel. This attractive smock mill figured charmingly in the recent film *Chitty Chitty Bang Bang* and in several shorter films, in which for effect it was fitted with four mock sails and a fantail.

Students of technology will, no doubt, regret the absence of interior machinery but without these conversions both mill and machines would eventually have vanished. Complete restoration is excessively costly yet it should still be the target of a few of the surviving derelict mills if voluntary labour were available. Although many windmills are on private land, most can be clearly seen from public roads and footpaths. The few open to the public are on or near the most beautiful rural scenery in the Midlands. The devotee of English life has much pleasure in store if he has not visited the watermills of the valley floors and the windmills on the hilltops.

CHAPTER FOURTEEN

The Victorian Reconstruction

Forget six counties overhung with smoke,
Forget the snorting steam and piston stroke,
Forget the spreading of the hideous town;
Think rather of the pack-horse on the down,
And dream of . . .
The clear Thames bordered by its gardens green.
(William Morris, *The Earthly Paradise*, 1869)

The Victorian age saw the virtual completion of enclosures and at the same time brought new life to the religion and education of rural and urban communities. This rejuvenation led to much new building and restoration in towns and villages that gave an air of well-being to agricultural counties that were in fact experiencing serious unemployment and overpopulation in purely farming districts. We will deal with the fate of the remaining common fields and forests before discussing the mansions, model villages, churches and schools that epitomise the Victorian achievement.

Final Enclosure of Common Fields and Forests

The enclosure of open fields and wastes of various kinds proceeded steadily but less rapidly in Victorian times. There were nearly 90 enclosure Awards for parts of Oxfordshire and Berkshire after 1835, the last being for Crowell (1882) and Steventon (1883). Many of these covered whole parishes but the majority aimed at tidying up or completing the enclosure of smaller parcels such as hamlets under the control of two or more parishes and meadows in which several parishes had rights of common. Most of the unenclosed hamlets were on the Chilterns, where the allocations under Awards between 1859 and 1863 included Pound Common, Christmas Common, Stoke Row and Stokenchurch. A few enclosures concerned marsh, as at Didcot, and many more affected floodplain meadows that had been used by several parishes for hay and winter feed since Anglo-Saxon times. Surviving open commons in or near boroughs also came under scrutiny and many were enclosed. At Chipping Norton the Southcombe and Great Commons were now subdivided and fenced in as also were Cowley Marsh, Bullingdon Green, Botley Meadow and Osney Mead (1853) at Oxford, much to the annoyance of students and citizens who had found them useful for horse riding.

The unenclosed forests and forest hamlets now experienced their final delimitation, so hastening a deforestation that had been active for centuries. Some of the royal forests had already disappeared. Bernwood, which once occupied the hummocky clayland between the Claydon villages and Wotton Underwood was disafforested and enclosed after 1623 and is today represented by about a dozen isolated woods. Shotover was disafforested in 1743-7 but contained many unallocated common tracts,[1] the ownership of which was sorted out by Awards of 1824 and, for the hamlet of Horspath and Shotover in Forest Hill parish, in 1858. Bagley Wood, which was part of three parishes, was enclosed in 1856.

The fate of Wychwood forest is typical of that of other royal hunting grounds in the English heartland. This vast woodland which once covered more than 102,000 acres (42,000ha) was greatly reduced by assarting and the acquisition of grazing rights by peripheral parishes especially during the twelfth and thirteenth centuries (*see* Chapter Four). In 1300 the Crown granted 'wastes' to would-be assarters and 'royal woods' were restricted to taller forest only or an area of about 50,000 acres (20,000ha) between the Evenlode and Windrush rivers from Woodstock west to Taynton. By the early nineteenth century the forest was in a poor condition with many extensive clearings and subject to much illegal cutting and widespread trespassing by pastured sheep and pigs in addition to the permitted horses and cattle. By tradition the Crown forest consisted of eighteen coppices or woods, each of which had its undergrowth cut in turn so as to give an eighteen-year rotation.

In 1791 a Commission on Woods and Forests recommended the enclosure of Wychwood, and the idea was favoured also by agricultural writers partly because of the prevalence of poaching, deer stealing, thieving and petty pilfering by nearby parishioners. The Parliamentary Award for the disafforestation of it and its purlieus was not passed until June 1857. Some 3,378 acres (1,367ha) were found to be subject to rights of the Crown, the hereditary ranger and commoners, half being in the coppices and half in the open forest; the purlieus comprised a further 3,000 acres (1,214ha). Between October 1856 and January 1858 the Crown allotment of just over 1,900 acres (769ha) was cleared of trees apart from a few stands left for shelter and ornamentation. The cost of clearing, about £6,000, was more than offset by the sale of timber, bark and cordwood worth £22,000. Seven fine new farmhouses with ample outbuildings were constructed of local stone at a total cost of £11,000. Then property and field fences were erected, water supply laid on, and the land made ready for tillage; finally 10 miles (16km) of fenced access road were made and cultivation began. The rents were high but the new farms were tithe free, and the newly created parish of Wychwood had as yet no poor needing parochial assistance. The purlieus included parts of Ascott under Wychwood, Asthal, Chilson, Crawley,

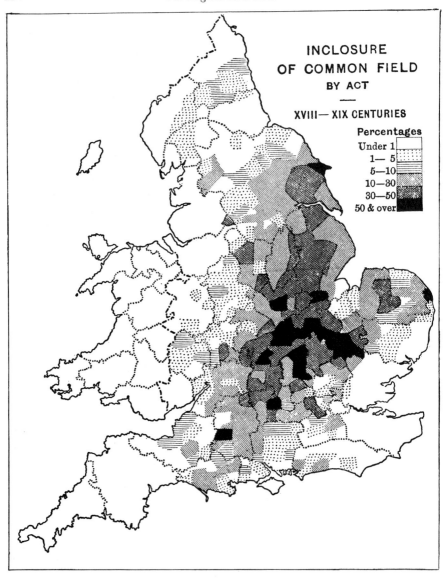

Enclosure in England by Act of Parliament in eighteenth and nineteenth centuries (from E.C.K. Gonner *Common Land and Inclosure*).

Finstock, Leafield, Ramsden, Shipton under Wychwood, Swinbrook and Widford, which were enclosed under various separate Awards between 1859 and 1863.

Today the great forest is represented mainly by woods of some 1,400 acres (570ha) incorporated into Cornbury Park estate, by a wealth of forestal place names, several parks and three or four former hunting lodges. Woodstock Park was walled in from the forest by Henry I about 1100 when he built or rebuilt its royal hunting lodge. Henry II founded New Woodstock and enlarged the lodge into a fine palace which was often used by him and later kings. The main buildings decayed in late Tudor times and after further damage in the Civil War were demolished about 1710. The ranger of Woodstock Park lived at Ditchley, in what was in Tudor times 'a low ancient timber house with a pretty bowling green'. Here in 1592 Sir Henry Lee entertained Queen Elizabeth with elaborate displays and masques, apparently so pleasing that the queen presented him with a portrait of herself standing upon a map of Oxfordshire.[2] James I stayed here three times, and his hunting skill is recorded in doggerel verse on brass plates beneath the mounted antlers of the six red deer killed. These trophies were retained when George Lee, second Earl of Lichfield, began to build a new Palladian mansion a few hundred metres away from the old in 1720. The house itself was designed by James Gibbs, but William Kent and many other famous contemporary artists worked on its richly decorated interior, which was not completed until about 1772. Recently it has been presented to the Ditchley Foundation as an Anglo-American conference centre, a use of which no doubt Sir Henry Lee would have approved, as a branch of his family emigrated in the reign of Charles I to Virginia and named their new estate 'Ditchley'. A descendant Robert E. Lee became the famous confederate general in the American civil war.

The ranger of Wychwood Forest, as distinct from Woodstock Park, lived at Cornbury Park where there was a stone and timber hunting lodge in 1337. Elizabeth granted the rangership to Robert Dudley, Earl of Leicester, who died here in 1588. In the next reign Henry Danvers, Earl of Danby, became ranger and he employed Nicholas Stone to design and supervise the building in local limestone of a new house, one of the first in rural England to have a classical facade. At the same time Cornbury Park was disafforested or placed outside the royal forest of Wychwood. In 1666-77 the mansion was greatly enlarged in a more purely classical or 'Wren' style which was widely followed elsewhere.

There was also a hunting lodge or palace at Langley near Leafield which dated from the thirteenth century and was extended after 1478 when the Crown took it over from the Nevilles. The Court stayed here as late as 1614, and the palace was not abandoned until Cromwellian times. Today its remains, including walls and a few windows, some bearing the initials H.E. for Henry VII and his wife, Elizabeth of York, are incorporated in a farmhouse.

The fate of other large forests or royal hunting grounds in the English heartland was similar to that of Wychwood. Near Towcester in Northamptonshire, Whittlewood forest has dwindled into various woods and a large park, much of which is now a wide expanse of oak-dotted meadow enclosed by iron railings and subdivided into extensive cattle pastures. Around this park strips of farm woodland and copses, served by straight roads, testify to recent

Wychwood Forest shortly before enclosure and its unenclosed purlieus in Milton, Shipton, Ascot and Chadlington parishes.

enclosure. The nearby Salcey forest is now little more than a broad circle of woods around a central clearing. Similarly Bradon or Braydon forest that once clothed the wide vale in north Wiltshire is today recalled only in place names, scattered copses and a few parks.

The great exception to the disappearance of forests in the English heartland lies along its southernmost fringes which in mediaeval times were densely wooded both on the Chilterns and in the drainage basins of the Kennet and Loddon. The whole of southeast Berkshire once formed part of Windsor forest which was Crown property in Anglo-Saxon times. These forests grew mainly on young Eocene strata such as London clay and Bagshot sands, the former favouring oak and hazel, and the latter conifers, birch and heath. In the early seventeenth century Windsor forest in Berkshire and the adjoining parts of Surrey consisted of sixteen walks, each under a keeper, and a vast surrounding

Woodland of silver birch and bracken on Bagshot Heath.

tract or *fines*. Numerous emparkments had been made as at Easthampstead and around Windsor where Little Park now forms Home Park, and Great Park and Moat Park are now incorporated in Windsor Great Park. Some other enclosures were called Rails, no doubt from the fencing round them. In the early nineteenth century the rights and properties of the Crown were more clearly defined, and after an Award of 1817 most of the broader forest was enclosed either as Crown land or as the estates of other owners. The process of enclosure of some 25,000 acres (10,000ha) was slow, and the development occurred mainly in mid and late Victorian times.

The Crown lands centred upon Windsor Castle, with its Home Park of 400 acres (162ha) and its Great Park of 4,800 acres (1,942ha). The former is private except for its northern meadows beside the Thames, while much of the latter, except the buildings, is open to visitors who can enjoy in it the finest expanse of regal landscape in Britain. The scenic features include the Long Walk that was planted with elms under Charles II in 1685 and has since 1945 been replanted with alternate plane and horse chestnut. The northern half of the park with its fine oaks and pastures stands mainly on London clay, while the southern part around Virginia Water, with its conifers, azaleas, heaths and other acidic flora lies on sandy Bagshot beds.

Ambarrow Hill near Sandhurst, Berkshire.

The same sands and gravels floor wide areas southwest of Windsor near the Blackwater and Loddon rivers. On these soils the scenery of vast tracts of coniferous woods and heaths, with shallow lakes and ribbons of villas and bungalows belongs to the London basin rather than to the English heartland. Lovers of forest walks will find plenty of access here in National Trust properties including Finchampstead Ridges, the pine-clad Ambarrow Hill, Heath Pool and Simons Wood which can be reached by way of a splendid avenue, 1,200m long, of towering Wellingtonias (*Sequoia gigantea*).

Much farther west at the non-metropolitan end of the Kennet valley near Marlborough, the cover of Eocene clays and sands peters out in small patches on hilltops before finally giving way to lofty chalk downs capped with clay-with-flints. Here Savernake forest is famous for its avenues of beech and the general beauty of its woodland glades. Covering 5,000 acres (2,000ha) within a perimeter of about 16 miles (25km), it has been a royal forest since the Norman conquest. The hereditary title of warder was held from 1083 to 1427 by the Esturmy family whose ivory horn, mounted in silver and ornamented with hunting motifs, is still preserved in the British Museum.

In 1427 the wardenship passed to the Seymours who lived at Wolf Hall just south of the present forest. In 1536 Sir John Seymour's daughter Jane became the third wife of Henry VIII and died in the following year giving birth to the future

Edward VI. During the mid-seventeenth century the Seymours emparked the southern part of Savernake forest and built a house there partly from materials removed from Wolf Hall which had been damaged in the Civil War. At the same time they probably planned a general layout for the woodland. In 1676 the wardership passed to the Bruces, Earls and later Marquesses of Ailesbury, who early in the next century began to remodel the forest in much the same way as was being done at Cirencester Park, woods being planned for commercial timber and open glades for cattle pastures. Charles, son of Thomas Lord Bruce, married the sister of Lord Burlington and no doubt under his influence began to plant long avenues of beech through the more open tracts and remodelled the house. Charles' successor continued the landscaping with some help from Capability Brown. The present Tottenham House and stables were built and furnished at a cost of over £250,000 in the early nineteenth century. A palatial Corinthian mansion, it is used today as a school and the woodland is administered by the Forestry Commission. The outstanding scenic features of the forest include several ancient oaks and a Grand Avenue that stretches for more than 3 miles from Forest Hill above Marlborough to the mansion. This impressive wide road is bordered by close-set ranks of old beech whose 'towering trunks and interlacing limbs form a vista of singular grandeur and beauty'.[3] So the English heartland, although having few woods or forests, is fortunate in preserving four exceptionally beautiful tree-lined avenues—the Broad Ride at Cirencester Park, the Long Walk at Windsor, the Wellingtonia avenue at Finchampstead and the Grand Avenue at Savernake, each with its own special qualities and each, as it happens, intended to be attractive.

Agricultural Boom and Decline

The continuation of the enclosure of open fields and of improvements in tillage methods increased the output from farms while the conversion of waste and forest to farmland raised the general agricultural yield. Rotations and crops suited to the local soils were now adopted and pre-enclosure conditions as at Kidlington where, on a large open field 'every man sows just what he pleases, which occasions such a confusion of headlands and abutments . . . as can hardly be conceived',[4] gradually became a memory in most parishes. The national yield per acre of wheat rose by 16 per cent from 1815 to 1836, and although the population of England increased by nearly 4 millions in the same time home growers supplied all the demand. During the Napeolonic wars farm prices soared and land was ploughed up irrespective of its nature. There followed an inevitable decline both in prices and extent of ploughland, especially on the clayey vales which did not begin to benefit from the production of cheap drainage tiles until after 1840. On the vast expanses of light, limey soils mixed farming, except in a few years, paid reasonably well either from livestock products or less frequently from grain.

In 1850, leading agricultural writers considered most of the English heartland

The Grand Avenue, Savernake Forest.

to be cattle and sheep country. The limestone belt had a grain-sheep economy and only the chalk downs of Berkshire and Wiltshire were grouped under a wheat-barley arable category. Livestock products were favoured by the growing home market and in some rural districts such as north Wiltshire by the coming of railways, which allowed fresh milk to be sent rapidly to London where the metropolitan dairies were decimated by a cattle plague in 1865-6. There seems no doubt that the period 1850 to about 1875, or from the repeal of the Corn Laws to the time when foreign wheat could undersell home-grown wheat even in good harvests, was the golden age of English agriculture. It was, however a less happy time for the small owner-occupier whose potential to keep stock was in practice lessened with the enclosure of commons and wastes. Farming was now more than ever dominated by landowners who subdivided their estates into suitable holdings and let them to tenants. Of all English farmers only 12 per cent lived and worked on their own estates. The incomes of landowners varied with farm rents which themselves were often tied directly or indirectly to the price of grain and malt. But land was also a fashionable investment especially in the form of a country estate, and many landowners in the Midlands had fortunes accumulated in trade, manufacturing, finance, professions and offices of state. Much of the building that was done bore no relation to local wealth; it represented the general financial prosperity of the realm and a fashion, or often a real desire, to live in rural countryside.

The distinction between wealth accumulated internally and externally is important because the golden age of farming was followed by a decline which was prolonged even if not serious enough to be called 'a great depression'. After a boom year in 1873 wholesale prices for farm products slumped and usually kept low until the late 1890s. Grains fell in price by one third and animal products by one seventh; the proportion of the national wheat consumption grown at home dropped from 61 per cent in 1870 to 27 per cent in 1880. By the end of the century wheat farming had decreased rapidly and, because low grain prices meant cheap feeding stuffs for livestock, and the growing industrial population elsewhere in England provided a ready market for fresh meat and milk, farmers went over more and more to pasture and at least to a strong animal bias. In the Vale of Evesham and near the few large towns market gardening and potato growing flourished, but the more clayey vales became expanses of greensward broken with patches of fodder crops. There were sidelines and specialities such as Aylesbury ducks, but the need for widespread grain crops was now met by the import of cheap cereals from the New World. The extreme run of corn prices and of incomes from arable estates may be judged from the parish of Westwell which lies on the edge of the Cotswolds near Burford. Here the main landowners, Christ Church, Oxford, received in rents 39s per acre in 1813, 26s in 1876 and 11s in 1894.

Victorian Mansions

Oscillations of this kind in the incomes of landowners are not represented immediately in the erection and repair of houses. Most building was financed from wealth accumulated during previous decades and, as already noticed, many of the new mansions were built from capital not acquired in agriculture. Victorian mansions were large, flamboyant and exuberantly detailed. Terms such as vulgar, misproportioned, debased and insensitive are widely used by opponents of the Victorian neo-Gothic, whereas those who tolerate or admire it see therein a pride in achievement, love of display, interest in the historic past and superb workmanship on excellent materials. There are, in fact, relatively few Victorian Gothic mansions, as distinct from additions, left in the English heartland largely because the great local landowners had already housed themselves grandly in the days of the Georgian squirearchy.

A few of the new mansions were replacements of older buildings destroyed by fire. Aldermaston Court was burnt down in 1843 and rebuilt a few years later of red brick diapered in blue in a Tudor style that was given more elaborate features in 1894. The mansion at Cliveden, the second to be constructed on the site, was burnt down in 1849 and was replaced in 1851 by a new house designed by Sir Charles Barry in what was for the time a very restrained Genoese style. An elaborate Victorian clock tower was added later. The styles became more elaborate and romantic as Victoria's reign progressed, and as increasing numbers of rich persons came to live on rural estates. Ettington Park, the chief high Victorian mansion in Warwickshire, was remodelled about 1860 in thirteenth century Gothic style in bands of yellow and grey stone in the manner liked by Ruskin. It was built for Evelyn Philip Shirley whose early ancestors lie in the mortuary chapel—formerly the south transept of the parish church—and whose family history is depicted in many reliefs in the mansion. Far north at Wroxall, the Abbey, once the home of Christopher Wren, was replaced in 1866 by a brick mansion built for James Dugdale of Liverpool. Its style is intermediate between late Gothic and late Tudor and makes ingenious use of oriel windows and columns of Aberdeen granite.

In Oxfordshire, the mansion at Heythrop was gutted by fire and rebuilt internally by Alfred Waterhouse in 1871 for Albert Brassey, son of a railway magnate but the exterior was little altered and in this county the most spectacular High Victorian houses outside Oxford are near Henley. Friar Park (1896) in the town owes much to Brighton pavilion, while Wyfold Court near Rotherfield Peppard is also constructed of red brick with yellow stone dressings and diapering in blue brick. The latter was built for Edward Hermon, a cotton magnate, to the design of a pupil of Sir Charles Barry, which is why its French flamboyant Gothic style has some features reminiscent of the Houses of Parliament. It is now the Borocourt Hospital.

In the north Cotswolds two Victorian mansions are outstanding and both are finely built of local oolitic limestone. Batsford Park was designed about 1890 by Sir Ernest George and Harold Peto in a Cotswold Elizabethan style on an E-shaped plan with a deliberate avoidance of prettiness and fussiness. Its clerk of works was Guy Dawber who went on to construct many graceful, smaller houses

Studley (former) Agricultural College, a castellar structure with Norman towers and Gothic motifs ranging from lancets to Perpendicular, designed by Samuel Beazley in 1834.

in the Cotswolds.[5] Rendcomb Park was rebuilt when Sir Francis H. Goldsmid, a financier, bought the estate in 1863. The architect was Philip Hardwick who built Aldermaston Court but now under the influence of Barry used an Italianate style. At the same time Sir Francis added to the park a new drive with bridges over the road and river, and beautified the village with six blocks of semi-detached stone cottages with barge boarding quite foreign to the Cotswolds but none the less attractive. Since 1920 the mansion has been a boys' college.

Buckinghamshire illustrates better than any other county the influence of outside wealth on a green countryside in Victorian times. The Rothschild family adopted and adapted to baronial splendour the pleasant countryside northeast of Aylesbury. Here they acquired Mentmore House that was designed by Sir Joseph Paxton and his son-in-law G.H. Stokes, with square angle towers and ornate Jacobean details. Built in Ancaster stone, it later became a home of the Roseberry family who in 1977 sold most of the contents and vacated the great mansion. In 1851 Sir Anthony de Rothschild bought a newly-built mansion at Aston Clinton and added in the village a hall and school, which remain while the great house has been demolished. The Rothschilds went on to acquire a timber-

Toddington Manor in the Vale of Evesham. Built in 1819-1835 and noted for its elegance, it was one of the last important wholly Gothic mansions.

framed house of about 1606 at Ascott which they greatly enlarged after 1874. Enlargements were also made on a separate estate nearby in the extensive grounds of Eyethorpe Park. Then Halton Park near Wendover was built in 1884 in a freely modified French chateau style with rich interior decorations, especially of white and gold in the central hall, which eventually graced the Royal Air Force. Still greater additions and alterations were made at Waddesdon which Baron Ferdinand de Rothschild bought as an empty estate in 1874. Within less than two decades the hilltop site had been levelled, formal gardens laid out and extensive tree planting completed. A French architect, Hippolyte Destailleur, devised a grand mansion resembling a chateau in Touraine (French Renaissance style) and embellished it with fine details outside and superb furnishings within. The beneficence was then extended to the village with estate housing, some of it half-timbered, together with hotel, almshouses, assembly hall, club and reading room. The mansions at Waddesdon and Ascott were later given to the National Trust and with their exquisite furnishings, gardens and grounds rich in unusual trees are open at certain times to the public. A full catalogue of the Waddesdon collections in fifteen sumptuous volumes is in course of publication.

Model Villages and Estate Housing

The large Victorian house gave employment to numerous indoor servants, gardeners and outworkers. Where its owner also ran a large estate he was responsible for many or most of the houses in the nearby village. Since the mid-eighteenth century the cottage had been the subject of improvement on several estates and now in Victorian times it became a veritable stylistic battleground, an integral part of the planning of a well-run property. It is no exaggeration to say that except in districts where cheap building stone and small farmers were or had been common, a large surviving part of many villages dates only from Victorian times.

The average workman who happened to own a cottage had nothing or little to spend on repairs and improvements. From 1850 to 1872 agricultural wages in Midland counties rose by 50 per cent, and some farm labourers benefited from the provision of allotment gardens, village schools, reading rooms, cottage hospitals and such fringe benefits, but the inadequacy of wages may perhaps be judged from the attempts to force landowners to raise them.[6] In 1872 Joseph Arch formed the National Agricultural Labourers' Union in face of bitter opposition. A mild, reasonable man, he was born at Barford in 1826 and died there, aged 92. Recently the 'Red Lion' has been re-named the 'Joseph Arch', an honour which in rural communities ranks above knighthood and canonisation.

Employment afforded by agriculture dropped rapidly throughout Victoria's reign partly because of mechanisation and partly because of falling prices and decreasing arable after 1873. Many workers migrated to manufacturing districts and abroad and in numerous rural parishes the population began to decline from 1840 or 1850 onward. There was an appreciable movement into the nearest towns, notably those with workhouses and railway workshops, but the chief salvation from permanent rural poverty was seen in the manufacturing north, in London and in the new lands being opened up overseas. At the censuses in 1851 and 1861 migration was so important that it was specially mentioned in at least 72 parishes in the English heartland. Typical entries record the departure of several families from Long Crendon to seek employment at needle manufacturing at Redditch, of plush weavers and families moving from Adderbury to Coventry, the home of silk power-weaving, and of no less than 40 families from Wootton to find work in Sheffield. In the same period at least 24 parishes experienced notable emigration. This had been an extreme method of countering poverty for many decades. At Bicester in 1830 an emigration committee organised free passages to the United States by borrowing £1,000 from the local rates. Seventy one adults and forty children were conveyed in wagons to Liverpool but some changed their minds before sailing and worked their way back to pauperism in Bicester. In the following year, Finmere ratepayers financed the emigration of several of its families to New York. The movement of both domestic and international migration was favoured by cheap

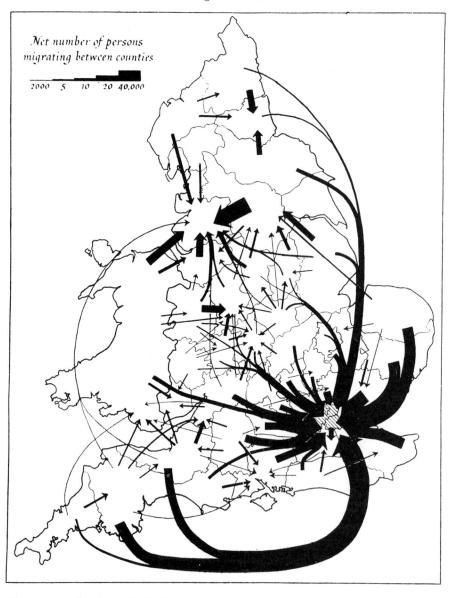

Net number of persons migrating between counties

2000   5   10   20 40,000

Inter-county migration in England, 1851–1861. Notice the strong movement to Birmingham, Coventry and London.

railway travel and by faster steamship crossings. In the 1850s the Bicester board of Poor Law guardians helped people from Lower Heyford to go to Canada and from Launton to go to Australia. On 23 December 1873 a party of 500 labourers and their families, including groups from Milton under Wychwood and many other Midland parishes, set out from Plymouth under the leadership of Christopher Holloway of Wootton near Woodstock. Their steamship, the *Mongol* of 2,252 tons and 400 h.p., arrived on 13 February 1874, and eventually the settlers went to Dunedin in the South Island. Holloway acted as an emigration agent and was a prominent member of the National Agricultural Labourers' Union which in time succeeded in raising the basic wage of farm labourers from 11s to 14s a week. Not all the emigrants arrived safely. A memorial on the tidy village green at Shipton under Wychwood remembers the 17 parishioners (five families) who perished with 400 others when the *Cospatrick* was gutted by fire off Tristan da Cunha on her voyage to New Zealand on 17 November 1874.

With such low wages farm hands with freehold or copyhold cottages lacked cash to improve their homes beyond the state of essential repairs while landowners in times of low rents were equally unable or unwilling to spend heavily on tenants' houses. Consequently in many rural parishes most of the labourers' dwellings were grossly overcrowded and left much to be desired. The years of prosperous farming from 1850 to 1870 saw widespread efforts to improve the homes of tenants. When Shipton on Cherwell parish was put up for sale in 1862 its vendors could boast that the land had been drained recently at a considerable expense and a bailiff's house, school house and several cottages lately erected. At Westwell, a small village on limestone suitable for building, the labourers' cottages were so decayed in 1855 that the rector asked Christ Church, the proprietors, to remove the worst and repair the others. The repairs consisted largely of propping up the roofs and adding a back door and a new privy. A few years later the rector requested that two dwellings unfit for habitation be replaced by cottages 'of a superior order, with a view to the encouragement of habits of decency and self-respect'. By 1869 Christ Church had pulled down four cottages and built two new ones which still adorn the village. There was, however, a long way to go to modern standards and in 1884 the diligent rector suggested that the two-roomed labourer's cottage set aside for the schoolmistress was 'quite unsuitable for a modern certificated mistress'.

In a time of acute rural unemployment and falling population numerous farm labourers' cottages became ruinous and landowners frequently found, as did Christ Church, that it was preferable to build a few new cottages rather than patch up the many old. As with Victorian mansions much of the finances for rebuilding the humbler dwellings came from outside sources. On the less backward holdings the idea grew up of beautifying all the buildings on the estate, especially those visible to visitors. The richer long-established squirearchy now vied with wealthy newcomers in the embellishment of mansion and cottage alike. The model cottage, model farm and model village go hand in hand with new mansions, agricultural improvements and often with a genuine sense of benevolence of landlord toward his tenants.

The largest example in the English heartland is Bear Wood in Berkshire

Bear Wood House near Wokingham.

where the Walter family of *The Times* acquired an estate of 7,500 acres (3,000ha) that included the villages of Finchampstead, Barkham and Sindlesham. In 1864 the third John Walter began to erect here, in a French Renaissance style, a huge mansion of brick with stout limestone dressings.[7] The woodwork was fashioned in the estate workshops and the red bricks from clay dug and baked locally. The landscaping included the extensive planting of conifers and hollies and the girdling of a large lake with rhododendron shrubberies. Five years later, when the mansion was completed, lesser buildings on the estate and cultural facilities in the whole neighbourhood received attention. For example, Walter built schools at Finchampstead, Sandhurst and Wokingham and the church of St Paul at the last named town. Perhaps the most charming addition was the model estate village at Sindlesham, with its school, inn and gabled cottages of red brick, diapered in black.

Elsewhere in the Midlands model estate housing is far more common than is generally believed and many favourite villages have had more than a touch of nineteenth century beautification. In Oxfordshire the chief local architect was William Wilkinson (1819-1901), son of a Witney family of builders and auctioneers, who became well known for his work in towns, particularly the

Victorian cottages, bailiffs' houses and model farms in the country. In rural areas he favoured a subdued Gothic style that according to his *English Country House* was suited to an English landscape. His influence may be seen on many estates in cottages of local stone, with, where possible, stone-slated roofs, constructed to generous proportions, as he often allowed on the ground floor an extra room for aged grandparents. A widely popular design for a model farm, complete with farmhouse, offices, stables, outbuildings and covered yard, may be seen, for example, at Chasewood Farm near Hailey, built in 1874 at a cost of £3,000 for the Duke of Marlborough.

Wilkinson also built farmhouses as far afield as Whittlebury in Northamptonshire, but the most notable series of farm lodges in this county was erected in the 1840s by another architect on the Duke of Grafton's estate in the parishes around Towcester. Here scattered over a wide area are at least ten fine farm lodges or houses of a Regency pattern, each with three widely-spaced bays with low-pitched roofs and lower wings, and some with a pedimented gable or doorway.

These isolated rural houses tend to attract less attention than planned groupings of dwellings, such as rows of cottages and model villages usually placed conveniently near a main road and not far from a lodge at the entrance to an estate. Examples abound, as at East Lockinge with its rows of pairs of high-gabled brick cottages of about 1860 and at Stockcross (just west of Newbury) with its pairs of pretty thatched cottages of brick and half-timbering built about 1900. The irregular grouping of new dwellings around a green is rare, the most picturesque example being Sulham (near Pangbourne) where about 1838 a delightful model estate village was laid out with a church of flint and stone and half-timbered cottages, some thatched, some slated, and with generous barge boards and wide eaves in a 'Swiss revival' style. At Buscot in 1897 Lord Faringdon built a model village of stone Cotswold-style houses, enhanced by a well with a pillared, gabled cover and a parish hall surmounted by a cupola.

In Wiltshire, a charming model village exists at Hilmarton (near Wootton Bassett) where the Poynder estate built plain cottages of cut stone in the 1830s and added rock-faced, gabled cottages and almshouses in the 1870s. In Oxfordshire, Cottisford, Hardwick, Churchill and many other villages show clear evidence of Victorian estate planning. At Mixbury near Finmere in the northernmost fringe of the county in 1800 the cottages were 'huts with here and there an upper room reached by a ladder'. Not surprisingly many were occupied rent free. Fifty years later the squire who owned the whole village and half the parish was old, non-resident and utterly neglectful of his property. In 1874 by order of the Court of Chancery the dilapidated cottages—thatched and of local limestone—were replaced by about forty semi-detached houses built of coursed rubble with red brick dressings, which with the lime trees newly planted between them, gave, and still gives, 'a neat and attractive appearance'. The population of the village reached its maximum of 402 in 1851 and then decreased steadily under the influence of agricultural unemployment and casualties in World Wars to a minimum of 184 in 1951.

Estate housing is equally common in southern Warwickshire. On Alscot Park, a property acquired in 1749 by James West, joint secretary to the Treasury, many pleasant red brick, Tudor-style gabled houses with diamond-leaded window panes were built about a century later at Alderminster and Preston on Stour. The latter village has a core of old timber-framed dwellings and is considered one of the few 'unspoilt' villages in the county. Nearby on the Foss Way, the hamlet of Walton was refashioned to the designs of Sir George Gilbert Scott who replaced the existing hall by a large stone mansion (1858-1864) in a late thirteenth century style and proceeded to replace all the cottages in his own Victorian idiom. Another fine example of a model village exists at Sherbourne (southeast of Warwick), where the beneficence of the Rylands, a wealthy Birmingham family of wire-drawers, transformed the village by adding a magnificent church and pleasant houses of brick with carved bargeboards, Tudor-style chimneys and half-timbering. In 1881 a Tudor Gothic school completed the scene which today with its neatly clipped yew hedges and general tidiness forms another testimonial to enlightened estate planning.

The reader may well wonder what happened to villages which were not attached to a large estate, and which had many small freeholders. The answer is that frequently they grew in population and acquired new houses, often of mediocre or poor quality, while the estate village declined in population and improved in housing conditions. Before the Union Chargeability Act of 1865 estate owners, already with a surplus of agricultural labourers, did not want newcomers who might become paupers. Such villages have been called by historians 'closed' as distinct from 'open' villages where the numerous small property holders did not deter new settlers.[8] In Oxfordshire by the mid-nineteenth century most closed villages were stagnant or declining in population whereas, according to the Poor Law Inspector, in 86 open parishes there had been a net increase of 1,352 cottages in the decade previous to 1849. Many of these new houses were small, poorly constructed, almost or quite gardenless, and built to rent by small landlords. Closed and open parishes or villages were often in close proximity. The estate-dominated Middle Aston decreased in population, while at Steeple Aston where about 100 cottages were owned by 25 different proprietors in 1869, newcomers were admitted. The same contingency existed at Sandford St Martin and the nearby hamlet of Middle Barton. Sandford St Martin is a charming village with some houses of Tudor age. The east side of its main street, nearest the park, was partly rebuilt between 1849 and 1880 by Edwin Guest, the master of Gonville and Caius College, Cambridge; the west side, nearest the manor, was improved by his ally and friend the Rev. Edward Marshall who made houses fit for villagers. At the same time the population of the village declined and several surplus houses were removed. Sandford became widely popular in the 1920s and today its marlstone walls, flowery gardens, landscaped eighteenth century park, manor house of about the same date with a multi-gabled Victorian facade, lych gate and village cross exude a charm that speaks of success and content.

Some people from Sandford migrated the short distance to the hamlet of Middle Barton where land could be had and houses rented in a community of many smallholders, some often absent, and where possibilities existed of squatting alongside the Bicester-Enstone turnpike.[9] By 1869 Middle Barton consisted of over 150 cottages owned by about 40 different landlords few of whom could rank as farmers. Of its young men no less than 30 were unemployed and supported by the Poor Law Union, a condition which the two main proprietors at Sandford St Martin had carefully avoided in their village.

The visitor will readily recognise the visual contrast between villages in closed and open parishes but may easily miss a rarer type of estate planning, the land schemes of the Chartists. Here the driving force was a socialistic land company intent on promoting self-reliance and a return to smallholdings. It was the practical expression of Chartism (1838-1850) which aimed at universal suffrage, vote by ballot, social equality, adequate clothing, food and drink, and a good house to live in with a garden. With this in view, a National Land Company directed by Feargus O'Connor was formed and on 1 May 1847 O'Connorville in Hertfordshire was opened to tenants who had been selected by lot from subscribers to the fund. Feargus in his *A Practical Work on the Management of Small Farms* (1843) ingeniously blinded his readers with science. Three acres, disposed one third under potatoes, one third wheat and the rest under cabbage, roots, tares, clover, flax and kitchen vegetables, would, he reckoned, produce enough to keep a family, two cows and six fatting pigs, and provide a surplus for sale equivalent to an overall credit balance of about £44 yearly. One acre of potatoes alone would, said the Irishman, yield 15 tons of which 2 tons would be fed to two cows in the colder months, 1½ tons to the family, 8 tons to six pigs and 3½ tons sold for £14. Feargus apparently did not realise that a milking cow does not give milk for a whole year, and if fed on potatoes would yield an unpalateable liquid or more likely die of diarrhoea. The subscribers also seemed unlearned in simple agricultural lore, for the money poured in, and by late 1847 about 42,000 shareholders had provided a paid up capital of £80,000. Eventually the number of subscribers nearly doubled, and the Company acquired four new estates which were divided into plots of 2, 3 or 4 acres, each plot being provided with a house and access road, and fenced and ploughed before being allotted to a lucky shareholder. Three of these estates, Lowbands near Redmarley d'Abitot; Dodford near Bromsgrove; and Minster Lovell near Witney, were in the Midlands. At Dodford the stiff red soil of the Keuper marl, although not well suited to intensive cultivation, proved ideal for strawberries which with tree fruits, vegetables and poultry afforded a reasonable living. The pull of industrial wages, especially in motor car factories, upset the smallholding subsistence in the 1920s and twenty years later the plots were eagerly sought for

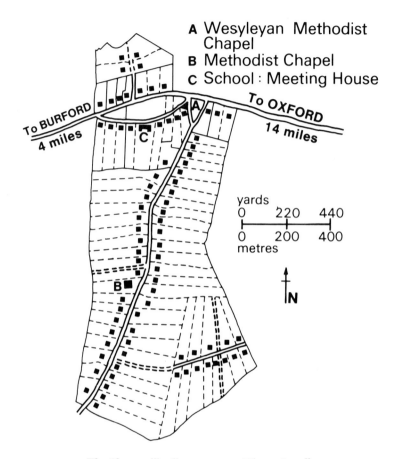

A Wesyleyan Methodist Chapel
B Methodist Chapel
C School : Meeting House

To BURFORD
4 miles

To OXFORD
14 miles

yards
0   220   440

0   200   400
metres

N

The Charterville allotments near Minster Lovell.

homes by non-agriculturalists. Today, as at Lowbands, the scheme is still distinguishable by its square road pattern and square fenced orchards and gardens but the subsistence ideal has faded, although a few skilled smallholders still make good on combined plots.

Charterville at Minster Lovell was the largest of the National Land Company schemes. Its farmhouse and 297 acres were bought for £10,878 and, after the homestead and 44 acres had been profitably resold, the remaining 250 acres were split up into 34 holdings of 4 acres each, 16 of 3 acres and 30 of 2 acres each. One storeyed cottages solidly constructed of local stone were built at a cost of £120 each. When the Land Company was declared an illegal lottery and dissolved by Act of Parliament in 1851 some of the Charterville smallholders had not paid their rent charge of 5 per cent on the original outlay, and O'Connor raged against them and obtained powers to eject them with a view to selling the estate. However, bona fide purchasers were not disturbed, and the colony made a reasonable, if hard-earned, livelihood mainly from sales of potatoes and livestock. Over the years the number of owner-occupiers gradually declined to 33 in 1889 and 26 in 1914 when there were 43 other occupants. So this scheme on the limestone plateau above the Windrush valley had provided work and homes for several scores of people on an area that would otherwise have employed a handful of farm labourers. The compact small stone bungalows, with the communal meeting house and school, widely spaced in rectangular plots along the main highway and side roads, remained virtually unaltered until the 1940s when a few of the occupants still kept stock on their smallholdings. Recently some of the cottages have been enlarged or rebuilt and part of the estate has been fronted with a semi-circle of new bungalows but the original Chartist plan survives with remarkable clarity to recall the time when a popular idea of an earthly paradise was 'three acres and a cow'.

Victorian Churches

By the nineteenth century most older churches were in need of extensive repair and restoration and this maintenance work was, and still is unless outside grants are available, a heavy burden on parishioners and estate owners. In addition in many newly developed parishes and hamlets, as in the former 'forest' lands of southern Berkshire, completely new churches were needed. Under the stimulus of a strong religious revival which aimed at taking the church to the people, the Victorians undertook those tasks with a remarkable vigour and thoroughness.

The English heartland played a leading part in both the religious change and in church building. The Oxford Movement germinated in the lower Coln valley. Many generations of the Keble family had been lords of the manor of Eastleach Turville, and John Keble senior was vicar of Coln St Aldwyn and lived in Fairford. His son, John, became curate of the twin Eastleach villages and of Southrop and it was in the rectory at Southrop that he and his friends began the Movement about 1825. Here too he wrote *The Christian Year* which between 1827 and his death in 1866 went into nearly one hundred editions. By then the Church of England had experienced a tremendous rejuvenation which flourished in Oxfordshire under Samuel Wilberforce, bishop from 1845 to 1869. During his episcopate many new churches and parsonage houses were built, several new parishes created and a wide programme of church restoration completed.

Most of the leading architects of the Gothic revival are well represented in churches repaired or built in the English heartland during this religious upsurge.

A.W. Pugin (1812-1852) had more influence than his few local buildings would suggest. He was responsible for the Catholic church of St Peter's, with school and schoolhouse at Marlow and for the small Anglican church at Tubney which cost only £649, including the coloured glass in the windows by the Hardman firm of Birmingham, the chief suppliers of coloured glass in Victorian churches.

Pugin's persuasive writings and illustrations strongly influenced George Gilbert Scott who was born in 1811 at Gawcott (near Buckingham) where his father was vicar, and in 1827 had designed the church in a Georgian classical style. After an apprenticeship in London, Sir Gilbert, as he later became, pursued a very active career for over forty years during which he 'built or interfered with'[10] nearly 500 churches, 39 cathedrals and minsters, 23 parsonages, 25 universities and colleges, 25 schools, 43 mansions, 26 public buildings and 58 monuments. In the English heartland he shared responsibility for Reading jail (1842-4), a battlemented castle in red brick, and then went fervently Gothic and set out to represent Tractarian ideas to the public. He did much work on Oxford colleges and at Buckingham where a street is named after him. On a parochial scale, he is at his best at the relatively austere church at Leafield (1860-74) and in the brick, flint and timber-framed parts of Bradfield College of the 1850s. His theme is seen to perfection at Sherbourne (1862-4), where at a cost of £20,000 he built a large sumptuous church of varied high-class materials. Today, still in perfect condition, it stands in an idyllic setting on the Smith-Ryland estate, surrounded by a tidy churchyard and facing across green fields to the deserted site of Fulbrook Castle.

Scott's chief architectural rival was William Butterfield (1814-1900), a confirmed bachelor and devoted Tractarian who restored the church at Cirencester and numerous other places, including Middleton Cheney where the Geometrical windows were later filled with beautiful coloured glass by the William Morris firm. Butterfield became famous for his vigorous and arresting use of Gothic shapes and brilliant colours. His polychromatic edifices of great originality include Keble College, many buildings at Rugby School, where his influence extended to much of the adjoining townscape, and, at the lesser end of the scale, the small church at Horton cum Studley, a microcosm, inside and out, of brilliant patterns in yellow, red and blue. He was often equally individualistic when working entirely in local stone as may be seen at Milton near Bloxham, an early church of 1856 and at Poulton nearly twenty years later.

George Edmund Street completes the trio of prolific mid-Victorian architects in the English heartland. He served for five years under Sir Gilbert Scott and early acquired an ingenious use of varied materials in a freely adapted Gothic style. A devoted Tractarian, he was attracted to live at Wantage from 1850-2 by the Rev. William John Butler, who was so High Church that his curates had to wear top hats and cassocks. Butler founded (in 1846) the Wantage Sisterhood, now with daughter houses in many countries, as well as a big school, a convent and two retreats. In a few years he had caused a vast transformation in the appearance and morals of the town 'rescuing it from its demoralised condition . . . and making it a model centre of church work'. Street designed many of the new buildings and skilfully extended the parish church. From 1852-1881 he served as official architect for the Oxford diocese and was responsible for the building, restoration or extension of numerous churches, schools and schoolhouses. Among his powerful designs is St Philip and St James (1862-6) in Victorian north Oxford. Built in a freely-adapted thirteenth century style, its exterior is of white limestone set off with bands of red sandstone while its interior includes polished pink granite columns and black marble shafts, all of which indicate how railway transport allowed Gothic Revivalists to revel in the glory of different stones. Street's church designs also show to advantage at Milton under Wychwood and at Westcott near Waddesdon, the latter an austere building with stone exterior and pale pink interior. It is often said, no doubt rightly, that he allowed some disastrously destructive restorations and overburdened some of his work with insensitive detail, but at Wantage his extensions seem perfect and at Hampnett near Northleach his restoration of a Norman church seems impeccable, even if one's judgment is favourably biased by the painting of the chancel by the vicar.

There were several other well known Victorian architects such as John L. Pearson (1817-97) who designed Freeland and Daylesford churches; T.G. Jackson who rebuilt much of the pleasant church at Bourton on the Water; Sir Arthur Blomfield who worked at Adwell, Ramsden and Heythrop; and Henry Woodyer (1816-96), a pupil of Butterfield, who was responsible for Christ Church, Reading and St Paul at Wokingham with its elaborate tracery and artistic font. But details of these and of public Victorian buildings in towns are now readily available although we cannot refrain from advertising Edward Godwin's town hall at Northampton which was strongly influenced by Ruskin's *Stones of Venice,* and has an impressive sequence of reliefs of the town's history.

This love of the past and of romantic or chivalrous deeds permeated Victorian life, and makes it hard to understand why some of the restoration and alteration in churches was carried out as much from conviction as from necessity. Undoubtedly a vast amount of repair and tidying up was needed but in some churches too much of historical interest was being destroyed, and inevitably opposition arose against overzealous restorers. The reaction found eloquent leaders among the pre-Raphaelites led by William Morris of Kelmscott, so the same district that gave rise to the Oxford Movement became the cradle of the Society for the Preservation of Ancient Buildings.

Burford church figures large in this revolt against the removal of the more awkward incrustations of many centuries. Its interior furnishings and fittings were rearranged in the early nineteenth century and again in the 1870s to plans by G.E. Street, with new seats, some heating apparatus, new flooring and new pulpit. In 1876 William Morris, when on his way to visit his friend Cormell Price at Broadway, passed through Burford and stopped to see the church. He was

The church at Barford largely rebuilt and heightened in 1844 at the expense of Miss Louisa Ann Ryland who also financed the building of the fine new church and estate house just across the Avon at Sherbourne. Elizabeth Stevenson (Mrs Gaskell) remembered vividly in later life the little, low-towered Norman church that she attended when at Miss Byerley's school in Barford from 1822 to 1824.

shocked at the interior renovations, especially at the hideous new tiles in the chancel, and at Broadway Tower wrote a letter which, through the agency of the Athenaeum, led to the foundation in 1877 of the Society for the Preservation of Ancient Buildings with the motto 'Protection instead of Restoration'.[11] Morris became its secretary. He had been articled to Street and never lost his architectural leaning. When an undergraduate at Exeter College, Oxford, he had seen the destruction of its mediaeval chapel and the start of its replacement with the present incongruous structure designed by Sir Gilbert Scott in the shape and style of the Sainte Chapelle, Paris. We must add that at Burford, the vicar, the Rev. Anthony Cass, considered that renovations were necessary and, annoyed at outside criticism, is said to have told Morris, 'The church, sir, is mine and, if I choose to, I shall stand on my head in it!'. The S.P.A.B., unconcerned with clerical athletics, soon called in question all Sir Gilbert Scott's theories and stemmed the flood of the drastic Victorian clean up. Eventually it saved, and still saves, from decay or destruction a large number of interesting buildings which otherwise lack finances adequate for repair and maintenance.

Victorian Schools

The mid- and late-nineteenth century were outstanding periods for the foundation and building of schools. At the lower levels of education were the various village schools, some complete with schoolhouse and built of the best local materials to the design of the diocesan architect. Several hundreds of these 'church' and 'charity' schools survive, either still used for teaching or, in villages where the children now go daily to larger schools nearby, converted into private dwellings.

For secondary education, and indeed for any form of education, people with money enough sent their children to private establishments or to grammar schools. Scores of academies and tutoring hostels provided board and tuition for young ladies and gentlemen. These were established widely both in towns and in villages where in some places the vicar provided learned assistance. Avonbank School near the entrance to Stratford upon Avon parish church was such an establishment. Here young Elizabeth Cleghorn Stevenson was educated.[12] Later, as Mrs Gaskell she began her literary publications with a chapter on Stratford in William Howitt's *Visits to Remarkable Places* (1840). The account includes Clopton House (3km to the north) which the schoolgirl visited and which is today, with its Elizabethan courtyard and associations with Shakespeare and the Gunpowder Plot, still open to the public. A year after Mrs Gaskell's death in 1865, Avonbank School was demolished which seems an unworthy fate for the seed bed of the author of *Mary Barton, Cranford* and *North and South*.

These academies for ladies and gentlemen bloomed and faded like flowers in spring, and the mainstay for secondary education was the old grammar school founded by potentates, gilds or burgesses to serve local needs. Several of these ancient schools, such as Warwick (914), Abingdon (1256), Eton (founded by Henry VI in 1440), Magdalen College School, Oxford (1478), Reading (re-founded in the Hospital of St John in 1486) and Chipping Campden (1487) survived the Reformation. Many more were founded soon after the suppression of chantries in 1547, among them Thame (1558), Rugby (1567), Burford (1571) and Wantage (1597). Burford will exemplify the high quality of these burghal societies and schools. Its seventeenth century pupils included Peter Heylin (1599-1662) and John Wilmot (1648-80). Heylin, who went on to become a fellow of Magdalen College, a Doctor of Divinity and to be buried in Westminster Abbey, wrote his famous *Cosmographie* (1652) at Minster Lovell after he had lost his library and other possessions in the Civil War. Wilmot, later Earl of Rochester, attended the school from his home at Ditchley and moved on to Wadham College and after 1667 to Adderbury House. He achieved considerable acclaim as a satirical wit and poet and his many memorable verses include the following *Epitaph on Charles II*:

> Here lies our sovereign lord the king
> Whose word no man relies on
> He never said a foolish thing
> Nor ever did a wise one.

After periodic decay in Georgian times, the Victorian age brought renewed prosperity to these old grammar schools, many of which were extensively enlarged to take boarders. Rugby, for example, flourished and expanded rapidly under Thomas Arnold (1828-42) and Dr Temple (1857-69) in spite of, or perhaps because of, Thomas Hughes' account of his life there in *Tom Brown's Schooldays* (1857). These older foundations were now joined by numerous new establishments mostly aimed specifically at high class education in boarding houses. In the English heartland the lead was taken by Sibford Ferris (Society of Friends, 1842) and by Cheltenham which in the 1830s was made a parliamentary borough and enriched by the establishment or laying out of two new spas, Old Wells and Pittville. Here a men's college was opened in 1842 and a ladies' college in 1853, the latter being a very early date for a large female academy. At Marlborough in Wiltshire a college was founded in 1843 in a mansion formerly belonging to the Seymours, Dukes of Somerset. The house stood beside the Bath Road and had been converted into the Castle Inn, a popular hostelry in the coaching era. The main Great Western Railway from London to Bristol had passed well south of the borough and was strangling the coaching trade when the mansion was turned into a school for 200 boys. It went from strength to strength, aided no doubt by easier access after the construction of a branch railway. Radley College originated in 1847 in a Queen Anne mansion, under Dr William Sewell, a devout Tractarian, who believed in the influence of beautiful surroundings. Bradfield College was established in 1850 by the Rev. Thomas Stevens on the site of an old manor house. Forty years later the additions included a Greek theatre fashioned out of a local chalk pit. Bloxham College, founded in 1854 in a farmhouse, was later re-created in large premises designed by G.E. Street. The story of mid-nineteenth century foundations continues with two exceptional ventures. The Royal Agricultural College, founded in 1846 at Circencester in spacious Tudor-style buildings, was the first of its kind in England. Wellington College, founded in 1853 as a national memorial to the great Duke, and built to the plans of John Shaw, is generally recognised to be of great architectural merit. Of red brick and creamy white Box limestone, it has two main square courtyards, designed in a style partly reminiscent of Wren's Hampton Court and partly of French buildings of Louis XIII. Later Gilbert Scott added a chapel.

The last quarter of the nineteenth century saw a resurgence of educational building. The Education Act of 1870 demanded new schools where necessary, and there was also a widespread improvement of the old, as at Thame, where the Elizabethan grammar school next to the almshouses and church, was re-housed in 1879 on the fringe of the borough in a new brick and stone Tudor-style building designed by William Wilkinson. Similarly at Cirencester the old grammar school, founded in 1457, moved in 1880 from its mediaeval classrooms to new spacious Jacobean-style premises in Victoria Road. But, above all, this was the period of ladies' colleges which, for example, at Oxford, Reading,

Rendcomb College, a grand mansion designed in the Italianate manner in the 1860s.

Northampton, Warwick, Wycombe and Caversham have just celebrated their centenary.

The popularity of the English heartland for would-be educationalists did not wane in the twentieth century when mansions too large for private families became available for other purposes. The grand houses in the parks at Rendcomb and Stowe were converted into colleges in the 1920s; the late Victorian mansion known as Pangbourne Tower became a nautical college in 1917; the fascinating Edwardian Court at Shiplake, with its brick diapering and extraordinary water tower, has been used as a boys' college since 1959. Today these and similar local foundations accredited to the Headmasters' Conference and closely related bodies educate over 25,000 students annually. By some quirk they are now called 'public schools' in spite of their dedication primarily to private education.

At the stage above these 'public schools' and the smaller grammar schools (which have recently been incorporated into a non-selective comprehensive system), come a variety of advanced technical and training colleges and the universities of which the English heartland has its full share. Apart from the longevity and pre-eminence of Oxford University, the oldest in Britain, the amazing thing about such education in the English heartland is the rise of a university at Reading barely 48km downstream. We have described elsewhere how the newly-formed Reading Extension College, under the aegis of Oxford University, took over premises in Valpy Street and a few years later began working in close co-operation with the Aylesbury Institute of British Dairy Farmers' Association, also newly-established at Reading. In 1904 the college moved to a spacious site with several Georgian dwellings on the London Road. Here with the financial aid of the Palmer family and Lady Wantage, a University College took shape with many residential halls on the terraced slopes above it. In January 1925 the university was incorporated by royal charter and soon plans were made to expand on to the plateau top at Whiteknights Park, an estate which had been embellished by the fifth Duke of Marlborough with a lake, sham ruins and a wealth of rhododendrons, azaleas and fine trees. The property was acquired in 1849 by the broker Sir Isaac Goldsmid who shortly afterwards divided it into six leaseholds, each with its own large country house. Two of these Victorian mansions, Whiteknights and Foxhill, still exist amid some features of the landscape gardening, and have, with the extensive flat grounds, been incorporated into a modern university complex which includes a fine Museum of Rural Life.

For other university foundations the English heartland has had mixed fortunes. The University of Warwick, founded in 1965, arose not near the county capital but in the populous north of the shire near Coventry, which in the Middle Ages was a great cultural centre. However, there have been some notable local gains. The Open University, founded in 1969, has its headquarters at Walton Hall, a late Georgian house near Bletchley in Buckinghamshire. About the same time an independent University College was started in Buckingham itself. The small town, long since displaced by Aylesbury as the county capital, deserves a fairy godmother, and it is to be hoped that the fledgling college will in its growth preserve the Georgian and Victorian architecture and in due course become the University of Buckingham.

CHAPTER FIFTEEN

The Railway Age

Son: I found the rails along the whole brook-side
          Left of that old stone bridge across yon Avon.
Father: That is the place.
Son: There was a house hard-by,
          And past it ran a furnace upon wheels,
          Like a mad bull, tail up in air, and horns
          So low ye might not see 'em. On it bumpt,
          Roaring, as strait as any arrow flits,
          As strait, as fast too, ay, and faster went it.
          (Walter Savage Landor, *A Railway Eclogue,* 1849)

Horse Tramways

The transport of freight and passengers was greatly cheapened and quickened by steam railways, which provided villagers with new horizons and farmers with distant markets. But this rapid locomotion was preceded in the English heartland, as on coalfields, by tramways. In 1798 such a tramway was laid down to serve the building stone quarries at the top of Leckhampton Hill near Cheltenham. The full trucks, descending the inclined plane to the main road at the scarp foot, pulled the empties up to the summit. During its construction the quarrymen left uncut at the upper scarp face an isolated column of limestone now known as the Devil's Chimney. Later this tramway was connected by a short branch to a horse-drawn Gloucester-Cheltenham Tramroad, which was opened in 1811 for the purpose of carrying coal and heavy freight from docks on the Severn to the growing spa.[1] The Tramroad was closed down in 1861 but the inclined-plane system for stone on Leckhampton Hill worked until 1924 when it was replaced by a short-lived railway to Charlton Kings. The old inclined plane now forms an energetic trail to Charlton Kings common.

The other notable horse tramroad in the English heartland ran from the dock at Stratford upon Avon 16 miles (26km) southward to Moreton in Marsh. William James, the canal promoter, intended it to be the first stage in a proposed steam railway from Stratford *via* Moreton, Oxford, Thame and Uxbridge to London. He obtained an Act for the scheme on 28 May 1821 only a few weeks after that for the Stockton and Darlington railway but in 1825 had to get another Act to raise more capital and in this a clause prohibited the use of steam engines where the line ran alongside the public road and through the village of

Alderminster. James went bankrupt, and the line was completed largely through the financial support of Lord Redesdale of Batsford Park. On its opening at Moreton in September 1826 a large concourse came, in the words of a local rhymster:

> To see our iron railway
> It makes our heart content
> To know what's saved in firing
> Will nearly pay the rent.

The track of about standard gauge consisted of fish belly rails resting on stone blocks. In 1836 a branch was built to Shipston on Stour and in 1889 this stretch from Moreton was straightened and modernised. The old horse-drawn tramway from Shipston to Stratford docks fell into disuse in 1904 but its embankments and bridge over the Avon near the theatre survive as well as one of the tramcars. The 'Railway Inn' on the Shipston Road, Stratford, has a sign showing a horse-drawn waggon with a load of top-hatted passengers, reminiscent of the passenger service in the 1850s. Elsewhere on the old track the wharves now form a block of cottages at Newbold and a house at Ilmington and the range of stables still stands at Moreton station.

The Early Main Line Network

The development of the main line railway network shows clearly the unimportance of the English heartland from a national point of view. The prime aim of the first railways here was to link London with Bristol and Birmingham and the first railway to cross the region ran from London *via* Bletchley and Rugby to Birmingham in 1838. The line followed much the same route as Watling Street and the Grand Junction Canal, and chose to avoid Northampton, largely, it is said, because of local opposition but primarily no doubt because the town lay at far too low an altitude to suit the general gradient of the railway. As a result the county town had to wait until 1845 for a branch line and until 1875 for a main line, and never recovered the wide regional dominance it held in previous centuries. On the other hand, Rugby soon had a large railway station and was ripe for industrial expansion. Similarly, Aylesbury benefited from a branch from the trunk line in 1839 whereas Buckingham, its chief local rival, had no railway connection until 1850, and actually began to decline in population about this time. The reason for Buckingham's decline is obvious. In 1838 the Midland Railway started its carriage works 8 miles (13km) away, at New Wolverton near Stony Stratford. Here, beside the Grand Junction Canal there arose a large factory backed by a gridiron pattern of streets of pleasant two-storeyed red brick cottages with bay windows.[2] The same pattern and style prevailed just east of the railway at New Bradwell where about 150 dwellings were built as well as a church and a school both designed by G.E. Street.

London was separated from Bristol by the southern fringe of the English heartland, across which the natural direct connection lay along the line of the old Bath Road and Kennet-Avon canal. However, Brunel, the chief engineer of the Great Western Railway Company, was probably well aware of the great flight of canal locks at Devizes and preferred a more devious route with a low gradient. So from Reading the line followed the valley of the Thames through the deep gap in the chalk downs at Goring, then turned westward along the flat Vale of White Horse to Swindon, southwestward to Chippenham (1839) and through the Box tunnel to Bath and Bristol (1841). Aptly nicknamed the Great Way Round, it brought fame and fortune to Swindon, and Brunel's red brick bridge at Maidenhead was immortalised in Turner's superb landscape 'Rain, Steam and Speed'. The straight track in the Vale of White Horse was some distance from most of the settlements, the chief of which clung either to the foot of the chalk downs to the south or to the hill tops of the Corallian ridge far to the north. Only at Swindon, at the narrow western end of the Vale, did the line closely approach a market borough. Here another reason for Brunel's choice of this circuitous route becomes clear. Gloucester and the flourishing Cheltenham Spa needed rapid communication with London, and their railway promoters were faced with surmounting the tall Cotswold escarpment. Brunel persuaded them to avoid a direct eastward route to Oxford and Tring in favour of a circuitous course down the Severn vale to Stroud and then up the Golden valley to a long tunnel at Sapperton and so down the dip slope to Kemble and Swindon. The Act for a Cheltenham and Great Western Union line was passed in 1836, but by 1841 the only part finished ran from Swindon junction to Kemble with a branch four miles long to Cirencester. The Sapperton tunnel proved costly and the line did not open at Gloucester until 1845 and at Cheltenham until 1847. Swindon now became an important junction of the broad-gauge Great Western Railway, and had greatness thrust upon it when that company chose the Wiltshire station as its locomotive workshop. Before describing its phenomenal expansion, we will outline the growth of the railway network in the English heartland and its recent decimation.

In the south, Reading grew rapidly in importance with lines up the Kennet valley to Hungerford (1847) and so to Westbury (1848) and Devizes (1862). Another route important for Berkshire ran south to Basingstoke (1848). Royal Windsor was connected to London in 1848 by an extension of the Richmond line to Datchet on the side of the Thames opposite the castle. In the following year the track was extended over the river to Windsor, after the South Western Railway had agreed to pay Prince Albert £80,000, the sum he needed to drain the Home Park. The money was well spent, for Queen Victoria loved railway travel, and soon broke down the prejudice many early railways had against passengers, who were considered rather a nuisance.

In the north of the English heartland a prime objective was Leamington Spa, then at the height of its popularity. The railway from Coventry reached it in 1844 and from Rugby in 1851, and although cutting ruthlessly through the town encouraged a large Victorian expansion. Expresses did not stop at Warwick and passengers wanting fast trains had to go, as they still do, to the fine station at Leamington. The spa has a wealth of Victorian buildings and iron work whereas the county capital actually declined in population from 1851 to 1861.

In the centre of the English heartland the situation at Oxford changed rapidly. Strong local opposition had rejected a proposed branch line from the Great Western Railway in the Vale of White Horse and the city was served by horse carriages to Steventon (Oxford Road station), ten miles (16km) away. The dramatic lowering of transport costs from 90s to about 30s a ton from London to Oxford and the saving of time converted many of the opponents. In June 1844 a branch line was opened from Didcot, and rail transport rates were halved again. The university town now became involved in the national mania for railway construction and the reckless competition between various companies. The G.W.R. supported an Oxford-Rugby line which would be part of a trunk route connecting northern and southern England. It went north up the Cherwell valley, crossing the meandering river six times in one stretch of 3km, and had reached Banbury (1850), when the pressure of rival companies caused it to be diverted away from Rugby and to proceed northwestward to Royal Leamington Spa and Birmingham (1852). As a result, from then until 1910 the main G.W.R. trains from London to Birmingham and Birkenhead passed through Oxford station, transferred at this time to the Botley Road. Opposition to the G.W.R.'s northward extension from Oxford induced the London and North Western Railway to construct a network of lines in Buckinghamshire, including a railway from Oxford via Bicester to Bletchley (1850) and so to Cambridge, linking the two educational cities at either end of a clay vale fondly called the Academic Lowland. A branch from this line at Verney Junction served Buckingham and Banbury. Oxford now became a railway terminus and its new additional station (later of the L.M.S.) was built of timber from the entranceway to the Great Exhibition.

The position of the English heartland between London and the Vales of Evesham and Worcester had long been significant and was now reflected in the construction, in 1853, of the Oxford, Worcester and Wolverhampton railway. It threaded the picturesque Evenlode valley to Moreton in Marsh and pierced the Cotswolds by a tunnel at Mickleton beneath a narrow col fashioned by glacial floodwaters and partly filled with glacial sediments. This tunnel was the scene of a notorious battle between two railway gangs when the men of a defaulting firm of contractors occupied the workings until driven out by a bigger gang of navvies hired by Brunel. The line still carries the main expresses from Paddington to Hereford.

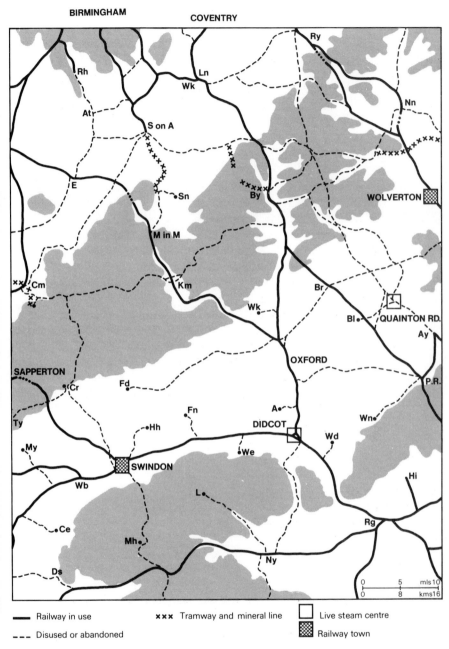

BIRMINGHAM

COVENTRY

Ry

Rh

Ln

Wk

Atr

S on A

Nn

E

Sn

By

WOLVERTON

M in M

Km

Cm

Br

Wk

Bl

QUAINTON RD.

Ay

OXFORD

P.R.

SAPPERTON

Cr

Fd

Fn

A

Wn

Ty

Hh

DIDCOT

Wd

My

We

Hi

Wb

SWINDON

L

Ce

Rg

Mh

Ds

Ny

| | 0 | | 5 | | mls 10 |
| | 0 | | 8 | | kms 16 |

—— Railway in use   ✗✗✗ Tramway and mineral line   ☐ Live steam centre

--- Disused or abandoned   ▨ Railway town

The railway network 1840–1978. Land over approximately 125 metres is stippled.

The Development of the Local Railway Network

The system described above left large areas of the English heartland more than 5 miles (8km) from the nearest station. Most of its ancient boroughs still relied on horse-drawn traffic and some were well content to be left in peace. Much depended on the wishes of local magnates and tradesmen. Within twenty years the trunk lines sprouted many branches, some solely of local intent and others part of the wide cross-country schemes that never materialised. The short spurs or branches included those from the nearest trunk line to Chipping Norton (1855), Abingdon (1856), Henley (1857), Stow (1862), Faringdon (1864), Brill (1872), Watlington (1872) and Wantage (1873). A longer branch line with single track ran from Oxford to Witney (1861) and to Fairford (1873). The cross-line connections were strengthened by a track from Princes Risborough to Thame (1862) that was soon afterwards extended eastward to Aylesbury and westward to Oxford.

Late Victorian and Edwardian Improvements

Another spurt of railway building occurred in late Victorian times, most of it concerned with shortening the connections between important termini and the remainder with new branch lines, as from Kemble to Tetbury (1889), Kidlington to Woodstock (1890) and Newbury to Lambourn (1898). Cheltenham made two brave efforts to shorten its circuitous connections with London. Under an Act of 1881 a single-line railway was built direct up the scarp to Andoversford, Cirencester and Swindon, where it linked with a railway to Marlborough, Andover and the south coast. The line reached Cirencester in 1883 but heavy costs, particularly of large embankments, delayed its completion until 1891. At Andoversford the Cheltenham and Banbury Direct railway crossed the high Cotswolds to Kingham and eventually traversed the redlands beyond Chipping Norton, reaching Banbury in 1887. This undulating upland track was perhaps no less extraordinary than the new line from Didcot which crossed the chalk downs through a high-level wind-gap to Newbury and Winchester, 1882-85. At about the same time some of the trunk lines were widened to three or four tracks, and the whole of the G.W.R. system by 1892 was converted from wide (7ft 0¾ in) to standard gauge (4ft 8½ in). In that year the Metropolitan Railway crossed the Chilterns to Aylesbury and strengthened the influence of London on southern Buckinghamshire.

The popularity of railway travel, encouraged by Queen Victoria, continued unabated in Edward's reign and, partly in response to improved technology and new markets, further efforts were made to shorten roundabout routes. The Severn tunnel line to south Wales from Paddington via Swindon and Wootton Bassett used a long tunnel through the Cotswolds and shortened the journey by 10 miles (16km). Opened in 1903, it cemented the importance of Swindon and Didcot as railway towns. The rail communications of Banbury were improved in 1902 by a short branch of the Great Central Railway which gave quick access to Rugby and Leicester. In 1906 Cheltenham strengthened its connections by the construction of a line along the foot of the Cotswold escarpment to Winchcombe, Broadway and Honeybourne junction and so to Stratford and Birmingham. Market gardeners in the Avon valley took full advantage of the new opportunities. The opening up of the forest of Arden by rail was delayed until this time. Henley in Arden had a short branch from the Birmingham-Leamington line in 1894, but the main development occurred after 1908 with the completion of a route from Birmingham direct to Henley in Arden and Stratford upon Avon. The G.W.R. company attracted new settlers by lush advertisements praising the beauty of the countryside and by issuing an excellent *Up to Date Property Register* of plots and dwellings for sale.

The last great positive change in the railway network took place in 1910, when a direct trunk line was built across the clay vale between Princes Risborough, Bicester and Banbury. Henceforth main line trains from Paddington to Birmingham used this quicker, shorter route instead of going through Oxford.

The Removal of the Local Network

The railways having impoverished the canals and put an end to turnpike trusts, all of which had disappeared by 1895, now themselves suffered drastically from the competition of motor car transport. The various competing railway companies were re-organised into a few large regional combines, and eventually in 1948 the whole system was nationalised in a vain attempt to halt its losses and to offset the growing popularity of the motor car. The shorter branch lines which had never been well patronised went first. The line from Brill to Quainton Road closed in 1935 and the Wantage tramway in 1948, but such pruning proved inadequate; between 1951 and 1967 all remaining branch lines and minor connecting routes were closed first to passenger traffic and then to freight. Finally these closed lines were abandoned altogether and their steel rails and bridge spans removed with indecent haste. Only the broad trunk line network survived, and even on this many local services were curtailed and some small stations demolished, including Adlestrop on the Oxford-Worcester route that on a sunny afternoon in late June evoked Edward Thomas's lovely poem:[3]

> No one left and no one came
> On the bare platform. What I saw
> Was Adlestrop—only the name.

The Scenic and Social Effect of Railways

In rural districts and towns railways provided new employment and in many country areas helped to lessen the population decline. They stimulated farming, especially dairying and market gardening, and early morning milk trains now regulated the lives of hundreds of farmers in the pastoral vales. The Vale of Evesham took on a new vitality in the 1850s when Richard Varden, surveyor for the Oxford-Worcester line, bought Seaford Grange, an estate of about 250 acres (100ha) at Peopleton, to produce fruit for sale in Birmingham and London. He planted more than half of it with Pershore Yellow Egg plums interplanted with 60,000 gooseberry and 100,000 currant bushes. At the same time Jonathan Thorpe, a director of the railway company, leased land at Offenham to James Myatt who had made money by growing strawberries and rhubarb at Camberwell in Surrey.[4] Myatt improved the vegetable production, especially of asparagus and brassicas, on a field rather than a plot scale. In 1872 a special goods station was built at Aldington near Evesham mainly to handle consignments of fruit and vegetables.

Quarrying was given a new lease of life, as although sales of local building stone did not increase, brick and tile making expanded rapidly and the exploitation of ironstone in north Oxfordshire took on a larger scale when the Banbury-Andoversford line (1889) provided a direct route to south Wales.

People's horizons and marketing habits were widened: the seaside resort began to replace the spa in popularity and old boroughs missed or badly served by railway, as at Burford, Deddington, Islip and Woodstock, gradually lost their ancient markets, while new ones arose at railway junctions such as Andoversford. In a general way railways tended to revive the clay vales and to neglect the uplands. Thomas Hughes noticed the change in the Vale of White Horse. Traditionally the irregularly placed houses of its straggling old-fashioned villages were built chiefly of good grey stone and thatched 'though I see that within the last year or two the red-brick cottages are multiplying, for the Vale is beginning to manufacture largely both brick and tiles'. At the same time most towns and villages on the uplands, preferring to use stone that came downhill from local quarries rather than brick that had to be hauled uphill from railway stations, retained their traditional appearance. But many of these upland towns began to lose the tight control of transport and trade that they had inherited from mediaeval times, and it was a long time before the motor car re-animated their streets and market squares.

The architectural legacy of the railways shows their preference for flat lowlands and riverine sites. Some surviving stations are interesting architecturally as at Reading, an Italianate or classical structure of pale yellow brick with pedimented windows and graceful cupola, but none excels the terminus with Queen Victoria's waiting room at Windsor. Designed in 1850 by William Tite in Tudor style, in red brick diapered in blue and set off with stone dressings, its waiting room part is now a chapel. Most isolated stations attracted to themselves a few houses and in towns a street pattern of small brick houses arranged parallel to the track. Everywhere railway inns and hotels sprang up, some of considerable elegance, as the 'Queen's Head', Swindon (1842) and the

'Great Eastern', Leamington, others more modest with delightful pictorial inn signs, such as the 'North Star' at Steventon and the 'Railway Inn' at Eynsham. At Hinton near Woodford Halse, the large half-timbered 'Railway Hotel' of 1900 is now a social club.

In the vales, new housing estates and factories sprang up at major junctions and at the railway company workshops. The economy at Reading went from strength to strength and today it has also become a rail feeder for London airport. At Didcot junction the transport facilities attracted large stores, military establishments, a huge thermal electricity generating station and a vast inland collecting depot. At Banbury national centrality and excellent rail connections have stimulated numerous industries and an exceptionally large livestock market. The direct and instantaneous economic effect of the railways was greatest at New Wolverton and New Bradwell on the London-Birmingham line and at Swindon on the London-Bristol route.

Swindon: The Railway Town

The old town at Swindon stands on the summit of a hill of hard Purbeck and Portland stone which gives wide views of the chalk downs and clay vale and was settled in Neolithic and Romano-British times. Its townsfolk acquired a market in the 1660s and were reasonably prosperous when the G.W.R. opened a station 1 mile (1½km) away. This Junction was 77¾ miles (124km) or just over halfway from Paddington on the Bristol route and barely 83m above its London terminus. The company built some Tudor-style houses nearby at Steventon for its board meetings and chose Swindon to be its chief refreshment centre where all trains stopped for 10 minutes. The catering at first was under the control of the proprietor of the 'Queen's Hotel', Cheltenham and Brunel's refreshment rooms matched the food in elegance. They occupied two long three-storeyed buildings of stone in a dignified late Classical style, the floors at platform level being for refreshments and the top floors, connected by a bridge until 1870, for a hotel with bedrooms on one side of the track and sitting rooms on the other. Today only the bedrooms survive, in a modernised state.

The stop for refreshments allowed locomotives to be changed, and in 1843 a large factory for engine repair and construction was opened. In its various shops, under the letters A to S, all processes of locomotive and tender construction went on. In 1862 a rail or rolling mill was built, which undertook the entire process from the puddling of pig iron to the production of up to 400 tons of rail weekly. Two years later a new engine shop (R), one of the largest, finest, and best arranged in the world, came into operation. Yet the expansion continued unabated and in 1868, after the citizens of Oxford had turned down the offer, an immense prison-like carriage and wagon factory enlarged the Company's works here to about 180 acres (73ha) and the pay-roll to nearly 2,000 hands. Swindon also became the chief depot for the stores department of the G.W.R. and in 1892 the scene, on 15 miles (24km) of extra new sidings, of the conversion of its rolling stock from broad to standard gauge. Eventually the works and sidings covered 300 acres (121ha) and employed about 14,000 persons who, among other activities, repaired nearly 1,000 locomotives annually and built two or three new ones every week.

The labour force needed for such a large industrial complex gave rise to a workers' housing estate on the flat land between the railway works and the hill-top market town. The original estate was laid out on a rigid rectangular plan of three long parallel east-west streets crossed midway by a north-south axis. It consisted of modest terraced houses built of local stone, each designed with a small entrance hall and suitable outbuildings. The dwellings were comfortable to live in, and the whole scheme had a dignity and quality that persuaded the borough council when it took over the estate in 1966 to renovate it sympathetically in a way that should be a model for all renovators of Victorian urban cores. The estate centred upon a Mechanics' Institution built in a Tudor style in 1853 and backed by a market hall, both private ventures. Nearby is a large stone-faced house erected in the 1840s as lodgings for Irish workmen and used later as a Methodist chapel until converted into a railway museum. The Company, at a total cost of £7,200, provided the new town with a church, vicarage and commodious schoolhouse, all designed by Gilbert Scott in a Decorated style. In the 1860s Cambria place was built just southwest of the original estate as lodgings for Welsh railway workers. By then 'New Swindon' had over 4,000 inhabitants or nearly double the population of the adjacent market town which had, however, derived some prosperity from its nearness to the new society of mechanics and engineers. At the turn of the century Old and New Swindon were combined into one administrative unit which by 1911 had 50,751 inhabitants and was by far the biggest borough in Wiltshire, and the only one experiencing rapid growth.

The town continued to expand in the twentieth century; boosted by the incorporation of Rodbourne Cheney village in the 1920s and by the arrival of several new firms during the Second World War, its population reached 69,000 in 1951. By then the railway industry was declining and considerable factory space was vacant, when for the second time in its history Swindon had greatness thrust upon it. Under the Town Development Act of 1952 it became an expanding or overspill town, expected and assisted to attract new industries and to accommodate eventually 19,000 extra persons, mostly from London. Estates totalling 1,000 acres (404ha) were acquired to house the newcomers in five distinct neighbourhood units, three built by the borough council and two by private enterprise. The scheme, aided by the existing superb network of railways, proved successful, and by 1961 over 91,000 people were living here.

In 1967 further expansion was decided on, and soon afterwards Swindon and the Rural District of Highworth with its 14 parishes were combined into a new district authority called Thamesdown (stretching from the Thames in the north

The restored railway village in Swindon, Thamesdown Borough.

to the Wiltshire downs in the south). By 1976 Thamesdown and a few outlying estates owned by it had nearly 150,000 inhabitants of whom probably no more than 3,000 worked for British Rail, mainly on repairs and refurbishing. This vast administrative unit differs widely from the dense conurbations on the coalfields of the Midlands and North, for within its boundaries are large expanses of farmland and several old villages including the former borough of Highworth. The present building programme envisages over 1,000 new dwellings each year to be arranged in 'urban villages' and a population of about 180,000 by 1986.

The new civic core between the railway village and Old Town is a tremendous complex of commercial and professional buildings, including a Civic centre and a vast Brunel shopping centre evocative of the great London railway architecture of the Victorian age, complete with a statue of the famous engineer. It would be impossible in a few words to describe the various housing and industrial estates, some of which are still under construction. A tinge of the local environment and its pre-railway rusticity peeps through even in the built-up areas. An enormous sarsen forms a monument in Sussex Square at Walcot East; Stratton St Margaret and Rodbourne Cheney have thirteenth century churches and other old buildings; Coate Water has pleasure activities and nearby the house, now a

The new Brunel shopping plaza, Swindon, Thamesdown Borough.

museum, where Richard Jefferies, naturalist and author, spent his early life. In *Round About a Great Estate* (1880) and *Bevis* (1882) he describes the locality and Burderop Park on the chalk downs to the south, and at Day House the remains of a stone circle he discovered survive as nine fallen monoliths. The cultural and spiritual value of these antiquities and open spaces will be enhanced if, as seems probable, Swindon becomes a city of 200,000 inhabitants by the end of the century.

Industrial Archaeology: The Preservation of Steam Traction

Swindon and some other railway towns and junctions acquired a special attraction when from 1955 onwards British Rail phased out steam traction. The last steam locomotive built for them, the Evening Star, was despatched from Swindon in 1960 and eventually in 1968 all services by steam-hauled passenger trains ceased on their standard gauge tracks. Numerous groups of local enthusiasts who deplored the closure of railways and especially of steam traction combined in 1965 to form the Association of Railway Preservation Societies, in order to encourage the preservation of certain lines, mainly narrow gauge, and of 1,000 steam locomotives. In addition, museums of railway technology and nine major live-steam centres have been established recently where locomotives are displayed and steamed for short rides on open days.[5] A few longer routes, including the lines from Oxford to Birmingham, Stratford upon Avon and Hereford, have been approved for occasional steam rides. The English heartland lacks an active narrow gauge railway, the nearest being at Leighton Buzzard, but it has a fine railway museum and much other industrial archaeology at Swindon and live-steam centres at Didcot and Quainton. The Great Western Railway museum at Swindon, founded in 1962, preserves among its wealth of exhibits some of the company's fastest expresses; a replica of the 'North Star', its first passenger train to run from Paddington to Maidenhead in 1838; and a special collection of items concerning Isambard Kingdom Brunel (1806-59).

At Didcot the Great Western Society has a fifteen acre site, where on open steam weekends train rides and footplate inspections may be enjoyed, and the largest collection of G.W.R. steam locomotives, together with a fully operational engine shed and numerous models, may be seen. Also on display is 'The Shannon' from the former Wantage tramway; built in 1857 it is probably the oldest engine in the British Isles still steamed, and was in active service till the tramway closed in 1948.

The Quainton Railway Centre, near Aylesbury, on the former Metropolitan/Great Central joint line, has a wide selection of locomotives and equipment such as was used on the railways before modernisation in the 1950s. These include, among others, two London Transport steam locomotives, a 102 year old well tank built for the London South Western Railway, an ex-Great Western Railway king class engine no. 6024 King Edward I (a class known as the

The railway museum, Swindon, Thamesdown Borough.

pride of the Great Western, as it was their fastest steam locomotive), and a London North Western Railway dining car built at the beginning of this century.

The centre has steam operations on the last Sunday in the month from April to October and on bank holiday weekends at Easter (not Good Friday), spring and late summer. In September 1977 a steam weekend with steam hauled rides and a cavalcade of steam locomotives and rolling stock — everything steamable in steam! — attracted 1,250 visitors.

Once again, in Stephen Spender's striking verses:[6]

> After the first powerful manifesto
> The black statement of pistons,
> Without more fuss
> But gliding like a queen,
> She leaves the station.
> (*The Express*, 1931)

CHAPTER SIXTEEN

The Growth of Towns

Towered cities please us then
And the busy hum of men.
        (Milton, *L'Allegro*)

The Reappearance of Towns

When Roman help and forces were withdrawn in the middle of the fifth century urban life in England was doomed. By 577, Cirencester, Gloucester and Bath had been captured by Anglo-Saxon invaders, and although a few persons may have inhabited their ruins they ceased to function as towns. The newcomers dotted the Midlands with small nucleated settlements, self-contained and utterly rural. Urbanisation had to begin again, and it was a long time before town life reappeared, for to become a town demands either a civic mentality, such as the Romans had, or the need for special functions beyond the scope of rural subsistence farmers. From the start the chief stimuli to urban growth were administration, defence and marketing on a regional or national scale, and it is often virtually impossible to separate the three.

For administration the royal manors had from the onset advantages over those of lesser lords with smaller holdings, because these *villae regales* collected the king's rent in kind from adjacent estates. This function fostered the early importance of Reading, Wantage, Blewbury and Lambourn in Berkshire and of Bampton, Bensington (Benson), Bloxham and four other places in Oxfordshire, where in 1066 the seven royal manors collected the profits of jurisdiction from nineteen Hundreds. Bampton had a market worth 50 shillings at *Domesday Survey*, and in 1315 its lord, Aymer de Valence, Earl of Pembroke, was given licence to crenellate his mansion. The parish covered more than 10,000 acres (4,000ha) and was served by three vicars, each of whom had a house near the church. But Bampton never acquired burgesses and the legal status of a borough.

The same can be said of Dorchester on Thames where the regional administration stemmed from a bishopric. Here on a riverine flat protected by earthen ramparts and a Roman wall, the first bishopric of Wessex was established by Saint Birinus in 634. For safety from Mercian attacks the see was transferred to Winchester in 705. However, from 886 to 1092 Dorchester replaced Leicester (captured by the Danes) as a cathedral city of Mercia and acquired large estates, especially near Banbury. In 1092 the see was transferred to Lincoln, and although fifty years later the bishop founded a house of Augustinian Canons in Dorchester, the Oxfordshire town never regained the importance or status it held in Romano-British times.

What regional administration failed to achieve the needs of national defence did. The growth of true towns in the English heartland was associated with the fortification of Wessex and the reconquest of the Danelaw by Alfred and his children during the years 871 to 925. Alfred decided to base his defences on fortresses, an idea long followed on the continent. By 892 when the Dutch repulsed a large army of Danes by this method and so deflected them to England, Wessex was dotted with fortified *burhs* in which the inhabitants could make a stand.[1] These burhs varied widely in size and wherever possible, as at Winchester and Bath, made use of Romano-British walls, but where walls were absent new fortifications were raised, in many places alongside or within water defences, as at Wallingford and Cricklade. They are generally considered to have been organised as garrison towns rather than as centres of civic administration but were no doubt already settled before they were fortified. They were repaired and garrisoned when necessary by people from the adjacent territory, assessed at a ratio of 16 hides to one acre's breadth of wall (that is 22 yards) or of one man per hide which would provide 4 men to each pole or perch (5½ yards) of wall or earthwork. This, a comfortable fighting space for each man along the whole perimeter, seems to have worked out reasonably well in practice. Cricklade was allotted 1,500 hides and its walls were probably 2,063 yards long; Wallingford was allotted 2,400 hides and its present rectangular perimeter beside the Thames exceeds 3,000 yards.

Alfred was too busy holding Wessex to try to gain full control of English Mercia and the Danelaw although he captured London and repaired its walls in 886. The securing of the south Midlands beyond the line of the Thames was the work of his children, Edward the Elder and Ethelfleda. Edward after 911 extended his control northward and took possession of Oxford, then under his sister's jurisdiction, and made it a burh. In October 914 he proceeded to build a fortress on each side of the Ouse at Buckingham and another farther north at Bedford. In the autumn of 917 he went with the west Saxon army to Passenham and stayed there while they surrounded the borough at Towcester with a stone wall. In the meanwhile his sister, Ethelfleda of Mercia, established ten fortresses in the Midlands, the chief survivors of which are Bridgnorth, Tamworth, Stafford and Warwick. In a contemporary document Oxford was allotted 1,500 hides, Buckingham 1,600 and Warwick 1,200 hides. Northampton remained securely Danish and was probably fortified by the Danes at this time.

During the tenth century these burhs began to change into market towns because their fortifications made trading safer, and their many houses owned by rural manors virtually ensured surplus agricultural products for sale. The Crown tried to restrict marketing and minting to specified places, as under Edward the

Elder, who wanted no one to bargain out of *port* (market centre), and Athelstan who wanted every market to be a city. With this encouragement the defensive burh slowly evolved into a market borough having economic, social and tenurial links with a wide rural area. Simultaneously, a new administrative arrangement or rearrangement appeared in the lands conquered by Wessex from Mercia and in the Danelaw. Whereas in Wessex the territory was divided into shires before Alfred's reign, in the southern Midlands shires are first recorded about 1010. However, these divisions, intended for fiscal and military purposes, probably originated between 912 and 939 and were focused upon the newly-fortified burhs after which they are named except for Berkshire, the origins of which are obscure. That the county capitals were not the only important towns may be judged from the meeting places of the Old English council between the years 930 and 1065. These include, in addition to Oxford (4 meetings), Buckingham and Northampton, the non-county towns of Cirencester (3 times), Winchcombe, Abingdon, Kirtlington, Headington, Sutton Courtenay, Wantage, Woodstock, Whittlebury and Cookham.[3]

Norman Boroughs and Towns

At the Norman conquest the king retained control of the burhs and strengthened their defences by constructing motte-and-bailey castles usually astride the existing fortifications, so destroying part of the old street pattern. About twenty years later, *Domesday Survey* gives an account of most of these towns and of the shires in which they were situated.

About 112 English towns were credited with borough status in the *Survey* but only twelve of these lay in the English heartland, namely Reading, Wallingford and Windsor in Berkshire, Cricklade, Calne, Marlborough and Bedwyn in Wiltshire, Winchcombe in Gloucestershire and the county boroughs of Oxford, Warwick, Buckingham and Northampton. The boroughs of Pershore, Tewkesbury, and Newport Pagnell lay just outside the territory we are describing. Some of the Domesday accounts are inadequate or incomplete, but the general picture is remarkably revealing. We are dealing largely with county towns and ancient *burhs*. Windsor and Bedwyn are each described as *villa* (town) rather than borough but the former had 95 hagae (houses) and must have been important, while Bedwyn, also the centre of a vast royal estate, had 25 burgesses or burgage plots. There is no information on Marlborough except that it paid the 'third penny', a sure sign of urban importance. Reading, a borough, had at least 59 burgage plots and Buckingham probably 53. The relatively small size of Buckingham then and later may be partly due to its site in the extreme north of its county being awkward for administration, a circumstance which caused the assizes to be held occasionally at Wycombe and more frequently at Aylesbury, which eventually displaced it as the county capital.

Domesday Survey contains much information on the other county towns and ancient burhs. Oxford with 990 burgesses or burghal holdings was the sixth most populous city in England, Wallingford with about 491 burgages the tenth, Northampton with 296 the nineteenth and Warwick with 244 dwellings the twenty fourth. These and most other boroughs had some 'waste' partly due to castle building, which in a few was offset by the arrival of new settlers (*franci*), or the addition of a new borough. Northampton and Oxford (*see* Chapter 19) had exceptional amounts of waste. Northampton, as we have seen, was in the Danelaw and in the tenth century its armies raided southward and extended the shire boundary in part south of Watling Street, the previously agreed limit. In 1065 Earl Morcar of Northumbria revolted against King Harold and, joined by Earl Edwin of Mercia, occupied Northampton. Eventually the leaders negotiated a peace at Oxford, but the rebels before they went back north harried the country round Northampton and took much spoil, including prisoners and cattle. In 1066 no less than 14 of the 61 burgage holdings in Northampton were waste. Apparently new building took place mainly in a new borough for in 1086 the town had 87 burgage plots (of which 40 were in the new borough), as well as 209 other houses and 35½ house-plots laid waste. The city had been walled and a castle built.

Most of these royal boroughs contained houses that were attached or belonged to outside manors whose owners thus had a secure foothold and a market in the nearby fortress. *Domesday Survey* reveals this network of tenurial tentacles or the territory contributory to the borough. Such boroughs inevitably became the chief towns of their neighbourhood, for to the natural advantages which led to their selection in the first place was added this artificial centrality. Winchcombe, which was formerly the capital of a Mercian shire and at one time the residence of its kings, is credited with 29 contributory burgesses, living as far away as Lechlade and including 10 from Hampnett. The *Survey* does not list Winchcombe's inhabitants but a contemporary survey by the clerks of Evesham Abbey enters 116 burgesses which seems a reasonable figure.

The extent of contributory manors or tenurial tentacles may be seen to perfection in the ancient boroughs of Cricklade and Wallingford. Cricklade stands on the south bank of the upper Thames where the Roman highway from Silchester to Cirencester and Gloucester crosses the river. It was on the frontier between Wessex and Mercia, and became an Alfredian fortress planned within a square enclosure defended by a wall, of which a stone footing can still be seen in the town cemetery. When in 903 a Danish force ravaged Mercia it crossed the Thames here but apparently did not take the town. *Domesday Survey* does not give an account of the borough beyond the general statement that the king received £5 from the 'third penny' and that St Peter's, Westminster had several burgages here which, with another 'third penny', brought in £9. However, the accounts of eleven neighbouring manors show that they held all told 33 burgages, 2 houses and 1 garden in Cricklade. The farthest away was Ramsbury, about 20 miles distant, with 5 burgages that rendered a total of 5s. Thus the

Cricklade viewed from the north across the valley floor of the upper Thames.

royal borough had many property owners and had close connections with a surrounding area of about 1,300 hides.

At Wallingford the town expanded within a rectangular rampart and ditch, and was arranged internally as four rectangles about a central crossroads. The fortress was built across the ancient all-weather routeway that led from the Marlborough and Berkshire downs to the Icknield Way along the foot of the Chilterns, less than 3km from the east gate and ford in the borough. For several millenia this thoroughfare was one of the most important in England and, until bridged, the firm-footed gravel ford never lost its popularity. William the Conqueror after the battle of Hastings did not cross the tidal Thames at London but preferred to march west to the ford at Wallingford whence he continued his destructive sweep to Berkhampsted and so approached the metropolis from the north. The castle he erected in Wallingford covered 25 acres (10ha) of the northeast quadrant, and unlike the south and east sides which were moated by diverting the Mill Brook, the ditch in this section was flooded by a sluice on the Thames. Today the mediaeval plan of Wallingford remains almost intact and some ramparts and gateways survive. The fortified borough covers about 112 acres (45ha) and ecclesiastically consists today largely of the parish of St Mary Le More, with small tracts in St Peter's and St Leonard's, whereas in the early thirteenth century it had eight more parish churches as well as St Nicholas in the castle and a chapel at the hospital of St John.

At the time of *Domesday Survey,* Wallingford was by far the chief town of Berkshire. According to it, Edward the Confessor had held 8 virgates here on which were 276 burgages or *hagae.* The burgesses did service for the king with horses or by water upstream to Sutton Courtenay, downstream to Reading and inland to Blewbury. In 1086, of the king's holdings 6 burgages were now quit of dues and service, 8 had been destroyed for the castle and 22 were held by Frenchmen. Altogether there were about 290 royal properties and at least 201 houses of other owners. Landowners in 16 or 17 rural manors in Oxfordshire held 68 houses in Wallingford, while twelve rural manors in Berkshire owned here a total of 88 *hagae,* and the village of Sonning had by right one church. These properties were presumably counted in the total of non-royal plots given above. It is difficult to equate burgages to population, as a burgage might be sub-divided and have more than one house on it, but multiplication by five gives 2,500 inhabitants which seems a reasonable estimate. The burgesses, who included a moneyer and blacksmith, held a market on Saturdays.

Of the property owners about 70 per cent had direct tenurial connections with the nearby countryside whereas at the newer boroughs of Warwick and Oxford the proportion was only 55 per cent and 35 per cent respectively. Thus it seems that with time the need for close connections with the adjacent territory had lessened, probably because the boroughs were now capable of defending themselves. Certainly Oxford was populous enough to do so, as by 1086 it had over 930 plots or dwellings (*see* Chapter Nineteen).

Domesday Survey records a market in a few quite large non-burghal towns or villages, including Cirencester, where the market was new, Cookham, Bampton, King's Sutton near Banbury, and Abingdon where ten merchants traded outside the abbey gates. But these places lacked the importance of the defensive boroughs described above.

The Golden Age of Borough Creation

From 1086 to 1348 the population of England increased from about 1½ million to over 4 million, and the internal trade in agricultural goods, cloth and metals grew with it. Cash rents became common and peasant farmers as well as manorial lords met their debts by producing surplus crops for market. Not surprisingly, markets began to arise or flourish in hundreds of small towns,

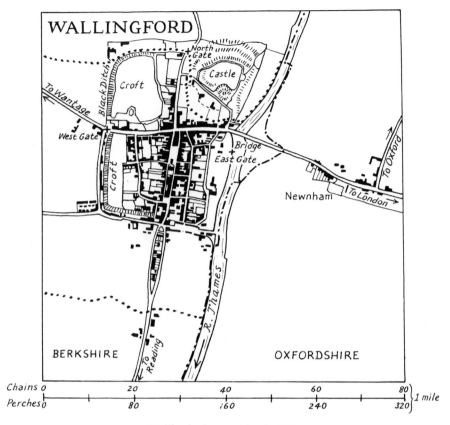

Wallingford: town plan in 1900.

nearly 300 such charters being granted or confirmed by the crown. Many villages grew into market towns and began to acquire some form of burghal status. There now co-existed towns called boroughs with varying degrees of independence or self government, some of which had little legal claim to the term except a market while others had both market and some burgesses, and others had by tradition or prescription wider and stronger privileges, including a trade guild and perhaps also the right to pay a fixed sum annually to the overlord in lieu of all his rents, dues and profits. By the death of King John in 1216, nearly 120 places in England had obtained charters either to confirm their borough status or to establish it. Half of these were not boroughs in *Domesday Survey*. From 1216 to 1334 about another 90 received charters either from the king on royal lands or on secular and ecclesiastical estates from feudal overlords.[4]

The benefits to both overlord and burgess seem obvious. Concentration of marketing into towns meant easy surveillance, control, protection, and

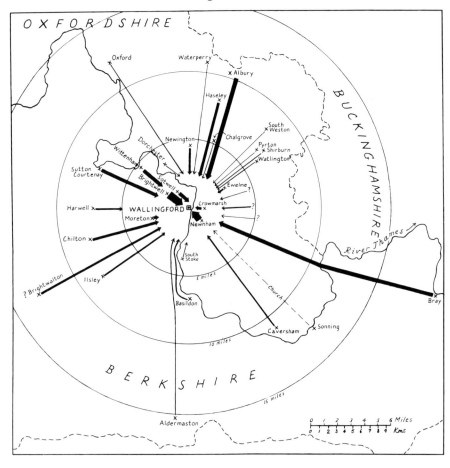

Wallingford: tenurial tentacles in 1086.

witnessing, for since the reign of Edgar twelve witnesses were appointed in small boroughs, and thirty six in large. The purchaser benefited from a wider variety and closer spacing of goods while the overlord by the close grouping of burgages greatly increased his rents or profits per acre. For the king, a borough provided an easily taxed unit which could afford to pay for special privileges. After the time of Simon de Montfort it could provide a means of selecting a parliament. The burgesses had the advantage of communal activity and protection of a civil, judicial and social kind, which, of course, could be a burden as well as a blessing. Probably the right, for a small cash rent, of burgage tenure as a freehold devisable to heirs and disposable at will, was the chief reason for the growth of boroughs. Here merchants and craftsmen flourished and the scholar, lawyer and scribe were needed most. The boroughs led the way in progress toward individual freedom, diverse occupations and mobility of people. Yet most boroughs had agricultural connections either with rural manors or with their own fields. Many holdings in scores of boroughs were small farmsteads, and the town had considerable agricultural wealth within its own perimeter or in the fields outside it. The great distinction between a borough and a rural town or village was that the borough was inhabited largely by burgesses who elected their own reeve and council and were tried by a court of their peers. Later only boroughs acquired merchant guilds and mercantile rights beyond those of a market and fairs. Over the centuries most alert boroughs paid large sums to the crown for the confirmation of their charters and the extension of their privileges. There were in addition numerous towns which for some reason never acquired a charter, among them Watlington which had two markets and a fair in 1302 but languished in later centuries.

The street pattern of towns and the layout of their house plots depended heavily on how they were founded and developed. Thus the old fortified boroughs of Wallingford, Cricklade, Oxford, Northampton and Warwick were greatly influenced by their surrounding walls with four main gateways leading to a central crossroads. But all the smaller towns were not walled and some grew almost haphazardly like a large unplanned village, as at Watlington and Bampton. In contrast to these, most mediaeval boroughs have patterns indicative of town planning on modern lines, either as an addition to an old town or as a virtually new creation. The new boroughs, as distinct from extensions of old towns, often seem to follow simple guidelines. Frequently they occupy small areas cut out from one large parish or from two adjoining parishes. The layout was simple; at one stroke a site was marked out in rectangular plots facing either a wide central street or a pattern of streets so settling easily problems of fencing, ownership and access. Commonly burgage plots were 15ft wide (4½ m) which seems to be about one rod, pole or perch (today 16½ ft) but in some towns, as at Burford and Chipping Norton, 20ft frontages are common as if intended to allow a side alleyway. Oxford seems exceptional as here some street frontages in the intramural built-up area were about half the usual width. Within this rectangular plan plots could be left vacant for market places, chapel, cemetery and other public facilities. The method minimised the risk of eavesdrip and was open enough for gardens, orchards, cartsheds, stabling, pigsties, crofts, and separate bakehouses or ovens. Often the mother parish church was outside the plan which thereby avoided conflict wth existing clerical rights, and internal religion was represented by a stone cross or chapel with a bell tower and perhaps later also by a monastic house. Subsequent infillings normally did not interfere with the plan except to bring greater continuity of houses on street frontages.

How many towns in the English heartland were planned in this way will never be known, as the records are not extant. Some planning occurred before *Domesday Survey,* as in the new borough at Northampton and probably also at

Newbury which occupies a site cut from two parishes and perhaps largely covered by Ulvritone, a place credited in the *Survey* with 51 *hagae*. It was probably called Newbury because it was new and needed to be distinguished from the ancient parishes around it. Numerous other towns in the English heartland bear strong or almost indisputable signs of mediaeval planning, but their historical records are not adequate to detail the new development. Among these are Alcester, Kenilworth, Marlborough, Wokingham, Chipping Norton, Hungerford and lastly Witney and Henley on Thames which we shall use as examples of undocumented borough planning.

Witney stands on a cornbrash limestone knoll surrounded by a wide ring of alluvium that marks a former meander of the river Windrush. The manor belonged to the Bishop of Winchester, a prolific borough founder, and was noted early for woollen cloth. The town appears to have been planned alongside a wide market strip (now the Green) sloping down from the church at the top of the knoll northward to the alluvium alongside the Windrush, which provided power for fulling. It continued to flourish on wool and textiles. On the opposite bank of the Windrush valley, in the manor of Cogges, Robert de Arsic in 1213 granted 23 holdings in plots of 2 acres on each side of the main Witney-Oxford road on condition that each tenant should build a house on his plot.[5] The privileges included right of access into the nearby wood and a rental of ony 1s per acre, but the new town of Newland was a failure and in 1279 only 7 men were still holding their plots. Today it is a suburb of Witney.

Obviously new boroughs needed powerful geographical advantages to succeed, such as existed at Henley on Thames which was a mere appurtenant of the royal manor of Bensington when a bridge was built here sometime before 1230. Within a few decades Henley had a fair, markets and a guild of 46 merchants. The town grew up on either side of a wide street stretching at right angles to the Thames up to a crossroads at the market place. Control of the river crossing and of water traffic proved sufficient to ensure its prosperity and the full occupance of its rectilinear layout.

New Planned Burgage Extensions, 1100-1348

There are plenty of more certain examples in the English heartland of the creation of new planned boroughs and of planned extensions to existing towns. We will discuss first planned extensions to pre-existing villages and small towns, as at Stratford upon Avon (*see* Chapter Seventeen), Banbury, Thame and Eynsham. At Banbury, Alexander, Bishop of Lincoln (1123-48) built a castle and laid out a new town between the river Cherwell and the older settlement. The town was extended further in the mid-thirteenth century when a planned suburb called Newland was built in the area of modern Broad Street.

Such mediaeval extensions are better seen at Thame and Eynsham than at the vigorous, expanding town of Banbury. At Thame the old nucleus stands on a gravel patch near the bridge over the river where a road leading south to the

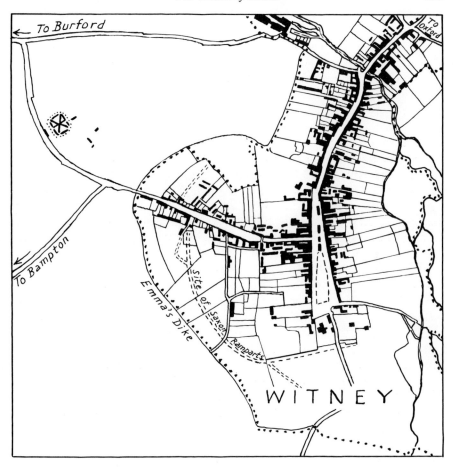

Witney: town plan in 1900; Dotted line shows parish boundary: the rectangle as in all the following town plans covers 1 square mile, or 640 acres or 260 hectares.

Icknield Way crosses a route along the valleyside. In the 1140s the overlord, Alexander, Bishop of Lincoln, founded a prebendal house near the church and gave a park some way to the south for the site of a Cistercian abbey. The old village expanded along the wide road leading to the abbey and here, at an unspecified date, the bishop of Lincoln laid out a planned borough. To foster it, in 1219 he obtained a licence to divert the valleyside route (Oxford-Aylesbury) from its direct course near the parish church into the centre of the High Street, thereby adding considerably to the distance but ensuring that traffic was forced to enter the market place. Soon afterwards he made 'on the king's highway in the *Forum* of Thame an encroachment where he built houses to increase his rent'. By 1258 about 76 burgesses were paying the 1s rent in the new borough and at least 18 shops had been erected in the roadway. Within a century the tax yield of New

Witney viewed from the south showing linear arrangements of plots facing on to the town green and market place.

Thame far exceeded that of Old Thame, so the fifty acres laid out in strips off the wide market place proved highly profitable. The burgesses could conveniently attend the parish church and, as was usual, some held property in both the new borough and the manor. Today the greater part of the town, apart from the church and prebendal house, aligns the wide High Street, in which the central island of shops and Town Hall recall the early encroachment. Many of the long narrow burgage plots survive and end in a back lane. Some, especially south of Cornmarket, show a slightly sinuous (reversed S) pattern which is considered characteristic of mediaeval ridge and furrow and may indicate that the plots were laid out directly on the open field. Travellers between Oxford and Aylesbury are still forced to make the circuitous detour shrewdly planned nearly eight centuries ago. In July 1925 Thame Urban Council bought the market

Thame viewed from the northwest, showing mediaeval planning beside the market square.

rights here for £1,000 from Lord Bertie, lord of the manor.

Some of these extensions to existing villages or towns proved less prosperous. In 1215 the Abbot of Eynsham marked out a *cultura* on each side of a road near the abbey adjoining the old borough, and divided its twenty acres into rectangular plots which he granted on burgage tenure at a rental of 4s per acre or *pro rata*. The liberties were similar to those granted by the king to the burgesses of Oxford but the venture was only moderately successful, perhaps

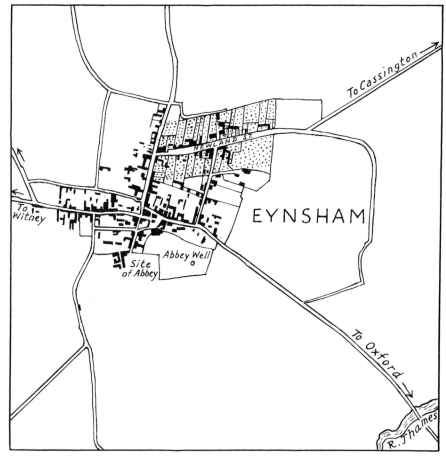

Eynsham: town plan in 1900 showing (stippled) mediaeval planned extension.

because the rents were high and the abbots none too popular. In 1366 the new borough had only 31 houses against nearly 300 in the old town, which it never seriously rivalled. Today they are conjoined, but the new creation stands out clearly as a patterned arrangement of houses along Newland Street.

New Planned Boroughs, 1100-1348

A clearer picture of planned boroughs or plantations is obtained from the many towns that were laid out on new sites rather than as extensions to pre-existing settlements. Henley in Arden consisted originally of a long string of burgage plots on each side of the main Birmingham to Stratford road within a short distance of the site of the Norman castle at Beaudesert. In 1296 it had 69 burgesses and two watermills and yielded over £15 annually. The borough site

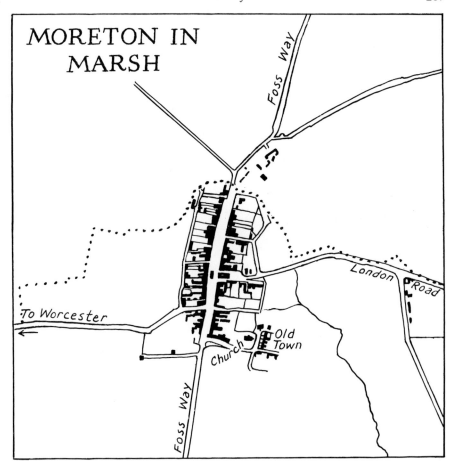

Moreton in Marsh: town plan in 1900. Dotted line denotes parish boundary. The settlement stands on a patch of glacial gravels.

was cut out of Wootton Wawen parish probably about 1220 and did not have its own church until after 1367. The High Street retains the fifteenth century market cross, church and guildhall, and a nice variety of Tudor houses, many of them timber framed.

A similar town plan exists at Moreton in Marsh on a gravel patch on either side of the Roman Foss Way in north Gloucestershire. Here in about 1226 the abbot of Westminster separated off a block of land in Bourton parish, whose inhabitants were recompensed for loss of commons by the gift of 4 acres of meadow nearby and 2 burgages at 6d a year in the new vill. The linear arrangement of plots is little disturbed by the entrance at right angles of the London-Worcester road nor by the church, presumably of the Domesday hamlet of Mortune, which stands separately in a small cluster called Old Town just

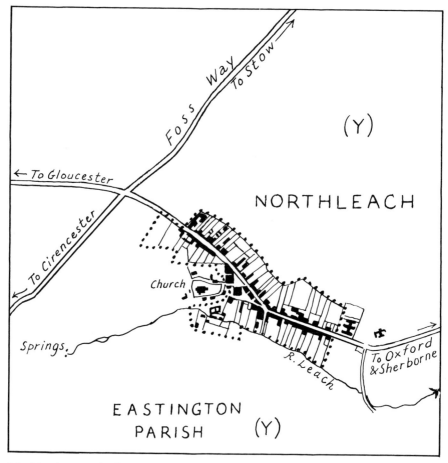

Northleach: town plan in 1900. The boundary of the borough which was cut out of Eastington parish (Y), is marked by a dotted line.

southeast of the planned borough.

The way mediaeval borough planners favoured busy roads may be seen also at Northleach in the Cotswolds, where in 1227 the Abbot of Gloucester, having granted a market and fair, took 43 acres (17ha) in Eastington parish on which to create a borough with burgage rents of 1s. The site was within a few hundred metres of the Foss Way and was also most conveniently astride the route between the Abbot's monastery in the vale at Gloucester and his chief summer residence at Sherborne on the limestone wolds. The small river Leach flowed through the town and gave an assured water supply in a land poor in permanent streams. Soon afterwards Northleach paid 8s annually for the right to try petty offences in its own court instead of the Hundred court. By 1267 there were about 80 burgages here as well as some other houses and stalls, and within a short time the

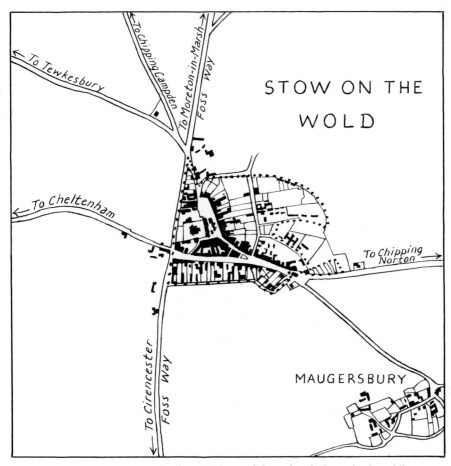

Stow on the Wold: town plan in 1900. Borough boundary is shown by dotted line.

town had become famous for Cotswold wool. The holdings are tightly packed end-on to the main road, except in the centre on the south side where a triangular space seems to have been left as a market place. The church is actually in Eastington parish just outside the borough boundary, but owes its magnificence entirely to Northleach wool staplers.

That the main highway did not always control the building pattern of a town may be seen at Stow, which stands beside the Foss Way only 9 miles (14km) from Northleach. This, the only true hilltop town in the Cotswolds, was the site of an Iron Age earthwork hence the name of its mother parish, Maugersbury (Maethelgar's burh). Here the Foss Way traverses the hilltop and the whole local road network focuses upon it. In 1107 the king granted the Abbot of Evesham at Stow the customs and liberties of all market places (*ports*) and boroughs. The urban district, for such it was until recently, covered 45 acres (18ha) and was cut out of Maugersbury parish at its junction with three other parishes. The built-up plan is largely triangular, but scarcely any building took place fronting the Foss Way which was the parish boundary.

A similar crudely triangular pattern occurs at Woodstock, probably the only borough in the world that owes its origin to one man's love of a woman. The royal park or forest at Woodstock was favoured by Norman kings, and Henry I about 1100 surrounded it with a stone wall seven miles (11km) long and kept a menagerie here including lions and camels. A straggle of dwellings, today called Old Woodstock, existed or grew up outside this wall on the north valleyside of the small river Glyme at some distance from the king's hunting lodge. Equally distant was the hamlet of Hensington some way to the east. Henry II fell in love with Fair Rosamond, daughter of Walter de Clifford, and housed her in Woodstock park, where he visited her frequently. The official record, the *Hundred Rolls* for 1279, states clearly that twelve witnesses swear that 'in the time of Henry le Veyl (H.II), King of England, the vill of Wodestok was first founded in this manner. At that time the king often resided in his manor of Wodestok for the love of a certain woman named Rosamund; and at that same time there was a certain empty plot outside the park of the same Manor, and because the King's men were lodged too far from this manor, the King, with the unanimous consent and counsel of his nobles, gave and granted divers portions of land of the desmesne, being void plots, to divers men for the purpose of building lodging houses therein, for the use of the King's men; and appointed therein, with the common consent of his nobles, the various rents underwritten; and gave to the men lodged therein a market to be held on the Tuesday of each week, of which market the King's bailiff shall collect the toll and answer therefor yearly to the Exchequer. At length came King Henry, son of John, who being moved with exceeding pity because of the poverty of the same vill, gave and granted an annual fair for three days at the feast of Saint Matthew the Apostle, free and without toll for the benefit of the said vill. And the whole vill of Wodestok holds freely in chief and their heirs of the Lord King for the rents under-written'.[6]

Thus New Woodstock was founded about 1163 or 1164 on a plot of thirty acres (12ha) acquired by Henry II from the Templars. As today it was hemmed in between the Park wall, the river Glyme and the village of Hensington and owned no land outside its own narrow confines. The borough contained 72 tenements ranging in annual rental from 18d for a house opposite the stone cross, to from 6d to 12d for other dwellings near the centre down to 2d or less for what appear to be terraced dwellings or divided tenements toward the periphery. In addition there were 33 cottages with rentals of up to 3½d but for the most part of ½d a year, as well as 30 messuages, 5 crofts, 19 vacant plots, 4 pigsties (at ½d each annually) and a row of 16 or 17 market stalls (at 1d each), of which at least one

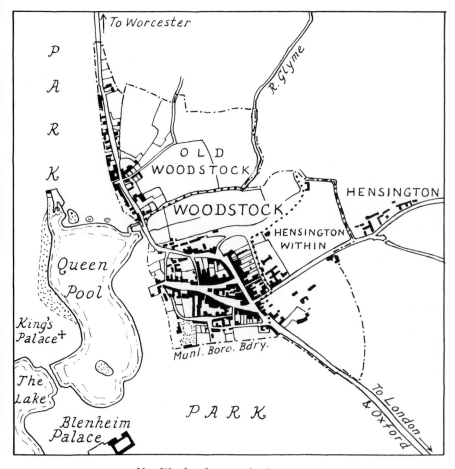

New Woodstock: town plan in 1900.

was a shamble. Also mentioned are a bakery (1d rental), an oven (½d), a cemetery, a chapel with a bell-tower (under the control of Bladon parish) and 2 smithies. All told, the borough had about 108 different householders, including several who owned a number of properties that were sub-let. The total resident population was about 540 and their occupations covered a wide variety of arts and crafts with perhaps a regal burghal tinge judging from the presence of a wymplare and a catchpoll. The total annual rental due to the King was 45s 3¾d, or about 1s 6d an acre, which seems a remarkably good yield considering that desmesne lands rented out in nearby parishes seldom brought in more than 1s per acre, and in most areas 6d to 9d an acre was the normal rental. The residents had come mainly from villages and hamlets less than fifteen miles (24km) away.

In 1453 New Woodstock received a royal charter of incorporation and the

New Woodstock from the Park. Old Woodstock climbs the valley slope just off the left of the photograph.

privilege of compounding the rents of the borough for a fixed communal sum. In Tudor times the borough became famous for gloves, a handicraft which expanded, especially in the nineteenth century, and still survives. The legal divorcement of the borough from the manor and adjacent parishes had interesting consequences in later years when the built-up areas of Old Woodstock and Hensington Without expanded to join up with New Woodstock. Houses on opposite sides of a street found themselves under different civil authorities, and new estates serving Woodstock borough were just outside the municipal boundary. However, most of these administrative differences have recently been resolved, and the borough after more than five hundred years of independence has lost its municipal status. The mayor and corporation are retained only as historic symbols of the former power of a borough that from 1553 to 1832 sent two members to parliament and then one till 1885.

Whereas the royal borough of Woodstock was divorced from agricultural

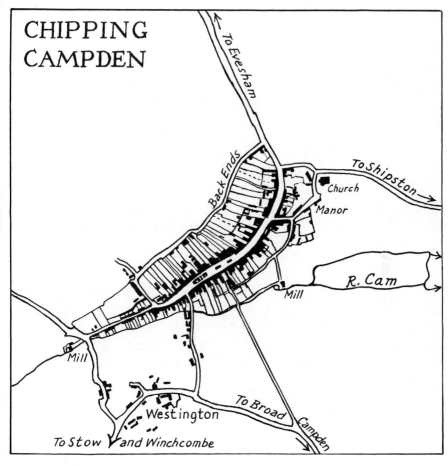

CHIPPING CAMPDEN

To Evesham

Back Ends

To Shipston

Church

Manor

R. Cam

Mill

Mill

To Broad Campden

Westington

To Stow and Winchcombe

Chipping Campden: town plan in 1900.

connections with adjacent parishes, our next example, Chipping Campden, is typical of new creations that had a close interest in the common fields. At *Domesday Survey* the parish of Campden had 50 villeins and 8 bordars, most of whom probably lived near the permanent springs in the hamlets or manors of Westington and Berrington, which included Broad Campden. About 1180 a charter (now lost) granted a fair to the burgesses of Campden and this was confirmed in 1247 in a grant of a weekly market and annual fair to Roger de Somery. The probability is that in 1180, Hugh de Gondeville, lord of the manor, laid out a new town of rectangular strip-like plots facing on to a wide central thoroughfare with market place and chapel, and backing on to a perimeter of Back Ends that gave direct access to the communal fields. The planned High Street curves gracefully along the contour upon a gentle slope to the Cam brook. Today in the north the planning ends near, but distinct from, a knoll in

Chipping Campden viewed from Westington Hill to the southeast, showing the mediaeval market street with linear plots leading to the Back Ends.

Berrington tithing on which the church and manor house stand; in the south it approaches the irregular cluster of houses at Westington and gets to within a short distance of the Norman chapel at Broad Campden. Thus in one operation the overlord created a borough in a large parish of 4,700 acres (1,900ha) that was supporting three tiny settlements. Not surprisingly the hamlets remained small while the borough developed into a flourishing town, with close access to a road along the Cotswold summit, the chief all-weather route from Coventry and Stratford to Winchcombe and Gloucester. By 1273 Chipping Campden had 75¾ burgages, 15 other houses and 7 shops. The manor contained extensive sheep pastures and by the late-fourteenth century the town was an important wool centre, with a woolstaplers' hall and the fine house of William Grevel, 'flower of the wool merchants of all England. Most of the traffic of the Cotswold ridgeway now came through the borough and as late as 1800 the standard *Description of All the Direct and Principal Cross Roads in England and Wales* still gave roads from Banbury to Campden, from Coventry to Gloucester via Campden, and from Salisbury via Marlborough, Lechlade and Burford to Campden. The last, a distance of 77 miles (124km), seems a relic of the wool trade.

Chipping Campden remained a seignorial borough and never achieved high burghal status. Its charter, as renewed by James I in 1605, provided for 14 chief burgesses, two of whom were to be bailiffs, and 14 inferior burgesses, who together made and enforced laws in the borough and tried actions involving amounts not exceeding £6 13s 4d. There were two serjeants-at-mace and a steward, learned in the law, who was elected and paid a salary by the burgesses for legal advice. In practice the court was held monthly but the corporation never bothered to apply for a seal and never sent a representative to Parliament. In 1851, the borough was still entered separately in the *Census,* with 356 inhabited houses and 1777 inhabitants, whereas the whole parish, including the adjacent hamlets of Westington and Berrington, contained 2,351 people. Already the corporation was languishing and the population declining and, later, investigations showed that the town was not suitable to be placed under the Municipal Corporations Act of 1883. The corporation was finally abolished in 1885, its income then being about £8 a year, derived mainly from tolls charged for use of the market place for amusement purposes. This small revenue and the regalia with other chattels were invested in a town trust which still survives. Eventually the unspoilt nature of the declining town proved its salvation, for in 1902 the Guild of Handicraft migrated from the East End of London to a disused silk mill in Sheep Street, bringing a group of skilled artists and craftsmen into the slumbering community. During the motor car age Chipping Campden was saved from commercialism and decay and it remains a Cotswold gem that many consider should be preserved intact as a National Town.

Such recognition of its historic and architectural qualities should certainly also be given to Burford in Oxfordshire, which is also built largely of local oolite in a Cotswold style. The manor here at *Domesday Survey* had 40 households and a mansion worth 5s. The site of the humbler dwellings is not known, but the mansion or manor house was almost certainly on the plateau just south of the present town at Bury Barns where until recently a rectangle of fences resembled the outline of a Saxon *burh.* The place names Bury Barns and Burford may recall the existence of a fortification. About 1100 the lord of the manor, Robert FitzHamon, Earl of Gloucester, created here a borough with market, and unusually for so early a date, a guild with the customs of the burgesses of Oxford. The borough was sited on the valley side facing north and sloping down to the Windrush beyond which were Fulbrook parish and Wychwood forest. Thus the site lay conveniently between the manor house and any dwellings near the ford which was soon to be bridged. The other main reason for placing the new borough on this slope in a terrain devoid of springs was probably the existence of a route northward, which the battle between Wessex and Mercia at Burford in 752 seems to indicate. This, the Southampton-Salisbury-Lechlade-Stow road of today, was almost certainly the stimulus but the motive was clearly profit. No doubt the population of the large manor was dispersed in several hamlets, for in addition to houses near the ford and near the mansion on the

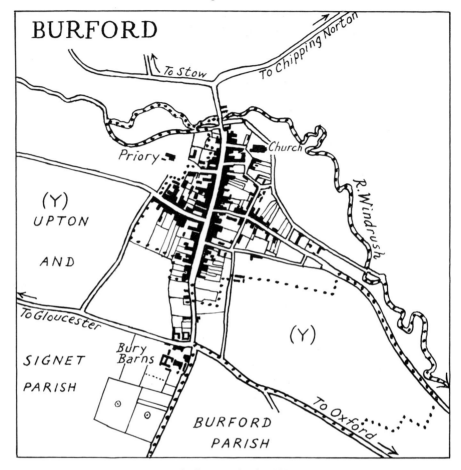

Burford: town plan in 1900.

plateau, there would also have been dwellings near the copious spring at Signett just south of Bury Barns and at Upton in the valley upstream. Presumably the overlord's agents could see no future for this dispersal of four tiny hamlets and decided to concentrate the manor's population into one township. Whatever the reason, the result was clear; within two centuries the economy, people and local road system were focused upon Burford and the stone bridge near its church.

The plan of the new borough consisted largely of rectangular strips fronting upon a wide central High Street and terminating outward at a back lane. The first burgages to be built on were those on the moderate slope at the foot of the valley side, and tenements already extended along two side roads, before, in the late sixteenth century, the pasture closes of the steep upper part of the valley side began to be inhabited. The number of mediaeval burgages corresponds almost exactly with present day holdings, and the street plan has scarcely changed except that some of the numerous cross-lanes have been built across. People from outside the manor took up some of the burgages, judging from the five messuages held in 1193 by Thomas de Langley, Warden of Wychwood. In 1299 there were about 500 inhabitants in the borough, another 75 in Signett and 40 customary tenants in Upton. By 1552 the town had 140 households living on 124½ burgages or at a reasonable estimate 750 inhabitants. None of the citizens achieved great success as woolstaplers but many became moderately prosperous as general traders and manufacturers especially of cloth and leatherwork. After 1435 much rebuilding was done in local stone and large quantities of oolitic limestone were taken from Kitt's quarries at Upton for the new St Paul's. Christopher Kempster, one of Wren's master masons, built a house in 1698 in the quarry and is buried in the church where his monument bears weeping cherubs, his personal mark. The hostelries in the town flourished especially between 1761 and 1812 when the main coach services from Oxford to Gloucester passed through the town. By 1830 the population had increased to over 1,600 while Upton and Signett had 250 inhabitants. Subsequently the railway did not come nearer than Shipton under Wychwood, 5 miles (8km) away, and the town began to decline. By 1901 it had only 1,146 residents, and Upton and Signett had dwindled to 177 persons. The decline was continuing when E.J. Horniman, a tea merchant, bought the priory ruins in 1911 and proceeded to restore them and any other old houses that fell vacant in the town. His example was followed by other residents and today the town attracts the admiration of throngs of tourists. Simultaneously Bury Barns has become the headquarters of a golf club, Signett remains a handful of houses, and at Upton the mill and cottages have crumbled away leaving only a farmstead and one or two dwellings. The ecclesiastic parish of Burford embraces them all, but Upton and Signett form a distinct civil parish from which Burford borough was cut as a separate administrative unit. The post-1918 extensions of Burford on to the top of the plateau lie in Upton and Signett parish.

The fate of the borough corporation has long intrigued historians. The first grant of liberties by the Earl of Gloucester about 1100 provided burghal tenure, a market, a merchant guild (rare at this date) and various free customs the same as those of the burgesses of Oxford. The Burford burgesses never tried to extend these privileges to any great extent, partly perhaps because they thought them comprehensive and utterly secure. A common seal was in use by the mid-thirteenth century, and the guild built its own chapel beside, but separate from, the parish church. The lord of the manor never lived in the district and over the centuries the burgesses unhindered gradually assumed that they had full and independent control of the borough. Unlike many other borough corporations, they never realised that they had not secured from the crown, by payment and new charters, such liberties as freedom from Hundred and Shire courts, the right to appoint their own bailiffs, and to pay their rents communally in a fixed annual sum. By 1600 the Burford corporation, consisting usually of 2 bailiffs, an

Burford viewed from the south looking down the steep valley slope to the church and floodplain of the Windrush. On the opposite valley side are (to right) the village of Fulbrook and (to left) the hamlet of Westhall Hill.

alderman and about 10 burgesses, was putting into its own coffers various sums for administration and services, which belonged by right to the lord of the manor. When the crown acquired the manor, as it did occasionally, the burgesses thought they were dealing directly with the king by ancient right, whereas they had never purchased this right and were dealing with him solely because as lord of the manor he appointed their bailiffs.

This misunderstanding passed virtually unnoticed and unchallenged until the king sold the manor, and it was acquired by Sir Lawrence Tanfield, Lord Chief Baron of the Exchequer, an avaricious lawyer who had already caused much distress among the parishioners at Great Tew. In the late sixteenth century Sir Lawrence bought Burford priory from the crown and built there, at a cost of about £5,000, a magnificent Elizabethan mansion in which he entertained James I. In 1617 he purchased the lordship of the manor and town and went on to buy nearly all the ancient manor. He could have advised the burgesses on the vagueness of their charters and have procured for them a charter of incorporation, instead someone—no doubt Sir Lawrence or his wife—secretly instituted proceedings against the legal authority of the borough corporation. The burgesses, relying on their early charters and prescriptive rights, stood no chance, and a Royal Commission in 1628 stripped them of all powers, except control of some former guild charities which they had wisely bought back in Elizabethan times. These charities were neglected in the nineteenth century, and in 1861 an Act of Parliament dissolved 'the existing corporation of the alderman, steward, bailiffs, and burgesses of the Borough of Burford'. The Tolsey or Court House, erected about 1560 during the zenith of burghal power, is now a museum, and Sir Lawrence Tanfield lies with his wife within a magnificent tomb in the former guild chapel in the parish church. Its rich canopy bears at its corners erect female figures representing the virtues, among them Law and Justice.

Abortive Boroughs and Monastic Towns

Many efforts of overlords to create new boroughs or to promote large villages to borough status failed, as at Newland near Witney. The picturesque village of Deddington had a new planned extension (New Street) on either side of the main Oxford-Banbury road in the thirteenth century but it never grew into a borough, probably because it was stifled by Banbury. Middleton Stoney had a weekly market and 14 burgage holders in 1279, most of whom paid 1s a year, and a few years later was granted a fair but it seems to have been almost wiped out by the Black Death.[7]

These abortive boroughs lacked the vitality and size of another form of settlement, the monastic town, which from a layman's point of view ceased to be or never became a normal borough. At Abingdon, Cirencester, Evesham and Reading the great monastery ruled the roost. At Winchcombe, a Saxon royal borough, apart from a short period in the thirteenth century, the bailiffs acted for the sheriff and the townspeople were virtually self-governing, but this freedom was quite exceptional in monastic towns. Elsewhere the abbot and citizens were constantly at loggerheads over their respective rights. At Evesham, where the Benedictine monastery was founded by St Egwin in the eighth century, the abbot had a market and commercial privileges before the Conquest and the townsfolk remained under his thumb till the dissolution. The divisive peculiarities of these monastic towns are well illustrated by Cirencester, Abingdon and Reading, all seats of mitred abbots.

At Cirencester, burgesses and some form of borough status almost certainly existed before Henry I reconstructed the Saxon College of Prebendaries into an Augustinian abbey, which he endowed with its old properties and one hide from his own manor here. The English kings stayed here frequently, partly for the good hunting, and the abbot had easy access to royal favour. Henry II allowed the abbot to enjoy the revenues and dues from the royal desmesne in Cirencester, and later the brethren paid the king £100 for a perpetual grant of the royal manor at a rental of £30 a year. In 1204 they gave the king another £100 for a renewal of the grant and for freedom from interference by the sheriff. The abbot now began to act as though he controlled the borough and in 1308 suppressed the borough court, so forcing the townsfolk to attend the court of the rural manor which he administered. The indignant citizens appealed to chancery, stating *inter alia* that the abbots had bought up many burgages in the town so making it a mere appendage of abbey property and that the abbot had got hold of their royal charter, which mentioned burgesses, and burnt it. The abbot denied this but refused to produce the charter and eventually paid the king £300 as a fine or bribe to close the dispute for ever. The best that the citizens could finally do was to form a social-religious Trinity Guild which was independent of the abbot.

In 1401 the townsmen and the abbot helped Henry Bolingbroke (Henry IV) against the forces of the rebellious Earls of Kent and Salisbury, both of whom they captured and after executing them in the market place, sent their heads to London. As Shakespeare says, with some exaggeration as the fire was merely an attempt by the rebels to cause a diversion:

> . . . the latest news we hear,
> Is that the rebels have consumed with fire
> Our town of Ciceter in Gloucestershire.
>   (*Richard II*, Act V. Sc. VI)

The citizens and abbot took rich spoils, and the king gave the townspeople monetary rewards and soon afterwards the right of a merchant guild, debt recovery and trade control in the town. However, in 1418 the abbot contrived to have this charter annulled and the townsfolk did not achieve independence and freedom from the lord of the manor until the early nineteenth century. The old town lacks any formal street planning and the fine market square in front of the parish church was made about 1832, by demolishing a jumble of narrow streets. According to some historians, the civic community never entirely overcame the handicap of four centuries of oppressive monastic control.

At Abingdon the abbot had absolute control and held a market outside his main gate from early times. In Henry II's reign the people of the royal boroughs of Wallingford and Oxford sallied forth and tried to smash this market because, they said, goods other than victuals were being sold there, but after long legal arguments the abbot won the day. In 1327 during the changeover from Edward II to Edward III, the Abingdonians revolted in an effort to control the organisation of the market. They set fire to the Geldhall recently erected in the market place, where the abbot collected dues, and attacked the main gate of the abbey. The armed defenders within the precincts retaliated and killed two

Central Abingdon in 1961, showing railway station (now gone), the Town Hall, and beyond it St Helen's church and the Thames.

townsmen and captured many others to bring them to justice. The riots soon took on a wider, more violent aspect. The mayor of Oxford with a large band of scholars, citizens and no doubt foot-loose hooligans marched to join the Abingdonians. On the way they burnt the manor of Northcourt which belonged to the abbey and entering the town 'made such horrid noises that the unusualness of it even frightened those who had invited them thither'.[8] Together the rioters stormed and burnt the abbey gates and thoroughly pillaged the conventual buildings. At an enforced meeting in Bagley Wood, the prior and few monks still available agreed to allow the citizens to elect their own provost and bailiff and to have certain other freedoms. But within a few weeks the abbot gained the support of the king and eventually royal officials rounded up many of the malefactors, twelve of whom were hanged at Wallingford and a further sixty saved from that fate only by the abbot's intervention. The reprisals and criminal trials continued for several years and many more citizens from both towns were hanged and a large number fined or imprisoned. The abbot regained complete ascendancy over Abingdon and in 1332 was given a royal licence to crenellate for defence his main gateway and the buildings near it.

The townsfolk now moved forward through a religious guild, the Brotherhood of the Holy Cross, which in 1416 undertook the construction of two bridges and a causeway across the Thames and Andersey Island. As a result the main road from London to Gloucester and the west now passed through Abingdon, so by-passing the older crossing at Wallingford which began to decay. The Brotherhood was incorporated into a guild in 1441 through the offices of Sir John Golafre who built at his own expense the fine stone bridge at Newbridge. After the dissolution of the abbey, Abingdon declined for a while and eventually in 1555 was incorporated as a free borough with a common council and the right to elect one member of parliament. The town lacks any regular plan, some roads converging on the parish church and others on the main abbey gate.

At Reading, which stands on the Kennet near its junction with the Thames, the abbey was founded by Henry I in 1121 and thereafter the citizens of the old borough struggled to keep their rights and privileges, including a merchant guild. In 1253 the abbot virtually gained control, but the frequent visits of royalty allowed the citizens to obtain and retain a few privileges. In 1301 when the chief officer of the guild assumed the name of mayor, the abbot refused to recognise the title just as later he refused the use of maces. In 1405 when the abbot granted the burgesses right of passage by boat on the Kennet alongside the abbey he restricted it to daylight with complete absence of 'play, riott or noyse'. The citizens struggled for more freedom throughout the fifteenth century but, although gaining some share of actual government, remained firmly under monastic supervision. After 1538 when the abbey became a royal palace they soon acquired a new charter with full rights of self-government, and Elizabeth added allowances sufficient to restore the corporation's finances, as well as 200 loads of freestone from the abbey ruins for the repair of bridges. Today central Reading has a chaotic street pattern that reflects the walled enclosure of the abbey and utterly lacks the rectangular patterns of old planned boroughs such as Oxford and Warwick.

Borough Development, 1348-1801

The creation of planned boroughs had already overstepped itself when the Black Death between 1348 and 1378 wiped out about one third of the population. The boroughs probably lost a greater proportion of their inhabitants than the rural villages but they recovered faster because their burgages passed to kin or would eventually find tenants. What happened to towns during the next few centuries depended largely on the amount of traffic passing through them, the quantity of goods they had for sale, especially wool and corn, and their production of

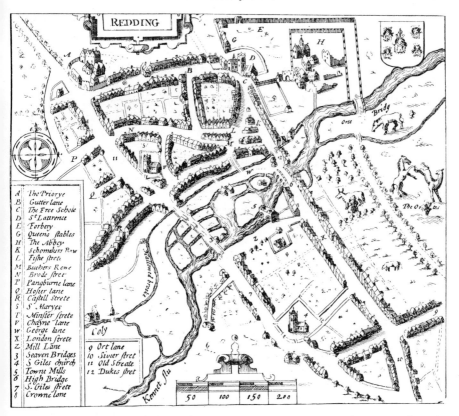

REDDING

A	The Priorye
B	Gutter lane
C	The Free Schole
D	S.t Laurence
E	Forbery
G	Queens stables
H	The Abbey
K	Schomakers Row
L	Fishe strete
M	Buchers Rowe
N	Brode strete
P	Pangburne lane
Q	Hoser lane
R	Castell strete
S	S.t Maryes
T	Minster strete
V	Chayne lane
w	George lane
X	London strete
Z	Mill Lane
3	Seaven Bridges
4	S Giles chirch
5	Towne Mills
6	High Bridge
7	S. Giles strett
8	Crowne lane
9	Ort lane
10	Sivier stret
11	Old Streate
12	Dukes stret

50   100   150   200

Reading: Speed's map of 1610 showing clearly that the town grew up on the Kennet where the river braided into numerous channels.

manufactures, mainly textiles and leather goods. Oxford's educational growth was an inexplicable peculiarity.

The national status of boroughs may be judged approximately from their taxation returns. In 1334, of about 106 towns in England assessed at £225 or more, only 10 were in the English heartland.[9] Oxford (£914) was ninth and Newbury (£412) twenty second in the national ranking; the remainder, Reading, Northampton, Abingdon, Banbury, Campden, Cirencester, Faringdon and Bicester at £243 to £293 did not come in the first forty. Bampton was assessed at £969 but that included a large number of contributory townships.

By 1527 the ranking of the towns had changed radically; partly due to the expansion of textile manufacturing, Reading was now tenth and Newbury still twenty second, but Oxford had slipped back to thirtieth and the other boroughs in the English heartland did not come in the first forty towns in England for wealth.[10]

We have described in earlier chapters how some of the towns in our survey experienced appreciable growth before declining or stagnating in the mid-nineteenth century. But the first official census of 1801 provides a fairly secure basis for the national ranking of towns. There were then in England about 50 towns with a population of over 10,000 and of these only Oxford (11,694 people; 35th in ranking) was in the English heartland, although Reading, with 9,742 inhabitants, was not far behind. Clearly the region was slipping gradually into nonentity and quite extraordinary factors would be needed to create large towns here. Prior to the coming of the motor car and the modern population explosion these factors proved to be the spas at Cheltenham and Leamington and the railway at Swindon, and only the latter lies well within the English heartland.

CHAPTER SEVENTEEN

Stratford upon Avon and Shakespeare

Triumph, my Britain, thou hast one to show,
To whom all scenes of Europe homage owe.
He was not of an age, but for all time!
    (Ben Jonson)

The New Borough

Stratford originated beside the Avon upon a large patch of river gravel which provided well drained sites for huts, light soils for ploughing and a clean water supply. The Romano-British settlers also had the advantage of a road (*street*) which crossed the Avon at a ford near the site of the present bridge. In the early sixth century AD the settlement was destroyed by Saxons advancing up the river valley, but before the end of the seventh century a monastery was founded here on or near the site of the present Holy Trinity church in what is still called *Old Town*. In 691 it was given by Ethelred of Mercia to the bishop of Worcester. Like many other English monasteries it died out during the Danish invasions, whereas the farming community around it managed to survive and by *Domesday Survey* in 1086 was apparently thriving. The manor then still belonged to the Saxon bishop of Worcester, the incumbent being the famous Wulfstan who was born at Itchington near Warwick, educated at Evesham abbey and later canonised by Innocent III. The bishop's estate at Stratford had land for 31 ploughs, of which 28 belonged to 21 villeins or tenants. There were also 7 bordars, or menial cottagers, and a priest. The meadow, obviously near the Avon, stretched for five furlongs by two and the mill was valued at ten shillings and one thousand eels annually. The community benefited indirectly from Wulfstan's submission to and alliance with William the Conqueror which ensured at least that these estates were not harried by the Normans. The friendly connections with the bishopric of Worcester continued to prove beneficial to Stratford.

In 1196 Bishop John of Coutances decided to create a new borough here in the manor not uncommon in England at the time (*see* Chapter Sixteen). The surveyors laid out six straight streets, three parallel with the edge of the flood plain, and three crossing them at right angles. Within this rectangular framework plots of about 12 perches by 3½ perches, or of about ¾ acre each, were demarcated and made available to any taker on burgage tenure of one shilling a year. At the same time the borough obtained a grant for a market. This new town was cleverly

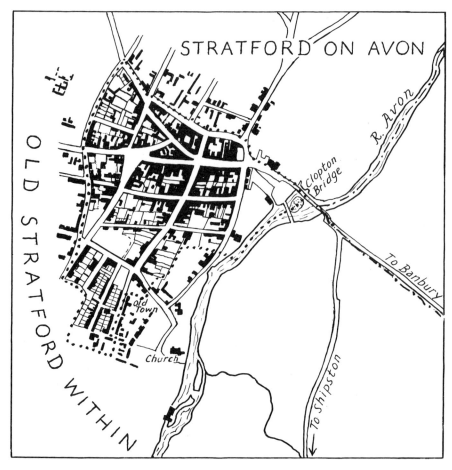

Stratford upon Avon: town plan about 1900. Dotted line denotes borough boundary. Railways are omitted.

sited between the old village and the main road from the ford. The highway actually went through its market place, then a triangular space west of the junction of High Street and Bridge Street, once the site of a market cross. So there was now an Old Stratford with a church and a large rural parish, and Stratford Town (*burgus*) with a small urban area inhabited by burgesses who paid well for the privilege of being freeholders and of looking after their own civic affairs. No doubt the bishop was popular and trusted for people migrated to the new borough from neighbouring villages up to 25 miles (40km) away.[1] In 1251-2 he received rents from nearly 250 burgages and 54½ other plots (*placae*) as well as from fourteen shop holders, ten stall holders and the tenants of two dye vats and of two bake ovens, the last named usually being separate structures well away from the houses. The burgesses paid a total annual rental of about £16 on

Stratford upon Avon, viewed from the east looking across the Avon to the Shakespeare Royal Theatre and Bancroft Gardens and beyond them to the mediaeval rectangle of nine planned streets.

what must have been an urban tract of about 70 acres (28ha), whereas the bishop's estates in Old Stratford, extending to over 250 acres (100ha) and with three corn mills and a fulling mill, yielded only £21. It was a remarkably successful venture although some difficulties were sure to arise later because the borough and rural parish were under separate jurisdictions.

The layout of the new borough survives clearly today opposite the Bancroft and Shakespeare Memorial Theatre. In 1216 the weekly market was augmented by the grant of a three-day annual fair and a few years later by two other yearly fairs. The weekly market and one fair survive, the latter as a mop or pleasure event.

From 1269 to 1547 the township was administered by the Guild of the Holy Cross which grew rich and included members with county and national reputations, such as the Duke of Clarence and Lord Warwick in the fifteenth century. With the aid of subscriptions, gifts and legacies it acquired many properties in the town and an income sufficient to contribute toward the repair of the wooden bridge over the Avon, to maintain priests to say prayers in its own chapel, to pay for a master to teach in its own school, to assist orphans, and to provide almshouses for ten poor folk.[2] The guild also controlled the manufacturing and trading functions of a wide variety of craftsmen and merchants, among them Hugh Clopton, a merchant who migrated to London and became its Lord Mayor in 1492. Clopton had the poor timber bridge over the Avon replaced by a fine stone structure of fourteen arches and a long walled-in causeway on four arches over the flood plain on the town side. The future prosperity of Stratford was now assured, as on this bridge there converged from the east main roads from Banbury and Oxford, and from the west main roads from Birmingham, Alcester and Evesham. The foresight of the bishops of Worcester and the generosity of Hugh Clopton had an unforeseen reward, for true to the adage 'to him that hath shall be given', the town attracted the Shakespeare family.

The Shakespeares in Stratford and Neighbourhood

At least since the thirteenth century, families called Shakespeare, Shakspeare or some other variant of the name have been common in England and especially in central Warwickshire. The name, although perhaps coming direct from the Anglo-Saxon Seaxberht, could be taken literally and so be open to martial puns and warlike innuendoes. In 1487 a certain Hugh Shakspere of Merton College, Oxford, considered his surname had so vile a reputation that he changed it to Saunders.[3] William was a favourite personal name of the Shakespeares and the sorting out of the poet's ancestors from the rest of the baptismal clan provides an unhappy hunting ground for scholars. The branches of his family tree only become clear back to his grandparents who were on the male side, Richard Shakespeare, a farmer of Snitterfield, and on the distaff side, the Ardens, substantial landowners of Wilmcote. The poet's mother, Mary Arden, was the youngest of eight daughters of Robert Arden by his first wife. In 1557 when she married John Shakespeare, the poet's father, she owned a farm called Asbyes at Wilmcote in the parish of Aston Cantlow. The charming farmstead at Wilmcote now called after her had been built a few years previously. It survives as an attractive half-timbered dwelling with a projecting gabled wing with herringbone strutting and extensive outbuildings including a square stone dovecot. The property now belongs to the Birthplace Trust and its barns form a museum of old implements, tools and utensils connected with rural life.

John Shakespeare was already living in Stratford when in 1556 he bought two

Mary Arden's house at Wilmcote.

freehold houses, one of which was the eastern half of the two tenements in Henley Street known today as the poet's birthplace. Probably he had already owned for some years the western half of the building, which traditionally is the birthplace proper. John was a glover and wool dealer who soon became prominent in Stratford life. He was elected an alderman in 1565 and within a few years became the high bailiff, or mayor, a post which carried with it the status and duties of a justice of the peace. William, the third and only then surviving child of the marriage, was born on or about 23rd April, a calendar date which is the same as that of his death and may be a confusion with it. Probably he was taught expertly at the local grammar school, but when thirteen or fourteen had his formal education curtailed by his father's financial difficulties. He did not proceed to a university and at the age of eighteen married Anne Hathaway, daughter of a farmer at Shottery, one mile (1.6km) west of his home. Anne's parents lived in a spacious farmhouse of twelve rooms, dating from the fourteenth or fifteenth century, and today called a 'cottage'. She was about eight years older than William and already pregnant. Their first child, Susanna, was born in May 1583 and was followed by twins, Hamnet and Judith, in February 1585.

The marriage could not have brought much comfort to John and Mary Shakespeare who had had five more children since the birth of William. John's

Anne Hathaway's farmhouse, Shottery.

financial troubles seem best explained by the rapid rise of Woodstock and Oxford as gloving centres. Oxford had a Glovers' Guild in 1461, and during Tudor times the burgesses often presented gloves to the monarchs and occasionally to their train also. Moreover the Earl of Leicester had a residence at Cornbury Park near the royal palace at Woodstock. Probably royal parties and troops of players journeying from London to Kenilworth now bought their gloves in Oxfordshire, to the great loss of Stratford glovers. What is certain is that John gradually ceased to attend corporation meetings and in 1586 lost his aldermanship. Shortly afterwards he was labelled a recusant as may be seen on a manuscript in Warwick county record office;[4] the reason for his absence from church, according to a similar list in the public records, was that he was avoiding public meetings in order to escape arrest for debts.

About this time William disappears from the scene. He may well have left Stratford with a company of travelling players on their way to London, as there had already been at least a dozen visits by such companies to Stratford during his life. Tradition has it that he was in danger of being arrested by Sir Thomas Lucy of Charlecote for some misdemeanour, having previously offended him by poaching in the extensive park at Fulbroke in Hampton Lucy parish. Sir Thomas had just built a fine house at Charlecote, and Fulbroke castle had been pulled down to provide bricks for it and Compton Wynyates. Probably most

Stratfordians regarded the deserted Fulbroke park as fair game for poachers. Shakespeare in *The Merry Wives of Windsor* parodied Sir Thomas as Justice Shallow who had a dozen louses in his old coat, the pun being on the name Lucy and their armorial crest which included several *luces,* the heraldic term for a small freshwater pike. Whatever the cause for his flight, Shakespeare, aged about twenty, left for London leaving behind a wife and three children, parents in difficulty and probably an unenviable reputation as a youthful hothead.

Within eight years he was beginning to make a name for himself as a poet and playwright. He had found in London several school-fellows from Stratford, including William Combe, a lawyer, and Richard Field, head of a publishing house, and above all had a patron in Henry Wriothesley, Earl of Southampton. His *Venus and Adonis* (1593) and the much longer *The Rape of Lucrece* (1594) were published by Field and dedicated to the Earl. He now became a prominent member of the Lord Chamberlain's Men formed in 1594 by Lord Hunsdon, gathering up actors from several previous companies scattered by the plague two years earlier. The Lord Chamberlain was responsible for entertainments at Court, and Shakespeare's company often provided these. In 1603 King James, newly arrived from Scotland, took the company under his patronage as 'The King's Men'. The company from 1594 to at least 1613, except for short intervals, played continuously in London, with Shakespeare writing on an average two plays a year and thirty seven or thirty eight in all.[5] The Lord Chamberlain's Men had acquired their own regular playhouse, The Theatre, but in 1598 tore it down, after a dispute with the landowner, and rebuilt it on the south bank, as 'The Globe'. In the new agreement between the shareholders then drawn up, Shakespeare had a ten per cent share of the profits, which would be considerable. In 1608 'The King's Men', after various legal delays, began to use their indoor theatre at Blackfriars and some critics would like to see this as marking a change in Shakespeare's style, the later plays giving more scope for special effects possible indoors. In 1613 The Globe burnt down during a performance of Shakespeare's *Henry VIII* which was being staged with great splendour but was soon rebuilt.

When William first began to visit Stratford regularly from London is not known. He was able to relieve the financial troubles of his father whose earlier application for a coat of arms, due to a high bailiff, was now confirmed. In 1597, William bought, for £60, New Place in Chapel Street, one of the largest houses in Stratford. In 1601, John Shakespeare 'a merry-cheeked old man', died peacefully on good terms with his son. William continued to invest his new won wealth in his native parish, and at various times bought, at a total cost of £760, about 127 acres (51ha) and rights of common in the open fields and half of the tithes of the township. When his mother died in 1608 he inherited the family home in Henley Street. He probably retired to New Place in 1610 though he seems to have often been in London after that date. Traditionally his last plays are thought to be the Romances: *Pericles, Cymbeline, The Winter's Tale,* and

The Shakespeare monument in Holy Trinity church.

The Tempest, written in that order between 1608 and 1612 although the evidence is slight. *The Tempest,* which because of its subject matter cannot have been written before 1610, is usually seen as Shakespeare's farewell to the theatre on his retirement, though he later contributed *Henry VIII.* It would be pleasing to be able to attribute the impression of moral serenity or peace of mind in the Romances to the quiet Stratford environment, but at least some of their unusual features may be attributed to their being written partly for the indoors Blackfriars theatre. Which plays were written at Stratford will never be known.

Shakespeare died of fever in 1616 at the early age of fifty two, his death, according to tradition, being hastened because he left his sick bed to carouse with Ben Jonson and Michael Drayton. As a tithe owner he was buried in the chancel of Holy Trinity Church where a few months later a life-size monument, by Gerard Johnson, was erected to him. This bust, a frontal demi-figure with hands resting on a cushion and a book, is one of the two undisputed or authentic surviving likenesses made when Anne Shakespeare (*ob.* 1623) was alive, but the destruction of the original colouring has blurred the features. The second undisputed likeness is the copper engraving by Martin Droeshout in the first folio edition of Shakespeare's plays (1622-3), edited by his fellow actors Condell and Heminge, a copy of which hangs in the birthplace. Other portraits and a wealth of Shakespeariana are on view in the museum adjoining the memorial theatre, and in the birthplace.[6]

In his riper years Shakespeare took a keen interest in Stratford affairs and by his will left £10 to the poor of the town. He tried to secure a lineage by leaving to his elder daughter, Susanna, under entail all his estates there, as well as his house at Blackfriars, London, and his best bed. Anne, his wife, would have been well satisfied with 'the second best bed', as it was probably the one she had brought with her from Shottery and she had dower for life in all the property that yielded an income. Susanna was married to Dr John Hall, a noted physician who had cured, among other patients, Michael Drayton, a frequent visitor to the manor house at Clifford Chambers, a small village three kilometres to the south. They lived in a lovely gabled Elizabethan building (Hall's Croft), still standing in Old Town. Their only daughter, Elizabeth, married first Thomas Nash and lived for some time next door to New Place in the dwelling that is now a museum. In 1649 she married as her second husband, John Bernard of Abington manor near Northampton, but by 1670 both she and the three children of Shakespeare's second daughter Judith had died childless, and with them the playwright's direct line ended.

No letter or writing in Shakespeare's hand has been found except a few signatures on his will and various title deeds and perhaps one scene in *The Book of Sir Thomas More.* The lack of original manuscripts encouraged the theory, first mooted in the mid-eighteenth century, that he lacked the education and practical skill to write such plays and poems. This critical extravaganza defeated itself partly because it stimulated laborious research into historical records and the texts. The whole theme has been dealt with recently by S. Schoenbaum, first in his *Shakespeare's Lives* (1970) and later in his monumental *Shakespeare: A Documentary Life* (1975).

Mr. WILLIAM

SHAKESPEARES

COMEDIES,
HISTORIES, &
TRAGEDIES.

Publiſhed according to the True Originall Copies.

LONDON
Printed by Iſaac Iaggard, and Ed. Blount. 1623.

The Droeshout portrait of Shakespeare.

Devotees of Warwickshire will be especially interested in the influence, conscious and subconscious, of that county's environment and society on the playwright. For example, Raphael Holinshed, who lived at Packwood, north of

Henley in Arden, produced his famous *Chronicles of England, Ireland and Scotland* in 1577 just when the schoolboy Shakespeare was at a most impressionable age. Shakespeare used the *Chronicles* for the historical background of at least nine plays. Except in some of the courtly tragedies of the playwright's metropolitan phase, there seems no end to the Stratford influence, for as the Countess de Chambrun says in her delightful *Shakespeare: a portrait restored,* 'The town of his birth, its countryside, its inhabitants, the fields, hills and forests of the Shire appear continually in his poetry, and it is this recourse to things seen and experienced which makes his work so alive and so human' (1957, p30).

Tudor and Jacobean Stratford

In Shakespeare's time the Old Town, as today, was dominated by the square tower and spire of Holy Trinity church, which stands beside the Avon. A graceful building, it dates back to the thirteenth century in its early English transepts, lower tower and some of the nave walls. The upper part of the tower with rose windows, the Decorated aisles and the columns of the nave were added in the fourteenth century. The south aisle with its original bossed ceiling was built for John de Stratford, later Bishop of Winchester, for the use of priests at the college he founded in 1331 just west of the churchyard. During the late fifteenth century the splendid chancel and clerestory and a two-storeyed north porch were added in the Perpendicular style. Of this period, twenty six stalls survive with their misericords, a weird collection depicting *inter alia* two bears and a ragged staff (the badge of the Earls of Warwick), a dromedary, a naked woman on a stag, a Tudor wife-beater, and a marital skirmish in which a woman has seized a man by the beard and raises aloft a saucepan to beat him.[7]

The numerous funereal monuments and inscriptions include those to Hugh Clopton, the Avon bridge builder, to Richard Hill, a grazier (*ob.* 1593) whose eulogy is written in Hebrew, Greek, Latin and English, and to John Combe (*ob.* 1614) who left £5 by will to Shakespeare and to whose nephew the playwright bequeathed his gentleman's sword. The font and entries in the parish registers associated with Shakespeare's baptism and burial are on display. The poet's monument is in the chancel and his gravestone with the inscription cursing anyone who moved his bones. No doubt he had often been through the existing door into the charnel house (now demolished) where bones taken from the vaults were stored. Among the other gravestones are those of Anne Shakespeare (*ob.* 1623), his wife, and of their eldest daughter Susanna (Hall), who died on 13 July 1649 aged sixty six, and whose inscription says:

> Witty above her sex, but that's not all,
> Wise to salvation was good Mistris Hall
> Something of Shakespeare was in that, but this
> Wholy of him with whom she's now in blisse.

In the Old Town, the chief surviving domestic buildings, all of late Tudor age, are the manor or dower house of the Cloptons, the adjacent Avon Croft, and Hall's Croft, formerly the residence of Shakespeare's son-in-law.

In burghal Stratford the architectural attractions also centre upon the religious core, here with a strong civic function. The dissolved Guild of the Holy Cross was replaced in 1553 by a chartered mayor and corporation, which inherited many notable buildings, most of which survive. The guild chapel, founded by Robert de Stratford, and partly rebuilt in the 1480s by Hugh Clopton, adorns the west end of Chapel Lane. Adjoining it in Church Street is the guildhall, built in 1417 and splendidly preserved. The ground floor, the meeting place of the guild or corporation, was no doubt the room where William Shakespeare saw his first theatrical performances, given by a troupe of travelling players on their way to or from London and Warwick. The overhanging upper storey was the grammar school where the playwright received what cannot be considered other than an excellent education for his day. Adjoining the guildhall and with the same timber studding and upper overhang is the long range of almshouses, part erected in 1427 and extended later. Elsewhere in the burghal town interesting timber-framed domestic dwellings also of the fifteenth century survive. Mason's Court, overlooking the market space in Rother Street, was originally a Wealden-type house with a lofty hall open to the rafters, flanked on each side by a wing divided into two storeys. It has been altered, but its crooked timbers and overhanging upper storey are for the most part original. Nearby is the 'White Swan', in which the former central hall was flanked with two projecting wings. Here the interior decorations include three Elizabethan paintings bespattered with large flowers on themes in the book of Tobit.

In Elizabethan times Stratford was 'a proper little mercate town', trading mainly in products of agriculture and manufacture such as brewing, leatherworking, particularly gloves, bell foundring and smithy work. However, it had its full share of plagues, fires and floods which apparently weakened its growth. In 1590 the manor contained 217 houses, most of which were situated in the streets nearest the main road and along Church Street. The southernmost streets of the burghal town such as Tinkers Lane (now Scholars Lane), Chapel Lane, and Swine Street (now Ely Street) were still bordered mainly with plots and barns. Trees and open spaces abounded and the corporation owned 1,000 elms and 40 ash trees dispersed among its properties. There now occurred a series of disastrous fires encouraged by the common use of thatch for roofing. Great fires broke out in 1594 and 1595 and a lesser conflagration in 1614. The chief guild properties and the isolated buildings escaped destruction, but the more built-up streets suffered severe damage. Luckily, Tudor domestic building was now at its best and Stratford added to its surviving structures a wealth of fine late-Elizabethan and Jacobean half-timbered houses that are a delight to the eye. The many gables, overhangs and porches with their variations in timbering, in the spacing of main uprights and crossings, and in the arrangement of struts in the intervening panels, beggar description. The strut details of concave-sided lozenges, ogee-shaped and diagonal crosses and other geometrical variants are caviare for architects. Take, for example, a stroll in High Street where Harvard House, built in 1596, has a one-bay front with decorated friezes, bressumers and corbels for the oriel windows, and panels adorned with crosses of struts. It was the girlhood home of Katherine Rogers, mother of the founder of Harvard University to which it was presented by Edward Morris of Chicago University in 1909. Next door the twin-gabled 'Garrick Inn' is a worthy rival in half-timbering. There are dozens of others including the lofty Shrieve's House in Sheep Street, the upper part of which was largely rebuilt after a fire in 1614. Some have been refaced and some, alas, destroyed (the fine chimney piece in the great hall at Packwood House came from a Stratford inn), but many have been only slightly altered and enough old buildings survive to make the town core essentially mediaeval.

Stratford and the Literary Pilgrimage

Shakespeare's influence on the growth of Stratford did not become significant until the late eighteenth century although the town became famous as his birthplace within a few decades of his death. In 1643, Queen Henrietta Maria stayed for three days at the home of Elizabeth Hall, Shakespeare's grand-daughter. Twenty years later the number of houses in the parish had risen to 421, but the ancient street plan was scarcely altered. In 1672 the improvement of navigation on the Avon, finished by William Sandys as far as Evesham in 1638, was completed by Lord Windsor upstream to Stratford and allowed boats of thirty tons to reach the quays near the present Memorial Theatre. Brick now begins to appear in house construction in the town which almost became a great river port. In 1677, Andrew Yarranton, a member of the Upper Avon navigation syndicate, proposed in his *England's Improvement by Sea and Land* the building of a commercial city called New Brunswick at Bridge Town on the Avon bank opposite Stratford. This emporium would, he suggested, be to the whole neighbourhood what Danzig was to Poland. However, his ambitious scheme as with a similar plan for a New Haarlem at the junction of the Avon and Stour, came to nothing although within a few decades Stratford could be reached by 40-ton barges and had a large water traffic, especially in coal.

The literary pilgrimage did not begin to assume real significance until the early eighteenth century when a wealth of Shakespeareana had arisen. Visitors to see the mulberry tree the poet was said to have planted in New Place gardens became so numerous that the then-owner, the Rev. Francis Gastrell, had it chopped down in 1756. Apparently the pilgrimage continued, for Gastrell, on the excuse of cutting taxes, later pulled down the house, an act which greatly enraged the townsfolk. Today only the foundations remain and the gardens, together with a mulberry tree and borders planted with all the flowers mentioned by the playwright. Next door is Nash's house with a fine mulberry and a charming knot garden of Elizabethan design.

Soon after the desecration of Shakespeare's home, Stratford enjoyed great prosperity and publicity. The timber spire of the church was rebuilt in stone and the town hall erected of Cotswold limestone in the Palladian style with a leaden statue of Shakespeare, by John Cheere, in the middle bay facing Sheep Street. This statue was presented by David Garrick, the celebrated actor, who organised on 6-7 September 1796 a magnificent jubilee to celebrate the bicentenary of the poet's birth. He spent lavishly on illuminations, decorations, feasts and a wide variety of entertainments including almost everything except, strange to say, the performance of a Shakespeare play. An elegant amphitheatre supported by a circular colonnade of columns of the Corinthian order, was erected without the town on the Bancroft; a part of the room was taken up with an orchestra and was illuminated by a chandelier of eight hundred lights hanging from the centre of the roof. On this occasion a prodigious number of the nobility and gentry resorted to Stratford. On the first day about 800 breakfasted in the town hall, 1,500 dined in the amphitheatre and about 2,000 attended the oratorio, ball and all-night masquerade on the following day. These crowds produced much confusion in regard to provisions made for their accommodation, especially with respect to lodgings and beds.

Subsequently Stratfordians have put right both the omission of a Shakespeare play and the inadequate facilities for visitors. They were helped by rapid improvement in transport and the town's nodality on highways from London to Birmingham and Gloucester to Coventry, the latter by way of Heydon's Elm, Bedlam and Chipping Campden. In 1817 the town had 24 main regular coaches calling daily. This carriage and turnpike era left its architectural mark in the small tower tollhouse alongside Clopton Bridge and in the high wide entrances to some of the burghal properties. About this time the Birmingham canal was extended to the Avon at Stratford, and its lock basin now forms part of the memorial gardens in Bancroft. In 1826 these wharfs were connected by a horse-drawn tramway to Moreton in Marsh (*see* Chapter 15). Its brick bridge still spans the Avon and its course in Stratford parish can be traced by the embankments. The former Market House, the first permanent theatre (1827), and some pleasant late Georgian houses, especially in Payton Street and Guild Street, reflect the town's prosperity. Not surprisingly the population of the parish rose from 2,418 in 1801 to 3,488 in 1831.

Thereafter, as with most rural boroughs the population began to decline, but prosperity was restored by the coming of two railways and of a Union Workhouse, all, like the racecourse, discreetly tucked away on the perimeter. In 1858 the birthplace, purchased by a trust about ten years earlier, was restored to the plan shown in a drawing in the *Gentleman's Magazine* in 1796. Today it is visited by more than 250,000 persons annually. There was a resurgence of building and commemoration after the third centenary in 1869. A new gothic theatre (now demolished), connected by a bridge to a library and art gallery was

Shakespeare's birthplace.

finished in 1881 and was matched by a large lecture room and scene dock on the other side of the street in 1887. A year later the fine bronze statue of Shakespeare on a high pedestal, supported by corner figures of Lady Macbeth, Hamlet, Prince Henry and Falstaff, was erected in the memorial gardens. There was a little Victorian gothicisation in the town such as in the redbrick Midland Bank in Chapel Street with its terra cotta relief scenes from Shakespeare's plays, but the result is awfully nice rather than nicely awful.

The motor age and faster liner travel brought increasing numbers of bardolators. In 1932, the new Shakespeare Royal Theatre, designed by Elizabeth Scott with external sculptures by Eric Kennington, replaced the old Gothic playhouse. It has always been packed, although the seating of its auditorium was enlarged in 1951. International air travel has greatly increased the number of foreign visitors, and the popularity of the plays shows no sign of abating. The town has stood up well to the invasion and to the recent population explosion. As with all progressive Midland communities, Stratford has acquired a few new industries, such as fruit canning, light casting and aluminium ware, and managed to enlarge one of its oldest industries, brewing. The canal and Avon navigation, fallen derelict after the coming of the railways, have been restored largely by public-spirited volunteers. The town abounds in starred hotels, of which it has more than Oxford which is seven times as populous. Visitors today find ample restaurants and gift shops, all of which in a quiet way pay some tribute to the bard. A certain decorum and charm pervades the whole scene that proves attractive to visitors and residents alike. In 1927 Stratford was enlarged by the incorporation of Alveston parish into the borough, including the fine half-timbered manor house, now an hotel, near the east end of Clopton Bridge. Subsequently its population has risen from 11,616 in 1931 to about 20,000 in 1971, but characteristically most of this increase has been accommodated in the periphery, and the Stratford that Shakespeare knew survives remarkably well. Although the play's the thing, the multitudes can still envisage the town and countryside that he loved.

CHAPTER EIGHTEEN

Warwick: Castle and Borough

This castle hath a pleasant seat; the air
Nimbly and sweetly recommends itself
Unto our gentle senses.
    (*Macbeth*, I, vi)

The Castle

Warwick castle, 'the flower of those fortresses of the Middle Ages which have been turned into peaceful dwellings' stands proudly on a sandstone bluff overlooking the Avon. Upon this eminence Ethelfleda constructed in 914 a fortified *burh* as part of her defences against Danish Mercia. This stronghold within its earthen ramparts had become a small township of about 1,200 inhabitants at the time of the Norman conquest. In 1068 William I, anxious to secure control of the Midlands before hurrying north, had the fortifications of the existing burh (Waerincwican) strengthened by the addition of a motte and bailey that necessitated the destruction of four houses. The motte, greatly altered today, stands at the southwest corner of the present walls of the castle and lies largely outside them. Probably the bailey extended mainly eastward on the bluff overlooking the Avon, as this is the site of the present castle with its strongly walled bailey about 142m long and nearly 84m wide. All the present buildings form part of the perimeter or curtain wall which is defended by a wide, deep moat except on the side rising from the Avon cliff.

William the Conqueror's motte, as at Oxford and Wallingford, was thrown up athwart the edge of the Anglo-Saxon burh nearest the water defences. Today it is mistakenly called Ethelfleda's mound. During the twelfth and thirteenth centuries there was considerable rebuilding in stone, and a house was erected at one side of the bailey. Some of the existing wall of the north curtain and of the base of the keep dates from the early thirteenth century or from the time when King John was greatly strengthening the rival castle at Kenilworth. Much of the early stonework at Warwick was destroyed by Sir John Giffard, the energetic castellan of Kenilworth, who 'beat down the walls from tower to tower' in 1264, the same year that his master, Simon de Montfort, issued writs for the first popular, representative English parliament. It appears that Sir John took Warwick castle by surprise and carried Earl William Mauduit and his Countess and family, prisoners to Kenilworth.

Warwick did not recover until the fourteenth century when the first and second Thomas Beauchamp virtually ensured that it would never be surprised again. Between 1331 and 1369 Thomas Beauchamp I constructed most of the northeastern quadrant with Caesar's tower, the gatehouse and probably also Guy's tower. His successor, Thomas II, had completed the northern curtilage by 1401. The whole facade is the glory of Warwick and has become a favourite subject with landscape painters. Inspired by French castellar styles and planned for effect as well as defence, it ranks as the superb achievement of English castle builders. Caesar's tower, on the corner of the curtilage east of the gatehouse, rises 133ft (40m) from the foot of a massive sandstone plinth which faces the moat and slopes, so it is said, at the correct angle to deflect missiles dropped from the embrasures above into the faces of assailants. This plinth, seen to perfection from the end of Mill Street, is cleverly faced with slight overhangs so as to afford no footholds. The tower has a trefoil or tri-lobed horizontal plan and is divided vertically into six storeys, the lowest being a prison 15m below the level of the bailey from which it is reached by a downward flight of steps. This basement has acquired over the centuries some graffiti and more recently a gruesome collection of instruments of torture. All storeys of the tower can be reached from the sentry walk at the top of the curtilage where a door at third storey level gives access to a spiral stairway that winds up to the higher storeys and down to the basement, where it forms a stone corridor round the dungeon with grills giving a full view of the prisoners. Each of the three storeys above the dungeon has a large rectangular room with a fireplace, a mural chamber for sleeping, and a latrine. The fifth storey consists solely of a rectangular room, presumably for storing ammunition or armaments and is surrounded by a platform with battlements that are machicolated and pierced with cross-shaped arrow slits or loops. The top storey comprises a large hexagonal guardroom with a flat roof, surrounded by plain battlements with ordinary embrasures and slits for archers.

Guy's tower at the opposite end of this main facade was completed in 1394 at a cost of £395 5s 2d. About 128ft (39m) high and with walls 8ft (2.5m) thick, it has a twelve-sided external plan and is divided vertically into five storeys. The uppermost storey consists of an octagonal guardroom, strongly vaulted and with a flat roof surrounded by a machicolated parapet pierced at intervals with apertures for discharging missiles onto invaders below. Each of the other four storeys has a large vaulted room with a mural chamber and, as in Caesar's tower, is reached by a spiral staircase from a door on the sentry walk at the third storey level. A further cunning defensive device involves the need to maintain a rapid sentry walk around the top of the whole of the castle's curtilage. This is done by means of a separate staircase which links the roof of each tower direct to the wall-top walk and without access to other floors.

Midway between these two fine towers is the gatehouse, itself a masterpiece of defensive devices. The approach, today along a gently graded curving defile cut deeply into the sandstone about 1800, was in mediaeval times up a steep incline

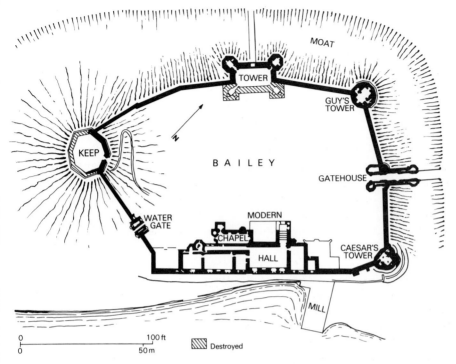

Plan of Warwick Castle.

direct from the town, leading to a flattish area fully exposed to the castle's defenders. Beyond this is the moat crossed formerly by a drawbridge that could be raised against the outer gateway. The gatehouse consists of a barbican or outer gate connected by a narrow sloping passage to the inner gate or clock tower. Each gateway has a strong door and a portcullis and sides pierced with loopholes for shooting at assailants. The exterior of the barbican gateway has downward facing apertures through which missiles could be showered on assailants; its inner side has a small gallery surveying the corridor to the inner gate and convenient for shooting at anyone who had succeeded in forcing the barbican.

After this demonstration of castellar skill, later reconstructions of Warwick tend to be less striking. In the late fifteenth century the north curtilage was modified by the addition of a massive rectangular structure with towers at its corners. Richard III probably built its northern tower, while its twin nearest the keep was begun by his brother the Duke of Clarence, but the bailey side was probably never completed. At the southwest angle of the castle the large Norman motte lies largely outside the present curtilage but three sides of the keep on it face the bailey or courtyard. The octagonal structure was drastically renovated and remodelled in the seventeenth and nineteenth centuries as part of

Warwick Castle from the Avon.

landscape gardening and looks, as it must once have been, truly formidable.

From the keep, the south curtilage with its water gate, leads to the southeast perimeter that overlooks the Avon and contains the main living quarters. Great alterations have been made in this domestic range over nine centuries. Parts of it date back at least to the late thirteenth century, and the ground floor remains largely early fourteenth century. The upper storeys, partly because of fires, were altered considerably or rebuilt between 1670 and 1890. These architectural details and historic furnishings are best left to the visitor's interests. The Great Hall, which measures 19 by 10m, suffered a disastrous fire in 1871. Its two tiers of windows, large below and small above, no doubt were inherited from the time when it had an upper gallery of rooms reached from the staircase in the nearby turret. Its furnishings include mediaeval armour, an enormous iron stewpot and fork for the garrison (later used as a punch bowl), a stupendous late Victorian chimney piece and a monumental sideboard carved by George Willcox, the local craftsman who supplied a similar tour-de-force to Charlecote House. The great dining room was rebuilt about 1765 and its interesting ceiling in an Elizabethan style is by Robert Moore, plasterer and sometime mayor of Warwick. The other state apartments with their fine portraits, include a splendid cedar drawing room with panelling of 1680, and Queen Anne's bedroom and a blue boudoir each with a most gorgeous ceiling.

The extensive grounds outside the castle walls were redesigned by Capability

Brown in 1753 and subsequently acquired an additional wealth of interesting features including a pleasant conservatory patrolled by peacocks. In 1978 Lord Brooke sold the castle, together with its rich remaining contents and 100 acres of the surrounding parkland, for £1½ million to Mme Tussaud's who will maintain it as an historic home that will, no doubt, deservedly, in spite of the absence of the Warwick vase and some other masterpieces, continue to attract more than 500,000 visitors annually.

The Earls of Warwick

The first constable of Warwick Castle under the Normans was Thomas, second son of Roger (de Newburgh) in 1068. The title Earl of Warwick was conferred on the family during the reign of William II but their direct line died out in the mid-thirteenth century. In 1263 the title descended indirectly to William Mauduit who sided with Henry III during the baronial wars and allowed the castle and himself to be taken by surprise by a troop from Kenilworth, then owned by Simon de Montfort. However the tide soon turned against the de Montforts after Simon was killed at Evesham, and in 1266 Henry III made Warwick his headquarters when conducting the famous six months siege of Kenilworth. Soon afterwards the Warwick estates passed by marriage to the Beauchamp family, and with Guy de Beauchamp, tenth Earl, the owners of Warwick step into the front rank of English history. Guy, who was nicknamed 'the Black Dog of Arden' by Piers Gaveston, Earl of Cornwall and favourite of Edward II, played a leading part in the struggle to rid the court of that hated courtier. In May 1312 Gaveston was captured at Scarborough and taken to Warwick castle where he was tried and condemned to death by the Earls of Warwick, Lancaster, Gloucester, Hereford and Arundel. On 9 June Gaveston was beheaded on Blacklow Hill about one mile north of the town.[1] This tenth earl is not to be confused with Guy of Warwick, the hero of a mediaeval romantic poem about a wealthy young noble married to the chatelaine of Warwick Castle, who went light-heartedly to the Holy Land and there enjoyed many fantastic adventures before regretting his misspent youth and returning to England to live incognito as a saintly hermit in the forest of Arden.

Thomas Beauchamp, eleventh Earl of Warwick (1315-1369) became Earl Marshal of England and France and fought at the battles of Crecy and Poitiers. His successor, the Thomas who completed the rebuilding of the fine northeastern facade of the castle, was imprisoned by King Richard II for many years in the Beauchamp tower in the Tower of London. He was followed by Earl Richard who regained the royal favour and became governor of Calais and Normandy, a post which caused him to preside in 1431 at the trial of Joan of Arc at Rouen. He was widely acknowledged the 'Father of Courtesy' and is unsympathetically portrayed in Shaw's *St Joan*. He became, by the expressed direction of King Henry V (*ob.* 1422), the preceptor of the baby King Henry VI and was no doubt responsible for this infant appearing at public functions and taking his rightful place in parliament when two years old. Richard Beauchamp bequeathed to posterity the exquisite chapel adjoining St Mary's church, Warwick and one of the most beautiful tombs of English mediaeval art. His son Henry was made premier Earl of England and Duke of Warwick but he died without a male heir in 1445, and the dukedom and Beauchamp male line ended with him. His estates and other titles passed through the distaff side to his sister Anne and so to her husband Richard Neville, eldest son of the Earl of Salisbury, and better known as Warwick the Kingmaker or in Shakespeare's words 'proud setter up and puller down of kings'.

At first the kingmaker supported the claims of Richard, Duke of York to the English throne against those of Henry VI who although the founder of King's College, Cambridge and of Eton, was now feeling the mental strain of a troublesome reign, and was grateful frequently to seek the rural safety of Kenilworth. The Earl of Warwick played a leading role in the ensuing Wars of the Roses. He greatly aided the Yorkist faction to set up a protectorate, but the king recovered from a bout of insanity and Warwick, with his cousin the Earl of March (later Edward IV) and other friends, was forced to flee to Calais. The following summer they returned to England and collected forces that defeated the royal army in a bloody battle at Northampton (1460). The war now assumed an unbelievable ferocity. Richard, Duke of York, was slain at Wakefield, but his eldest son, Edward, Earl of March, gained control of London partly through Warwick's efforts. The main battle took place at Towton near Tadcaster where at one stage Warwick, to encourage his men, is said to have stabbed his horse and sworn to win or die with them on the field. Some authorities attribute this action also to Edward but whoever did it he or they received no lasting recognition from the ungrateful English who, when in difficult circumstances, in later centuries talked of 'burning their boats' and not of 'slaughtering their horses'.[2] The slaughter at Towton decimated the baronage, brought Edward to the throne and raised Warwick to a position of outstanding power. The new king showered him and the house of Neville with rich rewards of titles, offices and vacant or forfeited estates.

The kingmaker was highly gifted, with a striking presence and a commanding personality. Almost as tall as Edward, who stood 6ft 3 inches (190cm), he had a lean and powerful build and wore his thick dark hair cropped short in typical Norman fashion. By instinct and upbringing a diplomat in a Machiavellian mould, skilled in political and dynastic intrigue, he was by nature an organiser of armies rather than a great warrior. As captain of Calais he became a successful privateer, a forerunner of Hawkins and Drake, and was as much at home at sea as on land. He took the helm of the ship that carried the fugitive earls from Bridgwater along the Channel to Calais. On land he never moved without at least one hundred retainers, who wore his livery emblazoned with his badge, 'the rampant bear chained to a ragged staff'.

As they were cousins it is not surprising that Edward IV also possessed good looks and strong personal charm, and that from the company of his uncle he had acquired considerable military and political skill. Two such powerful personalities with a generation gap, for Warwick was thirty three and the king nineteen at his accession, were eventually almost bound to disagree over some decisions. For three years Warwick ruled in all but name, and when the rift came it did the king little credit. It may have been started by the king's seduction of one of Warwick's wards, probably his daughter, at a time when the Earl, convinced that an alliance with France was a political necessity, was in the midst of secret diplomatic activities to arrange a marriage between Edward and Bona of Savoy, sister of Louis XI of France. The rift widened in May 1464 when Edward IV secretly married Lady Elizabeth Grey, the charming widow of a slain Lancastrian, with two young children to boot.[3] The public announcement of this wedding was made in the following September at a Great Council at Reading, when secret negotiations for the French marriage were well advanced. Warwick put as good a face as possible on the affair and along with the Duke of Clarence presented the new queen to the council but he had lost faith in Edward's judgment. The king proceeded to grant great power and estates to the queen's family, the Woodvilles, and to elevate them as a counterpoise to the Nevilles. Other disagreements followed, and Warwick tried to raise a rebellion around the king's brother, the Duke of Clarence, now secretly married to the Earl's eldest daughter. The in-fighting that follows beggars description. A reconciliation ended with a revolt after which Warwick and Clarence fled to France whence, after making an alliance with their old enemies the Lancastrians, they invaded England. Edward fled to Flanders but soon returned to northern England and marched on London where the gates were opened by the perfidy of the Earl's brother, Archbishop Neville. On 14 April 1471 Warwick lost his life fighting the king's forces at Barnet. Edward permitted the body to lie in state in St Paul's, and then to be buried in the Neville vaults at Bisham Abbey, Berkshire. At the Reformation all traces of the Neville funerary monuments were destroyed, except some battered alabaster figures supposedly of the kingmaker's parents now in Burghfield parish church. His fame, however, rests on more than Bulwer Lytton's *The Last of The Barons* (1843), as his beneficence peeps through the cultural geography of fifteenth century England in places as far apart as York and Burford. In York he and his brother founded in 1461 St William's College to house the chantry priests of the cathedral; a delightful half-timbered, quadrangular structure with a stone gateway it serves today as the meeting place of the northern convocation. At Burford in Oxfordshire, where he was lord of the manor, the Earl leased two crofts to Henry Bishop, for 7s 6d a year, and gave him licence to build almshouses on them in 1456. This licence has one of the only two known specimens of the signature of the kingmaker. The almshouses still stand in the shadow of the church near the spot where it is rumoured that the Earl met the future King to offer him the throne of England. During the restoration of the almshouses in 1828 an inscribed plaque was added, stating wrongly that they were founded by Richard, Earl of Warwick. Nearby in the High Street a fifteenth century hostelry with a fine gateway sported until recently the sign of the Bear and Ragged Staff.

On the kingmaker's death, the Warwick estates passed through the female line and eventually after a long period of abeyance were conferred in 1547 on John Dudley, later Duke of Northumberland, who was beheaded for his part in a plot to put Lady Jane Grey on the throne. The forfeited estates and title were granted by Queen Elizabeth to his eldest son Ambrose who died without heir in 1590, whereupon they reverted again to the Crown. In 1618 the earldom, as distinct from the estates, was revived for Robert Rich, whose wife Penelope was the beloved Stella of Sir Philip Sydney's poem of courtly love *Astrophel and Stella*. This remarkable woman, the sister of Robert Dudley, Queen Elizabeth's favourite who was granted Kenilworth Castle, already had six children by Rich when she decided in 1595 to go to live with Lord Mountjoy; she finally separated from her husband six years later. Mountjoy acknowledged fatherhood of five more offspring born to Penelope after 1595, and in 1605, aided by his chaplain, William Laud, arranged an irregular marriage with her, only to be promptly banished from the court by James I.

The estate and castle, now in considerable disrepair, were granted by James I to Sir Fulke Greville, a descendant of a cadet branch of the Beauchamp family. Sir Fulke, later Baron Brooke, spent over £20,000 on repairing and beautifying the castle, particularly the south range, and entertained the king here on four occasions. During the Civil War Lord Brooke favoured the Parliamentarians and Warwick Castle easily withstood a half-hearted Royalist siege lasting fourteen days. At the peace it was spared the fate of Kenilworth and most other Midland fortresses. When, in 1759, the Rich family died out, the Earldom of Warwick was granted to Earl Brooke whose descendants held the castle until 1978. Today it welcomes graciously throngs as great as in the days when it housed the retainers of Warwick the kingmaker.

Warwick Borough

There was probably an Anglo-Saxon settlement on the gravels on the south bank of the Avon at Warwick two or three centuries before Ethelfleda constructed here in 914 one of the ten fortified *burhs* she built to defend English Mercia against the Danes. She had already fortified Tamworth against the Danish army based on Leicester, and Warwick was an obviously useful second line of defence, being less than 5 miles (8km) west of the Foss Way that ran direct from Leicester to Bath. The burh was on a sandstone bluff rising 70ft (21m) above the Avon floodplain, and the general circular shape of the first earthworks was probably represented by the mediaeval defences, and the present circular pattern of streets round the borough's core. This Anglo-Saxon fortress, as at Oxford and

Wallingford, is known to have had some tenements attached to rural properties. It had to send 4 sailors or £4 in lieu thereof when the king went on an expedition by sea. The administrative County of Warwick was artificially created around it during the tenth century and it has remained the shire capital ever since.

In 1068, when William the Conqueror threw up a strong motte and bailey here, four houses were destroyed, indicating that the castle impinged on the old burh. At this time, according to *Domesday Survey*, Warwick was held by Turchil of Arden, one of few Englishmen who kept extensive lands at the Norman Conquest. The borough contained about 248 houses of which 22 were burgages with privileges granted by Edward the Confessor. Twelve rural manors in Warwickshire held all told 26 houses or plots in the town while at Coton End just outside the borough 100 bordars with their gardens paid 50s annually.[4] The total population would have been about 1,200 or 1,250. The town was reached from the south by a ford across a natural sandstone weir in the Avon, but a bridge is recorded in 1208. This river crossing was controlled by the castle and the siting of the fine many-arched mediaeval stone bridge that spanned the Avon for four centuries was a little way upstream so as to be reached by skirting the castle walls. The county town no doubt grew steadily in population and acquired walls instead of an earthen rampart and ditch. Its original plan seems to have consisted of two main streets crossing each other at right angles at the site in Tudor times of a 'right goodly cross' in the centre of the burh. On the town's perimeter each main street ended at a gate in the walls. Speed's map of 1610 shows that circular streets had evolved or been planned both inside and outside the circular ramparts. The foundation of the castle and castle precincts had typically quite destroyed this simple plan in the southern part of the borough.

Although most of the town wall had been demolished by the early sixteenth century, there survive, in addition to the alignment of the circle of streets around the old core and the street names Wall Ditch and Northgate, a bastion behind the Butts, a stretch of wall, mostly fourteenth century, on the southwest, and two of the four gates. The west gate with a chapel on it was recorded in 1129. Cut in solid rock, it forms today a most impressive building, with an eastern entrance probably of the early fourteenth century, and a western part in the early Perpendicular style surmounted by the tower of its chapel, St James', later incorporated into the Leycester Hospital. The east gate dates from the early fifteenth century and was capped by the chapel of St Peter, which was replaced in 1788 by a delightful, highly decorative structure now embodied in the Girls' High School.

Ecclesiastical Warwick

The fortress functions of Warwick seem to have undermined its ecclesiastical importance. Before the dissolution it had a friary, two hospitals and a monastic establishment, all founded by the owners of the castle, but none grew to any size

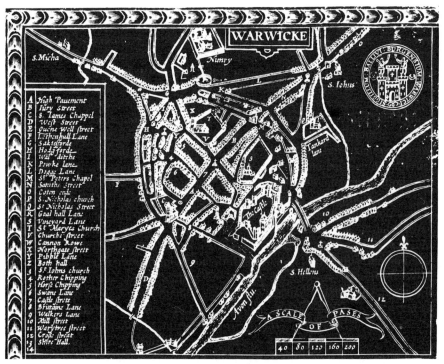

The map legend reads:

A High Pauement
B Iury Street
C S. Iames Chappel
D West Street
E Quene Well street
F Lithenhull Lane
G Saktesforde
H Hodgforde
I Wall ditche
K Powke lane
L Diggis Lane
M S.t Peters chapel
N Smiths Street
O Coten end:
P S. Nicholas church
Q S.t Nicholas Street
R Goal hall Lane
S Vineyard Lane
T S.t Maryes Church
V Churche street
W Cannon Rowe
X Northgate street
Y Pibble Lane
Z Both hall
1 S.t Iohns church
2 Rother Chipping
3 Horse Chipping
4 Swane Lane
5 Castle street
6 Brittaine Lane
7 Walkers Lane
8 Hall street
9 Warstree street
10 Crosse street
11 Shire Hall.

Warwick: Speed's map of 1610, when a cross stood at the central crossroads.

or wealth and most were outside the town walls. The largest, the Augustinian priory of St Sepulchre, owned a large estate north of the walled town (Priory Road), stretching northward far beyond the borough boundary. After the dissolution a mansion was built on the priory site and this Tudor structure was remodelled about 1620 being given a long west facade with a row of six ogee-headed gables above its parapet, a style characteristic of Warwick architecture. In 1709 Henry Wise, gardener successively to William III, Queen Anne and George I, bought the whole estate and lived there from 1727 to his death in 1738, when he left £200,000. He and his son planned a garden with a parterre and a crescent of trees but nearly all has vanished.[5] In 1851 the southern part of the estate, with the priory, fish ponds and mills, was sold to the Birmingham and Oxford Junction railway while the large northern part remained private until purchased in 1935 as a public park by Warwick Corporation. The shell of the priory building was bought in 1925 by A.W. Weddell, later US ambassador to Spain, who used it and other antique fragments to construct a house in Richmond, Virginia. The surviving masonry on the site at Warwick consists only of a wall of a forecourt, a lodge and a brick cottage. The estate has had a remarkable influence on the development of the built-up area in the borough as it prevented all expansion to the north just as effectively as did the castle on the south and common lands on other sides.

In early times the dominant church at Warwick was All Saints, within the castle precincts, but before 1153 St Mary's college had gained control of it and 9 other churches or chapels in the town. By the end of the fourteenth century the borough, as today, consisted of two parishes, St Nicholas' outside the walls, with a church said to have been founded in Norman times on a nunnery destroyed by the Danes, and St Mary's which serves the walled area. The latter, established as a collegiate church for the use of secular canons, was founded in 1123 by Henry Newburgh and completed by his son. The earls of Warwick showered St Mary's with benefactions and embellishments, and the extensions of the church summarise the mediaeval history of that earldom.

The massive vaulted crypt shows the scale of the Norman building and reveals at its east end the later supports for the chancel built by the earls of Warwick about 1365 to 1392. In the middle of the chancel is a rectangular tomb chest surmounted by the recumbent alabaster effigies of Thomas Beauchamp (*ob.* 1369) and his wife. The sides of the tomb are beautifully enriched with thirty six small mourners, many of which are original and delicately carved in a realistic style. At the feet of the effigies, two large bears stand guardian over the group. The adjacent south transept contains the magnificent brasses of Thomas Beauchamp the Second (*ob.* 1401) and his wife, with figures elongated to 6ft 3 inches (190cm).

Off the south transept and virtually separated from it is the Lady Chapel, now known as the Beauchamp Chapel, built in 1442 to 1465 at a cost of £2,481 4s 7½ d. The great expenditure, six times that on Guy's tower in the castle, is explained by the richness of decoration, vaulting, wall panelling and sculpture in this late Gothic masterpiece. The executors of Richard Beauchamp (*ob.* 1439) spared no expense in employing the best artists and materials they could procure. In the middle of the chapel stands a high tomb chest of Purbeck marble, which supports a copper gilt or bronze effigy of Earl Richard, shown recumbent in plate armour with his head on a helmet and his feet on a muzzled bear and griffin. The long delicately veined hands are raised, but not clasped, as if in prayer and the furrowed brow, bluntish nose, protruding upper lip and truncated earlobe reveal how faithfully he was portrayed. The effigy is protected by a herse or guard of copper gilt hoops over which a pall could be draped when desired. The tomb chest bears enamel armorial shields at its foot and above them a continuous row of delicately cast mourners, seven men and seven women interspersed at above waist height by a tier of small angels holding inscribed scrolls. Each mourner may be identified by the coat of arms beneath.

The surrounding chapel matches the quality of this exquisite tomb. The glass in the windows was designed to order by John Prudde, the King's glazier, using 'the best, cleanest and strongest glass of beyond the seas that may be had in England, and of the finest colours' with the proviso that white, green and black glass should be avoided as far as possible. The surviving lights have incredible detail, including musical notation on the scrolls held by the tracery angels and separately coloured jewels in the borders of the robes. The mullions and jambs of the east window are elaborately carved into tabernacles enshrining numerous statues. The present wall painting of the Last Judgment dates from 1678, but some of the original fifteenth century figures were incorporated into it. The chapel was used again as a mausoleum for a while after John Dudley, descendant of Margaret daughter of Richard Beauchamp, became Earl of Warwick in 1547. The alabaster monuments include recumbent effigies to Ambrose Dudley; to Robert Dudley who died aged three and whose suit of armour is in the castle; and to Robert Dudley, Earl of Leicester, who is portrayed in armour and cloak, lying beside his second wife, Lettice. Leicester died in 1588 at his home in Cornbury Park, Oxfordshire, while on his way to Kenilworth from the east coast where a few weeks earlier he had been in charge of the troops mustered at Tilbury to repel invasion from the Spanish Armada. Countess Lettice survived until the morning of Christmas day 1634 and is remembered here also by a very long inscription on a wooden tablet describing *inter alia*:

> She that in her younger yeares
> Marcht with two great English peares
> She that did supply the warrs
> With thunder and the court with stars
> She that in her youth had bene
> Darling to the Maiden Queene

The next owner of Warwick after the Dudleys, Sir Fulke Greville, has for a monument, a black sarcophagus in a six poster frame standing in the chapter house north of the chancel.

On 5 September 1694 a fire broke out in central Warwick and in a few hours reduced the greater part of the town to ashes, the damage being reckoned at £120,000. The tower, nave, aisles and transepts of St Mary's had to be rebuilt; the citizens contributed £11,000 towards the cost and Queen Anne sent £1,000. Although Sir Christopher Wren submitted a sketch for the new church, the work was eventually done to the designs of Sir William Wilson, and carried out from 1698 to 1704 by the Smith brothers of Tettenhall and Warwick. At an early stage the base of the west tower began to lean and Wren's mason was called in to correct the fault. Today this tower rises 174ft (53m) and has a simple Gothic form with classical detail, as in the statueless niches, and a pleasant modesty conditioned perhaps by the expense involved in correcting the structural weakness. About this time a very decorative portal was pierced into the Beauchamp chapel and blends nicely with its mediaeval opulence.

Burghal Warwick

Warwick sent two members to the parliament in 1295 and continued to do so until its representation was reduced to one member in 1885. Today it forms part of a wider parliamentary constituency. In Tudor times its affairs were altered appreciably at the Reformation, when the college was dissolved and St Mary's handed over to the burgesses by Henry VIII who also refounded the school. By Elizabeth's reign the borough had grown to between 2,600 and 3,000 inhabitants and was a flourishing market centre without any special industries except malting. Speed's map of 1610 shows a considerable expansion of houses alongside the roads leading to the ancient nucleus. The fire of September 1694 came at a time of great prosperity, aided no doubt by extensive rebuilding at the castle. In the conflagration 460 buildings were destroyed and 250 families rendered homeless, particularly on the hilltop where only more isolated houses and the south side of Jury Street escaped severe damage, although some other dwellings in central streets can have been only partially destroyed, since they show remains of timber construction behind their later fronts.

Thereafter Warwick can almost be divided into pre- and post-fire structures. Mill Street escaped the fire and consists today largely of timber-framed and stone Tudor houses. On the other side of the river at Bridge End is Brome Place, a fine timber-framed, four gabled dwelling owned in the mid-fifteenth century by John Brome who held and partly erected the lovely moated manor house at the nearby village of Baddesley Clinton. The south end of High Street also escaped the fire and is mainly Tudor. Here on a low terrace stands the delightful grouping of mediaeval buildings belonging to Lord Leycester's Hospital. It includes the chapel of St James built over the west gate in the early twelfth century and the other meeting rooms of the town's three combined guilds that were dispersed in 1546. The present chapel is basically fourteenth century but was largely restored in 1864 when an east window and flying buttresses were added. Most of the property was granted to the borough corporation shortly before the guild's dispersal, and the burgesses met here until 1571 when they were persuaded to make it over to Robert Dudley, Earl of Leicester, under threat that otherwise he would found his projected hospital at Kenilworth. So there was created here the Lord Leycester Hospital for a master and twelve disabled ex-servicemen, with an annual endowment of £200. The present front on the street has an overhanging first floor and a facade richly decorated with moulded crossbeam or bressumer and close-spaced studs. The courtyard is galleried in part and surrounded on three sides largely by the fifteenth century guildhall (now a museum), the chaplain's dining hall (now a regimental museum) and the master's house to which a fairly recent restoration has added ornate strutting and painted armorial reliefs. On the fourth or west side is the great hall still used as in guild times for social functions. Here in 1617 the burgesses entertained James I at a banquet that put them in debt for several years. The garden shelters a fine Norman arch almost certainly the chancel arch of the original chapel over the west gate.

Warwick has many other mediaeval houses that have escaped fire or serious

Lord Leycester's Hospital and the West Gate, Warwick.

alteration, among them the gabled Oken's House in Castle Street, now a museum of dolls. The notable early seventeenth century buildings include St John's, also today a museum, and Tudor House in West Street. The second half of this century brought several fine dwellings such as the half-timbered, triple-gabled Eastgate Cottage (1686), Marble House built of local sandstone and now sadly neglected, and Landor House of brick. The town hall, constructed in 1670 as a market hall on stone pillars, has been converted into the county museum that includes among a wide range of exhibits a large Sheldon tapestry map of Elizabethan Warwickshire.

The great fire of 1694 cleared the ground for a wealth of pleasant eighteenth century architecture which although lacking in the picturesque half-timbering of earlier times has a symmetry and dignity all its own. Moreover the needs of the castle ensured that Warwick abounded in skilled masons and craftsmen. Within a few years most of the devastated area had been rebuilt in a handsome way. By 1720 the town, with its 'spacious regular streets, constantly clean' was 'esteemed a place of agreeable retirement for gentlemen of small estates, and in its neighbourhood are frequent horse races'. It had three charity schools in which no less than 62 boys and 42 girls were clothed and taught, as well as four hospitals or almshouses, including the Leycester where twelve decayed gentlemen had £20 a year each and the chaplain £50. There were markets on

St John's Museum, Warwick.

Saturdays and four fairs annually for horses, cows and sheep, that in September dealing also with cheese. Many of the civic buildings acquired a Georgian splendour. In 1725, Francis Smith completed the Court House with its fine ballroom that houses, among other treasures, a notable Elizabethan coffer. The Shire Hall in Northgate Street (1753-8), designed by Sanderson Miller, consists of a range of nine bays of only one tall storey and containing a single room 28m by 10m. It is rivalled in length by the nearby county goal (1777-1783) which extends for eleven bays with stout unfluted Doric columns that its architect, Thomas Johnson, meant to be fluted. Now used as county offices, this was one of the earliest Greek Revival buildings in Europe. A few years later a new single-span bridge with a graceful balustrade was constructed some distance upstream from the many-arched mediaeval structure and a new road pattern made to serve it. A large part of the old bridge was swept away in 1795. About this time Warwick found itself near a hub of canals, the chief being the Grand Union, and these encouraged industrial growth well away from the ancient core.

By 1801 the population of the borough had increased to 5,600 and with the aid of light industries such as engineering and worsted spinning had grown to nearly ten thousand by 1841. The coming of the railway maintained the civic growth and today Warwick has 20,000 inhabitants. As previously the modern industries are tucked away in the outer suburbs of the extensive borough and its ancient core survives remarkably well compared with those of other old towns in the Midlands. The future is bright as there is a watchful Warwick Society, and new expansion on a large scale is occurring on the borough's perimeter at Woodloes. The Warwickshire capital has long been noted for education and a school, according to tradition founded either by Ethelfleda or Edward the Confessor, was first recorded here in 1123 when it served the sons of Warwick burgesses. Among the town's noted scholars was Walter Savage Landor who seems to have gone elsewhere for a classical education. Born here in 1775 in a house at the Eastgate, now part of a girls' school, he soon showed an outstanding talent for elegant prose and impeccable dramatic verse but unfortunately had an impatient and quarrelsome nature that denied him the full praise he deserved. Expelled from Rugby and rusticated from Trinity College, Oxford, he was always at loggerheads with his associates, which may explain why, in his opinion:

> There may be cities who refuse
> To their own son the honours due.

Ironically one of his best remembered verses runs:

> I strove with none; for none was worth my strife.
> Nature I loved and, next to Nature, Art;
> I warmed both hands before the fire of life;
> It sinks, and I am ready to depart.

CHAPTER NINETEEN

Oxford: Town and Gown

For place, for grace and for sweet companee,
Oxford is Heaven, if Heaven on Earth there be.
    (Sir John Davies, *c.* 1610)

The Natural Setting

Early Oxford had few natural advantages except the river for fish, defence and later for transport, and a flat gravel terrace for building on. The site was not favoured in prehistoric times when the main national routes ran along the chalk to the south and the Jurassic limestone to the north. There was a south-north trackway making use of the small Corallian uplands and crossing the Thames near the site of Oxford but it remained insignificant until mediaeval times. In the Romano-British period the road from Dorchester north to Alchester passed over the hills at Cowley and Headington, where several potteries have been found, but again the low-lying site of Oxford was little occupied, so the city lacks antiquity and is an Anglo-Saxon foundation, late at that.

The reasons seem fairly obvious. The place is far distant from the coast and being almost river girt was difficult to reach except from the north. The Thames valley hereabouts has a vast floodplain that from Portmeadow narrows southward to about 3km at the walled city and to half that width near Sandford where the tall valley sides are clearly intervisible. The Thames with its various distributaries or braidings runs down the west side of this plain and the Cherwell down the east, to their junction just south of the city core. During late glacial times the rivers made in this valley a series of gravel terraces, patches of which now protrude above the clayey river alluvium. The chief, called the second or Summertown-Radley terrace, rises at most about 8m above mean river level and slopes gently southward for over three kilometres from Summertown to Carfax. There is another patch of this gravel east of the Cherwell on the Plain. Everywhere it has a thickness of 3 to 10m and rests on Oxford clay, an impervious layer which holds up ground water that can be tapped by shallow wells in the gravel. Below this terrace, at heights of 1 to 3m above normal river level, are patches of a lower floodplain terrace such as occurs at the foot of the short descent down St Aldate's, in the housing estate of St Ebbe's. The original city was on the southern tip of the main patch of the second terrace in the doab or angle of the Thames-Cherwell junction. The site is surrounded except on the north by

Present day Oxford, viewed from the south, showing the road over the Thames at Folly Bridge leading north to Christ Church (at the former south gate) and so through the mediaeval borough to its former north gate and St Giles', beyond which the highway divides into Woodstock Road (to left) and Banbury Road.

floodable alluvium and in times of high river flow still forms a narrow peninsula jutting into a shallow lake. Only on the north side was access easy and only there did nonfloodable plots abound. Communications elsewhere were tied to fords and later to bridges and causeways over the marshy alluvium, so providing a very restricted access which was ideal for defence but raises serious traffic problems today.

The uniqueness of Oxford's site lies not so much in its doab location, a feature seen also at Abingdon and Reading, as in its position on the north bank. Oxford is the only large town on the north bank of the freshwater Thames. For centuries when the river formed a boundary between southern and midland tribes or kingdoms it found itself, with London, just inside 'northern' territory. During the post-Roman unification of England, Oxford became a frontier fortress convenient as a meeting place between north and south. The phase soon passed but characteristically the influence seems interminable. For example, its university arose at the southern perimeter of the diocese of Lincoln while the town itself was far enough from London for the crown to feel secure there from metropolitan dominance.

Atmospherically the site suffers from the Anglo-Saxon preference for low lying gravel patches. On calm clear nights colder air tends to gravitate down the adjacent valley sides and to fill the valley floor with mist or fog which persists long after sunrise. On hot days, admittedly few, the air seems moister and more stagnant than at Headington and Cumnor on the nearby hilltops. The eulogies of Robert Plot, 'a place of so sweet and wholesome an Air' (1705) and of Daniel Defoe, 'so eminent for the goodness of its air, and healthy situation' must be seen against the wiser strictures of Anthony Wood: 'Colds become very frequent in Oxon; many sick; cold without coffing or running at the nose: only a languidness and faintnesse. Certainly, Oxford is no goode aire . . .'. However, climate is incidental to diseases spread by creatures and water, and great plagues struck hard here. The colleges had their country refuges from the plague; Exeter scholars went to Kidlington, Corpus Christi to Witney, and Oriel to St Bartholomew's, Cowley, a hospital founded by Henry I and given to the college in 1328 'for the use of wholesome air in times of pestilential sickness'. The more subtle psycho- and physiological effect of the 'meadows' moisture' cannot be distinguished, and the general conclusion may be safely left to Max Beerbohm, who, in *Zuleika Dobson* (1911) writes 'If the colleges could be transferred to the dry and bracing top of some hill, doubtless they would be more evidently useful to the nation. But let us be glad there is no engineer or enchanter to compass that task'.

The Anglo-Saxon Burh

According to tradition St Frideswide founded a nunnery at Oxford in about 727, and recent excavations have revealed that within a century a settlement existed near the south end of St Aldate's where the nunnery stood. This village had expanded considerably when the king of Wessex, presumably Edward the Elder, decided to fortify it and make it the capital of a shire. The Thames on the south and west made a suitable county boundary with Berkshire and the northern location of the fortress was useful in repelling Danish raids. It is not improbable that the first crude fortifications were thrown up around a square enclosure and that later the fortified area was extended to embrace the walled city. Whatever the sequence, the existing street pattern of the central parts of Oxford consists of squares, as at Wallingford and Cricklade. Perhaps this was the first garrison town which in a contemporary record was equated to men from 1,500 hides, whereas the larger enclosure was associated with the shire of 2,400 hides.

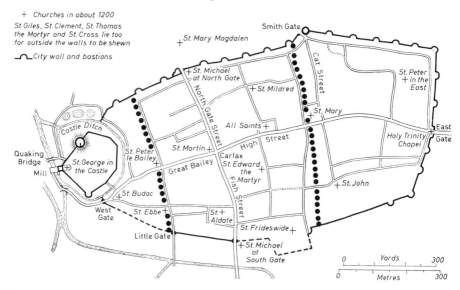

Plan of mediaeval Oxford. The dotted lines show suggested east-west extent of the original defended burh.

The date of the original fortification and of shire status remains uncertain but was probably just before 911-12 when Edward the Elder took over from his sister Ethelfleda the control of London and Oxford and all lands tributary to them. Judging from the mediaeval walls, the defended *burh* was an oblong of about 1,100 yards (1,000m) from east to west and half that length from north to south, covering about 110 acres (44ha) or nearly exactly the size of Wallingford. However, unlike Wallingford, it was not astride any national routeway although the track from Southampton to Winchester northward passed through it and may now have begun to assume importance.

The main street pattern within the ramparts was based on the four main gates and consisted of two thoroughfares crossing each other at a central Carfax (? *quatuor furcas*). The whole seems to have been oriented on the north-south route leading to the site of St Frideswide's church and the ford over the Thames here. The roads to the former gates still dominate the traffic of the town, whereas streets along the inner side of the walls have been almost obliterated by later building. At the same time several streets arose parallel to or alongside the outer side of the walls, as Broad Street and Longwall Street exemplify.

The fortifications were rebuilt or repaired many times, the surviving towers dating from the eleventh century and the walls from about 1226-40. The only Anglo-Saxon tower is part of St Michael's church but was against the north gate and provided at least a look-out post. It has twin bell-openings and a small doorway half way up its north face which seems to have had some defensive purpose. Many stretches and bastions of the city wall survive, but it is seen to perfection in New College, especially in the lovely gardens where a long stretch, with bastions, complete with wall walk, battlements and loop-holes, is carefully preserved, as part of a repair agreement undertaken by William of Wykeham when he purchased the site in 1380. A less bastioned stretch forms the boundary between Merton and Christ Church meadow and shelters Dead Man's Walk where the Norman wall made a southward salient round St Frideswide's priory.

In spite of Danish raids Oxford flourished in late Anglo-Saxon times and seems to have recovered quickly from the destruction in 1009 when the Danes, repulsed at London, crossed the Chilterns and burnt the town. About this time there was a bridge (Pettypont) over the Cherwell and suburbs were springing up outside the four gates. Several national assemblies were held here including a spectacular parliament (*gemot*) by Cnut in 1018. On Cnut's death his illegitimate son Harold Harefoot was crowned and three years later buried here. Edward the Confessor found Oxford convenient for dealing with northern troubles and no doubt felt at home as he was born at Islip. In his reign the town had 7 moneyers or minters, a number exceeded by only five other English cities. Late in 1065, a few months before his death, he called a great council of state here to negotiate with the leaders of a Northumbrian and Mercian revolt who were harrying the country round Northampton.

The Norman Borough: Secular Growth

In *Domesday Survey* the king's borough of Oxford was called a *civitas* and with between 930 and 1070 houses was the sixth most populous town in England. In Edward the Confessor's time the citizens had paid annually £20 and 6 sextaries of honey for toll and gable and all other customs. When the king went to war 20 burgesses went with him in lieu of the rest or gave £20 for freedom from that service. Oxford now (1086) paid £60 annually. In the town, within and outside the walls, were 243 houses paying geld and 478 so waste and destroyed that they could not pay tax. The king owned 20 mural mansions which, when need arose, helped to repair the city wall, but extra lists show that all told 225 houses had to undertake this duty. The overlappings of the survey are hard to disentangle and it seems best to assume that the *civitas* contained about 946 houses of which nearly half paid tax. If five persons are allowed to each taxable property there were between 2,000 and 2,500 inhabitants, but if most of the decayed dwellings were inhabited 4,000 residents would be a more reasonable estimate. Only a small fraction of the waste can be attributed to the castle built upon the western parts of the city. The urban-rural interconnections were wide, and the list of 13 rural manors recorded in the *Survey* as having properties in Oxford is known to be incomplete.[1] The burgesses held in common the wide alluvial pastures of Portmeadow that covers 500 acres (200ha) just northwest of the town and was then assessed at 6s 8d yearly.

The Normans soon radically altered Oxford. In 1071 Robert d'Oilly, the new sheriff, constructed a motte and bailey castle across the western defences. The motte, about 73m in diameter at its base and 20m high, survives and retains its well and well-chamber. To the south as part of the walled defences, d'Oilly built the chapel of St George which, with its low massive crypt and tall tower still stands above its moat. Tradition dies hard in Oxford, and the castle complex is part of the county prison, a most unimaginative use of a site in the core of a tourist city. Robert d'Oilly was also responsible for a causeway and bridge, (Grandpont) which gave dry passage southward over the Thames near St Frideswide's. With this bridging Oxford was entered dryshod from all sides except the west, where the ancient route from the Corallian upland crossed a ford at North Hinksey.

The castle, as with all such strongpoints, proved a mixed blessing. During the civil war in the twelfth century Oxford, with Wallingford, Faringdon, Newbury and Marlborough declared for Matilda, and Windsor and Northampton for Stephen. In the winter of 1143 the would-be queen was cornered in Oxford and escaped, it is said, camouflaged in white robes over the frozen river.

Either the decay recorded in *Domesday Survey* was greatly exaggerated to avoid taxation, or else Oxford made a very rapid economic recovery in Norman times. Probably the burgesses who held Portmeadow formed the dominant group that founded the merchants' guilds. There was a weaver's guild here before 1130 and in 1155 Henry II granted the burgesses a charter of free trade in all his realm and the same customs and privileges enjoyed by citizens of London. The Merchant Guild had a seal in 1191, the first guild to use a seal in England. It was inscribed as belonging to all citizens of the city of Oxford and, incidentally, may well have misled the guild at Burford into thinking that they too represented all the inhabitants. The Oxonians continued to buy privileges. In 1199 the Guild Merchant procured from King John the right of *firma burgi*, whereby in return for 200 marks and a fixed annual fee of £63 0s 5d they held the town as tenant-in-chief, paid the rent direct to the crown instead of through his sheriff, and elected two bailiffs to collect the rentals. The first mayor was appointed in about 1204 and after 1229 the corporate meetings, hitherto nomadic, were held in a guildhall on the site of the present Town Hall.

This progressive community had in the meanwhile received a royal fillip. Henry I about 1128 built a mansion outside the north gate at the west end of what today is Beaumont Street, a name typical of Norman French disregard for accuracy in place names, for the area is dead flat. The mansion grew into a small palace where later kings stayed often and Richard I and John were born. It has vanished almost without trace and of thirteenth century secular architecture in Oxford the only notable remains are the city walls, the rib-vaulted cellar at the Mitre and perhaps the well house, also with chamfered rib-vaulting, on the motte.

Ecclesiastic architecture is better represented, although the two great abbeys have virtually disappeared. In the city each sizeable rectangle of streets had its own church, there once being seventeen parish churches. Some of these have gone, among them St John the Baptist which was replaced by Merton College chapel, and St Martin of which only the tower survives at Carfax. In the outer parts of the present borough, apart from the incomparable church at Iffley (*see* Chapter 4), St James', Cowley and St Andrew's, Headington have some Norman work; in the inner wards, St Aldate's has reset arcading, St Giles' two shafts with capitals, St Cross a chancel arch and St Ebbe's a rich doorway of this period. But the chief Norman survivals are St Peter in the East and the present cathedral. St Peter's seems to have developed in the tenth century from a small timber and stone structure into an aisleless stone building. Its present crypt (open to visitors) has tiny windows, short columns and groin vaulting of about 1135 and was topped shortly afterwards by the existing chancel and nave with a fine doorway enriched with beakhead and zigzag. In the next century this church and that of St Michael at the north gate were enlarged in an early English style.

St Frideswide, the present cathedral, is the surviving building on a site used first for a nunnery and later for a house of secular canons. In about 1112 these were replaced by regular Augustinians, whose property and rights were confirmed by Henry I ten years later. The king's grant included the chapel of Holy Trinity beside the east gate, and the right to an annual five-day fair. The priory soon owned the advowson of seven Oxford churches and became rich partly from the offerings of pilgrims to St Frideswide's shrine. The monastic church was rebuilt between 1180 and 1210 and of this work, in spite of a fire during its construction, there survive the lower tower, part of a cloister and a fine doorway rich with zigzag in the chapter house. The second stage of the tower and the delightful chapter house are Early English additions. The contemporary monuments comprise fragments of the shrine of St Frideswide, cleverly pieced together in Victorian times, and the lid of the coffin of Ela, daughter of William Longespée.

Although the citizens of Oxford sent representatives to the parliament of 1295 they seem thereafter to have suffered a gradual decline in prosperity. They strongly opposed the claim of the prior of St Frideswide to control the fair and never succumbed in any way to monastic control but in practice found their corporate dominance threatened and weakened by the growth of clerical or non-commercial interests within their city. Their cause was not helped when the king's residence passed into monastic hands. Beaumont palace was in bad repair and in 1308 Edward II gave the sheriff permission to take timber and lead from it to repair the castle. Ten years later the king gave 'the mansion of our manor near the north gate of Oxon outside the walls, and also two tenements between the palace and the road near Gloucester College' to the Carmelite Friars. The guild of weavers, more than 60 strong in 1130 was now almost defunct due no doubt to a minor industrial revolution that had spread clothmaking away from old boroughs into rural districts with overshot waterwheels. Yet in 1334 the national lay subsidy found Oxford taxed as a city at one-tenth of its wealth and Oxfordshire as the richest county in England after Middlesex. The town paid

£914 and only eight cities in England paid more; the county tax worked out at about £27 per square mile against £21 per square mile in Berkshire (the fifth richest county), £18 in Gloucestershire and £14 in Warwickshire and Buckinghamshire.

This rich society was then shattered by the plague, which in bubonic and more lethal pneumonic forms, entered the southwest ports in August 1348 and spread via Bristol and Gloucester to Oxford by October. Within eight months probably 3,000 persons or nearly half the resident population had been buried. Thereafter plagues of various kinds, notably sweating sickness, black fever or typhus, and smallpox, broke out at intervals particularly in Tudor times. The Tudor monarchs, and indeed kings and queens from 1300 to the reign of Charles I, preferred to stay at Woodstock palace although Henry VIII in 1518 patronised Abingdon Abbey. Henrietta, wife of Charles I was fond of Woodstock palace and when virulent plague broke out in London in 1625, Oxford was the scene of a short-lived parliament. There is no doubt that the economy of Oxford suffered grievously from the Black Death and the loss of the royal palace at Beaumont, but the proximity of Woodstock had some compensatory effects until the Civil War.

The decline of industrial functions in Oxford coincides with the growth of the university, but exactly when the academic and clerical side became overwhelming remains uncertain. In 1380 the city had 25 weavers and 14 fullers, which suggests the existence of several mills in addition to that long established at Osney. In the fifteenth century it became, with Woodstock, famous for gloves, but by 1546 the local economic environment was unsuitable for what would have been a large scale industrialisation. Then William Stumpe, clothier of Malmesbury, rented Osney Abbey with the intention of finding work for 2,000 persons 'from time to time in clothmaking for the succour of the city of Oxenford and the country about it'.[2] Stumpe did not succeed and a century later Sir William Davenant, the poet laureate, who was born (1606) and lived at the Crown Inn in the Cornmarket, looked upon Banbury and not Oxford as the home of weavers. It seems as if the university took root in a thriving civic community and gradually sapped its vitality.

The Rise of the University

The college founded by Robert d'Oilly in St George's-within-the-Castle was for secular canons and had a learned provost. The local monastic influence did not begin to be noticeable until 1122 with the founding of St Fridewide's Priory for Augustinian canons. Its early priors included the scholarly Robert of Cricklade. The next great foundation, Osney Priory, soon became the richest abbey in Oxfordshire and invested heavily in property in the town where, for example, it built about 1200 the Golden Cross hostel, the successor of which adorns its own yard off Cornmarket. By 1279 the abbey owned about one-tenth of all property in Oxford and so had numerous buildings it could hire out as schools for clerks, a function which it greatly encouraged.

The earliest large school in Oxford actually pre-dates these monastic bodies, for in 1117 Theobald of Étampes was lecturing in the town to over 60 students. More significant for the future university was the arrival in 1167 of some of the English scholars ordered by Henry II to return home from Paris University. Probably the choice of Oxford was mere chance, unless distance from Westminster and from the Bishop's seat at Lincoln, as well as isolation from important national routes, were considered advantages. By the early thirteenth century the numbers of scholars and teachers had increased so fast that the townsfolk complained of the difficulty of providing enough food. In 1209 a young clerk shot and killed a woman, probably accidentally, whereupon the townsmen lynched two other clerics for a crime they did not commit. The king at first was disinclined to help the students, nearly all of whom then left Oxford, some going to Reading and others to Cambridge where they remained. Five years later the pope took a hand in the affair and the citizens had to apologise to the papal legate and pay as penance an annual fee of 52 shillings for the relief of poor scholars. It seems that some of the students then returned, and in nearly all future troubles between them and the corporation the monarchs favoured the clerks. In any event the students being priests were subject to ecclesiastic law and seldom suffered the severe penalties meted out to offending laymen.

In the thirteenth century academic life at Oxford was strengthened by the arrival of the Friars, the Dominicans or Blackfriars coming in 1221 and the Franciscans or Greyfriars three years later, among them Agnellus (one of the companions of St Francis of Assisi) who is buried here. Eventually there were seven friaries in the town.

The thirteenth century also brought the decline of the rivalry of Northampton as an academic centre. This city has an early history very similar to that of Oxford but was far more popular with the crown for which it provided an impregnable fortress in a strategic position. Henry II visited Northampton fifteen times, including the occasion of the trial of Thomas à Becket in 1164, and King John and later Edward II also looked upon the castle as a favourite residence. Between 1230 and 1258 many students from Oxford and Cambridge migrated here and it looked as if a university might be taking root when Henry III disbanded the scholars partly because many of them had supported Simon de Montfort against him and perhaps partly as a sop to royalist Oxford. Parliament met in Northampton castle in 1338, but soon afterward the Black Death caused havoc, the castle became ruinous and only two more parliaments met in the town, which languished until it was rejuvenated by trade in wool and footwear several centuries later.

In contrast to the decline of Northampton, Oxford's academic growth and its recovery from the Black Death were ensured or hastened when great abbeys elsewhere began to set up houses in the city for the education of their own brethren. Gloucester College, the first such establishment, was founded in 1283 by St Peter's, the Benedictine monastery at Gloucester, for 13 monks, but it soon widened the territory of its student intake as the mediaevel coats of arms over its surviving suites of terraced rooms at what is now Worcester College testify. By 1437 Durham College, Canterbury Hall, St Bernard's College and St Mary College had also been established for regular canons, and have influenced the siting of existing colleges.

These regular priests who lived in their own enclosed houses were few in number compared with the numerous students who lodged in small groups in small halls or schools hired by a teacher or regent master. From 1214 onwards students were under the authority of a chancellor who represented the Bishop of Lincoln, and was elected by the regents of the various halls and the two proctors. Estimates put their number in the early thirteenth century at nearly 1,500 as against about 4,000 citizens. The townsfolk generally over-charged the students or at least asked prices which the scholars thought excessive, and there was considerable hostility between the two parties. In 1290 the citizens appealed to parliament against the oppressive rule of the chancellor of the university, but the crown confirmed his rights and privileges, including authority over all crimes involving scholars, except murder and mayhem (maiming). The youthful students also had their own internal vendettas, the chief being between northern and southern gangs which became so disruptive that in 1334 some scholars went for peace to Stamford. They were ordered back by the king and until 1827 every Oxford M.A. had to take an oath not to teach at a hypothetical University of Stamford.

The friction between town and gown grew red-hot on St Scholastica's Day, 10 February 1355. Two students insulted the innkeeper of the Swyndlestock tavern and soon each side tolled its bell to call its partisans to battle. The chancellor could do nothing to stop the skirmish and the mayor rode off to inform the king at Woodstock. In the next two days the townsfolk, with the aid of numerous villagers from outside the walls, got the upper hand and many clerks were chased to their rooms which were sacked and burnt. All told 63 scholars and an unknown number of citizens were slain. The Bishop of Lincoln laid an interdict on the town, and the mayor and scores of burgesses were imprisoned. The university in a new charter was given control of the assizes of bread, ale, wine, and weights and measures and the chancellor was granted some jurisdiction over townsmen, who were fined and had also to pay an annual penance of 100 marks. The mayor had in future to take an oath to uphold the liberties and privileges of the university. This public penance by the mayor and 63 burgesses, one for each slaughtered clerk, went on in a modified form until 1825 and the oath until 1859.

The First Corporate University Buildings

By the time of the slaughter on St Scholastica's day the university already owned

The church of St Mary the Virgin, viewed between the Radcliffe Camera (to left) and Brasenose College.

some corporate buildings. The first such building was the late-thirteenth century congregation house, a rib-vaulted room attached to the north side of St Mary's.

About 1320 Thomas Cobham, Bishop of Winchester, added over this room an upper storey to house the university library. Both survive facing across Radcliffe Square to the site of the next university buildings, the Divinity School with its extensions in the Bodleian library. The Divinity School was begun about 1420 and not completed until 1490, a delay explained by the need for legacies and the elaborate nature of the decorations. The designer of the general frame may have been Richard Winchcombe, while the constructor of the richly-embossed vault was William Orchard. It is one of the glories of English architecture and, with its upper storey in Duke Humphrey's library, is still in regular use. During the early seventeenth century projections were added to each end of the Divinity School, on the west the convocation house and chancellor's court and on the east a vestibule or proscholium which forms part of the schools' quadrangle of the Bodleian built in 1613 to 1624 through the generosity of Thomas Bodley.

St Mary's church must also be included in these corporate buildings. It was mentioned in *Domesday Survey* and remained in the hands of the crown until 1326 when its then rector, Adam de Brome, obtained royal consent to give it to his new foundation, Oriel College. The university had long made use of the church for lectures and ceremonies and had paid for some of its repairs. In the late fifteenth century they and Oriel College raised enough money to rebuild almost all the fabric, except the tower and spire (of about 1280-1325) in a splendid Perpendicular style.

The Rise of the College System

During this period of increasing corporate wealth the university changed radically also in organisation and cohesion. By 1415 attempts were made to force all undergraduates to live in halls, and as the Black Death from 1349 onwards had killed off over one third of the citizens there were plenty of empty or derelict houses available, especially as the abbots of Osney did all they could to provide scholastic premises. In 1444 there were about 69 of these small halls, usually with 12 to 20 students under the control of a master. The citizens complained to the king that the fee-farm was too high as scarcely one-third of the laymen had survived and much of Oxford was inhabited by scholars and their servants who were exempt from payment. Yet there is no doubt that the number of students had now decreased from 1,500 to about 1,000, partly due to the rival attraction of Cambridge.

At this stage a small but highly significant change in organisation becomes apparent. Some students now lived in colleges as distinct from small halls run by masters in hired properties. From the first the colleges were intended to be impressive residences, expressive of the desire of rich benefactors to acquire heavenly grace by promoting good works and a godly education. In 1249 William of Durham, who had returned from Paris University because of a clash between clerks and citizens there two decades earlier, left 310 marks to be invested in property to keep 10 or more needy masters studying divinity in

Oxford. Various buildings were bought and eventually in the 1280s were unified into University College. In the meanwhile John Balliol (*ob.* 1269) and his wife, the Scottish princess Dervorguilla, gave money for sustaining scholars at Oxford, and a college was set up outside the north gate. About the same time, Walter de Merton, Chancellor of England and opponent of Simon de Montfort, planned a college for his numerous kin and eleven older men from Winchester diocese studying at Oxford. Between 1277 and 1311 the surviving hall, treasury, quadrangle and choir of the great church with its superb traceried windows were built on a splendid scale for about 40 fellows and 25 scholars.

The idea of establishing colleges flowered in the fourteenth century. Exeter College was founded about 1315 by Walter de Stapleton, Bishop of Exeter, for the benefit of West Country youths; Oriel by Adam de Brome under titular cover of Edward II in 1326; and The Queen's College, with preference for natives of Cumberland and Westmoreland, by Queen Philippa under the inducement of Robert de Eglesfield, chaplain to her at Woodstock, in 1341. On a grander scale was New College, founded in 1379 by William of Wykeham for the completion of the education of 70 poor and indigent scholar clerks from the school he had already created at Winchester. William, a Surveyor of the King's Work and a keen architect, probably designed the college himself. Between 1380 and 1400 there arose the great quadrangle, cloisters and bell tower flanked on the north by the city wall. A gate tower with warden's chamber above gives access to a quadrangle enclosed by all the structures essential to the functioning of a scholastic community: on the north side the magnificent chapel with an antechapel and, on the first floor, the dining hall; in the east range a four-storeyed muniment tower, bursary and library; on other sides sets of rooms for both students and fellows, an innovation at Oxford where earlier colleges had been virtually for fellows only. The cloisters and bell tower are set off the west end of the antechapel, as an adjunct to the quadrangle. The whole is a skilful combination for educational purposes of a monastic house and a courtyard fortress such as William of Wykeham owned at Broughton. Its plan and convenience had a great influence on future college architecture.

The idea of a chapel consisting only of a choir and nave of two bays that formed an antechapel or vestibule which could be used for lectures and disputations became widely popular. At Merton the original plan for a great minster with nave and aisles was now curtailed to choir, crossings and transepts above which a magnificent Perpendicular tower was built about 1450. The chapels at many future Oxford colleges followed the New College design even to the use of pinnacles. Within a few decades the skyline of the university core had become a forest of crocketted pinnacles topped by pinnacled towers and spires.

The fifteenth century brought three more colleges. Lincoln was founded in 1427 by Richard Fleming, Bishop of Lincoln, to train theologians to combat heresy, particularly Lollardry. Its charming two-storeyed front quadrangle survives little altered. All Souls' College was founded by Archbishop Chichele in

Magdalen College viewed from the Botanic Garden.

1438 and within four years over £4,000 was spent on its construction. Magdalen College owes its foundation to William Waynflete, Bishop of Winchester, who in 1456 was granted the hospital of St John Baptist and two years later proceeded to enlarge it for a president and 40 scholars. By about 1510 the main buildings, including the chapel and cloisters by William Orchard and the bell tower, were completed. The cloisters are notable as they form a verandah inside the quadrangle and so provide dry access to the sets of students rooms whereas at the New College the cloisters were for burials. Magdalen is sited outside the east gate of the city and the college was able to buy the adjacent meadows on the floodplain of the Cherwell. Its deer park and Addison's Walk are among the coolest and quietest oases of modern Oxford.

In the early sixteenth century the number of colleges increased by three. Brasenose grew out of the enlargement of an ancient hall by endowments in 1509, and Corpus Christi arose also partly on the site of an old hall in 1517. The third, Cardinal College, was particularly magnificent in conception and scale, being planned for about 180 persons and having an endowment of £2,000 annually. The pope gave Wolsey permission to suppress St Frideswide's priory

Christ Church, Tom Quad.

and several small religious houses such as Littlemore priory, and to incorporate their estates and revenue into the college. Various buildings on the main site, including the church of St Michael at Southgate, the south gate itself and half the nave of Frideswide's priory church were demolished. Within six years of the granting of the royal licence in July 1523, part of Tom Quad, the kitchen and the great hall with its magnificent hammerbeam roof, were completed. Wolsey had already appointed about 30 of the 100 intended canons when he fell into disgrace. Henry VIII then turned the establishment into a collegiate church but in 1538, after the destruction of St Frideswide's shrine, he regained control of the endowments and soon saw in them a chance to perpetuate his memory and acquire eternal grace in a magnificent way. He had already set up a bishopric in Oxford and made the huge church at Osney Abbey the cathedral with Robert King as the first bishop, when he changed his mind and established Christ Church by transferring the cathedral status to St Frideswide's church and uniting it with the college. Thus Christ Church became the most splendid of Oxford colleges and acquired through Osney large properties in Oxford.

The Reformation marked the point of no return for the city of Oxford. It became the head of a diocese but did not seize the chance of large scale industrialisation provided by the empty monastic buildings, and thereafter developed into a university town, with an increasing amount of its space passing into college hands. By about 1550 the university had also changed from a multitude of tiny halls into a collection of well-endowed colleges. Of the halls, once 70 in number, all but eight, with less than one third of the total students, had been swallowed up by the colleges or closed because of the great decline in the student population. Today the only independent academic survivor is St Edmund Hall, which passed from Osney Abbey to Queen's but remained independent, and became a college in 1957. 'Tackley's Inn' in High Street with its rib-vaulted cellar also occupies the premises of a mediaeval hall.

University colleges continued to attract benefactions, as they provided the personnel of the civil service as well as of the church and in the years to come educated the kin of the landed gentry and successful merchants. The reformation by destroying monastic estates and chantries deprived the rich of a traditional means of disposing charitably of their wealth. Simultaneously the purchase cheaply of large monastic estates enriched many families who disposed of some of their income in legacies to colleges. These bequests were facilitated by the presence of empty monastic colleges dissolved at the Reformation. Of the five colleges established at Oxford between 1550 and 1630, four were by wealthy laymen, and at least three were born on the spacious sites of monastic buildings and had founders who had benefited greatly from the purchase of former monastic estates. Trinity College was founded in 1555 by Sir Thomas Pope, a rich civil servant who had purchased the former estates of Wroxton priory. The site included Durham College which the Crown had seized in 1544, and the extensions were made partly of stone taken from Blackfriars. In the same year Sir Thomas White, a wealthy London merchant, bought St Bernard's College from Christ Church, which had acquired it at its dissolution, and refounded it as St John's College. The monastic building forms much of the front quadrangle, and in the extensions over 1,000 wagonloads of timber and stone were brought from the Carmelite friary in Beaumont Street. In 1610 Nicholas Wadham and his wife Dorothy, rich West country landowners who had profited considerably from the purchase of monastic estates, created Wadham College partly on a typically spacious site used by Austin Friars. Within three years they had completed this perfect Jacobean gem. The indirect influence of monastic houses in Oxford is seen also in Christ Church in Canterbury quadrangle which arose on

Canterbury College, and in Frewin Hall, in New Inn Hall Street, which was founded in 1435 for Augustinian canons and remained a private hall until 1580.

The strength of the Reformation is reflected in the creation in 1571, on the site of the former White Hall, of Jesus College, a protestant foundation endowed by Dr Hugh Price, son of a rich butcher. The fifth college of this period was Pembroke, founded in 1624 as an enlargement of Broadgates Hall, partly by Thomas Tesdale, a wealthy Abingdon maltster who owned Glympton Manor.

So by the early seventeenth century the university consisted materially of several notable corporate buildings, 18 colleges and 6 private halls including Hart Hall and Magdalen Hall which were combined and refounded as Hertford College in 1874. The colleges were flourishing and many added splendid new quadrangles as at Merton, St John's, Oriel and University. That at St John's (1631-6), with its arcades of elegant columns and fine statues of Charles I and Queen Henrietta, is the finest of its date in Oxford, while the chapel on the quadrangle at University has glass by Abraham van Linge (1641) of a surprising richness and boldness. Full details of architecture and furnishings will be found in *Oxfordshire* (1974) by Nikolaus Pevsner and Jennifer Sherwood, while academic aspects are aptly summarised in V.H.H. Green's *History of Oxford University* (1974). Suffice it to say that although still essentially clerical nearly half of the student population consisted of sons of gentry. The future seemed bright until in October 1642 Charles I chose Oxford as his headquarters. The king and court resided at Christ Church, and Queen Henrietta, until near childbirth, lived conveniently close at Merton. The royal presence was stimulating but disruptive, and when in June 1646 the city mildly surrendered to the parliamentary forces, although material damage was negligible, the general effect on the town and neighbourhood had been disastrous.[3] Thereafter the university slowly settled down to nearly two centuries of sterile comfort.

Gown and Town: 1650-1850

The number of entrants to Oxford University rose to a peak of about 575 a year just before the Civil War and then declined to about 455 by 1650 and to below 300 by 1700. The earlier peak was not regained until Victorian times. Yet at first this falling recruitment was not matched by stagnation in building, largely because of the presence of Oxford's greatest architect, of generous benefactors and of artists working at Blenheim palace.

Christopher Wren was professor of astronomy and fellow of All Souls' when he designed for his friend Archbishop Sheldon a new meeting place for university ceremonies till then held in St Mary's. Sheldon gave the £12,000 required and Wren provided a classical design based largely on Serlio's illustration of the theatre of Marcellus. The building, with its main facade facing the Divinity Schools, was completed in 1663-9, and Wren then went on to complete Tom tower in Christ Church to a Gothic design suited to the quadrangle left

The Sheldonian Theatre and Clarendon Building.

unfinished by Wolsey. Wren was a key figure in Oxford science and used to meet with Robert Boyle and other scientists in the rooms of John Wilkins, Warden of Wadham, where they formed in 1648 a Philosophical Society, which twelve years later combined with a similar group in London to found the Royal Society.

Wren's classical innovations in architecture at Oxford were eagerly followed by Thomas Wood, a local mason who built the graceful Old Ashmolean to house the natural curiosities collected by John Tradescant and Elias Ashmole. Today it is a museum of the history of science. The appeal of classical motifs spread and are seen to perfection in Queen's College library and in Trinity College chapel with its superb wood carvings. The early eighteenth century brought the inspiration of artists working at Blenheim. In 1711-15 Nicholas Hawksmoor built the massive Clarendon building with its huge Tuscan columns and proceeded to design the north quadrangle of All Souls'. He may also have added the spire of All Saints' Church to the main fabric designed by Dean Aldrich of Christ Church. This delightful edifice, once the city church, has now been cleaned and repaired as a library for Lincoln College. There are many other buildings of this period elsewhere in the university and town, including the baroque Vanbrugh house in St Michael's Street. The architectural florescence was prolonged by the great benefactions of Dr John Radcliffe, who gave £40,000 for the massive rotunda or camera built from designs by James Gibbs in 1737-49, and provided finances for the erection off the Woodstock Road of the Radcliffe Infirmary (1770) and the delightful observatory, a copy of the Tower of the Winds at Athens, as well as a quadrangle at University College.

The town seems to have experienced a brisk rejuvenation about the time when the university's building efforts waned. In 1771 a Mileways Act, the first of five such acts before 1848, saw the straightening and widening of some streets and, unfortunately, the demolition of the east gate and the north gate together with the Bocardo prison. The market was moved from the streets to a new covered site over which the citizens gained some control. The bridges were improved and movement of traffic to the west was greatly eased when the ferry over the Thames at Eynsham was replaced by a toll bridge in 1769. A canal from the Midland coalfields reached Oxford in 1790 (*see* Chapter 10) and within a few years 77 boats from Staffordshire and Warwickshire were registered for use to the wharfs near the castle mound.

During the first four decades of the nineteenth century the population of Oxford, in spite of outbreaks of cholera, rose from 12,000 to 24,000, and the built-up area expanded rapidly under the influence of successful tradesmen and printers. Between 1820 and 1832, at least 125 new houses of well-to-do business men were built upon the open gravel terrace alongside and between the Banbury and Woodstock turnpikes about 2km north of the city. Soon the settlement had a church of its own and became the parish of Summertown which remained independent of Oxford until 1889. The few surviving original dwellings include the 'Dew Drop Inn' and a grand Italianate villa now the Freemasons' hall.[4]

A new industrial housing suburb arose in Jericho when the third Oxford University Press moved to palatial premises in Walton Square in 1827. This move from the Clarendon Building in Broad Street was necessitated by the large production of bibles, for the Press, with Cambridge University and the royal publisher, enjoyed, and still enjoys, the exclusive right to publish the authorised version of the English Bible and the Book of Common Prayer. The whole front and south wing of the large new printing office were devoted solely to this purpose, and by 1865 over one million bibles were being printed annually.[5] Eighty years later about two-thirds of the printing work done was religious in character, a condition which would have pleased Thomas Combe, Superintendent of the Clarendon Press from 1838 to his death in 1872. Combe was a friend of Newman and Pusey and a devout Tractarian. About 1857 he began to transfer some of his patronage from pre-Raphaelite art to religious architecture, and was financially responsible for the rebuilding of Wolvercote church, and the building of the chapel at the Radcliffe Infirmary and the church of St Barnabas in Jericho. The last-named, with its varied anglicised motifs on an Italian Romanesque theme, stands in Cardigan Street near the canal, and its tall campanile makes a fine sight from the railway tracks.[6] It was designed by Arthur Blomfield, the architect under whom Thomas Hardy served for five years. In *Jude the Obscure,* Jude Fawley during his stay in Christminster (Oxford), took

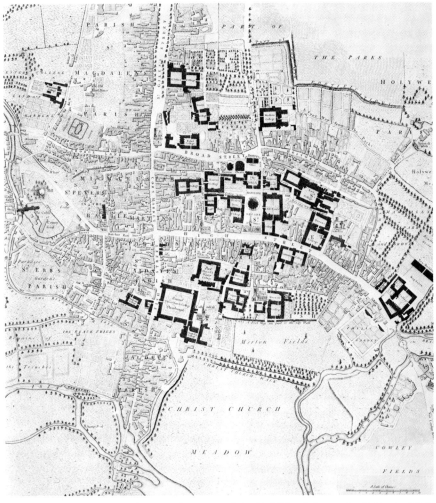

Late eighteenth-century Oxford showing some of the Civil War defences (by R. Davis, 1794).

cheap, modest lodgings in Beersheba (Jericho) and like his cousin, Sue Brideshead, worshipped at St Silas (St Barnabas), then noted for its High Church ritual. After their quarrel Sue went to St Silas' where Jude found her sobbing in front of the large jewelled cross, which still stands there.

The expansion of the street pattern was associated with the reform of the city council, and in 1835 the ten aldermen and 30 councillors were elected by about 3,000 ratepayers instead of by half that number of freemen. Although the change did nothing to lessen the powers and privileges of the university, when the railway came from Didcot in 1844 a new spirit and stronger economic potential existed in the township.

Resurgence of Town and Gown, 1850-1900

Within ten years of the coming of the railway from Didcot, Oxford had lines to Worcester, Banbury, Birmingham and Cambridge, and in the following decade was linked also to Fairford and to Thame and Princes Risborough (*see* Chapter 15). The town, with its two railway stations, became the chief railway centre of the south Midlands. In 1865, the GWR wished to set up its carriage works here, and the citizens eagerly offered it a large meadow near the station as a site, but the university crushed the scheme and the works went to Swindon. So the town lacked any notable manufacture or trade apart from printing, paper making, some engineering and iron working and boat building, all small concerns except the press. The university dominated the economic and social life, but the citizens were becoming less subservient. The oath of fealty by the mayor was discontinued in 1859, and a decade later a Police Act established one constabulary force for the whole area under a committee in which the Town had the majority. In 1889 when the city was made a county borough with extended boundaries and a new council, the university relinquished its exclusive right of policing the streets after sundown. By 1901 the city had increased in population to nearly 50,000.

In the meanwhile the university had recovered from its earlier decline and had reached new peaks of popularity. By 1875 about 695 students matriculated annually and by 1900 the number had risen to 840. This growth was accompanied by a reformation in the nature of the university society and a great excrescence of material wealth. By various Acts and reforms the conditions of student entry were widened, religious tests for most degrees were abolished and colleges allowed their fellows to marry without resigning their fellowships. The latter on the domestic front is represented by the remarkably large Victorian dwellings in the Woodstock and Banbury Roads, fantasies in brick and stone offset by a profusion of flowering shrubs.

Oxford is particularly fortunate in Victoriana. The new Ashmolean Museum and Taylorian Institution of 1841-5 is Grecian, a 'grand pile in the Ionic order'. Its powerful, dignified facades look across to the Martyrs' Memorial, the herald of Victorian Gothic in Oxford. Designed by Gilbert Scott as an eyecatcher at the town end of St Giles, it stands some way from the spot in the town ditch, now Broad Street, where Ridley and Latimer were burnt in 1555. Scott went on to design Exeter College chapel (based on the Sainte Chapelle in Paris), the library here and at University College, and, for example, the range of New College facing Holywell Street.

Then Oxford developed its own eccentricities when Ruskin and the pre-Raphaelites left their unmistakeable touch. John Ruskin, Slade professor of art at Oxford from 1869 to 1879, was the dominant influence on the University museum which was designed in Venetian Gothic by Benjamin Woodward, while the adjacent laboratory for chemistry was copied from the Abbot's kitchen at

Oxford, the university core.

Glastonbury. Ruskin was largely responsible for the interior details, an artistic riot of iron and varied building stone, so perfect and elaborate that it was never completed as he envisaged. His influence can also be seen in the Meadow buildings at Christ Church, designed in Venetian Gothic by Thomas Deane. But many people will find more delight in the ideals and smaller artistic achievements of the pre-Raphaelites, which, as John Christian points out in a recent booklet (Ashmolean, 1974), can be recaptured most vividly at Oxford.

Thomas Combe, Printer to the University, was deeply attracted by the work of John Everett Millais who had come to Oxford to paint a portrait of Mr Wyatt who kept a picture shop in High Street. Combe soon became the patron of both William Holman Hunt and of Millais from whom he commissioned *The Return*

William Morris.

of the Dove to the Ark. The painting was displayed in Wyatt's window where it was seen in 1853 by two undergraduates of Exeter College, William Morris and Edward Burne-Jones. The two friends became devotees of mediaeval craftsmanship, and after various grand artistic ventures Morris lived from 1871 to 1896 beside the upper Thames at Kelmscott manor, where the house and its furnishings are carefully preserved. It lies a day's trip by boat up the stripling Thames and close to Buscot Park with the famous Brier Rose series of Burne-

Jones' paintings of the Sleeping Beauty. The Ashmolean has a rich collection of pre-Raphaelite paintings based on the legacy of Thomas Combe who bought direct from the artists. The original of Holman Hunt's *Light of the World* hangs at Keble, Exeter College chapel has an exquisite tapestry and the cathedral beautiful glass, and, although the Union murals have faded, there are numerous other survivals of this idealistic reaction to an over-industrialised Britain.

Another reaction, this time against the apparent sterility of the university's religious belief, led, as we have seen, to the Tractarian Movement which is reflected in the establishment of Keble College from funds donated in memory of John Keble, who died in 1866. A striking symphony of polychrome brick, it is the master work of William Butterfield.

In late Victorian times both town and gown began to disregard William Morris' advocacy of restraint and refinement and showed a great partiality for the work of Sir Thomas G. Jackson. In the new Examination Schools (1876-1882) Jackson mixed Italian and English motifs with rare gusto. He went on to enlarge, among others, Brasenose, Corpus, Hertford, Lincoln, Somerville and Trinity colleges and his disciples built, for example, the Town Hall (Henry Hare) and the Indian Institute (Basil Champneys). Eventually he set what Pevsner calls 'his elephantine feet' over much of central Oxford. Recently many of his buildings have been cleaned and repaired, and hybrids they may be and repulsive to some modern architects, but as reminders of an opulent age and as welcome contrasts to the dull expanses of plain brick, concrete and plate glass of modern international styles they seem delightful extravaganzas. Hertford College with its 'Bridge of Sighs' alone suffices to convince ordinary mortals of the lasting success of Jackson's ingenuity.

The mention above of Somerville College serves to recall that the late Victorian age saw the admission of women to the university. Between 1878 and 1893 Lady Margaret Hall, Somerville, St Hugh's, St Hilda's and the Society of Oxford Home Students (later St Anne's) were opened for women who took the usual examinations, but until 1920 were refused degrees. They lie around the fringe of the main cluster of old colleges and suffer, or perhaps enjoy, a much undeserved neglect by tourists as their modern buildings are among the most successful in Oxford. They have other attractions such as pleasant Georgian premises (Cowley Place) and a fine position above the Cherwell at St Hilda's, a small range by T. G. Jackson at Somerville, a beautiful triptych by Burne Jones in the Byzantine style chapel at Lady Margaret Hall and the delightful garden planned by Annie Rodgers at St Hugh's, a choice addition to a city of lovely gardens. Today several women's colleges and the vast majority of men's colleges are residential for both sexes.

The Twentieth-Century Explosion

In 1900 the university admitted 840 students and had a total residential population of less than 3,000 undergraduates. By 1978 the number in residence

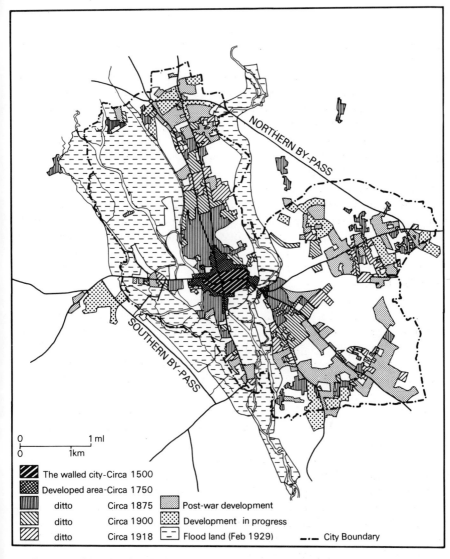

The walled city-Circa 1500
Developed area-Circa 1750
  ditto   Circa 1875   Post-war development
  ditto   Circa 1900   Development in progress
  ditto   Circa 1918   Flood land (Feb 1929)   —·— City Boundary

Development of the City of Oxford to 1935. Post-war development refers to 1918–1933. To avoid confusion some of the floodplain water channels have been omitted.

had risen to about 12,000 of whom 3,000 were postgraduates engaged in some form of research. This fourfold increase was due largely to the expansion of science and research, to the enlargement of existing colleges, and to the creation since 1958 of eight new colleges, the latest being Green College for clinical students. The present university consists of 35 colleges and 5 permanent halls, namely Campion, Greyfriars, Mansfield, Regent's Park and St Benet's. These and the corporate buildings are clustered in or around the old walled city within a few minutes walk of St Mary's and the Bodleian.

So far in the twentieth century the city population has increased from about 40,000 to approximately 120,000, a quite staggering growth, most of which must be imputed to the exploits of William Richard Morris, a Cowley mechanic who later became Lord Nuffield. As described in Chapter 20, Morris made Cowley and a huge fortune. At the time of his death he had donated nearly £30 million to worthy causes. A practical man, who had 'come up the hard way', he expected immediate results such as came from supplying components to a factory line, and for a long time he had no love for Oxford and distrusted intellectuals. However, he gave about £4 million to the university, mainly to medicine, St Peter's College, and to Nuffield College which he founded in 1937 and which inherited a further large sum at his death. Nuffield College, as its founder insisted, is plain architecturally and quite attractive.

Today motor car manufacturing, although the dominant single employer, by no means swamps Oxford economic life. In 1971, of the city's total working population, 21,000 or nearly 30 per cent were employed in the vehicle industry, against 19,200 or 27 per cent in professional and scientific services. The former operate mainly on the plateau top and the latter on the valley floor in the university quarters and near the town hall where the various county offices and the chief shops and markets are also situated. In recent years the numerical ranking of occupations given above has probably been reversed because the motor car trade has been hit by strikes and overseas competition, while the professional and research side has gone from strength to strength. For example in addition to the Oxford University Press, Pergamon and Blackwell, many other printing firms have offices here and in the educational sphere a grand Polytechnic, numerous College extensions and institutions for teaching English have arisen. At the same time, the stimulus of an environment rich in expertise and reference facilities has encouraged the expansion of concerns dealing with bookselling, research, business consultancy and management studies.

The city has been surrounded by ring roads and by a Green Belt about 5 miles (8km) wide aimed at restricting excessive ribbon development and urban sprawl.[7] Within this belt ten villages have been selected for growth and since 1961 all have increased in population by one third and several by double that amount. This preservation of green countryside around the city was conceived by the Oxford Preservation Trust, which for over fifty years has also played a major role in protecting listed domestic architecture such as Alice's shop in St Aldate's, some seventeenth century houses in Turn Again Street and the gateway of Blackfriar's Priory in St Ebbe's.

The abundance of colleges and the diligence of the Trust have ensured that large areas of the inner city have not been draped in the international style that dulls the redeveloped centres of so many other towns. Yet the new constructions, mainly in St Ebbe's and outside the former walled city, are sufficient in

East Oxford: early twentieth-century planning.

themselves to be an attraction. A recent walk-round guide by David Reed and Philip Opher (*New Architecture in Oxford*, Oxford Polytechnic, 1977) demonstrates that for every arrogant and over-assertive new building foisted on the Oxford townscape it has had another that is elegant and conformable. But, as said, the misfits are minimal in the university quarters.

Tourists abound at all seasons and the town is a 'must' on the international tour from London to Stratford upon Avon. For Shakespearean addicts the attractions include the Painted Room at No. 3 Cornmarket, with its wall paintings of about 1570 when the place was the 'Crown Inn'. The innkeeper then was William Davenant whose son William, born here in 1606, later became poet laureate. Shakespeare stayed here often when travelling between London and Stratford and was young Davenant's godfather, and it is said also probably his natural father.

Facilities for visitors have been improved, although hotels are few and a brave attempt by one college to build a grand hotel on the bank of the Thames was turned down because the site was just within the Green Belt. The colleges themselves have become favourite venues for conferences and societies; the old city library has been converted to a museum and efforts are being made to improve the long waterfront, as has been done so imaginatively in the cool riverside gardens of Fisher Row. The city atmosphere has been cleaned of much

The High Street, Oxford, before the motor car mania.

of its pollution and the fine stonework, after costly cleaning or refacing, now gleams with a new brightness. The High but for its motor traffic still merits Wordsworth's praise: 'the stream-like windings of that glorious street'. The older parts within a short distance of St Mary's remain a microcosm of civilised arts, with so many fine buildings and gardens, such a wealth of small treasures and beautiful vistas that inevitably, as Gerald Gould says:

> . . . All discover, late or soon,
> Their golden Oxford afternoon.

CHAPTER TWENTY

The Machine Age

And now, if you will set us to our task,
We will serve you four and twenty hours a day!
We can neither love nor pity nor forgive,
If you make a slip in handling us you die!
We are greater than the Peoples or the Kings—
Be humble, as you crawl beneath our rods!—
Our touch can alter all created things,
We are everything on earth—except the Gods!
(Rudyard Kipling, *The Secret of the Machines*)

Events during the twentieth century brought at first stagnation and decay to the English heartland and then, when its rural nature proved attractive to would-be residents and manufacturers, proceeded to restore its vitality. The industrial parts of coalfield England suffered from excessive congestion and pollution, and in comparison the neglected heartland was clean, thinly-peopled, pleasant to look at and peaceful to live in. The official *Censuses* clearly reveal the great relative decline of Oxfordshire in Victorian and Edwardian times. Between 1851 and 1901 the population of the county grew by less than 10,000 persons (5.7%) and was now outpaced by the inhabitants of Berkshire and Buckinghamshire, which increased in population by 89,000 (52%) and 31,000 (19%) respectively. During the next three decades Oxfordshire began to make a belated recovery but its total population growth was only 16 per cent against 20 per cent in Berkshire and 30 per cent in Buckinghamshire.

The Years of Rural Decline

Throughout the early twentieth century farms went over increasingly to grass and livestock and agricultural employment continued to fall. The population of most rural parishes and of many towns declined until the mid-1920s and in some continued to stagnate for another decade. Oxfordshire was exceptionally backward and oppressed; from 1891 to 1901 the county decreased in population by 4,670 persons and from 1911 to 1921 the number of its inhabitants scarcely changed at all. The chief exceptions to this stagnation lay in the south of the English heartland near Henley, Windsor and the lower Chilterns, where commuting to London was growing and in the far north, where the great expansion of Coventry and Birmingham had a similar effect.

The architectural results, apart from restorations in a traditional style, are visible mainly in and near the Thames valley where it cuts through the chalk downs. The river and its riverside scenes, beloved by the Victorians, were now popularised further by Kenneth Grahame's *Wind in the Willows* (1908). In Edwardian times Goring, for example, expanded rapidly with rich dwellings and gabled balconied boat-houses; Wargrave enjoyed a similar prosperity; Medmenham saw the erection of Danesfield, a palatial stone structure in Tudor style, the masterpiece of Romaine Walker who had just been responsible for the restoration of the nearby abbey; Shiplake was embellished by the White House, reminiscent of Brighton's marine parade, and by the Court, one of the most vigorous and pleasing of Ernest George's designs. The outstanding local dwellings designed by Sir Edwin Lutyens are Deanery Gardens, Sonning, built in 1901 for Edward Hudson, owner of *Country Life,* and Folly Farm at Sulhamstead, extended in 1906 and 1912, part in Tudor and part in William and Mary style. At the latter the gardens were laid out with the help of Gertrude Jekyll, who was a great friend and patron of Lutyens from his early days.

The dearth of Edwardian buildings elsewhere in the English heartland reflects the poor profits from agriculture, and Eynsham Park, rebuilt by Sir Ernest George in a Jacobean style in 1904, is a rare sign of prosperity. In the north Cotswolds estates with good sporting facilities continued to attract buyers with wealth enough to refashion their homes. Lutyens was employed to remodel Copse Hill and eight cottages near the churchyard at Upper Slaughter, and to rebuild Abbotswood at Lower Swell, where he laid out the grounds with floral terraces and a characteristic water garden. Sir Guy Dawber also designed many comely modest-sized mansions in local stone, including Eyford Park and Burdocks near Fairford, both in Queen Anne style, and Lower Swell manor (now Hill Place School) in a Jacobean style. But these Edwardian additions suggest that the day of the huge mansion was past. Lutyens expressed himself abroad in the grandeur of New Delhi and his famous disciple, Henry Medd,[1] who was born at North Cerney in 1892, became chief architect to the Indian government, 1939-47.

The scarcity in the upper Thames, or William Morris countryside, of homes built under the direct influence of the Arts and Crafts movement is more surprising. At Kelmscott the William Morris memorial cottages by Philip Webb and the village hall by Ernest Gimson are traditional Cotswold. C.R. Ashbee built a house at Wroxton and another, By Ways, at Yarnton while Baillie Scott designed Home Close at Sibford Ferris and White Lodge at Wantage in an Arts and Crafts version of the Cotswold style, but perhaps the most striking effort is the Working Men's Club at Nettlebed, a red brick structure round three sides of a courtyard.

In fact there was little money available and little demand for working class dwellings. Nearly all villages and towns on the wolds and in the remoter clay vales had many empty houses. To see humbler dwellings of Edwardian times the visitor should go to east Oxford, where between the Iffley and Cowley Roads a suburb of considerable architectural interest was planned for low paid artisans. When this extension was arising most small towns and rural villages outside easy reach of London were decaying unless they had by chance attracted to them some newcomer willing to spend large sums on repairs without regard to profit.

At Stanton in Gloucestershire the estate was bought in 1906 by an architect, Sir Philip Stott, who, until his death thirty one years later, bestowed his skill and wealth on restoring and beautifying the small Cotswold village. Besides restoring the dwellings, many of which dated from Elizabethan and Jacobean times, he enlarged the malthouse cottages, brought in bodily three old timber-framed barns, and carefully laid on essential services, including a communal swimming pool. The whole village now has an idyllic and harmonious tidiness which displays to perfection the colourful garden fringes and the subtle variations of the Cotswold stone.

At Burford, E.J. Horniman and other residents inspired by his example saved the town from decay and ensured the restoration of its ancient frontages. In Chipping Campden parish forty one dwellings were unoccupied when in 1901-2 the Guild of Handicraft migrated from the East End of London to the old silk mill in Sheep Street. The beauty and unspoilt nature of the quiet Gloucestershire town seemed an ideal setting for individualistic craftsmen and artists. The guild had been founded in Whitechapel in 1888 to practise the principles of a class at Toynbee Hall, imbued with the ideas of Ruskin, Morris and Carlyle. The enterprise was guided by Charles Robert Ashbee, pupil in architecture of G.F. Bodley and highly-skilled disciple of the pre-Raphaelite brotherhood, who had already taken over the Kelmscott Press from William Morris and used it as the basis for his own Essex House Press. Eventually about fifty working guildsmen and one hundred women and children came to live in the Cotswold town. The variety of their crafts ranged from handwork in precious metals, iron, copper, stone and wood to stained glass and printing. Ashbee converted and restored the Norman chapel at Broad Campden,[2] retaining its original doorways and chancel arch and after completing this work in 1907 he handed over the Essex House Press there to an Indian artist and craftsman, Dr A.K. Coomaraswamy, and went to live temporarily in the Woolstaplers' Hall, which he also carefully restored. The guild, run as a limited liability company, flourished at first and then failed financially, whereupon Joseph Fels, an American philanthropist, came to its rescue by presenting it with a local farm of seventy acres, so enabling the members to pursue Ashbee's original idea of combining handicrafts and husbandry at least in years when craft sales were poor. But very few of the artists and craftsmen proved able or willing to undertake farm work — by now they had been long enough in the countryside to realise that farming requires exceptional skill and stamina — and in 1921 the farm was sold. The town continued to benefit from the presence of skilled craftsmen and in 1924, owing largely to the enthusiasm of F.L. Griggs and Ashbee, the Campden Society, a purely amenity group, was formed. This society gradually faded away and in 1929 the Campden Trust Limited was founded by Griggs and others, with the share capital provided largely by Sir Philip Stott and William Cadbury. The Trust has, by practical example and peaceful persuasion, managed to preserve the appearance of Campden down to details such as artistic shop signs and to maintain its reputation for arts and crafts. Some of the direct descendants of the original craftsmen carry on the family tradition, notably in silver work and furniture making, which have acquired, here and at Broadway, a national reputation.

The Campden guild barely survived the World War of 1914-18 which struck especially hard in rural parishes already declining in population due to decreasing employment in agriculture. The young men enlisted patriotically in droves and some rural villages were almost emptied of active males of military age. The ploughing up campaign[3] and other farm work depended mainly on women who now 'kept the home fires burning' and broke free for ever from the male dominance inherited from Victorian moralism. The visual effects of this terrible war are small but widespread. The slaughter of unbelievable numbers of men in the muddy trenches in Flanders is recorded in the war memorial and Roll of Honour in each parish. Visitors with similar memorials in their own parishes may perhaps be excused for giving these sad new historical sights no more than a passing glance, but many have great artistic merit and they mark the change from an old to a new Britain. At the little village of Iffley 21 men never returned; at Shipton under Wychwood 27, at Burford and Fulbrook, 44 and so the sad story goes on to every hamlet and town. In addition, many of the survivors were grievously wounded. By the armistice in November 1918 the nation had lost a considerable proportion of its virile males, and homes and education facilities had been utterly neglected. It seemed that a miracle would be needed to revive the material well-being of rural villages and towns. As always the inspiration, except in agricultural matters, came from outside, this time in the form of the internal combustion engine.

The Coming of Motor Cars and Aeroplanes

The use of free-roaming steam waggons or coaches was almost eliminated from British roads by hostile Acts of parliament from 1831 onward. These included the 'Red Flag' Acts of 1861 and 1865, which required a man to precede the steam waggon carrying a red flag by day and a red lantern at night. About thirty years later Karl Benz made a successful internal-combustion-powered tricycle and Gottlieb Daimler patented his own internal-combustion engine. These high-speed petrol machines soon proved more satisfactory than those driven by steam, other gases or electricity but they could not be introduced into Britain until 1896 when the 'Red Flag' Acts were repealed and the maximum speed limit for motor-drawn vehicles raised from 4 to 12 m.p.h. In that year the Daimler Motor Company (founded by Benz and Daimler at Kannstatt in Germany in 1890) searched in Cheltenham and Birmingham for suitable premises, before being offered on favourable terms a disused cotton mill in Coventry. The site proved ideal for the Daimler Company and the Great Horseless Carriage Company, as the Black Country factories already made a vast variety of small metal wares, including bicycles and gas engines. Coventry immediately became the chief British centre for motor car manufacture with Birmingham second, the latter being the prime source of components. The industry employed only 151 persons in 1900 but grew rapidly and with the raising of the maximum legal speed limit to 20 m.p.h. in 1903 was assured of success. By 1905, irrespective of small engineering concerns, 22 Coventry manufacturers had entered the industry, and most of them made bicycles as well as motor cars.[4] The great English pioneers were Henry Royce, Herbert Austin and William Hillman. Royce of Manchester produced a car in 1904 and two years later, after merging with C.S. Rolls of London, designed the famous Rolls-Royce Silver Ghost with a 40-50 h.p. side-valve engine. Austin began designing his first car on returning in 1893 from Australia, where he had foreseen the future of mechanical road transport while managing a sheep farm. By 1906 he had moved to a more spacious site at Longbridge on the outskirts of Birmingham. Hillman was a Coventry cycle manufacturer who, after entering a car in a Tourist Trophy Race and establishing a track record in 1907, began to construct his own cars. Among other cycle firms who took up motor car building and later became household names were Swift, Lea and Francis, Allard, Singer, Rover, Riley and Humber. By 1914 the industry had spread to a few other towns, and about 53,000 workers supplied the market with no less than seventy different models of light cars. The new makers included William Richard Morris, a cycle mechanic who had grown up in east Oxford, where numerous small workshops tucked away in back gardens were run by craftsmen skilled in the repair and production of wood and metal objects largely for Oxford colleges.[5] In 1893, Morris, at the age of sixteen, started to make bicycles from Midland components and gradually moved on in 1900 to motor cycles and so in 1903 to selling and hiring out automobiles from a garage in Longwall Street. Nine years later he began producing from components bought from Coventry and Birmingham engineers, a 'bullnosed' Morris with a body made by Oxford coach-builders. The outbreak of war in 1914 halted production, and the firm went over to other work but the internal combustion engine, although not then produced in the English heartland, had a considerable impact upon its scenery.

On land this war was fought at first with foot- and horse-power and had become a disastrous stalemate when motorised transport, particularly in the form of tanks and aeroplanes, began to be introduced. The internal combustion engine revolutionised warfare and later reformed the western way of life. Its earliest scenic effects were small and widespread and lacked the massive impact of military barracks and Ordnance depots such as raised the population of Didcot parish from 707 to 2,164 between 1911 and 1921. The petrol machine after 1904 perpetuated the aeroplane, originally a light contrivance with a single small engine and a frail carpenter-built frame. The World War encouraged the development of aircraft, especially of aero-engines by Rolls-Royce, and in 1919 the North Atlantic was crossed non-stop. In these early days any extensive flat pasture was adequate for take off and landing, and the personnel were usually lodged in small rectangular bungalows alongside the perimeter. The airfields near Oxford included the floodplain at Farmoor; the flat cornbrash plateau used by the De Havilland Aircraft Company at Curbridge near Witney; an open expanse of 285 acres created in 1915 at Weston on the Green by Canadians with the aid of German prisoners of war; and the R.A.F. station at Bicester, constructed in 1917 as a training depot for Southern Army Command. Here and elsewhere a few of the sites and most of the temporary hutments were to prove permanent in a post-war age starved of adequate housing.

The Inter-War Recovery, 1918-1939

The period following the first World War was notable in the English heartland for a great building of domestic homes, a relapse to pastoralism, and the rise of new industries.

The building, apart from the need to repair four years' neglect, was primarily to provide dwellings fit for heroes to live in. During previous centuries rural communities had been responsible for the parish church (except the chancel) and a 'poor' house or two, while the citizens of boroughs had also to provide for defences, jail and town hall. In Victorian times the larger boroughs also acquired a Corn Exchange and a workhouse, the latter being maintained by rates on town and country. In the twentieth century all local councils undertook the erection of dwellings to be rented mainly to ex-service men. The council houses usually took the form of well-spaced blocks of semi-detached dwellings with sizeable gardens aligned beside a road on the fringe of the main built-up area of villages and towns. They were well built, where possible of good local materials, stone in the wold and brick, sometimes with pebble dash, in the vales. At Burford the twelve dwellings were constructed of oolitic stone dug in the nearby fields. Small 'towns' of this kind and the larger boroughs were allotted more council houses than were less populous villages and, in fact, many isolated rural parishes needed employment much more than new dwellings. The result was a continued drift of labourers and craftsmen from outlying villages into the ancient boroughs. These council dwellings of the 1920s survive as distinctive groupings and often mark in a pleasant way the halting of the visual decay of the English heartland. However, they did not bring prosperity to the economy, least of all to that of rural villages declining in population.

The ploughing-up campaign of the first World War was merely a brief halt in the long decline of arable farming that continued until 1939. By then the area under tillage had decreased by one-half since the prosperous farming era in mid-Victorian times, and the extent of grassland had doubled. Except in the Vale of

Evesham, nearly two-thirds of the improved farmland was under grass, and ominously increasing amounts of land were being left as rough grazing or being taken for housing and other non-agricultural uses. More and more farmers were dependent on dairying and other livestock products and, although sheep flocks decreased drastically in number, the popularity of cattle and pigs offset the decline. Except in favoured localities, agriculture provided neither a rich living nor much employment; farmland was relatively cheap and the inhabitants of rural districts were desperate for new occupations.

These unfortunate circumstances appear less disastrous when seen against the marked decline of the major older manufacturing industries, such as cotton textiles, ship building and coalmining, on coalfields elsewhere, especially during the severe economic depressions of the mid-1920s and early 1930s. Industrial magnates, well aware of the spread of the electric power grid and of fast road transport, now began to find·rural localities attractive for large new ventures. Economists stressed the virtues of centrality, and humanists extolled the value of clean and pleasant surroundings for workers. Yet industrial growth in the English heartland was slow except in heavy local products.

The great national demand for construction materials led to the establishment of many brickworks and cement factories. For example, Oxford clay was used for brick making on a large scale at Calvert and Woodham from 1928 onwards, while cement making flourished and expanded, sometimes from pre-existing limeworks, as at Chinnor on the middle chalk and Shipton on Cherwell on the great oolite. However, quarrying of the calcareous ironstone near Banbury ceased for some years partly because more use was now made of the ferruginous sands in Northamptonshire. By 1936 these sands were providing 26 per cent of the United Kingdom's output of iron ore (against 18 per cent in 1913) and several blast furnaces had been established at Wellingborough, Kettering and, complete with a steel works, at Corby. The rapid expansion of iron and steel and of footwear industries in northern Northamptonshire attracted workers from, and emphasised the rural nature of, the southern parts of the county which we have included in the English heartland.

The establishment of new metal-using concerns in the heartland did not depend on local ores. The plant of the Northern Aluminium Company, that was established on a spacious site at Banbury in 1931, used ingots imported from Canada. The success of this large firm, especially in building up its own labour force from a wide area, provided a portent for other firms seeking a central location in England. Elsewhere in Oxfordshire and nearby counties the new industrial employment depended heavily on the development of the aeroplane and motor car. Flying, both private and military, grew in popularity and light aeroplanes became almost as cheap as motor cars. Old airfields were retained and new aerodromes, and bombing ranges, added. For example near Oxford, part of the rough grazing ground at Otmoor was acquired in 1920 by the R.A.F. as a bombing range; De Havillands continued to use their airfield near Witney;

a new R.A.F. station was opened at Upper Heyford in 1927; and Bicester R.A.F. station, after temporary closure, was re-opened in 1928 as a bomber station. Within a few years the English heartland contained at least a dozen airfields, civilian and military.

The growing popularity of motor cars had most affect on districts within easy commuting distance of Coventry and Oxford. Warwick and Leamington were connected by rail to Coventry station, whence the trains continued to Nuneaton stopping en route to serve car workers at Daimler halt. In 1931 a large proportion of the 1,300 employees in manufacturing living at Warwick worked in Leamington and Coventry.

At Oxford after the First World War William Morris formed Morris Motors Ltd and took over the vacant Military College at Cowley which was soon turning out, from Coventry components, over fifty cars a week. More importantly he had gained a reputation among bankers as a man who paid his debts promptly and put an adequate share of profits back into his business. Consequently when many older car firms in the Midlands closed down during the general slump in the 1920s, Morris joined the relatively few survivors who could obtain credit enough to modernise their production methods. These few, by adopting flow production and standardisation of parts, raised the national output, lowered production costs by about one quarter and broke the hold of American cars on British markets. Morris' idea of a 'square deal' for his workmen was to enable them to work as hard as himself. At Oxford he paid relatively high wages to men who had little hope of finding other employment locally but did not hesitate to dismiss them temporarily whenever immediate sales slowed down. In 1923 he took over the firm at Coventry that had been making for him about 300 engines a week, and within four years its weekly output for Morris vehicles was 2,000 engines and gearboxes. At about the same time be bought and enlarged a motor bodies factory at Coventry. By 1927 the Cowley factory at Oxford was producing nearly 1,000 cars a week, and a radiator branch had been opened in the Woodstock Road in north Oxford. In the meanwhile the Pressed Steel Company had established a factory for steel motor car bodies on the plateau adjoining the Morris works at Cowley. William Morris was responsible for the arrival of this development, as he had persuaded a noted Philadelphian company who were applying new techniques to the manufacture of steel car bodies to join with him in the venture. Within a few years the Morris interest was withdrawn and Pressed Steel began to supply steel bodies to other car manufacturers also.

The Morris firm struck a boom period for car sales abroad as well as at home, and by 1934 were exporting no less than 450 vehicles weekly. At Cowley the labour force commuted from within a radius of about 20 miles (32km) and immigrants from many parts of the British Isles settled in the Oxford district.[6] Between the two World Wars 10,000 new houses were built in Oxford, and its outer suburbs and the number of people living within the extended city boundary rose by 30,000. At least one third of all insured workers in the Oxford area were employed by the Nuffield and Pressed Steel Organisations and there was an important offshoot of special Morris Garages cars at Abingdon.

By 1938 the annual production of private and commercial motor cars in Britain had reached 447,000, or double that of ten years earlier, and the general increase in road traffic was widening the choice of residence or commuter radius and revitalising some parts of the rural countryside. At the same time pleasure trips by motor car became a habit with people of modest means so that pleasant spots and scenes such as Cotswold villages, Chiltern beechwoods, ancient monuments and spring blossoms in the Vale of Evesham, began to be frequented at holidays and weekends.

Only the great mansions and the more isolated villages seemed to derive no direct benefit from the new middle class mobility. Rising costs of maintenance and of rates oppressed owners of mansions and the last to be built in the English heartland, perhaps in England, was at Middleton Stoney. Here in 1938 the ninth Earl of Jersey replaced the large Georgian building with a magnificent dwelling designed by Sir Edwin and Robert Lutyens in a clever combination of early Georgian, French classical and Queen Anne styles. The luxurious fittings included elegant bathrooms, an abundance of marble and, as became the British Empire, a wealth of teak.

We must, however, mention one other extraordinary stroke of good fortune. In 1939 Mrs Anthony Gillson, a rich American, took the tumbledown hamlet of Cornwell, Oxfordshire, under her care. She employed Clough Williams-Ellis to extend the manor house and lay out elaborate terraced gardens and a pool and to repair or rebuild almost all the village except the vicarage. The model hamlet may seem to some pretty or precious but it is built of traditional material and has a charming air of picturesque perfection.

The Impact of the Second World War

The second world conflict of the twentieth century had a much greater effect than the first on the landscape and future of the English heartland. Acute shortage of food encouraged a ploughing-up campaign of unprecedented speed and extent because it was done mainly by tractors. Between 1939 and 1945 the percentage of all farmland under tillage almost doubled and approached that of the golden age of farming a century earlier. However, in spite of this expansion of tillage the amount of farmland increased little and in some counties actually fell because of the extraordinary growth of military airfields and depots. Civil airfields were converted for service uses, existing service airfields were enlarged and over ninety new airfields created and equipped with hangars and personnel barracks. Some of these were constructed in the clay vales, but to suit the increasing weight of aircraft many more were placed on flatter parts of the well-drained limestone uplands, especially where long runways could be laid out for take off into prevailing westerly winds.[7] Whereas the eastern and southeastern seaboard counties of England were ideal for stations for interceptor and fighter planes, the inland Midland counties were better suited for storage depots and training and bomber planes which needed large expanses of several hundred acres, often with concrete runways. As there were 38 airfields in the Oxford-Swindon district alone, a few examples must suffice. At Bicester the bomber station became an operational training airfield after 1939; Bomber Command also took charge of the airfield at Upper Heyford, using Weston on Green as its satellite; at Culham a Royal Naval Air Station, named *H.M.S. Hornbill*, was commissioned in 1941. Although large, these airfields were dwarfed by some of the military depots, such as that built by the Ordnance branch of the War Office on a site conveniently near two main railways in Ambrosden parish near Bicester. Eventually this scheme absorbed 8,000 acres (3,200ha), much of it farmland, but the loss to agriculture was partly offset by improvements in drainage which prevented almost annual floods and raised the productivity of the land left for farming. The employment provided by the depot affected all the surrounding parishes, and the consequent spate of housing may be judged from the total population of Ambrosden, Arncot and Blackthorn which numbered 937 during the good farming years of the 1850s, had dropped to 474 by the slump of 1931, and rocketted to 5,879 by 1951. These airfields and depots acquired housing for service personnel when new civilian building was prohibited, and although much of the military constructions was obviously not meant to be permanent, a surprising proportion of it survived tenaciously in post-war years.

The English heartland suffered relatively little from enemy bombing while the industrial belt outside its northern fringes was heavily bombed quite early in the war. Coventry, one of Britain's leading centres for aircraft components, was the first British provincial city to be selected by the German airforce for a highly concentrated aerial bombardment by explosives and incendiaries.[8] On the night of 14-15 November 1940 an intense blitz killed 554 citizens and seriously wounded 865 others, and the unwelcome term 'to coventrate' passed into the English language. In further concentrated air-raids in early April in the following year the city suffered nearly the same number of casualties. Devastation such as this and in Birmingham and metropolitan London heightened the safety of the English heartland which, as would be expected of a thinly-peopled rural area, experienced relatively little destruction. Not surprisingly, the region was used for the reception of old and young evacuated from the chief industrial cities around its periphery. In addition many manufacturing firms moved or were driven from urban sites into the small towns of the rural Midlands. In Warwick, motor, aircraft and allied industries increased; at Banbury and Swindon several new factories sprang up; at Cirencester the Mycalex Group arrived in 1940, while at Witney, Crawford Collets took over the spacious old Workhouse in 1941. Also significant, though less enduring, was the use of great mansions and their grounds for evacuated schools, hospitals and service headquarters. For example Nuneham Park, considered by Horace Walpole 'a paradise on earth', was occupied by the Air Ministry and part of the grounds became *H.M.S. Hornbill* for Admiralty aircraft. The influx took many other forms but its general significance from our point of view was that, in spite of wartime deficiencies, multitudes of newcomers grew to appreciate the charm of the English heartland.

The Population Recovery

The end of hostilities in 1945 saw the return to their own homes of many evacuees and service personnel, some pleased to renew the more compact humanity of big cities and others sad to leave. The demobilisation of military forces was rapid, especially from airfields. By 1955 over sixty airfields in the English heartland had been closed down and put to other uses; by the mid 1960s only 25 remained in active service here, about half of them military and the remainder civilian with municipal and special flying uses, as at Kidlington the airport for Oxford, and Haddenham the airport for Thame and Aylesbury. Most of the military stations tended to mature and grow with the increasing size and complexity of modern aircraft. The buildings for their personnel took on a more permanent, more humane aspect, and, for example, a well-built village sprang up on the plateau top above Little Rissington. At Bicester the R.A.F. station continued active as a supply centre for British forces in Germany, but the airfield was spacious enough also to provide extensive agriculture, particularly pig breeding and root cultivation. In 1950 the War Office decided to base a garrison in the town and proceeded to erect a barracks, which with 300 new council houses built by the local authority caused the population to expand from 4,171 to 5,521 in the following decade. The town changed appreciably in nature from an old market and fox hunting borough into a part-garrison centre with almost as many cafés as inns and a population of over 15,000 in 1978. A few miles away at Upper Heyford the aerodrome went over to parachute training before being leased to the United States' Airforce and provided with extensive new housing complete with a children's school. The population of the parish, which had dwindled to 319 in the early twentieth century, rose to 1,504 in 1951 and 2,976 in 1971. A still more staggering growth occurred around the R.A.F. aerodrome at Brize Norton, on the flat fields of the upper Thames vale. The installations kept pace with the size of modern transport aircraft and since 1967 have included one hangar, measuring 318m by 65m, said to be the largest in Europe and, as the historically minded will notice, about seven times as long as the gigantic tithe barn at Great Coxwell. More recently a large air transit centre has been added, and over the last few decades the whole district has been transformed by the addition of housing both on and near the airfield. The nearby village of Carterton was founded by William Carter in 1901 when be bought land to divide up to enable a colony of smallholders to live off the produce from their plots. In the 1920s the hamlet consisted mainly of four ribbons of widely-spaced houses, some with glasshouses for market gardening. Today under the influence of the aerodrome Carterton is a vast congerie of dwellings, mainly tidy bungalows with fruitful gardens front and rear. The population of the parishes of Brize Norton and Carterton with Black Bourton rose from about 3,000 in 1951 to over 10,000 in 1971. The influence extends to Witney and much farther afield, until it meets strong competition from Oxford commuters and week-enders at Standlake. A less concentrated, but equally persistent, aeronautical influence is seen near Fairford where the aerodrome became the testing base for British supersonic Concorde aircraft.

Most of the scores of airfields that did not continue as military or civilian flying bases were eventually reclaimed for agriculture, and their unwanted concrete structures were gradually dismantled. The reclamation was speeded up after the late 1950s when concrete runways could be sold profitably as hardcore for road making. In 1963 the neglected and derelict airfield at Great Horwood near Buckingham was reclaimed for agriculture by a farming company by means of poultry, pig and sheep rearing combined with cereal growing.[9] Large areas of concrete were sold as hardcore at a price equal to the cost of the land beneath them, but enough was retained to provide ideal foundations for poultry and pig breeding units.

Many surplus airfields found non-agricultural uses, such as car racing at Silverstone and go-karting and gliding at Shenington. Several others became research establishments, the most impressive of this kind being for nuclear research at Aldermaston and Harwell, both large institutions that have quite transformed the appearance of their sites and enhanced the prosperity of villages within a wide radius. The large airfield at Culham, recently associated with nuclear research themes, has also quickened the demand for dwellings. In this part of the Vale of White Horse and neighbouring hills several villages increased in population by more than one third in the decade following 1951, and nearly half of all employees were engaged in skilled professions and research. These highly-qualified groups were eight times as numerous as agricultural workers, although the district is noted for horticulture and has at Kingston Bagpuize the only hopfields in the English heartland.

A few of the disused airfields became industrial estates. At Witney the former De Havilland airfield, which had proved too small for the regular operation of large planes in the Second World War, was sold in 1949 to a motor accessory company who built a large new housing estate and, with other firms, ensured that metal trades now dominated the employment of the ancient blanket making town. The population of the urban district or municipal borough soared from 6,554 in 1951 to 12,552 in 1971.

In several other towns also the influence of former airfields and military depots seems never ending. For example, at Wantage in 1978 the possible choice of a new site for future industrial growth was either the disused Admiralty depot or the former airfield at Grove.[10]

The growth points sparked off by these aerodromes mainly affected small towns and rural districts that otherwise would probably have suffered a post-war unemployment malaise. In the few larger towns local councils tried to attract and diversify their industries by setting up industrial estates.[11] At Cirencester several companies making precision equipment and plastic mouldings bolstered the employment already afforded in the manufacture of small electric motors and electric insulating materials. At Banbury the new industrial growth which began in a big way in the 1930s has been exceptional, but this town has never been characteristic of the English heartland. Between 1790 and 1820 the fine mediaeval church was rebuilt in ironstone, in an impressive Romantic Classical style with a semicircular portico and a cylindrical tower topped with a cupola. From the early nineteenth century onward the town experienced surges of industrialisation and expansion especially at Neithrop and Grimsbury. Since 1950 its population has grown at five times the national average, and it boasts of being the largest livestock market in Europe. In the late 1970s it was completing two supermarkets on a grandiose scale when most towns of its size would have been more than content with one. Reading, the county capital of Berkshire with 133,000 inhabitants in 1971, has experienced a similar expansion of light industries and international-style civic developments. The open spaces near the main railways have been filled with new factories, including the light industrial estate which has replaced the brilliant glitter of flowers and greensward of Sutton's seed beds. Northampton has also grown recently at a phenomenal rate and, according to advertisements persuading new companies to go there, has added 13,000 new homes since 1971 and will have 173,000 inhabitants by the mid-1980s.

At Warwick about half the industries operating in the town in the 1960s had been established since the end of the Second World War. Here and at Leamington and Oxford the motor car industry continued to flourish. At Oxford William Morris had gradually extended his empire so that Morris Motors of Cowley had manufacturing branches at Coventry (engines and bodies), Birmingham (Wolseley cars and commercial vehicles), Abingdon (M.G. and Riley cars) and Oxford (radiators and Morris cars). In 1952 the Nuffield Organisation merged with Austin Motors to form the British Motor Corporation with Lord Nuffield as its honorary president. Over the years the company combinations proliferated, and in 1968 when British Motor Holdings, which included the descendants of the old Pressed Steel Company, merged with Leyland, including its Austin-Morris division, British Leyland became the largest British-owned organisation producing motor vehicles. Cowley was Leyland's main single production area and the assembly plant here had a target of nearly 6,000 cars a week in late 1977. The effect of the motor car and other manufactures on the appearance and populousness of the country within twenty miles of Oxford has been staggering. Villages such as Sutton Courtenay and Cumnor have doubled or trebled in population since 1931, while Kidlington, a

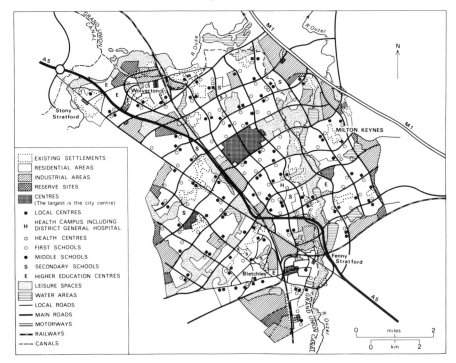

Development plan for Milton Keynes, a new twentieth-century city.

few miles to the north, although within the protective green belt, has grown
from 1,683 inhabitants in 1931 to over 10,000 in the 1970s.

The Housing Boom

The rapid growth of population in the English heartland since 1945 has led to
the building of more new houses than in any previous generation. The
commonest housing schemes were the council houses erected by local
authorities, not infrequently fairly close to those built after the first world war.
These rented dwellings complied with a high standard of health requirements
but except in richer parishes on limestone consisted of brick or concrete,
sometimes roughcast. As a rule they were neither as well built nor as widely
spaced as their predecessors.

The cheap motor car and cheap petrol encouraged commuters to live in rural
villages where numerous older dwellings needed repair and modernisation. The
new owners transformed the village scene by spending much money and effort
on tidying up their homes and beautifying their gardens. Except for the
occasional over-zealous or indifferent alteration and demolition, the newcomers
brought a welcome tidiness and floral prettiness without destroying the old
heritage. However, in most villages space had to be found for extra dwellings

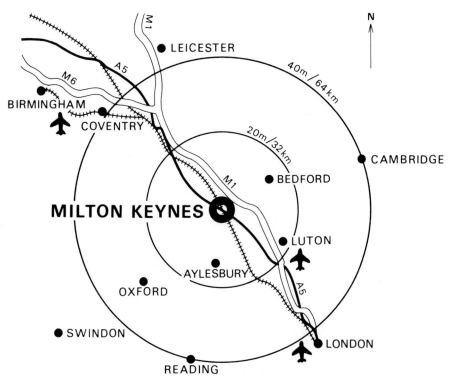

Advertised locational advantages of Milton Keynes.

and this could be done best by additions alongside roads outside the ancient core or by filling in vacant plots within the older parts. The results are pleasing more often than not, and although some villages have preserved their old-world character better than others, everywhere, with rare exceptions, the tidy fences, green verges and abundance of flowering plants give an undeniable air of well-being.

However, the observant visitor will soon notice that the rapid growth described above is largely restricted to parishes favoured by commuters and retired persons and providing all modern services. In many of the small, more isolated hamlets, especially those lacking sewerage systems and adequate schooling for infants, the population has increased little or actually decreased. Here, owing partly to high costs of converting old properties to modern standards, some dwellings may still be empty and gardens overgrown. In a few small, charming villages the uninhabited properties may not be for sale and the proud property owner finds himself being overtaken by inflation. The greatest accretions of new buildings are, as said, near the bigger towns and at artificial growth points in the rural countryside. The large extensions to Warwick, Kenilworth, Alcester, Henley in Arden and Shipston on Stour demonstrate that the northern fringes are as much affected as the southern near Swindon, Newbury and Reading.

This unparalled expansion of population and housing within a welfare state has generated much planning on local, regional and national scales. Apparently the wider plans envisage only two large cities in the English heartland—the expanded Swindon and a new creation, named 'Milton Keynes' after a local village. The latter, a loosely-knit amalgamation of old and new settlements stretching over a large area of slightly undulating clay plain in Buckinghamshire, embraces Bletchley, Wolverton and Stony Stratford as well as several old villages. The city of Milton Keynes obtained ministerial planning approval in January 1967 and was then expected to grow in population from about 40,000 to nearly 250,000 by the close of the century. It will be an administrative combination of well-spaced nucleated settlements, rather than a compact city in the Victorian sense, and will depend heavily for success on its mid-way position on rail and road between London and Birmingham. For some reason the idea of founding small new towns, as distinct from housing estates, has not been used in the English heartland except at Berinsfield near Oxford. Here in 1960, to a general plan drawn up by Sir William Holford, a small new town was begun on the flat site of a former airfield. The result, as might be expected, given the finances available for landscaping and building, was according to Pevsner not a failure but 'an opportunity missed'. Recently the council in a 'culture move' allotted a house and salary for a whole year to a poet who, alas, found more inspiration in the local inn than in the unremarkable brick houses and flat sprawl of commonplace streets.[12]

The reader will be familiar with the wide variety of dwellings typical of the second Elizabethan age and will realise that most local councils today are intent on supplying accommodation at a cheap or reasonable rent. Because of the high burden of local rates most new houses are small, and for the same reason large houses are expensive to maintain. So an age of proliferation of small dwellings has caused the decline of mansions. Several big houses have been totally destroyed, among them Estcourt Park in Shipton Moyne parish (except the stables) and Fairford Park, now the site of a school. The latter, a seventeenth century mansion, was altered by Sir John Soane in 1789, which explains why one of its fireplaces went to the Victoria and Albert Museum and its magnificent orangery has been stored pending re-erection elsewhere by the National Trust. The former landscaping here may be judged from the lake and bridge in the grounds, and an eyecatcher, a tall isolated column, on the plateau above Quenington. Some large mansions have been shorn of unwanted wings; others have survived by subdivision into private apartments, and many more as institutions for education, welfare services and research.

With few exceptions, the remainder open their grounds and gardens, regularly or occasionally, to the public for a small fee which helps toward their upkeep. As in the days of holy pilgrimages, tourism has become a major source of income.

The Cloth Hall Museum, Newbury, built in 1626 at the expense of John Kendrick of Reading as a municipal cloth-weaving workshop to employ the poor.

The Blossoming of Tourism

The cheap motor car gave a new mobility to society and opened up rural areas far from railways to multitudes of families of modest means and to visitors from all over the world. The extent of the general movement may be judged from statistics of motor vehicles of all kinds registered in Great Britain, which rose from nearly 5 million in 1953 to over 18 million in 1978. Inevitably the English heartland, already popular since coaching days with visitors to Stratford, Oxford, Warwick and Cotswold villages, attracted more than its fair share of this new mobility. The general response may be seen both in the spread of commuting and the enormous increase in visitors. The local response usually takes the form either of extra catering and attractions, maybe in the simple planting of flowers, as at daffodil time in the Leach villages, or of new amenities and diversions, such as the miniature model village and aviary at Bourton on the Water and local museums as at Burford, Filkins and a score of other places. Everywhere the more significant historic public buildings, mainly churches, are with rare exceptions kept in a state of perfect cleanliness and often adorned with native needlework. On a broader scale, the new attractions include the outdoor parks for wild life at Bradwell Grove near Burford and at Pangbourne, and for old breeds of farm animals near Temple Guiting. The National Trust, a private society run by voluntary subscriptions and gifts, now owns or has protective covenants on properties in more than sixty places in the English heartland. Where and when possible most of these are opened to the public, who thus have access to properties ranging in character from old manor houses, to ancient monuments, scenic beauty spots, and sites of scientific and industrial interest.

Preserving the Past

The rapid growth of housing and of tourist traffic since 1945 has emphasised the need to preserve the more interesting features of our cultural past and more beautiful facets of the existing landscape. This aim is made difficult by pressure of numbers and the modern desire to combine freer access to the countryside with its preservation against wear and tear. Recently the conservation efforts of numerous private trusts and subscription societies have been backed by government decrees initially expressed in the Town and Country Planning Act of 1947 and strengthened by the National Parks and Access to the Countryside Act of 1949. These and subsequent decrees, aimed at preserving high quality landscapes and townscapes, were consolidated in the Countryside Act of 1968 which included powers to foster and improve facilities for recreation. In a brief space we can draw attention to only a few of the planning problems and achievements in the English heartland, which by nature and inheritance is a prime conservation region.

The greatest official preservation move came in 1966 with the designation of the Cotswolds and Chilterns, or the major part of them, as Areas of Outstanding Natural Beauty. Thereafter the local planning authorities concerned had extra powers including the right to government grants of up to 75 per cent of costs for tree planting, reclamation of derelict spaces, removal of eyesores such as ruinous

A typical Chiltern walk at Great Wood near Hambleden.

military structures and telephone poles, and for any other scheme which would maintain or enhance the existing natural beauty.

For scenery of exceptional natural qualities the English heartland after four

Coombe Hill, the highest point of the Chilterns, near Wendover. The acidic clay with flints on the flat summit supports silver birch, heather, gorse etc. while the adjoining steep chalk slopes are clothed in juniper and a lime-loving flora.

millenia of cultivation has relatively little to show, and by nature its landscapes are neither wild nor spectacular, compared with those of mountainous terrains, but on a small scale it provides many fine viewpoints and scenic spots. The National Trust has acquired covenants over many of these, ranging from riverine meadows, as at Pangbourne, to Dover's Hill on the North Cotswolds and Coombe Hill (852ft; 260m), the highest viewpoint on the Chilterns.[13] Recently the Nature Conservancy or National Environmental Research Council has classified and designated sites that are of national importance for natural or biological reasons. Of 735 such sites in Britain only 24 or 3 per cent were in the English heartland, and most of these were already either National Nature Reserves or controlled by the National Trust or some local scientific committee.[14] They comprised 8 sites of woodland, 14 of lowland grass and scrub, 2 of open water sites and 1 of peatland.

Four woodland sites were classified Grade I, or of prime national importance biologically; namely, Bradenham woods, mainly of tall oak and beech on the Chiltern dipslope above High Wycombe; Windsor forest, parts of which consist of old oak woodland noted also for its beetles; Wychwood forest, dominated partly by oak-ash and partly by hawthorn and other scrubs; and Waterperry wood near Stanton St John, a pedunculate oak-ash community now mainly under conifers but still famous for its butterflies.

Four other woodland sites were classified Grade 2: the remnants of Whittlewood forest of oak and ash; Savernake forest with its many old oaks and rich epiphytic biota; and Aston Rowant woods and Windsor Hill on the Chilterns, dominantly old beech with oak-ash locally. Surprisingly, the fine woods at Wytham managed by Oxford University were not included in the list.

For lowland grassland and scrubs, 14 sites in the English heartland were classified of national importance. On the Chilterns, Aston Rowant was selected for its juniper and mixed scrub and chalk pastures, Ellesborough Warren for its extensive box scrub and Coombe Hill for its junipers. On the Lambourn downs Aston Upthorpe was also classified for its extensive stands of juniper.

For grassland on the Jurassic limestones of the Cotswolds, Cleeve Hill common at the top of the scarp and the Warren on the dipslope near Barnsley are classified Grade I. The latter consists of several small valleys with a wide variety of ecological slopes, one of which is famous for its pasque flowers (*Anemone pulsatilla*). Two other sites in the north Cotswolds, Brassey near Lower Harford on the upper Windrush and the hummocky abandoned quarry tips at Hornleasow Roughs near Snowshill are conserved as Grade 2. Each supports a number of rare local plants, including *Thlaspi perfoliatum* (perfoliate pennycress), of which this is the main British habitat.

The lowland riverine grasslands worth conserving, because they show the effects of centuries of haymaking and grazing on the botanical composition of the sward, are Pixey Mead, Yarnton Mead and Port Meadow near Oxford, Clattinger Farm near Oaksey and North Meadow, Cricklade. The last two are noted for their fritillaries (*Fritilleria meleagris*) and North Meadow, like Yarnton Mead, has been managed for centuries by customary laws. Certain inhabitants of Cricklade may graze their stock on it from 12 August to 12 February when the meadow is left for hay to be cut by the owners of 'hay doles'. These cutting rights can be put on the market and today belong to eight people. A recent Grade 2 addition to the conservation of these grassland sites concerns two meadows of old ridge and furrow at Draycote in Warwickshire.

For open water of national biological importance the only sites in the English

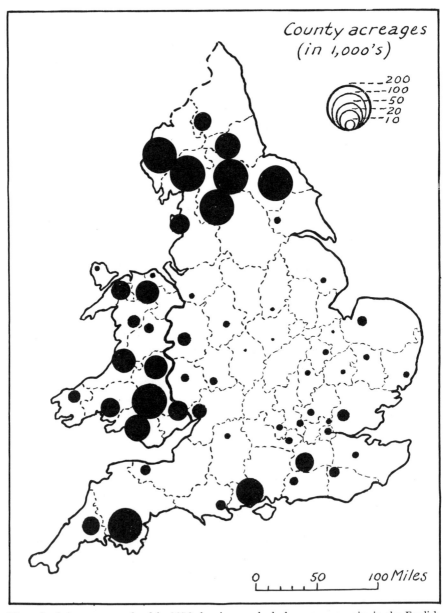

Map of existing common land in 1956 showing marked absence or paucity in the English heartland counties (from *Royal Commission on Common Land;* Report cmd. 462. 1959).

heartland are the large Cotswold Water Park near Fairford and the four small artificial ponds (Grade 2) in Wychwood forest with an interesting fauna. For peatlands the only site is Cothill Fen with Parsonage Moor near Abingdon, where the flora of the calcareous mire is rich in insectivorous plants.

The brevity of the above list demonstrates clearly that the English heartland is primarily a humanised landscape in which the beauty of the buildings and villages play a vital role. For buildings in town and country alike, an important preservation step was taken in the late 1940s when a national survey provided photographs and detailed lists of structures of historic and architectural significance. The assessment of buildings into classes according to their national importance virtually ensured that in future structures in the highest group must not be destroyed under any circumstances, and those in the next group must be neither altered radically nor demolished without special planning consent. Oxfordshire has about 3,500 Grade I buildings and the borough of Oxford alone has 185 of that category and a further 1,210 listed structures, irrespective of churches which do not come under these provisions. The lists are not yet complete and in our opinion need to be extended to include many more Victorian and Edwardian buildings, but the chief weakness of the system remains its lack of finance, for although local authorities have powers to order the repair of a listed structure and, if such instructions are ignored, can serve a compulsory purchase order on it, they often cannot afford to prevent its decay.

In 1967 the Civic Amenities Act allowed suitable villages and parts of towns to be designated 'Conservation Areas' in which the amenities and special architectural characteristics had to be maintained and if possible enhanced. Many of the prettier and older settlements in the English heartland fell clearly into this protected category, and in most of them the Act merely gave support to what local pride, good taste and preservation trusts had already achieved. However, all these government decrees are open to interpretation, and in some places conservation has not meant preserving the existing condition unchanged. For example, since Iffley, now a suburb of Oxford, was made a conservation area in 1969, ninety new housing units have been added and planning permission given for a further one hundred and fifty. Such extensive infill, although perfectly legal and maintaining the traditional land use, seemed to many residents incompatible with the real spirit of conservation, and apparently 'a beautiful village was being devoured by a voracious city desperate for housing'.[15]

Conservation and continued development seem to pose insoluble problems in the English heartland because so many people want to live in and visit it. Fortunately government legislation does not kill private initiative, as witnesses the recent creation of the Warburg Reserve on the Chilterns near Bix. The inhabitants can do much for themselves in a local sense but their influence fades rapidly in schemes of regional or national scale. Among the regional problems is the digging of gravel, which has been active on a vast scale in the Thames valley since the 1920s; today there is increasing demand for gravel for use in construction.[17] Although legally the diggings should be returned to agricultural uses, in practice, low-lying quarries, especially on the floodplain terraces,

Henley Royal Regatta. First held in 1839 it remains the mecca of oarsmen from all over the world for one week in mid-summer. The finish of the racing course (shown here in 1923) lies to the right of the phalanx of punts and other small boats moored in midstream.

rapidly fill with water to form lakes for fishing and boating, which near towns prove more profitable to owners than would the reclaimed farmland. A notable development of this kind concerns the extensive flooded gravel pits in the upper Thames vale, near the lower Coln, downstream of Fairford and between the lower Churn and stripling Thames south of Cirencester. Here 400ha of flooded gravel pits already exist, and planning permission will nearly quadruple the water area before the turn of the century. It is proposed to develop the whole water surface and its surrounds as a Cotswold Water Park for aquatic sports, angling, nature studies, picnicking and so on. Already two areas within it have been designated 'County Parks', one being specifically for sailing and other quiet pursuits.[18] Eventually the complex of artificial lakes will provide a wide variety of recreational amenities, and the Cotswold Water Park, created by gravel excavators in the aeroplane age, may well become a serious rival to the Norfolk Broads made by peat diggers eight centuries earlier.

National needs are often hostile or troublesome to regional planning. Attempts to submerge Otmoor and the Enborne valley as precautionary links in a national water supply scheme were successfully opposed by local preservationists, as also was the suggestion to make Cublington in

The Ridgeway on the Lambourn Downs.

Buckinghamshire the site of a third national airport. More often this opposition only modifies or delays the national intent. Recently the erection in rural countryside of a colossal 2,000 Mw thermal power station near Didcot at one end of the Vale of White Horse shows the national strength. This high structure dominates the vale, adds volcanic symptoms to an otherwise placid landscape and depends on supplies of fuel from distant coalfields. The expansion of Swindon and the creation of Milton Keynes are also expressions of national needs. With regard to new roads, the English heartland suffers or benefits little according to your point of view. The super motorways follow much the same course as the early main railways. The M1 (London-Leicester north) lies roughly parallel to Watling Street and the chief railway and cuts across the northeastern tip of the English heartland near Wolverton and Milton Keynes. The M5 (Bristol-Birmingham) keeps largely to the vale and runs west of Cheltenham. The M4 (London-Bristol-south Wales) crosses the Berkshire wolds south of Swindon and thence proceeds westward to a new bridge over the Severn. The M40 (London-Birmingham) cuts a great gash through the Chilterns near High Wycombe and continues almost to Oxford, but the route northward over the lovely Cherwell 'country is still not decided, partly because of strong local opposition which considers it symptomatic of an age of mechanical chaos in which a road mania dictates highways that are unnecessary. In 1978 the remaining Oxfordshire unbuilt section was demoted from a motorway to a high standard dual carriageway.

Hostility to destructive swathes of motorways intended primarily for fast transit traffic is understandable when the railways are seriously under-used, and certain long distance pleasure routes and nature trails need more definition and completion. The Ridgeway on the Berkshire and Wiltshire downs already provides an incomparable ramble, but the public Thames-side walk from Kemble to Teddington is not yet complete and the Jurassic Way remains fragmental in spite of its high tourist potential.

The English heartland also faces regional problems associated with changes in social habits and farming techniques. Decline in attendance and rising costs of repairs have made the upkeep of some churches and chapels in small villages and depopulated city parishes practically impossible.[19] Under the 1955 Inspection of Churches Measure, the Church of England provided for regular inspection of every church by an architect followed by a sustained programme of conservation. The magnitude of this task led indirectly to the Pastoral Measure of 1968 whereby the Church Commissioners could declare unused churches redundant. Within ten years over 640 Anglican churches in Britain had suffered that fate, and in addition, in a similar but quite independent way, probably four times that number of nonconformist chapels had been closed. In the Oxford diocese, which also includes Berkshire and Buckinghamshire, out of 850 Anglican churches 35 have already been declared redundant, among them the chapel of ease (1861) at Asthall Leigh, now a dwelling; St Peter's (1890) in the late Victorian part of Didcot, now a community centre; and East Hanney, built to the design of Street in 1856. Fewcott church, erected in 1870, and Holy Trinity, Oxford, were among the few demolished. This pruning, although regrettable, helps toward the preservation of churches of greater architectural and historical importance, such as the redundant St Peter's, Wallingford (1760-9), which is preserved, partly for its delightful spire and its associations with Sir William Blackstone, the famous jurist. Unique redundant churches such as the fine chantry chapel at Rycote, built in 1499 and adorned in the early seventeenth century with two magnificent pews, are maintained as historical monuments by the Department of the Environment. Notable ecclesiastic buildings in use, other than cathedrals, may in the future be eligible for partial State grants toward their repair, but their upkeep will still depend mainly on private gifts and institutional resources.

The chief new farming technique that has affected both society and landscape is the use of motor tractors and elaborate power-driven machines, which has revolutionised arable farming and further decreased the demand for manual labour. Because these expensive large machines operate most efficiently in fields of 20 to 50 acres (8-20ha) or more, many farmers have uprooted long stretches of hedgerow in order to combine their small fields. Although many of these fences

COTSWOLD GAMES

Pub.d by Caulfield & Herbert 1794.

Cotswold games on Dover's Hill near Chipping Campden (from *Annalia Dubrensia*).

dated back only to Georgian and Victorian enclosures, they had become a favourite feature of the scenery, and their removal was regretted, especially by naturalists.[20] Some stretches of the cultivated chalk now have a breathtaking spaciousness with monochromatic expanses of grain and roots unbroken by bush, tree or hedge.

This openness has been increased in the extensive areas affected by elm disease. Probably three or four million elms have died recently in the English heartland and in spite of urgent clearance their bare lifeless trunks and branches rise as lofty trellises above the few surviving fences. Very few elms have escaped and their removal reveals in the flat vales a width of vision never seen before in living memory. On the Feldon and Vale of White Horse the flatness now seems more impressive, and the adjacent scarp rises with a more startling clarity. A great replanting is planned, so a fresh landscape topped by oak, beech, ash and perhaps some horticultural species will eventually mature in the stricken regions.

In the meanwhile the scenic heritage of all the more rural parts of the English heartland outside the Areas of Outstanding Natural Beauty will need better protection. Surely many of them should be legally defined as of 'Particular' or 'Special' beauty, at least until the distant time when the nation has, with Wordsworth, learned:

> To look on nature, not as in the hour
> Of thoughtless youth; but hearing oftentimes
> The still, sad music of humanity.

Acknowledgments, references and selective bibliography

General Works

The fundamental reference is *The Victoria History of the Counties of England* which since 1902 has been published for almost all of the English heartland.

For architectural details, *Buildings of England* (Penguin) edited since 1960 by N. Pevsner and others for each county.

The main relevant 1:50000 Ordnance Survey sheets are, in numerical order: 150 Worcester and the Malverns (small part only); 151 Stratford upon Avon; 152 Northampton and Milton Keynes; 163 Cheltenham and Cirencester; 164 Oxford; 165 Aylesbury and Leighton Buzzard; 173 Swindon; 174 Newbury and Wantage; 175 Reading and Windsor.

Some County Volumes

Beckinsale, R. P. 1951/72. *Companion into Berkshire,* Spurbook, Bourne End. 1948/72. *Companion into Gloucestershire and the Cotswolds,* Spurbook, Bourne End.

Cave, L. F. 1976. *Warwickshire Villages,* Hale, London.

Emery, F. 1974. *The Oxfordshire Landscape,* Hodder and Stoughton, London.

Ireson, T. 1974. *Northamptonshire,* rev. edtn., Hale, London.

Jessup, M. 1975. *A History of Oxfordshire,* Phillimore.

Smith, B. and Ralph, E. 1972. *A History of Gloucestershire,* Phillimore.

Steane, J. 1974. *The Northamptonshire Landscape,* Hodder and Stoughton, London.

CHAPTER 1
REGIONAL LANDSCAPES

Reference

1. Bishop, W. W. 1958. The Pleistocene geology and geomorphology of three gaps in the Midland Jurassic escarpment, *Phil. Trans. Roy. Soc.,* B. No. 682, **241**, 255-306; Dury, G. H. 1951. A 400-foot bench in southeastern Warwickshire, *Proc. Geol. Assoc.,* **62**, 167-73; Shotton, F. W. 1953. The Pleistocene deposits of the area between Coventry, Rugby and Leamington . . . *Phil. Trans. Roy. Soc.,* B. No. 646, **237**, 209-60.

Selective Bibliography

Arkell, W. J. 1947. *The Geology of Oxford,* Clarendon Press, Oxford

Beckinsale, R. D. 1972. Recent progress in geology, in L. Richardson, rev. edtn. *A Handbook to the Geology of Cheltenham and Neighbourhood,* P. B. Minet, Chicheley, Bucks., 270-294

Beckinsale, R. D. 1976. Glaciation and periglaciation in the Cotswolds, *Proc. Cot. Nat. F. C.,* **35**, 194-205

Coppock, J. T. 1962. *The Chilterns,* Geogr. Assoc., Sheffield

Dreghorn, W. 1967. *Geology explained in the Severn Vale and Cotswolds,* David and Charles, Newton Abbot

The English Heartland

Edmonds, E. A. *et al.* 1965. *Geology of the Country around Banbury and Edge Hill,* Mem. Geol. Surv. H.M.S.O.

Goudie, A. S. & Hart, M.G. 1975. Pleistocene events and forms in the Oxford Region, in *Oxford and its Region,* ed. C. G. Smith and D. I. Scargill, O.U.P., 1-13

Kellaway, G. A. *et al,* 1971. The development of some Pleistocene structures in the Cotswolds and upper Thames, *Bull. Geol. Surv. Great Britain,* **37**, 1-28

Kellaway, G. A. & Welsh, F.B.A. 1961. *Bristol and Gloucester District,* British Regional Geology, H.M.S.O.

Naish, M. C. 1978. *Cheltenham and Cirencester District,* Geogr. Assoc., Sheffield

Paterson, K. 1971. Weichselian deposits and fossil periglacial structure in north Berkshire, *Proc. Geol. Assoc.,* **82**, 455-67

Richardson, L. 1929. *The Geology of the Country around Moreton in Marsh,* Mem. Geol. Surv., H.M.S.O.

1933. *The Geology of the Country around Cirencester,* H.M.S.O.

1946. *The Geology of the Country around Witney,* H.M.S.O.

Shephard-Thorn, E. R. & Wymer, J.J. 1977. *South East England and the Thames Valley,* Guidebook A5, INQUA, Geo Abstracts, Norwich

Sherlock, R. L. 1947. *London and the Thames Valley,* British Regional Geology, H.M.S.O.

1977. *The English Midlands,* Guidebook A2, INQUA, Geo Abstracts, Norwich

Small, R. J. 1970. The periglacial rock-stream at Clatford Bottom, Marlborough Downs, Wiltshire, *Proc. Geol. Assoc.,* **81**, 87-98

Thomas, M. F. 1961. River terraces and drainage development in the Reading area, *Proc. Geol. Assoc.,* **72**, 415-36

Webster, R. 1966. The drifts in the Vale of White Horse, *Proc. Geol. Assoc.,* **77**, 255-62

Williams, B. J. & Whittaker, A. 1974. *The Geology of the Country around Stratford upon Avon and Evesham,* Mem. Geol. Surv., H.M.S.O.

Wills, L. J. 1948. *The Palaeogeography of the Midlands,* Hodder and Stoughton, London

Wood, P. D. 1968. *The Oxford and Newbury Area,* Geogr. Assoc., Sheffield

Vale of Evesham (dominated by intensive agriculture)

Adlam, B. H. 1974. *The Worcester District,* Geogr. Assoc., Sheffield

Buchanan, K. M. 1944. *Worcester,* Pt. 68, *The Land of Britain,* Geogr. Publics., London

Fekete, E. B. 1953. *Vale of Evesham and An Economic Study . . . 1951/2,* Dept. Agric. Econ. Vol. 4, No. 2 Univ., of Bristol

Gaut, R. C. 1939. *A History of Worcestershire Agriculture . . .,* Littlebury and Co., Worcester

Lodge, R. S. 1974. Horticulture in the Vale of Evesham *Worcester and its Region . . .,* ed. B. H. Adlam; Geogr. Assoc., Worcester

CHAPTER 2
EARLY SETTLEMENT: PREHISTORIC AND ROMANO-BRITISH

Of the many museums well worth frequent visits that at Long Street, Devizes is outstanding for prehistory and those at Cirencester and Reading for Romano-British times.

References

1. Wilson, D. R. 1975. 'Causewayed camps' and 'interrupted ditch systems', *Antiquity,* **49**, 178-86

2. Atkinson, R. J. C. 1967, 1970. Silbury Hill, *Antiquity,* 41, 259-62; 44, 313-4

3. Rhodes, P.P. 1950. The Celtic field systems on the Berkshire Downs, *Oxoniensia,* 15, 1-28

4. Cotton, M. A. 1962. Berkshire hill forts, *Berks. Archaeol. Journ.;* **60**, 53-61; Sutton, J. E. G. 1966. Iron Age hill forts and some other earthworks in Oxfordshire, *Oxoniensia,* 31, 28-43

5. Bradley, R. 1968. The South Oxfordshire Grim's Ditch and its significance, *Oxoniensa*, **33**, 1-12
6. O'Neil, H. E. 1971-2. A Roman bathing establishment at the Grove, Ebrington. *Proc. Cots. Nat. F. C.*, **36**, 87-93
7. Frere, S. S. 1962. Excavations at Dorchester on Thames, *Archaeol. Journ.*, **119**, 114-49
8. Young, C. J. 1975. The defences of Roman Alchester, *Oxoniensia*, **40**, 136-170

Selective Bibliography

Ashbee, P. 1970. *The Earthen Long Barrow in Britain*, Dent, London
Benson, D. & Miles, D. 1974. *The Upper Thames Valley: An Archaeological Survey of the River Gravels*, Oxfordshire Archaeol. Unit, Oxford
Boon, G. C. 1974. *Silchester: The Roman Town of Calleva*, David and Charles, Newton Abbot
Burl, A. 1976. *The Stone Circles of the British Isles*, Yale Univ. Press
Case, H. 1963. Notes on the finds and on ring-ditches in the Oxford region, *Oxoniensia*, **28**, 19-52
Clifford, E. M. 1960. *Bagendon, A Belgic Oppidum*, Heffer, Cambridge
Collingwood, R. G. & Richmond, I. 1969. *The Archaeology of Roman Britain*, Methuen, London
Cunliffe, B. W. 1974. *Iron Age Communities in Britain*, Routledge and Kegan Paul, London
Dyer, J. 1973. *Southern England: An Archaeological Guide*, Faber, London
Grinsell, L. V. 1939. *White Horse Hill*, St Catherine's Press, London
    1966. *Belas Knap*, Dept. of Environment pamphlet, H.M.S.O.
Harding, D. W. 1972. *The Iron Age in the Upper Thames Basin*, Routledge and Kegan Paul, London
Head, J. F. 1955. *Early Man in South Buckinghamshire*, J. Wright, Bristol
Hawkes, C. F. C. & Smith, M.A. 1957. On some buckets and cauldrons of the Bronze and Early Iron Ages, *Antiquaries Journ.*, **37**, 131-198
O'Neil, H. E. & Grinsell, L.V. 1960. Gloucestershire barrows, *Trans. Bristol and Glouc. Archaeol. Soc.*, **79**, 1-149
Margery, I. D. 1955-7. *Roman Roads in Britain*, 2 vols, Phoenix House, London
Ordnance Survey, 1967. Map of *Southern Britain in the Iron Age;* 1978. Map of *Roman Britain*
Peake, H. 1931. *Archaeology of Berkshire*, Methuen, London
Piggott, S. 1954. *The Neolithic Cultures of the British Isles*, C.U.P.; 1962. *The West Kennet Long Barrow . . .*, Min. of Works Archaeol. Report No. 4, H.M.S.O.
Powell, T. G. E., ed. 1969. *Megalithic Enquiries in the West of Britain*, Liverpool Univ. Press
Renfrew, C. (ed.) 1974. *British Prehistory*, Duckworth, London
Rivet, A. L. F. 1958. *Town and Country in Roman Britain*, Hutchinson, London
Rivet, A. L. F. (ed.) 1969. *The Roman Villa in Britain*, Routledge and Kegan Paul, London
Rodwell, K. & Rowley, R. T. (eds.) 1975. *The Small Towns of Roman Britain*, Oxfordshire Archaeol. Unit, Oxford.
Rodwell, K. 1975. *Historic Towns in Oxfordshire*, Oxford. Archaeol. Unit., Oxford
Royal Comm. Hist. Monuments, 1976. *Iron Age and Romano-British Monuments in the Cotswold Area*, H.M.S.O.
Smith, I. F. 1965. *Windmill Hill and Avebury . . .* Clarendon Press, Oxford
Thom, A. 1971. *Megalithic Lunar Observatories*, C.U.P.
Thomas, N. 1977. *Guide to Prehistoric England*, Batsford, London
Vatcher, F. & L. 1976. *The Avebury Monuments*, Dept. of Environment, H.M.S.O.
Wacher, J. 1971. *Corinium*, Ginn, Aylesbury
Wilson, R. J. A. 1975. *A Guide to the Roman Remains in Britain*, Constable, London
Wymer, J. J. 1974. *Lower Palaeolithic Archaeology in Britain, as represented by the Thames Valley*, J. Baker, London

CHAPTER 3
ANGLO-SAXON AND DANISH SETTLEMENT

References

1. Gelling, M. 1967. English place names derived from the compound 'Wicham', *Mediaeval Archaeology*, **XI**, 87-104
2. From 'Blossom gatherings out of St Augustine', B. M. Vit. A, XV, f.1; given in Seebohm, F. 1883. *The English Village Community*, C.U.P., 169.

Selective Bibliography

Ashmolean Museum, 1971. *The Alfred and Minster Lovell Jewels.*
Baker, A. R. & Butlin, R.A. 1973. *Studies in the Field Systems of the British Isles*, C.U.P., 619-56
Clemoes, P. (ed.) 1972. *Anglo-Saxon England*, C.U.P.
Dolley, R. H. M. (ed.) 1961. *Anglo-Saxon Coins*, Methuen, London
Finberg, H. P. R. 1955. *Roman and Saxon Withington, A Study in Continuity*, Leicester Univ. Press
Grundy, G. B. 1933. *Saxon Oxfordshire, Charters and Ancient Highways*, Oxfordshire Rec. Soc., 15
Harden, D. B. (ed.) 1956. *Dark-Age Britain*, Methuen, London
Helm, P. J. 1963. *Alfred the Great*, Hale, London
Hinton, D. A. 1977. *Alfred's Kingdom. Wessex and the South 800-1500*, Dent, London
Loyn, H. R. 1962. *Anglo-Saxon England and the Norman Conquest*, Longman, London
Meaney, A. 1964. *Gazetteer of Early Anglo-Saxon Burial Sites*, Allen and Unwin, London
Myres, J. N. L. 1969. *Anglo-Saxon Pottery and the Settlement of England*, Clarendon Press, Oxford
Ordnance Survey, 1974. Map of *Britain in the Dark Ages*
Rice, D. Talbot 1952. *English Art 871-1100*, Clarendon Press, Oxford
Stenton, F. M. 1971. *Anglo-Saxon England*, (3rd edn.) O.U.P.
Sturdy, D. 1963. Saxon nomadism near Oxford, *Oxoniensia*, **28**, 95-98
Taylor, H. M. & J. 1965-78. *Anglo-Saxon Architecture*, 3 vols. C.U.P.
Wainwright, F. T. 1959. Aethelflaed, Lady of the Mercians, in *The Anglo-Saxons*, ed. P. Clemoes, London, 53-69
Whitelock, D. 1954. *The Beginnings of English Society*, Pelican, London
Wilson, D. M. (ed.) 1977. *The Archaeology of Anglo-Saxon England*, Methuen, London

Place Names
English Place-Name Society, C.U.P.
Vol. 3 Mawer, A. & Stenton, F. M. 1925 *Buckinghamshire*
   10 Glover, J. E. B. & Mawer, A. 1933 *Northamptonshire.*
   13 Glover, J. E. B. & Mawer, A. 1936 *Warwickshire*
   Glover, J. E. B. & Mawer, A. 1939 *Wiltshire*
   Gelling, M. 1953-4 *Oxfordshire*
   Smith, A. H. 1964-5 *Gloucestershire*
1 Pts. 2 & 3 Gelling, M. 1974-6 *Berkshire*
Gelling, M. 1976. The evidence of place names, in ed. P. H. Sawyer, *Medieval Settlement*, Arnold, London
Smith, A. H. 1956. *English Place-Name Elements*, 2 vols., C.U.P.
   1956. Place-names and the Anglo-Saxon settlement, *Proc. British Acad.*, **42**, 73-80

CHAPTER 4
THE NORMAN CONQUEST AND ITS AFTERMATH

References

1. Darlington, R. R. 1933. Aethelwig, Abbot of Evesham, *Engl. Hist. Rev.*, **48**, 1-22; 177-198
2. Bazeley, M. L. 1922. The extent of the English forest in the thirteenth century, *Trans. Roy. Hist. Soc.*, 4th ser. **IV**, 140-172; Neilson, N. 1940. The Forest, in *The English Government at Work, 1327-1336*, ed. J. F. Willard & W. A. Morris, Harvard Univ. Press, Cambridge, Mass., I, 394-467
3. O'Neil, H. E. 1962-3. The Norman motte at Upper Slaughter, *Proc. Cot. Nat. F.C.*, **34**, 32-36
4. Ford, W. J. 1976. Some settlement patterns in the central region of the Warwickshire Avon, in *Mediaeval Settlement*, ed. P. H. Sawyer, Arnold; Harley, J. B. 1964. The settlement geography of early mediaeval Warwickshire, *Trans. Inst. Brit. Geogr.*, **34**, 115-130; Roberts, B. K. 1968. A study of the mediaeval colonisation in the forest of Arden, *Agric. Hist. Rev.*, **16**, 101-113
5. Glassock, R. E. 1974. *The Lay Subsidy of 1334*, Brit. Academy, London

Selective Bibliography

Addy, S. E. 1933. *The Evolution of the English House*, Allen and Unwin, London
Bennett, H. S. 1937. (paperback 1960.) *Life on the English Manor*, C.U.P.
Boase, T. S. R. 1953. *English Art, 1100-1216*, Clarendon Press, Oxford
Bridbury, A. R. 1962. *Economic Growth: England in the later Middle Ages*, Allen and Unwin, London
Brieger, P. H. 1957. *English Art, 1216-1307*, Clarendon Press, Oxford
Brown, R. A. 1955/59. Royal castle-building in England 1154-1216, *Engl. Hist. Rev.*, **70**, 353-98; **74**, 249-80
Colvin, H. M. 1963. *The History of the King's Works*, 2 vols., Min. of Works, H.M.S.O.
Darby, H. C. 1973. Domesday England, being Chapter 2 in *New Historical Geography of England*, C.U.P.
1977. *Domesday England*, C.U.P.
Darby, H. C. & Campbell, E. M. (eds.) 1962. *The Domesday Geography of South-East England*, C.U.P.
Darby, H. C. & Terrett, I.C. (eds.) 1971. *The Domesday Geography of Midland England*, C.U.P.
Hilton, R. H. 1967. *A Mediaeval Society: The West Midlands at the end of the Thirteenth Century*, Weidenfeld and Nicolson, London
1968. *The Decline of Serfdom in Mediaeval England*, (Studies in Econ. Hist.), Macmillan, London
Knowles, D. 1948-59. *The Religious Orders in England*, 3 vols., C.U.P.
Knowles, D. & Hadcock, R. N. 1953. *Mediaeval religious houses: England and Wales*, Longman, London
Lennard, R. 1959. *Rural England, 1086-1135*, Clarendon Press, Oxford
Long, E. T. 1940-1. Mediaeval domestic architecture in Berkshire, *Berks, Archaeol. Journ.*, **44**, 39-48, 101-113; **45**, 28-36
Loyn, H. R. 1968. *The Norman Conquest*, Hutchinson, London
Powicke, M. 1953. *The Thirteenth Century, 1216-1307*, O.U.P.
Renn, D. F. 1968. *Norman Castles in Britain*, J. Baker, London

Roden, D. 1969. Desmesne farming in the Chiltern Hills, *Ag. Hist. Rev.*, **17**, 9-23
Stenton, D. M. 1952. *English Society in the Early Middle Ages, 1066-1307*, Pelican, London
Vollans, E. C. 1959. The evolution of farmlands in the central Chilterns in the twelfth and thirteenth centuries, *Trans. Inst. Brit. Geogr.*, **26**, 197-241
Wood, M. E. 1965. *The English Mediaeval House*, Phoenix, London

CHAPTER 5
GENERAL DECLINE AND RECOVERY, 1335-1550

We are grateful to the Mediaeval Village Research Group of the National Monuments Record, Fortress House, 23 Savile Row, London who kindly supplied us with a full list of deserted and shrunken villages for all the south Midland counties.

References

1. Anon., in *Four Supplications*, Early Engl. Text Soc. Extra ser. 13, 1871, 95-102. Refers mainly to Oxon., Bucks. and Northants.
2. Lloyd, T. H. 1964-5. Some documentary sidelights on the deserted Oxfordshire village of Brookend, *Oxoniensia*, **29-30**, 116-128
3. Taylor, A. J. 1958. *Minster Lovell Hall*, Dept. of Envir., H.M.S.O.
4. Emery, F. V. 1962. Moated settlements in England, *Geography*, **47**, 378-88

Selective Bibliography

Allison, K. J. *et al* 1965. *The Deserted Villages of Oxfordshire*, Leic. Univ. Press
  1966. *The Deserted Villages of Northamptonshire*, Leic. Univ. Press
Baker, A. R. H. 1966. Evidence . . . of contracting arable land in England during the fourteenth century, *Econ. Hist. Rev.*, 2nd ser. **19**, 518-32 (deals with Buckinghamshire in 1341)
Ballard, A. 1916. The manors of Witney, Brightwell and Downton, in *The Black Death on the Estates of the See of Winchester*, ed. A. E. Levett, Oxford Studies in Social and Legal History, **V**, 181-216
Beresford, M. W. 1953-60. Glebe terriers and open-field Buckinghamshire, *Records of Bucks*, **16**, 5-28
  1963. *The Lost Villages of England*, Lutterworth Press, London
Beresford, M. W. & Hirst, J. G. (eds.) 1971. *Deserted Mediaeval Villages*, Lutterworth Press London
Biddle, M. 1961-2. The deserted mediaeval village of Seacourt, Berkshire, *Oxoniensia*, **26-27**, 70-201
Bond, C. J. 1969. The deserted village of Billesley Trussell near Stratford, *Warwickshire History*, **I**, No. 2, 16-24
Brooks, J. 1969. Eaton Hastings: A deserted mediaeval village, *Berks. Archaeol. Journ.*, **64**, 1-8
Crossley, F. H. 1921. *English Church Monuments A.D. 1150-1550*, Batsford, London
Esdaile, K. A. 1941-2. English sculpture in some Berkshire churches, *Berks, Archaeol. Journ.*, **45**, 45-52, 86-92; **46**, 22-27, 69-73
Esdaile, K. A. 1947. Renaissance monuments of Buckinghamshire, *Records of Bucks.*, **15**, 32-38
Evans, J. 1949. *English Art 1307-1461*, Clarendon Press, Oxford
Finn, R. W. 1971. *The Norman Conquest and its Effects on the Economy 1066-86*, Longman, London
Fletcher, J. 1968. Crucks in the West Berkshire and Oxford Region, *Oxoniensia*, **33**, 71-88

Harvey, P. D. 1965. *A Mediaeval Oxfordshire Village: Cuxham 1240-1400*, O.U.P.
Hassall, W. O. 1962. *How They Lived: 55B.C. to A.D. 1485*, Blackwell, Oxford
Leadam, I. S. (ed.) 1897. *Domesday of Inclosures, 1517-18*, 2 vols, Longman, London
Morley, H. T. 1924. *Monumental Brasses of Berkshire*, Electric Press, Reading
Shrewsbury, J. F. D. 1970. *History of the Bubonic Plague in the British Isles*, C.U.P.
Stone, L. 1955. *Sculpture in Britain in the Middle Ages*, Penguin, London
Thirsk, J. 1950. *Tudor Enclosures*, Hist. Assoc., London
Ziegler, P. 1969. *The Black Death*, Collins, London

CHAPTER 6
THE GOLDEN AGE OF DOMESTIC BUILDING AND CHURCH MONUMENTS,
1550-1645

References

1. *V.C.H. Oxon.*, **VI**, 1959. It is interesting that the peasants in Northamptonshire did not revolt until 1607.
2. Portman, D. 1960. Little Milton, the rebuilding of an Oxfordshire village, *Oxoniensia*, **25**, 49-63
3. Havinden, M. A. 1965. *Household and Farm Inventories in Oxfordshire, 1550-1590*, Hist. Mss. Comm. H.M.S.O.

Selective Bibliography

Barley, M. W. 1961. *The English Farmhouse and Cottage*, Routledge and Kegan Paul, London
Bott, A. 1964. *Monuments in Merton College Chapel*, Blackwell, Oxford. (Especially monument of Sir Henry Saville (*ob.* 1622). See also monument of John Blagrave (*ob.* 1611) in St Laurence, Reading; R. P. Beckinsale, *Companion into Berkshire*, 154)
Curtler, W. H. R. 1920. *The Enclosure and Redistribution of Our Land*, Clarendon Press, Oxford
Ellwood, Thomas 1714. *The History of the Life of Thomas Ellwood . . .*, (among many issues, Headley Bros., London 1906. A story of an Oxfordshire quaker who was born and lived at the manor house at Crowell at the foot of the Chilterns)
Fussell, G. E. (ed.) 1936. *Robert Loder's Farm Accounts, 1610-1620*, Camden Soc., 3rd ser., **53**, (Loder farmed at the Manor Farm at Harwell, then in Berkshire)
Havinden, M. A. 1961. Agricultural progress in open-field Oxfordshire, *Agric. Hist. Rev.*, **9**, 73-83
Hoskins, W. G. 1953. The rebuilding of rural England, 1570-1640, *Past and Present*, **4**, 44-59; reprinted in *Provincial England*, 1963
Prince, H. C. 1959. Parkland in the Chilterns, *Geog. Rev.*, **49**, 18-31
1967. *Parks in England*, Shalfleet, I.O.W.
Roden, D. & Baker, A. R. H. 1966. Field systems in the Chiltern Hills . . . *Trans. Inst. Brit. Geogr.*, **38**, 73-88
Thirsk, J. (ed.) 1967. *The Agrarian History of England and Wales*, Vol. IV, 1500-1640, C.U.P.
Wood-Jones, R. B. 1964. *Traditional Domestic Architecture in the Banbury Region*, Manchester Univ. Press
Yelling, J. A. 1968. Common land and enclosure in east Worcestershire, 1540-1870, *Trans. Inst. Brit. Geogr.*, **45**, 157-68
1969. The combination and rotation of crops in east Worcestershire, 1540-1660, *Agric. Hist. Rev.*, **17**, 24-43

CHAPTER 7
GREAT MEDIAEVAL HOUSES

Each of the inhabited mansions has its own historical booklet, usually well-illustrated, and including description of special contents. For Chipping Campden house, which is in ruins and private, *see* Rushen, P.C. 1911. *History . . . of Chipping Campden,* private, London; Whitfield, C. 1958. *A History of Chipping Campden,* Shakespeare Head Press, Eton; Clark, G: (ed.) 1959. *The Campden Wonder,* O.U.P.

For Grey's Court; National Trust booklets, and Parry, E.A. 1925. *The Overbury Mystery,* Fisher Unwin, London. Sir Thomas Overbury (1581-1613), poet and essayist, was born at Compton Scorpion near Ilmington, Warwickshire, the son of Nicholas Overbury of Bourton on the Hill. For the donkey wheel *see* Brunner, H. & Major, J.K. 1972. *Water Raising by Animal Power,* 2 Eldon Road, Reading, reprinted with addenda, from *Industrial Archaeology,* **9,** 117-151, 209-14.

For the Washington family and Sulgrave *see* 1972 *Sulgrave Manor,* English Life Publ., Derby; Clifford Smith, H. 1933. *Sulgrave Manor and the Washingtons,* Jonathan Cape, London; *The Times,* 5 May 1977. The visitor should also see St Mary's, Great Brington where the floor slabs include that of Laurence Washington (*ob.* 1616) who had 8 sons and 9 daughters, and is reckoned to be the great-great-great grandfather of George Washington, the American president. The Washingtons originated at Washington in County Durham and migrated to Northamptonshire. We are indebted to Drs S. and C. Mitchell of Washington, D.C. for assistance on the American connections.

CHAPTER 8
THE CIVIL WAR AND THE END OF CASTLES

References

1. In Finberg, H.P.R. (ed.) 1957. John Chamberlayne and the Civil War, in *Gloucestershire Studies,* 184-189, Leics. Univ. Press
2. The Verney tomb was erected in 1653. It is the work of Edward Marshall, later the Royal Master Mason, and cost £130.
3. It seems that Cromwell was at Andover when he heard of the Levellers' march. He reached Burford, about 80 km, in one day.

Selective Bibliography

Ashley, M. 1952. *England in the Seventeenth Century,* Pelican, London
　　1974. *The English Civil War,* Thames and Hudson, London
Aylmer, G. E. (ed.) 1975. *The Levellers in the English Revolution,* Thames and Hudson London
Brailsford, H. N. 1961. *The Levellers and the English Revolution,* ed. C. Hill, Cresset Press, London
Burne, A. H. & Young, P. 1959. *The Great Civil War: A Military History . . .* Eyre and Spottiswood, London
Hyett, F. A. 1891-2. The last battle of the first Civil War, *Trans. Brist. and Glouc. Archaeol. Soc.,* **16,** 61-67
Jennings, R. W. 1976. *The Cotswolds in the Civil War,* (booklet) Corinium Museum, Cirencester

Sorrell, A. 1973. *British Castles,* Batsford, London

Thames and Chilterns Tourist Board, 1978. *Civil War Heritage Trail,* a map pamphlet with practical information, St Aldate's, Oxford

Toynbee, M. 1962. *The Papers of Captain Henry Stevens, Waggon-Master-General to King Charles I,* Oxfordshire Rec. Soc., **42**

Toynbee, M. & Young, P. *Cropredy Bridge, 1644, the Campaign and Battle,* Roundwood Press, Warwick

Varley, F. J. 1932. *The Seige of Oxford 1642-6,* O.U.P.

Wedgewood, C. V. 1958. *The King's War 1641-47,* Collins, London

Young, P. and Holmes, R. 1974. *The English Civil War: A Military History. . .,* Eyre Methuen, London

Young, P. 1967. *Edgehill 1642: The Campaign and the Battle,* Roundwood Press, Warwick

CHAPTER 9
TRANSFORMATION OF THE RURAL SCENE AND LIFE, 1660-1835

References

1. Fussell, G. E. 1973. *Jethro Tull: his Influence on Merchanised Agriculture,* Osprey, Reading
2. Arkell, W. J. 1947. (reprint 1970). *Oxford Stone,* Faber, London
3. Barley, M. W. 1961. *The English Farmhouse and Cottage,* Routledge and Kegan Paul, London, 257
4. Full returns are in Jukes, H.A. Ll. (ed.) 1957. *The Primary Visitation of Dr Thomas Secker, 1738,* Oxfordshire Rec. Soc., **38**
5. 'The Removal of the Village at Nuneham Courtenay', quoted in Batey, M. 1968. Nuneham Courtenay . . . , *Oxoniensia.* **33**, 123
6. For Yarnton lot meadows, *Oxford Times,* 15 July 1899; Gretton, R. H. 1910-11. *Econ. Journ.,* **20**, 38-45; **22**, 53-62; *Oxford Mail* 2 July 1974
7. Martin, J. M. 1964. The cost of Parliamentary enclosure in Warwickshire, *Univ. Birmingham Hist. Journ.,* **9**, 144-162, reprinted in Jones, E. L. (ed.) 1967. *Agriculture and Economic Growth in England, 1650-1815,* Methuen, London. Tate, W. E. 1952-3. The cost of Parliamentary enclosure . . . *Econ. Hist. Rev,* 2nd ser., **5**, 258-265 (with special reference to Oxfordshire)
8. Bruce, M. R. 1972. An Oxfordshire enclosure, 1791-94, *Top. Oxon.,* **18**, 2-5
9. Brown, A. V. 1967. The Last phase of the enclosure of Otmoor, *Oxoniensia,* **32**, 34-52
10. From 1701 to 1801 the population of Berkshire and Buckinghamshire increased by 47 per cent, of Oxfordshire by 35 per cent, of Northamptonshire by 21 per cent, and of all England and Wales by 57 per cent. From 1801 to 1841 the national average growth of all Rural Districts and small towns was over 10 per cent and for all areas 14 per cent per decade.
11. Neuman, M. D. 1969. A suggestion regarding the origins of the Speenhamland plan, *Engl. Hist. Rev,* **331**, 317-22

Selective Bibliography

General

Burke, J. 1976. *English Art 1714-1800,* Clarendon Press, Oxford

Butlin, R. A. 1978. *The Transformation of Rural England, 1580-1800,* O.U.P.

Chalkin, C. W. & Havinden, M. A. 1970. *Rural Change and Urban Growth, 1500-1800,* Longman, London

Coleman, D. C. 1976. *The Economy of England 1450-1750,* O.U.P.

Darby, H. C. 1973. The age of the improver 1600-1800, in *New Historical Geography of England*, 302-88, C.U.P.

Mingay, G. E. 1963. *English Landed Society in the Eighteenth Century*, Routledge and Kegan Paul, London

Whinney, M. & Millar, O. 1957. *English Art 1625-1714*, Clarendon Press, Oxford

Agriculture and Enclosures

Chambers, D. & Mingay, G. E. 1966. *The Agricultural Revolution 1750-1880*, Batsford, London

Curtler, W. H. R. 1922. *The Enclosure and Redistribution of Our Land*, Clarendon Press, Oxford

Elrington, C. 1964. Open fields and inclosure in the Cotswolds, *Proc. Cot. Nat. F.C.*, **34**, 37-44

Gonner, E. C. K. 1966. *Common Land and Inclosure*, 2nd Edn., Cass, London

Gray, H. L. 1915. *English Field Systems*, Cambridge, Mass; O.U.P.; new edn.
    1969. Merlin, London (deals especially with Oxfordshire)

Johnson, A. H. 1963. *The Disappearance of the Small Landowner*, 2nd edn., Clarendon Press, Oxford

Jones, E. L. (ed.) 1967. *Agriculture and Economic Growth in England 1650-1815*, Methuen, London

Kerridge, E. 1967. *The Agricultural Revolution*, Allen and Unwin, London

Martin, J. M. 1967. The Parliamentary enclosure movement and rural society in Warwickshire, *Agric. Hist. Rev.*, **15**, 19-39

Mingay, G. E. 1968. *Enclosure and the Small Farmer in the Age of the Industrial Revolution* (studies in Econ. Hist.), Macmillan, London

Roberts, B. K. 1973. Field systems in the West Midlands, in Baker, A. R. & Butlin, R. A. *Studies in the Field Systems of the British Isles*, 619-56, C.U.P.

Roden, D. 1973. Field systems of the Chiltern Hills and their environs, in Baker and Butlin, *op. cit.*, 325-76

Tate, W. E. 1967. *The English Village Community and the Enclosure Movement*, Gollancz, London
    1946. W. E. Tate has compiled *Handlists* of the Enclosure Awards of each county. For Oxfordshire see new *Handlist of the Inclosure Acts. . .*, Oxfordshire C.C. Rec. Publ. 2, 1975, County Hall, Oxford

Yelling, J. A. 1977. *Common Field and Enclosure in England 1450-1850*, Macmillan, London

Ridge-and-Furrow and its Problems

Harrison, M. H. *et al.* 1965. A Midland ridge-and-furrow map, *Geogr. Journ.*, **131**, 366-69

Mead, W. R. 1954. Ridge and furrow in Buckinghamshire, *Geogr. Journ.*, **120**, 34-42

Orwin, C. S. & C. S. 1967. *The Open Fields*, Clarendon Press, Oxford

Sutton, J. E. G. 1964-5. Ridge and furrow in Berkshire and Oxfordshire, *Oxoniensia*, **29-30**, 99-115

Poverty and Poor Law

Longmate, N. 1974. *The Workhouse*, M. T. Smith, London

Marshall, J. D. 1968. *The Old Poor Law 1795-1834*, (studies in Econ. Hist.) Macmillan, London

Neuman, M. D. 1972. Speenhamland in Berkshire, *Comparative Development in Social Welfare*, ed. E. W. Martin, Allen and Unwin, London

Oxley, G. W. 1974. *Poor Relief in England and Wales 1601-1834*, David and Charles, Newton Abbot

CHAPTER 10
TURNPIKES, CANALS AND DOMESTIC INDUSTRIES

We are grateful to the County Archivist of each of the shires involved and to Miss J. M. Swann, Keeper of the Shoe Collection at the Central Museum, Northampton, for help and information. Fig. 28 is taken from *Glovemaking in West Oxfordshire* by N. L. Leyland & J. E. Troughton by kind permission of the Oxfordshire County Council Department of Museum Services. Figs. 22 and 23 of Cheltenham and Leamington Spas were kindly supplied by Professor J. A. Patmore (*see* reference 6).

References

1. Young, A. 1809. *View of the Agriculture of Oxfordshire,* 324, R. Phillips, London
2. Jordan, J. 1857. *A Parochial History of Enstone,* 308, Alden, Oxford
3. Shaw, S. 1789. *A Tour to the West of England . . .,* Robson and Clarke, London
4. Anon, 1769. *Description of England and Wales,* I, 64, Newbery and Carnan, London. The Hare and Hounds retains its five-bay front with pedimented gables and the date 1756.
5. Hart, R. J. 1973-4. A survey of the milestones in western Berkshire, *Berks, Archaeol. Journ.,* **67**, 71-77
6. Patmore, J. A. 1968. The Spa Towns of Britain, in *Urbanisation and its Problems,* ed. R. P. Beckinsale & J. M. Houston, Blackwell, Oxford, 47-69; Chaplin, R. 1972, The rise of Leamington Spa, *Warwickshire History,* **II**, No. 2
7. Paine, E. M. S. 1861. *The Two James's and the Two Stephensons,* reprinted 1961, David and Charles, Newton Abbot
8. Beckinsale, R. P. 1937. Factors in the development of the Cotswold woollen industry, *Geogr. Journ.,* **90**, 349-362
9. Evans, R. Ll. 1975. The Bliss Mills . . . Chipping Norton, *Top. Oxon.,* **20**, 6-12
10. Beckinsale, R. P. 1963. The plush industry . . ., *Oxoniensia,* **28**, 53-67. Hodgkins, V. 1975. The plush industry in Shutford, *Cake and Cockhorse,* (Banbury Hist. Soc.) **6**, 59-76
11. Mounfield, P. R. 1977. The place of time in economic geography, *Geogr.,* **62**, 272-5. Has maps of general distribution of employment in footwear manufacturing in England and Wales 1841-1971. The Central Museum Northampton has a full bibliography of shoes and leathercraft.
12. Andrews, P. W. & Brunner, E. 1965. *The Eagle Ironworks, Oxford: The Story of W. C. Lucy & Co.,* Mills and Boon, London
13. Among other towns that became noted for ironwork and agricultural machinery were Reading (*see* Corley, T.A.B. 1973-4, *Berks. Archaeol. Journ.,* **67**, 79-87) and Wantage which produced the Berkshire plough.

Selective Bibliography

Turnpikes
Albert, W. 1972. *The Turnpike Road System in England, 1663-1840,* C.U.P.
Copeland, J. 1968. *Roads and Their Traffic 1750-1850,* David and Charles, Newton Abbot
Cossons, A. 1941-2. Warwickshire Turnpikes, *Trans. Birmingham Archaeol. Soc.,* **64**, 82-95 has full list, with map, of turnpikes in Warwickshire.
Duckham, B. F. 1967. *The Transport Revolution 1750-1830,* Hist. Assoc., London
Jackman, W. T. 1916. *The Development of Transportation in Modern England,* 2 vols., C.U.P., reprinted 1962, Cass, London
Ordnance Survey, 1930. Map of *XVII Century England*

Paterson, D. 1771-1829. *A New and Accurate Description of All the Direct and Principal Cross Roads in England and Wales,* Longman, London (the latest editions were under E. Mogg)

Villiers, E. de 1969. *Swinford Bridge, 1769-1969,* White House, Eynsham

Webb, S. and B. 1913. *The Story of the King's Highway,* Longman, London, reprinted 1962, Cass, London

Canals and River Waterways

Compton, B. J. 1977. *The Oxford Canal,* David and Charles, Newton Abbot

Hadfield, C. 1969. *The Canals of South and South East England,* David and Charles, Newton

Hadfield, C. 1970. *The Canals of the East Midlands,* David and Charles, Newton Abbot

Hadfield, C. & Morris, J. 1962. *Waterways to Stratford,* David and Charles, Newton Abbot

Household, H. 1969. *The Thames and Severn Canal,* David and Charles, Newton Abbot

Thacker, F. S. 1914-1920. *The Thames Highway,* 2 vols.; reprinted 1968, David and Charles, Newton Abbot

Willan, T. S. 1936. *River Navigation in England, 1600-1750,* O.U.P.

1936. The navigation of the Thames and Kennet 1600-1750, *Berks. Archaeol. Journ.,* **40**, 1-9

Domestic Industries

Herbert, G. 1948. *Shoemaker's Window,* Blackwell, Oxford

Leyland, N. L. & Troughton, J. E. 1974. *Glovemaking in West Oxfordshire,* Oxford City and County Museum and Kegan Paul, London

Plummer, A. 1934. *The Witney Blanket Industry . . .,* Routledge and Kegan Paul, London

Plummer, A. & Early, R. E. 1969. *The Blanket Makers, 1669-1969 . . .,* Routledge and Kegan Paul, London

Sibbitt, C. 1968. *Bells, Blankets, Baskets and Boats: a survey of crafts and industries in Oxfordshire,* Oxford City and County Museum

Spenceley, G. F. R. 1973. The origins of the English Pillow Lace industry, *Agric. Hist. Rev,* **21**, 81-93

Woods, K. 1921. *Rural Industries round Oxford,* O.U.P.

CHAPTER 11
COUNTRY MANSIONS AND LANDSCAPE GARDENING

We are grateful to Mr Charles Cottrell-Dormer for kind permission to reproduce from his *Guide to Rousham Park* William Kent's plan for the gardens there.

References

1. Anon, 1971. *A Guide to the Oxford Botanic Gardens,* Clarendon Press, Oxford; Gunter, R. T. 1912. *Oxford Gardens,* Parker, Oxford

2. Malins, E. 1966. *English Landscaping and Literature, 1660-1840,* O.U.P., 7

3. Wood, A. C. & Hawkes, W. 1969. Sanderson Miller, *Cake and Cockhorse,* Banbury Hist. Soc., 79-110

4. Bickham, G. 1753. *The Beauties of Stowe,* Bickham, London; Whistler, L. 1956. *Guide to Stowe Garden*

5. In 1603 when James I and his Queen (Anne) stayed there the royal family occupied the gatehouse, but some members of the household had to lodge in tents on ground that Robert Cecil, Earl of Salisbury, said was watery and smelt of pigs and cows. Lodge, E. 1838, reprinted 1969. *Illustrations of British History,* Vol. 3, 186

6. Green, D. 1956. *Gardener to Queen Anne,* O.U.P.; 1972, *Blenheim Park and Gardens*

7. Batey, M. *Nuneham Courtenay,* Oxford

Selective Bibliography

Clark, H. F. 1948. *The English Landscape Garden,* Pleiades Books, London

Clifford, D. 1966. *A History of Garden Design,* Faber, London

Dutton, R. 1937. *The English Garden,* Batsford, London

Hussey, C. 1967. *English Gardens and Landscapes 1700-1750,* Country Life, London

Jekyll, G. 1899. *Wood and Garden,* Longman, London

Jekyll, G. & Weaver, L. 1914. *Gardens for Small Country Houses,* Country Life, George Newnes, London

Jones, B. 1953. *Follies and Grottoes,* Constable, London

Jourdain, M. 1948. *The Work of William Kent,* Country Life, London

Loudon, J. C. 1804. *Observations on the function and management of useful and ornamental plantations . . .,* Constable, Edinburgh

1806. *A Treatise on forming, improving and managing Country Residences,* 2 vols., London

1812. *Hints on the formation of Gardens and Pleasure Grounds*

1836. *Encyclopaedia of Cottage, Farm and Villa Architecture . . .* Longman, London

Malins, E. 1966. *English Landscaping and Literature, 1660-1840,* O.U.P,

Mason, W. 1782. *The English Garden: A Poem in Four Books,* London

Prince, H. C. 1967. *Parks in England,* Shalfleet, I.O.W.

Repton, Humphry, 1794. *Sketches and Hints on Landscape Gardening,* London

1803. *Observation on the Theory and Practice of Landscape Gardening,* J. Taylor, London

1806. *An Enquiry into the Changes of Taste in Landscape Gardening,* London

1907 (ed. J. Nolen) *The Art of Landscape Gardening,* Constable, London

Robinson, W. 1892. *Garden Design and Architects' Gardens,* J. Murray, London

1883. *English Flower Garden,* Murray, London

Stroud, D. 1975. *'Capability' Brown,* Faber, London

1962. *Humphry Repton,* Country Life, London

Whistler, L. 1954. *The Inspiration of Vanbrugh and his Fellow Artists,* Batsford, London

Willis, P. 1976. *Charles Bridgeman and the English Landscape Garden,* Pinhorns, London; (ed.) 1974. *Furor Hortensis . . .,* Elysium Press, London; & Hunt, J. D. 1974. *Genius of the Place: English Landscape Gardens 1620-1820,* Elek, London

CHAPTER 12
WATERMILLS

We are greatly indebted to J. Kenneth Major for much help with this chapter and for information to the Wind and Watermill Section of the Society for the Protection of Ancient Buildings, 55 Great Ormond Street, London W.C.1, who welcomes new members. Fig. 33 of watermill interior mechanisms is reproduced from Miss Katharine S. Woods' *Rural Crafts of England* with the kind permission of the authoress and George G. Harrap & Company (*see* reference 8).

References

1. Calendar of Liberate Rolls, 48 H3
2. For full account of millstone transactions *see* Rogers, T. E. T. 1866. *A History of Agriculture and Prices in England,* Vol. I, 505-8, Clarendon Press, Oxford; for other details Harvey, P. D. A. 1965. *A Mediaeval Oxfordshire Village: Cuxham 1240-1400,* O.U.P. An alternative probable source of the millstones is the volcanic region of the Eifel near the Rhine which has exported blue/black basalt stones since pre-Roman times.

These whole stones or blocks were exported from Andernach and sent down the Rhine via Cologne, hence the term Cullen stone.

3. Hilton, R.H. in Finberg, H. P. R. (ed.) 1957. *Gloucestershire Studies*, 102, Leics. Univ. Press

4. Hudson, K. 1965. *The Industrial Archaeology of Southern England*, 82, David and Charles, Newton Abbot

5. For example as *The boke of Husbandry*, 1767. Its last publication was in facsimile in 1974

6. Among the 9 English firms granted the first licences to install Fourdrinier machines in 1807 were the proprietors of Eynsham mill, Marlow mill, and the large four-storey brick mill newly built beside the Alne at Wootten Wawen.

7. Kenneth Major, K. 1970. River Barn, Bucklebury, Berkshire, *Berks. Archaeol. Journ.*, **65**, 49-51

8. Woods, K. S. 1975. *Rural Crafts of England*, E. P. Publishing, Wakefield (1st edn. Harrap, London, 1949)

9. Alfred Humphris, the local millwright, installed a waterwheel, brought from Berrick, here in 1913, and worked repeatedly on the machinery until May 1923. The manuscript of his day journals (1910-23) is in Oxford City library. He had two donkeys and carts for moving heavier stuff.

10. Major, J. K. 1962-3. Berkshire watermills *Berks. Archaeol. Journ.*, **61**, 81-91

11. Valuable recent surveys of mill sites and mills include Carter, J. 1968. Watermills in North Oxfordshire, *Cake and Cockhorse*, **3**, No. 12, Banbury Hist. Soc.; 1969 Witney Watermills, *Bull. Industrial Archaeology in C.B.A.*, *Group 9*, No. **10**, 2-3; and Starmer, G. H. 1970. Check List of Northamptonshire Wind and Watermills, *ibid.*, No. **12**, 11-38. With the preserved mills should be included the interior of Coldron mill, Spelsbury, Oxfordshire, which with its eighteenth century overshot wheel, was re-erected in the Science Museum, London, in 1938.

12. *Oxford Mail*, 24 June 1969.

13. Brochure and information from Sam Mackaness, Little Billing.

14. For details see Shadwell, L. L. 1912. *Enactments in Parliament specially concerning the Universities of Oxford and Cambridge . . .*, Vol. I, 245

15. There was also an ancient mill at Oxford at Holywell on the Cherwell and in late Tudor times a fulling mill near Rewley Abbey. Among accounts of Oxford mills are Carter, H. 1974. *Wolvercote Mill*, 2nd edn., Clarendon Press, Oxford; Cornish, C. J. The ancient mills of Oxford, *Country Life Illustrated*, 7 April 1900, 427-8; Taunt, H. W. *Iffley Mill and Its Story*, 2nd edn., Oxford, n.d.; Belsen, K. 1975. *The Story of Botley Mill*, Hunt and Broadhurst, Oxford

16. Letters and Papers, Henry VIII, Sir Richard Rich to Thomas Cromwell, 22 February 1538; Thomas Cade to Thomas Cromwell, 4 March 1538.

17. Slade, C. F. & J. Kenneth Major, 1971-2, Excavations at Reading Abbey, *Berks. Archaeol. Journ.*, **66**, 65-116

Selective Bibliography

Ordnance Survey maps , and non-official county 18th century maps for locations.
Bennett, R. & Elton, J. 1899. *History of Corn Milling*, Vol. 2, *Watermills and Windmills*, Simpkin and Marshall, reprinted by E. P. Publishing, 1973.
Smeaton, John, 1759-60. An Experimental Enquiry Concerning the Natural Powers of Water and Wind to Turn Mills and Other Machines Depending on a Circular Motion, *Phil. Trans. Royal Soc.*, London, **51**, 100-174
Skilton, C. P. 1947. *British Windmills and Watermills*, Collins, London

Syson, L. 1965. *British Water-Mills*, Batsford, London
Wilson, P. N. 1955-7. The Waterwheels of John Smeaton, *Trans. Newcomen Society*, 30, 25-48

Paper Making
see especially the following, which contain full references:
Carter, H. 1974. *Wolvercote Mill, Oxford*, Clarendon Press, Oxford, 2nd edn.
    1967. Papermaking in the neighbourhood of Oxford, *Seventh International Congress of Paper Historians*
Coleman, D. C. 1958. *The British Paper Industry 1495-1860*, Clarendon Press, Oxford
Shorter, A. H. 1957. *Paper Mills and Paper Makers in England, 1495-1800*, Paper Publicns., Hilversum
Shorter, A. H. 1966. *Water Paper Mills in England*, Soc. for Protection of Ancient Buildings, London
Shorter, A. H. 1971. *Paper Making in the British Isles*, David and Charles, Newton Abbot

CHAPTER 13
WINDMILLS

We are greatly indebted for much assistance to J. Kenneth Major and for information to Dr W. C. Allan of the County Museum, Warwick and Mrs. J. Costigan of the Avoncroft Museum of Buildings, Stoke Prior, Bromsgrove. Fig. 37 of the interior of Brill post mill is reproduced from Stanley Freese's *Windmills and Millwrighting* by kind permission of the author and the Cambridge University Press.

References

1. Clarke, E. (ed.) 1907. *The Chronicle of Jocelyn of Brakelond . . .*, 75
2. Salter, H. E. (ed.) 1935. *Cartulary of Oseney Abbey*, Oxford Hist. Soc., V, charter 692
3. *Cal. Charter Rolls, 111, 319*, presumably of 1163-81 mentions a windmill. Beedell *(op. cit.)* mentions a rental of 1185 with a windmill in Weedly, Yorks. let at 8s a year.
4. For details, 1959. *V.C.H., Oxon.* VI
5. Starmer, G. H. 1970. Checklist of Northamptonshire Wind and Watermills, *Bull. Ind. Archaeol. C.B.A. Group Nine*, No. 12, 11-38
6. Baxter, E. G. 1971. Chesterton windmill, *Warwickshire History*, I, No. 6
7. *The Times* 29 April 1977
8. *The Times* 8 September 1976

Selective Bibliography

Beedell, S. 1975. *Windmills*, David and Charles, Newton Abbot
Freese, S. 1957. *Windmills and Millwrighting*, C.U.P., reprinted 1971 David and Charles, Newton Abbot
Hopkins, R. T. & Freese, S. 1931. *In Search of English Windmills*, Cecil Palmer
Paddon, J. B. 1925. *Windmills in the Midlands*, Oxford
Seaby, W. A. & Smith A. C. 1977. *Windmills in Warwickshire*, County Museum, Warwick
Skilton, C. P. 1947. *British Windmills and Watermills*, Collins, London
Smith, A. C. 1976. *Windmills in Buckinghamshire and Oxfordshire*, Stevenage Museum, Hertfordshire
Smith, D. 1932. *English Mills*, Vol. 2, Architectural Press, London
Vince, J. N. T. 1977. *Discovering Windmills*, Shire Publications, Tring

1978. *Windmills in Buckinghamshire and the Chilterns,* Format, Thames Ditton
Wailes, R. 1967. *The English Windmill,* Routledge and Kegan Paul, London

CHAPTER 14
THE VICTORIAN RECONSTRUCTION

Fig. 40 of internal migration is reproduced from *The Geographical Journal,* June 1951 by kind permission of Professor Clifford T. Smith and The Royal Geographical Society.

References

1. 17 Geo. 2 c. 3 private.
2. Now in the National Portrait Gallery, London, as also is a fine portrait of Sir Henry Lee by Antonio Mor, 1580.
3. Murray, John 1869. *Handbook for Travellers in Wiltshire . . .* 47
4. Young, Arthur 1809. *View of the Agriculture of Oxfordshire,* 127. Board of Agriculture
5. Davie, W. G. & Dawber, E. G. 1905. *Old Cottages, Farm Houses . . . in the Cotswold District,* Batsford, London
6. For Trade Union movement *see* Horn, P. L. R. 1968. Christopher Holloway, *Oxoniensia,* 33, 125-136; 1971, *Joseph Arch,* Roundwood Press, Kineton; 1974. *Agricultural Trade Unionism in Oxfordshire, 1872-1881,* Oxfordshire Rec. Soc., 48
7. Girouard, M. 1968. Bearwood, Berkshire, *Country Life,* 17 October, 964-6
8. Holderness, B. A. 1972. 'Open' and 'Close' parishes in England . . ., *Agric. Hist. Rev.,* 20, 126-139
9. Stevenson, G. R. 1975. Open village: Victorian Middle Barton, *Cake and Cockhorse* (Banbury Hist. Soc.) 6, 39-47
10. Goodhart-Rendel, H. S. 1953. *English Architecture since the Regency,* 95
11. Another and perhaps the main cause of Morris' letter was a report of the proposed restoration of Tewkesbury Abbey in *The Times.*
12. Elizabeth Stevenson went to Miss Byerley's excellent school at Barford House, 4km south of Warwick, from 1822 to May 1825 when the school moved to larger premises at Avonbank, a Tudor building with 23 bedrooms once owned by Shakespeare's cousin, Thomas Greene, who moved into it from New Place in 1611 when the dramatist decided to live permanently in Stratford. *See* Gérin, W. 1976 *Elizabeth Gaskell,* Oxford
13. We should mention also the Abbey School in the Gatehouse of the former Reading Abbey where Mrs Latournelle, a French *émigrée* ran a very successsful academy that from 1785-7 was attended by Jane Austen and her elder sister and ten years later by Mary Russell Mitford who described so delicately the Reading countryside.

Selective Bibliography

Boase, T. S. R. 1959. *English Art 1800-1870,* Clarendon Press, Oxford
Church, R. A. 1968. *The Great Victorian Boom 1850-73,* Macmillan, London
Young, G. M. 1977. *Victorian England,* O.U.P. (new annotated edn.)

Forests
Belcher, C. 1863. On the reclaiming of waste land as instanced in Wichwood Forest, *Journ. Roy. Soc.,* 24, 271-285
Watney, V. 1910. *Cornbury and the Forest of Wychwood,* Hatchards, London

Agricultural Boom and Decline

Chambers, J. D. & Mingay, G. E. 1966. *The Agricultural Revolution 1750-1880,* Batsford, London

Fisher, A. S. T. 1972. *A History of Westwell, Oxfordshire,* Bear Court Books, Burford

Jones, E. L. 1968. *The Development of English Agriculture 1815-1873,* Macmillan, London

Saul, S. B. 1969. *The Myth of the Great Depression 1873-1896,* Macmillan, London

Thompson, F. M. L. 1963. *English Landed Society in the Nineteenth Century,* Routledge and Kegan Paul, London

Thompson, Flora. 1945. *Lark Rise to Candleford,* Everyman (description of rural hamlet of Juniper Hill and village of Cottisford in north Oxfordshire)

Mansions, Model Villages, and Estate Housing

Brooks, S. 1839. *Designs for Cottage and Villa Architecture . . .,* T. Kelly, London

Buchanan, K. M. 1944. *Worcester; the land of Britain,* **68**, 572-5 for Dodford

Hadfield, A. M. 1970. *The Chartist Land Company,* David and Charles, Newton Abbot

Harrison, J. F. C. 1977. *Bibliography of the Chartist Movement,* Harvester Press, Hassocks

Jones, D. 1975. *Chartism and the Chartists,* Lane, London

Redford, A. 1964. *Labour Migration in England 1800-1850,* (2nd edn.) revised by H. W. Chaloner), Manchester Univ. Press

Roberts, H. 1860. *The Dwellings of the Labouring Classes, their Arrangements and Construction, Royal Commission on the Employment of Children, Young Persons and Women in Agriculture, 1867-69,* Parl. Reports, 1868-9, Vol. 13

Smith, C. T. 1951. The movement of population in England and Wales in 1851 and 1861, *Geogr. Journ.,* **117**, 200-210

Tyack, G. 1970. Ettington park, *Warwickshire History,* **I**, No. 4; 1972. Victorian country houses of Warwickshire, *Warwickshire History,* **II**, No. 1

Ward, T. J. 1973. *Chartism,* Macmillan, London

West, J. 1920. *A History of the Chartist Movement,* Constable, London

Wilkinson, W. 1870. *English Country Houses . . .,* Oxford

Victorian Churches and Architects

Clarke, B. F. L. 1938. *Church Builders of the Nineteenth Century,* S.P.C.K., London

Rendel, H. S. G. 1953. *English Architecture since the Regency,* Constable, London

Street, A. E. 1888. *Memoir of G.E. Street,* Murray, London

CHAPTER 15
THE RAILWAY AGE

For information we are indebted to Reg and Janice Uphill of the Quainton Railway Society.

References

1. The Birmingham and Gloucester Railway (53 miles; 85 km) ran via Lansdown Junction at Cheltenham to Tramway Junction at Gloucester in 1840. Gloucester was connected with Bristol in 1844. At Cheltenham Lansdown Junction was connected with St James in 1847.

2. Richards, P. 1962. The influence of railways on the growth of Wolverton, Buckinghamshire, *Records of Bucks.,* **17**, 115-126

3. Adlestrop, 1975 in *Edward Thomas, Poems and Last Poems,* (ed.) E. Langley, MacDonald and Evans, London

4. Gaut, R. C. 1939. *A History of Worcestershire Agriculture . . .,* Littlebury & Co., Worcester, 424; Robinson, G. M. 1976. *Late Victorian Agriculture in the Vale of Evesham.,* Booklet 16, School of Geography, Oxford University

5. Grimshaw, P. N. 1976. Steam railways: growth points of leisure and recreation, *Geogr.*, **61**, 83-88
6. In Spender, S. 1954. *Collected Poems,* Faber, London

Selective Bibliography

Bick, D. E. 1968. *The Gloucester and Cheltenham Railway and Leckhampton Quarry Tramroads,* Oakwood Press, Blandford Forum
Carter, E. F. 1959. *A Historical Geography of the Railways of the British Isles,* Cassell, London
Christiansen, R. 1973. *The West Midlands,* Vol. 7 of Regional History of Railways of Great Britain, David and Charles, Newton Abbot
Clinker, C. R. 1960. *The Railways of Northamptonshire . . . 1800-1960,* C. Clinker, Rugby
Davies, R. & Grant, M. D. 1975. *Forgotten Railways: Chilterns and Cotswolds,* David and Charles, Newton Abbot
Gilks, J. S. 1955. The Cheltenham and Banbury Direct Railway, *Railway Magazine* (Aug.)
Hadfield, C. & Norris, J. 1962. *Waterways to Stratford,* David and Charles, Newton Abbot. (Has full account of Stratford and Moreton Tramway by John Norris)
Harloe, M. 1975. *Swindon: A Town in Transition,* Heinemann, London
Hawke, G. R. 1970. *Railways and Economic Growth in England and Wales, 1850-1870,* Clarendon Press, Oxford
Household, H. G. 1950. Sapperton Tunnel, *Railway Magazine* (February)
Hudson, K. 1968. The early years of the railway community in Swindon, *Transport History,* **I**, 146-150; 1967, *An Awkward Size for a Town. A Study of Swindon . . .*, David and Charles, Newton Abbot
Lingard, R. 1973. *The Woodstock Branch, G.W.R.,* Oxford Publ. Co.
MacDermot, E. T. 1927. *History of the Great Western Railway,* G.W.R. (revised by C. R. Clinker, 1964, Allan, Shepperton)
Oxfordshire County Council, 1964. *Handlist of Plans, section . . . for proposed Railways in Oxfordshire, 1825-36,* Record Publ. 3
Swindon Borough Council, 1950. *Studies in the History of Swindon*
Tonks, E. S. 1961. *The Ironstone Railways and Tramways of the Midlands,* Locomotive Publ. Co.
White, H. P. 1961. *A Regional History of the Railways of Great Britain: Vol. 2 Southern England,* Phoenix House, London
V. C.H. Wiltshire, IX, 1970, Swindon, 104-168

CHAPTER 16
THE GROWTH OF TOWNS

We are much indebted to A. D. M. Cox of University College, Oxford, Mrs Mary D. Lobel and Professor H. Loyn for generous help with this chapter.

References

1. Robertson, A. J. (ed.) 1939. *Anglo Saxon Charters,* 246-9, 494-6, C.U.P.
2. *See* Bibliography Chapter 3 for references.
3. Map in Stenton, F. M. 346
4. Ballard, A. (ed.) 1913. *British Borough Charters, 1042-1216;* Ballard, A. & Tait, J. (ed.) 1923. *British Borough Charters, 1216-1307;* Weinbaum, M. (ed.) 1943. *British Borough Charters, 1307-1660,* C.U.P.

5. Loyd, L. C. & Stenton, D. M. (eds.) 1950. Sir Chris. Hatton's Book of Seals, *Northants. Rec. Soc.* XV, 76-78
6. *Rotuli Hundredorum,* II, 839-42 (Record Commission, 1818), our translation and analysis.
7. *V.C.H. Oxon.* VI, 1959, 247
8. *Egerton Mss.,* (B.M.), 282, 21; quoted in Trenholme *op. cit.*
9. For 1334 *see* Glasscock, R. E. in Darby, H. C. (ed.) 1973. *New Historical Geography of England,* ed. H. C. Darby, C.U.P. 177-181
10. For 1523-7 assessments *see,* Baker, A. R. H. in Darby, *op. cit.,* 243; Cornwall, J., 1953-60, An Elizabethan Census, *Records of Bucks.,* **16**, 258-273; 1962-3. English country towns in the fifteen-twenties, *Econ. Hist. Rev.,* 2nd ser. **XV,** 54-69; Sheail, J. 1972. The distribution of taxable population and wealth in England during the early sixteenth century, *Trans. Inst. Brit. Geogr.,* **55,** 111-126

Selective Bibliography

Beckinsale, R. P. 1968. Urbanisation in England to A.D. 1420, in *Urbanisation and Its Problems,* Blackwell, Oxford, 1-46
Beresford, M. 1967. *New Towns of the Middle Ages,* Lutterworth, London
Colvin, H. M. 1958. Domestic architecture and town-planning, in *Mediaeval England,* ed. A. L. Poole, I, Clarendon Press, Oxford, 37-97
Darby, H. C. 1977. *Domesday England,* C.U.P. 289-320
Finberg, H. P. R. 1957. The Genesis of the Gloucestershire Towns, in *Gloucestershire Studies,* Leics. Univ. Press, 52-88
Lobel, M. D. (ed.) 1969. *Atlas of Historic British Towns,* (with text, numerous maps and large scale plans etc. for each town), The Historic Towns Trust & Scholar Press. Banbury and Reading are in Vol. 1, 1969; Vol. 2, 1975
Loyn, H. R. 1962. *Anglo-Saxon England and the Norman Conquest,* Longman, London
Rodwell, K. (ed.) 1975. *Historic Towns in Oxfordshire,* Oxfordshire Archaeol. Unit
Tait, J. 1936. *The Mediaeval English Borough,* Manchester Univ. Press
Trenholme, N. M. 1927. English Monastic Boroughs, *Univ of Missouri Studies,* **II,** No. 3, 1-119

Some Selected Towns, in alphabetical order. For Stratford on Avon *see* Chapter 17, for Warwick Chapter 18, and for Oxford Chapter 19.

Abingdon. Biddle, M. *et al* 1968. The early history of Abingdon, *Mediaeval Archaeol.,* **12,** 26-69; Cox, M. 1975. *Abingdon: Abbey to Borough;* Lambrick, G. M. 1965. Abingdon and the riots of 1327. *Oxoniensia,* **29-30,** 129-141; Trenholme, *op. cit.*
Banbury. Harvey, P. D. A. 1969 in Lobel, M. D. (ed.) *Historic Towns Atlas,* I, 1-8. 1972. *V.C.H. Oxon.,* **10,** 5-127
Buckingham, Elliott, D. J. 1975. *Buckingham,* Phillimore
Burford. Gretton, R. H. 1920. *The Burford Records,* Clarendon Press, Oxford; Laithwaite, M. 1973. The Buildings of Burford, *Perspectives in English Urban History,* ed. A. Everitt, 60-90
Chipping Norton, Meades, E. 1949. *The History of Chipping Norton,* Alden, Oxford
Cirencester. Finberg, 1957. *op. cit.,* 74-79; Fuller, E. A. 1878-1894. *Trans. Bristol and Gloucs. Archaeol. Soc.,* **2,** 285-319; **9,** 298-344; **18,** 32-74, 175-6; *The Cartulary of Cirencester Abbey,* ed. C. D. Ross, 1964. I – II; Devine, M. 1977. Vol. III, Clarendon Press, Oxford
Cricklade. Loyn, H. 1961. The origin and early development of the Saxon borough with special reference to Cricklade, *Wilts. Archaeol. and Nat. Hist. Mag.,* **58,** 7-15; Haslam, J., Cricklade: Saxon defences, *The Times,* 2 Jan. 1976, suggests that the wall was slighted by Cnut in 1016

Deddington.   Colvin, H. M. 1963. *History of Deddington,* S.P.C.K., London
Eynsham.   Chambers, E. 1936. *Eynsham under the Monks,* Oxon. Record Soc., **18**; Salter, H. E. 1906-8. *Cartulary of the Abbey of Eynsham,* 2 vols., Oxford Hist. Soc., **49** and **51**
Henley in Arden. Cooper, W. 1946. *Henley in Arden,* Cornish, Birmingham
Henley on Thames. Briers, P. M. ed. 1960. *Henley Borough Records,* Oxon. Record Soc., 41; Burn, J. S. 1861. *History of Henley on Thames,* Longman, London
Northampton.   V.C.H. Northants, III, 1930; Lee, F. 1953, A New theory on the origins . . . of Northampton, *Archaeol. Journ.,* **CX**, 164-74; Williams, J., Northampton: Remains of Saxon Church found, *The Times* 13 June 1977
Reading.   Slade, C. F. in Lobel, M. D. (ed.) 1969 *Historic Towns Atlas,* Vol. I; Guilding, J. M. (ed.) 1892-96. *Records of the Borough of Reading,* 4 vols., Parker, London; Trenholme, *op. cit.*; *V.C.H. Berkshire,* Vol. 3, 1923, 336-384
Stony Stratford.   1948. Hyde, F. E. & Markham, S. F. *History of Stony Stratford,* McCorquodale, Wolverton
Thame.   *V.C.H. Oxon.* VII, 1962, 160-219
Wallingford.   Biddle, M. & Hill, D. 1971. Late Saxon planned towns, *Antiquaries Journ.,* **51**, 70-85; Rodwell, K. (ed.) 1974, *Historic Towns . . .,* 155-58
Windsor.   Bond, S. 1970. The mediaeval constitution of New Windsor, *Berks. Archaeol. Journ.,* **65**, 21-39
Woodstock.   Ballard, A. 1896. *Chronicles of the Royal Borough of Woodstock,* Alden, Oxford

CHAPTER 17
STRATFORD UPON AVON AND SHAKESPEARE

For generous help we are much indebted to Dr Glenn Black of Oriel College and to Dr Levi Fox and his colleagues at The Shakespeare Centre at Stratford upon Avon.

References

1. Carus-Wilson, E. M. 1965. The first half century of the borough of Stratford upon Avon, *Econ. Hist. Rev.,* 2nd ser. **XVIII**, 46-63
2. *Minutes and Accounts of the Corporation of Stratford upon Avon, 1553-1592,* 4 vols., Dugdale Soc., 1921-29
3. 3 May 1487. 'Hugo Sawnder alias dictus Shakspere, sed mutatum est istud nomen ejus, quia vile reputatum est'. *Registrum Annalium Collegii Mertonensis, 1483-1521,* ed. H. Salter, Oxford Hist. Soc., **LXXV**, 98
4. Formerly Warwick Castle Mss. 2662. List of recusants at Stratford upon Avon in 1592 includes John Shakespeare. The castle archives have been transferred to the Warwickshire County Record Office where, Mr. M. W. Farr, the archivist, tells us that this manuscript is now catalogued as CR1886/B1 2662.
5. He may have had a hand in one more. John Fletcher, who succeeded him as the Company's dramatist and Thomas Dekker each wrote or collaborated in about 60 plays.
6. The Chandos portrait in the National Portrait Gallery, probably of the early seventeenth century, has the best claim to be an authentic painting from life.
7. White, M. F. 1974. *Fifteenth Century Misericords in the Collegiate Church of Holy Trinity, Stratford upon Avon,* Philip Bennett, Stratford upon Avon

Selective Bibliography

Bearman, R. 1969. A history of Stratford's finest mediaeval house: Mason's Court, *Warwickshire History,* **I**, No. 2. 25-36

Chambrun, Clara L. de 1957. *Shakespeare, a Portrait Restored.* Hollis and Carter, London

Fox, L. 1967. *Stratford upon Avon,* Jarrod, Norwich, and numerous booklets and pamphlets issued by the Shakespeare Centre.

Ford, B. (ed.) 1955. *The Age of Shakespeare,* Penguin, London

Hadfield, C. & Norris, J. 1962. *Waterways to Stratford,* David and Charles, Newton Abbot

Jones, Emrys L. 1977. *The Origins of Shakespeare,* Clarendon Press, Oxford

Schoenbaum, S. 1975. *Shakespeare: A Documentary Life,* Clarendon Press, Oxford

1977. *William Shakespeare: A Compact Documentary Life,* (reduced version of above)

V.C.H. Warwickshire Vol. 3. 1945, 221-282, Stratford upon Avon, by Philip Styles

Wilson, J. Dover (ed.) 1944. *Life in Shakespeare's England,* Penguin, London

CHAPTER 18
WARWICK: CASTLE AND BOROUGH

We are much indebted for generous help and information to the late Philip Styles and to John Gould of the Warwick Society.

References

1. The beheading spot, Gaveston's Cross in Leek Wootton parish, is marked by a thick short cross on a high pedestal of four stout square piers, designed by J. C. Jackson in 1832. Its inscription reads, 'The minion of a hateful king, in life and death a miserable instance of misrule.'

2. The Spanish conquistador Hernan Cortes when invading Mexico in 1519 had his ships run aground and dismantled, an action which gave rise to the legend that he had burnt his ships in order to show his men that they must win or perish.

3. The wedding took place in great privacy in the chapel of the Woodville's manor house at Grafton Regis on the edge of Whittlebury Forest in Northamptonshire. They had ten children, including the two princes murdered in the Tower and Elizabeth of York who married Henry VII. This king's badge of a Tudor rose with red petals (Lancaster) and white (York) is used as the emblem of Northamptonshire. Excavations on the site of the manor house revealed the outline of a mediaeval cloistered or courtyard building with a chapel with some tiles bearing the Woodville arms.

4. For tenurial tentacles or rural-urban interconnections *see* Chapter 16.

5. For Henry Wise *see* Green, D. 1956 *Gardener to Queen Anne,* O.U.P.

Selective Bibliography

Abercrombie, P. & Nickson, R. 1947. *Warwick: its Preservation and Redevelopment,* Architectural Press, London.

Cronne, H. A. 1951. *The Borough of Warwick in the Middle Ages,* Dugdale Soc. Occas. Papers **10**, Oxford

Harvey, P. D. A. & Thorpe, H. 1959. *The Printed Maps of Warwickshire 1576-1900*

Kemp, T. (trans. and ed.) *1898. The Black Book of Warwick,* Cooke, Warwick

Kendall, P. M. 1957. *Warwick the Kingmaker,* Allen and Unwin, London

Styles, P. 1936. The Corporation of Warwick, 1660-1835. *Trans. Birmingham Archaeol. Soc.,* **59**, 9-122

V.C.H. Warwickshire Vol. 8. 1969. The Borough of Warwick; 417-556. K. J. Allison, R. W. Dunning *et al*

Warwick County Museum. 1977. *Town Maps of Warwick* (with explanatory text)

CHAPTER 19
OXFORD: TOWN AND GOWN

We are greatly indebted to Mrs Mary D. Lobel for much help with this chapter.

References

1. To manors with Oxford properties attached to them recorded in *Domesday Survey* can be added Lyford, Steventon, and Streatley in Berkshire and Tadmarton and Pyrton in Oxfordshire. Jope, E. M. 1956. Saxon Oxford and its region, in *Dark Age Britain,* ed. D. B. Harden, 234-258
2. Bodl. Ms. Top. Oxon. c.22 42 a-b; 43; 69-72
3. *See* Chapter 8
4. Full details are in Fasnacht, R. 1977. *Summertown Since 1920,* St Michael's Publications, Summertown, Oxford
5. For the History of the Oxford University Press *see* Carter, H. 1974. *A History of the Oxford University Press Vol. I to 1780;* Barker, N. 1978. *The Oxford University Press and the Spread of Learning, 1478-1978,* Clarendon Press, Oxford. Among the notable helpers of the Press was William Blackstone, of Wallingford, who rescued it after it had declined in the eighteenth century.
6. Quinault, R. 1974. Jericho and St Barnabas, *Oxford,* **26,** Dec., 34-55
7. See Scargill, D. I. 1975. The Urbanisation of Oxford's Green Belt, in *Oxford and its Region* ed. Smith, C. G. & Scargill, D. I., O.U.P., 77-82

Selective Bibliography

Cordeaux, E. H. & D. H. Merry, 1976. *Bibliography of Printed Works relating to the city of Oxford* Oxford Hist. Soc., n.s. **25**
Crossley, A. (ed.) 1979. *V.C.H. of Oxfordshire* Vol. 4. *The City of Oxford*
Davis, R. H. C. 1973. The ford, the river, and the city, *Oxoniensia* **38,** 258-267
Fasnacht, R. 1954. *A History of the City of Oxford,* Blackwell, Oxford
Green, V. H. H. 1974. *A History of Oxford University,* Batsford, London
Hassall, T. G. 1972. *Oxford: the City beneath your feet,* Oxfordshire Archaeol. Unit
Lobel, M. D. (ed.) 1954. *V.C.H. of Oxfordshire* Vol. 3. *The University of Oxford;* 1967, Some Oxford borough customs, in *Miscellanea Mediaevalia in Memoriam J. F. Niermeyer,* 187-200, J. B. Wolters, Groningen
Oakeshott, W. F. (ed.) 1975. *Oxford Stone Restored,* University Offices, Oxford
Pantin, W. A. 1947. The development of domestic architecture in Oxford, *Antiquaries Journ.,* **27,** 120-150
1964. The halls and schools of mediaeval Oxford, in *Oxford Studies Presented to Daniel Callus,* Oxford Hist. Soc., n.s. **16,** 101-134
Piper, D. 1977. *The Treasures of Oxford,* Paddington Press, London (Has accounts of beautiful and interesting objects in museums etc.)
Prior, M. 1973. St Thomas's and its waterways, *Oxford,* **25.** Dec., 36-43
Rodwell, K. 1974. *Historic Towns in Oxfordshire,* 133-146. Oxfordshire Archaeol. Unit, Oxford
Royal Commission on Historical Monuments, 1939. *Oxford,* H.M.S.O.
Saint, A. 1970. Three Oxford architects, *Oxoniensia,* **35,** 53-102 (includes William Wilkinson)

Salter, H. E. 1936. *Mediaeval Oxford,* Oxford Hist. Soc., **100;** *Survey of Oxford, 1 and 2,* eds Pantin, W. A. & Mitchell, W. T., 1960; 1969. Oxford Hist. Soc., new series, **14** and **20**

Sherwood, J. & Pevsner, N. 1974. *Oxfordshire* (with separate section on Oxford), Penguin, London

Stone, L. (ed.) 1975. *The University in Society,* Vol. I, O.U.P.

Woolley, A. R. 1975. *The Clarendon Guide to Oxford,* O.U.P.

William Morris and the Pre-Raphaelites

Christian, J. 1974. *The Pre-Raphaelites in Oxford,* Ashmolean Museum, Oxford

Clark, F. 1973. *William Morris: Wallpapers and Chintzes,* Academy Editions, London

Duffy, A. R. 1963. William Morris and the Kelmscott Estate, *Antiquaries Journ.,* **43,** 97-115

Mackail, J. W. 1899. *Life and Letters of William Morris,* 2 vols., Longman, London

Needham, P. 1977. *William Morris and the Art of the Book,* O.U.P.

Renton, J. D. 1977. The Oxford Union murals, *Oxford,* **29,** Dec., 38-42

Sewter, A. C. 1974. *The Stained Glass of William Morris and his Circle,* Yale, New Haven

CHAPTER 20
THE MACHINE AGE

We are grateful to the Oxford and Cambridge Schools Examination Board for their kind permission to reproduce Figs. 60 and 61 of Milton Keynes from their 1977 Geography papers.

References

1. Obit, *The Times* 31 Oct., 1977
2. Nelson, J. P. 1971. *Broad Campden,* private
3. About 70,000 acres (28,000 ha) were returned from grassland to ploughland.
4. For early history of the motor car *see* Castle, H. G. 1950, *Britain's Motor Industry,* Clerke and Cockeran, London; Fenelon, K. G. 1925. *The Economics of Road Transport,* Allen and Unwin, London; *Report Royal Comm. on Motor Cars* Cd. 3080, (Parl. Papers, 1906, 48); *V.C.H. Warwickshire,* Vol. VIII, Coventry, 177-186
5. For William Richard Morris *see* Andrews, P. W. S. & Brunner, E. 1955. *The Life of Lord Nuffield,* Blackwell, Oxford; Taylor, A. M. 1964. *Gilletts: Bankers at Banbury and Oxford,* 199-200, Clarendon Press, Oxford
6. Gilbert, E. W. 1947. The industrialisation of Oxford, *Geogr. Journ.* **109,** 1-25
7. For location *see* Ordnance Survey Maps, and Blake, R. N. E. 1969. The impact of airfields on the British landscape, *Geogr. Journ.,* **135,** 508-28
8. *V.C.H. Warwickshire,* VIII, 1969, 12-15
9. K. Robertson, A vigorous new life for a derelict airfield, *Oxford Times,* 20 May 1966
10. For long-lasting effect see also the continued use of the airfield on Greenham Common, near Newbury in *The Times,* 17 March 1958; 22 March 1978. In October 1978 it became apparent that Greenham had escaped the introduction there of large re-fuelling tanker aircraft and that these heavy aeroplanes would be based at Fairford.
11. For the towns specially selected by national policy for growth (which now includes Northampton) see D. I. Scargill, 1968. The Expanded Town in England and Wales, in *Urbanisation and its Problems,* ed. R. P. Beckinsale & J. M. Houston, Blackwell, Oxford
12. Scannell, V. 1977. *A Proper Gentleman,* Robson Books, London
13. See *National Trust, Properties Open.,* National Trust, 42 Queen Anne's Gate, London. Regional Offices at Hughenden Manor, High Wycombe; Church Street, Tewkesbury; and London Street, Faringdon. Each county has also its own Open Gardens Scheme of normally private estates open occasionally, partly or wholly for charitable purposes as listed

in *Gardens of England and Wales open to the Public,* National Gardens Scheme, 57 Lower Belgrave Street, London. Information on other Stately Homes will be provided by the regional Tourist Office. Among the recent gifts to the National Trust is Basildon Park, near Streatley, a fine Classical Georgian house designed by John Carr.

14. Ratcliffe, D. A. 1977. *A Nature Conservation Review,* Vol. 2, C.U.P. (A large volume with a description of each site).
15. Helen Turner, *Oxford Times,* 28 Oct. 1977
16. *See,* for example, Brett, Lionel, G.B. 1965. *Landscape in Distress,* Architectural Press, London and numerous Reports by the Council for the Preservation of Rural England.
17. Each county has its mineral extraction plan and map, with later amendments, prepared by its Planning Department.
18. Collins, N. R. & McDonic, G. F. 1969. *Cotswold Water Park,* Gloucester C.C. and Wiltshire C.C.; Ratcliffe, D. A. 1977. *op. cit.* O.W.9
19. For the problem of the preservation of places of worship see Binney, M. & Burman, P. 1977. *Chapels and Churches; Who Cares,* British Tourist Authority, London; 1977. *Change and Decay: The Future of our Churches,* Studio Vista, London; Duncan, S. Decline and fall of a cherished empire, *Oxford Times,* 29 July 1977
20. Baird, W. W. & Tarrant, J. R. 1972. Vanishing hedgerows, *Geogr. Mag.,* **44**, 545-51; C.P.R.E. 1971, *Loss of Cover through Removal of Hedgerows and Trees;* Pollard, E., Hooper M. D. & Moore, N.W. 1974. *Hedges,* Collins, London

PHOTO ACKNOWLEDGMENTS

The authors are grateful to the following for kindly allowing the use of photographs: Eagle Photos, Cheltenham, with special thanks to Bill Bawden, 2, 17, 22, 28, 29, 30, 31, 32, 35, 37, 38, 39, 42, 43, 44, 45, 46, 49, 51, 53, 54, 57, 59, 68, 70, 74, 75, 76, 82, 83, 85, 86, 87, 89, 98, 115, 119; Cambridge University Collection (copyright reserved), with special thanks to Professor J.K.S. St Joseph, 1, 3, 4, 8, 9, 10, 13, 15, 16, 25, 58, 92; Aerofilms Limited, 5, 6, 7, 14, 90, 91, 93, 94, 95, 96, 97, 106, 111, 118; Patrick Baron, Jury Street, Warwick, 103, 104, 105; British Waterways Board, 61, 62; Butt Studies, Bourton on the Water, Gloucs., 71, 72; Department of the Environment (Crown copyright reserved), 55; Martyn J. Harris, 113; A.F. Kersting, 11, 20, 23, 40, 41, 52, 64, 84, 116, 117; Peter Masters, 33; National Portrait Gallery, London (copyright reserved), 112; National Trust, 65; Oxford Central Library and J.H. Taunt, 110, 114; Oxford Mail and Times Ltd., 12, 19, 36, 50, 63, 67, 77, 78; John Peacock, 107; The Shakespeare Centre, Stratford upon Avon, with special thanks to Dr Levi Fox, 99, 100, 101, 102; Thamesdown Borough, Public Relations Officer, Swindon, 88; The Times, 18, 24, 26, 27, 48, 60, 66, 69, 73, 79, 80, 81; Thomas-Photos, Oxford, 21, 56, 108, 109.

Index

Numbers in bold type refer to page numbers of diagrams and photographs. After an entry D.O.E. denotes in care of the Department of the Environment, N.C. denotes Nature Conservancy or some other nature conservation form, body or society, such as National Nature Reserve; N.T. denotes National Trust; S.P.A.B. denotes the Society for the Preservation of Ancient Buildings; and Bucks C.C; Warws. C.C. denotes in care of the relevant county council or city council. The natural areas under the Nature Conservancy and National Trust often adjoin, or overlap or coincide. For full details consult the relevant County Council's planning maps and booklets.

W 3 P.